Flavours
of Greece

Flavours of Greece

Rosemary Barron

GRUB STREET · LONDON

Published in 2010 by
Grub Street
4 Rainham Close
London
SW11 6SS
Email: food@grubstreet.co.uk
Web: www.grubstreet.co.uk
Twitter: @grub_street

Reprinted in 2012

Designed and formatted by Sarah Driver
Photography by Michelle Garrett
Food styling by Jayne Cross
Cover design LizzieBdesign

A CIP catalogue record for this book is available from the British Library

ISBN 978-1-906502-60-7

Printed and bound in Slovenia

This book has been printed on paper from sustainable sources

Contents

Foreword

It is impossible for me to think of Greece without thinking of the colours, sights, aromas, and, above all, the flavours of Greek cooking. So many of my happy memories of the country are linked with food enjoyed in the company of good Greek friends or of new food experiences associated with out-of-the-way or exotically beautiful places – high in the mountains, by the glistening blue Aegean Sea, or in medieval ports, picturesque villages, or the heart of cosmopolitan Athens.

Yet my interest in this fascinating, many-layered, cuisine began by accident: On an archaeological dig on Crete, cut off by rugged mountain passes from all but the most durable of supplies, my fellow 'diggers' and I found ourselves eating the same foods our 'subjects' had enjoyed some 4,000 years earlier. This was the beginning of a passionate and lifelong curiosity about Greek food and its history, and its place in our own culinary culture.

Fifteen years after this first prophetic encounter, I was back on Crete, this time to set up a cooking school. *Kandra Kitchen* was based in an old house which, 450 years earlier, had been rebuilt with stone rescued from a ruined monastery. Its wood-burning oven still worked, the huge wine press remained intact, remnants of once-elegant antique columns supported the steps, and the flagstone floor was gloriously shiny and worn. *Kandra Kitchen's* programme ensured that each student enjoyed Greek foods, wines, and culture within the daily, seasonal, and festive rhythms of village life. I did, however, make one contribution to this otherwise idyllic state of affairs – I installed a 'state-of-the-art' kitchen, at that time the only one on Crete, to provide the 'classroom' for testing and experimenting with Cretan foods and dishes.

Kandra Kitchen attracted enormous interest, in the United States (where I was living at the time) and Canada in particular, and the six years I ran the school on Crete and on Santorini (Cyclades) were very happy ones for me.

The constraints of family life, although perfectly enjoyable in their own way, prevented further long-term travel, so I turned to writing, teaching and lecturing on Greek foods and culinary culture, past and present. My 'itchy-feet' were reasonably well-taken care of though, as these new activities entailed plenty of travel – to the United States and Greece, to Canada, Australia, France, Argentina, Thailand and elsewhere. During this time, I wrote *Flavours of Greece*.

I hope my recipes here will pay some tribute to the wonderful spirit of friendliness that has engulfed me, and warms any visitor in Greece; that they will revive happy memories in those who have already travelled to Greece or her islands and in the Greeks who now live abroad.

As a visitor to Greece I was automatically awarded the status of a *xsenos*, which means a "stranger-friend"; with this comes, for any traveller, the "protection of the gods" and a magnificent welcome to match. Such a welcome always includes the sharing of food. You are not just given food by Greeks but asked to share with them the food they enjoy (somehow there is always enough!). In few other countries are food and its traditions so much part of the fabric of life, playing an important role in the rituals associated with birth and death and everything in between.

Of course, just because a recipe is ancient, there is no guarantee that it will taste wonderful. But, with Greek food, much of it does. When I open a recipe book I often recall that the first recorded collection of recipes dates from the days of ancient Greece, that Greeks established the first schools for chefs, and that a fastidious Greek gourmet invented the fork. And each time I hear the issues of the day discussed over dinner, my mind is drawn back to the scholarly dinners of antiquity when food, philosophy and conversation were considered inseparable companions.

My hope is that some of this enthusiasm for Greek food and culinary history will inspire my readers to discover more about both. Perhaps too it will persuade others to visit that beautiful and hospitable country and experience the delights of Greek food for themselves.

Rosemary Barron

Introduction

Those who know Greece, even if only from a brief acquaintance, are aware that there is a vigorous culinary tradition in the country, with a distinct identity and character. There is a robust regional and local cuisine and an informed and lively interest in food and flavour. All these aspects are linked, in an amazing continuity of tradition, with the ancient world of over two thousand years ago.

Ancient Greece is universally accepted as the cradle of Western civilization, with its highly developed political and social system and rich intellectual and cultural life. In such a civilization could it have been possible that food and its preparation would not have been taken seriously? A remote possibility indeed. In fact, the ancient Greeks regarded cooking as both an art and a science and throughout the ancient world Greek chefs were accorded the status and reputation that French chefs now enjoy. The principles and practice of fine cooking and gastronomy as we know them today were first established in the abundantly stocked and highly creative kitchens of ancient Greece, and modern Greeks still enjoy the foods and tastes that inspired the chefs of antiquity.

What makes the style and flavour of Greek food essentially different from that of other Mediterranean countries? To discover that we need to take a brief look at the country's history, since Greek cooking is greatly influenced by the twists and turns of its turbulent past.

Until around 3500 BC the early inhabitants of Greece grilled the food they had gathered, hunted, and fished over wood fires, baked it in glowing embers, or, like their Etruscan neighbours, cooked it in clay ovens. But with the advent of what has been called the "Greek miracle" – the budding of the sophisticated Minoan civilization on the islands of Crete and Santorini – Greek cuisine began to develop a strongly individual style.

At the height of its influence (around 1700 to 1400 BC) the Minoan state dominated the Aegean, and its culture spread throughout the Mediterranean. Trade links with North Africa brought dates and onions to the islands and forests were cleared to make way for widespread planting of vines and olives. Then, as now, Crete was a true "Garden of Eden", producing some of the richest honey and sweetest fruits to be found anywhere, so it is no coincidence that the first sweetmeats were made in Minoan kitchens. The well-known Mediterranean sweetmeat *membrillo*, made from quince paste, is almost undoubtedly Minoan in origin, although it is often thought to come from Spain. Quinces were grown on Crete before the days of the ancient Greeks and archaeological research has established that the Minoans made pastes from fruits.

The creative and organizational skills of the Minoans, and their systematic approach to land cultivation and trade, laid the foundations for the successful economy of classical Greece and, as the Greek civilization developed, so also did a culinary culture. Gastronomy became a subject for serious study, and skilled technicians were required to put into practice the food theories formulated by scholars. These technicians, soon highly regarded as chefs, developed many of the cooking techniques and basic sauces we still use. Just as importantly, civilized Greek society developed the framework in which we enjoy food – the art of dining and of dinner party conversation.

As classical Greece declined and the Roman Empire grew in power and influence, Rome supplanted Athens as the centre of the civilized world. Educated and affluent Romans, anxious to improve their gastronomic and cultural standards, employed Greek teachers for their children and Greek chefs in their kitchens. Under the tutelage of Greek chefs the Romans developed their own distinctive cuisine and laid the foundations of Italian cooking, which, of course, has many similarities with Greek food.

Later, the expansion of the Byzantine Empire, with its centre in Constantinople (now Istanbul), spread the influence of Greek cooking northwards and eastwards throughout the Balkans and the area that is now Turkey. Even today, many Turkish and Eastern Mediterranean communities rely on Greek bakers and pastry cooks for a variety of breads, pastries, and sweetmeats. In its turn, Greek cuisine absorbed Balkan and Eastern influences.

Then came the "dark years" for Greece when she found herself at the mercy of a succession of invaders. Parts of the country were occupied in turn by Franks, Venetians, and Ottomans, who all influenced native food, and smaller invasions – for example, by the Vlachs and Slavs – brought new flavourings, such as paprika, to occupied towns and villages.

After the fall of Constantinople in 1453 AD Greece was under the sway of the expansionist Ottoman Empire. This occupation naturally brought a renewed Eastern influence to bear on Greek food, although this influence was not so profound as is generally thought. During this period (which lasted until 1830), Greeks were forced to use Turkish names for foods and dishes; this practice has led to a widespread, but mistaken, belief that Greek dishes with eastern-sounding names, for example *dolmades* and *borekakia*, are, of Turkish origin. Four hundred years of culinary habits based on expediency have left Greece with a legacy of native foods with Turkish names and a few dishes, such as *moussakas*, that are popular in both countries.

During the Turkish occupation many Greek chefs took refuge in monasteries, both for their own safety and to safeguard centuries of culinary knowledge and practice. To distinguish them from the monks, who wore the black hats still associated with the Greek Orthodox church, they wore tall white toques – the chef's hat now familiar throughout the world and an accepted professional symbol.

Over the centuries migrations, invasions, trade customs, and personalities all have contributed to the magnificent expansion of the early Greek diet of olives, wheat, figs, grapes, wild greens, fish, and a little meat, to the colourful abundance evident in Greek food today. Lemons, potatoes, aubergines, tomatoes, spinach, and okra, for example, none native to Greece, were introduced over the centuries as a result of trade, war, or occupation. Even in the last century, drastic changes took place in Greek culinary life. A brief German occupation during World War II was responsible for a devastating reduction of the Greek Jewish community and thus its influence on food, and today the European Union, although, of course, not similar in tragic human terms, is making a decisive impact on Greek agriculture and food choices. The production of "ancient" crops is giving way to the demands and patterns of mechanisation and export, and inexpensive foods from other European countries are replacing more expensive traditional ones. In many towns, for example, the transatlantic hamburger is unfortunately supplanting the centuries-old *souvlaki* as a favourite street food. However, fine imaginative cooking and good natural ingredients are still to be found in Greece if the visitor cares to look beyond the bland hotchpotches commonly offered to tourists.

Greek tables today

Greek food is inspired by the heady perfumed fragrances that float on the Greek air. Then there is the colour and novelty of Greek food. On shopping trips to the market, shapes, textures, and colours assault the senses, excite and entice – glossy multicoloured vegetables and lush juicy fruits; plump nuts and seeds; boxes of dried fruits; strange-shaped sausages and meats from every part of an animal; sea-fresh fish you have never seen before; barrels of salted fish and *tarama*; hard and soft cheeses, crumbly white or creamy golden, some wrapped in animal skins; and more kinds of olives and beans than you ever imagined. Even the water in Greece seems special; Greeks say that some dishes, particularly those based on vegetables, cannot be made properly outside Greece because the water is not the same.

In the villages the traditional way of dining is still observed, and very pleasant and relaxed it is. A table is set up in a courtyard and on it is spread a variety of *mezedes* for guests and family to nibble on for an hour or two while they chat and wind down. Every meal is preceded by *mezedes*, "to prepare the stomach for the onslaught to come," as one ancient Greek writer explained. When the *mezedes* are finished, bread, salad, and a main course are placed in the centre of the table. Vegetables are usually served later, separate from the main course. Family and guests alike are expected to serve themselves to the food provided and to pass their wine glasses to the host to be filled.

But there are strict rules of etiquette at work here, very different from our own. For example, taking large helpings of everything at the start of the meal, to show appreciation of the food, would actually be an insult to the host, implying that there might not be enough food to go around! Instead, the diners help themselves to the same dish several times, proving to the host that they are enjoying themselves and the food he/she offers.

Even the most sophisticated world-travelled Greek approaches a village table laden with foods such as wild greens, spit-roasted lamb, and sweet cheese pies with relish and enthusiasm. At such a feast he instinctively feels in touch with generations of Greeks who have enjoyed these traditional aromas and tastes before him; these are the flavours of home and here he knows he will find good companionship and a special communal pleasure and appreciation.

The preparation of food for others, a generous and loving activity, is experienced at its most lavish and hospitable at a Greek table; no one is ever turned away.

Feasting and fasting, richness and frugality, especially among traditional and religious Greeks, is still the pattern of gastronomic life; food cannot be truly valued unless, at some other time, it has been denied. Hence, the strict observance of the Lenten and Advent fasts, and the explosion of rich ingredients and exotic flavours lavished on Easter and Christmas meals.

Dining in Greece is an activity that stimulates all the senses; the food – aromatic, pungent, and colourful – is consumed with great gusto. Whether the occasion is an ordinary family supper or a splendid festive celebration the dining table is the place to enjoy each other's company. At home, in a taverna, or at a restaurant, a meal is accompanied by animated conversation, and appreciation of the food is loud and unequivocal. Good food entwines people in a bond that remains long after the meal is finished.

This brief introduction to Greek gastronomic history and present-day culinary practices gives just a shadowy outline of the rich character and tradition of the country's cuisine. But the way to really appreciate the variety, flavour, and sheer pleasure of the best Greek food is to try it. And since much of this is to be found in out-of-the-way tavernas or on domestic tables, rather than in ritzy restaurants, trying your hand at some of the regional and national specialities in this book is the ideal introduction to the expressive Greek attitude to food and cookery, and to enjoy some of the unpretentious, flavoursome foods that Greeks delight in. From appetizers to desserts you will find strength and subtlety, verve and vigour in these flavours of Greece and discover the wonderful legacy that Greek cooks of the past have left us.

Traditional flavours on modern tables

For me, Greek food is beautiful in its honesty, its healthy indifference to trends (although many basic tenets of traditional Greek cooking are now both medically approved and highly fashionable) and in its ability to promote a feeling of wellbeing in everyone at the table. In this book you will find no "haute cuisine" but much fine food. Many recipes are simple, based on good fresh ingredients and the aromatic scents of the Greek countryside; many are highly flavoured; all taste even better when shared with friends. Most of these dishes are straightforward to prepare and do not call for unreasonable culinary artistry and skill. And each recipe is in some way personal to me and evokes wonderful memories of the person who gave it to me.

When we serve Greek food at home, some traditional customs can pose problems. Our guests, used to spending less time relaxing before dinner, can easily misjudge the pace of the meal and become quite full just on *mezedes*. Thus, it is better to serve just a few *mezedakia* such as olives, *feta* cheese, salted almonds, and peppered figs with drinks. Then, at the table, serve two or three more substantial *mezedes* as a first course.

In traditional Greek homes no separate first or soup courses are served (a soup is usually served as a complete meal), so the main course is served immediately after the *mezedes*. However, this does not mean that you have to do the same: I often serve a few *mezedes*, followed by a soup or vegetable bake, bread and salad. Fresh fruit or perhaps pudding or ice cream usually completes the meal. After the meal, and away from the dining table, Greeks often enjoy honey-rich pastries, sweetmeats, or syruped fruits (*glyka*) with coffee. For us these treats make delectable desserts.

If you find balancing your Greek menu a problem you may find my menu planner (page 352) helpful. As you become more familiar with Greek food, however, you will begin to recognize instinctively which dishes complement each other best.

Map

The Greek Kitchen

ingredients

Olives / *Elies*

For modern Greeks olives and bread are the basic necessities of life, as they have been for centuries. The olive groves of modern Greece – still, mysterious, and peaceful places – date back to around 450 BC when olive oil was first recognized as a valuable export commodity and the land was given over to olive cultivation. As Lawrence Durrell put it, olives have "a taste older than meat, older than wine. A taste as old as cold water."

Olives thrive in the Mediterranean climate of long hot summers and mild winters with only short periods of frost. The difference in flavour and texture are to some extent influenced by their situation – olives grown on the arid rocky hillsides, for example, tend to be small and the richest flavoured, while those grown on the coastal plains are fatter and fleshier.

The taste is also affected by the degree of ripeness when an olive is picked and by the curing method used. Some Greek producers, using centuries-old methods, still supply olives of a very high standard and a great diversity of flavour. In each olive-producing area the local people delight in the flavour variation that makes their olives different from others and, they claim, better.

All olives are bitter and inedible when picked. As an olive matures it changes from green to black. Most olives are picked when young or just mature but, if local taste and custom dictates, some olives are harvested at a very late stage when their skins are leathery and wrinkled. In the two-stage traditional curing process the olives are first soaked in water for 3-30 days to remove any bitterness, then immersed in brine, the strength of the brine determining the saltiness of the cured olive. Occasionally the olives are packed into rock salt rather than steeped in brine.

Olives are usually harvested in autumn and considered sufficiently cured by early spring. They are then packed in either fresh brine, brine and vinegar, olive oil, or olive oil and vinegar for storage. They can be used straight from the pot or marinated in herbs, lemon juice or vinegar, and olive oil to serve as a *meze*.

It is worth seeking out imported Greek olives to give an authentic flavour to the recipes in this book. Although there are only a few commercially important types of olive grown in Greece, regional preferences for ripeness and curing method, as well as the local environment, give an imposing variety of olives for sale. Most are not exported and can only be sampled in their place of origin, but here is a list of those more commonly available in Greek shops, good supermarkets, and speciality shops:

Amfissa   From the olive groves surrounding Delphi. Picked when ripe and oil-rich, Amfissa olives are round and black with a mellow, pleasantly nutty flavour. Perfect with cheese and crusty country bread.

Atalanti   Large, luscious, and fruity olives in shades of purple and greenish-purple. Atalanti are gathered half-ripe and cured in brine. The effort and time required to produce these lovely olives means that they are particularly at risk to modern lye-curing methods; check before buying. Exquisitely flavoured, they can be served straight from their brine or sprinkled with a few drops of red wine vinegar, olive oil, and a little dried *rigani* or thyme.

Cracked Green   The ubiquitous countryside olives, picked just before their colour changes from light to dark green. This olive too is at risk from modern 'short-cuts' in curing; buy from a reputable supplier. Strong and sharp, they are an ideal *meze* to serve with ouzo. Or marinate them for a few hours in olive oil, a few drops of red wine vinegar, bay leaves, a little crushed coriander seed, and slivered garlic.

Elitses   Tiny, sweetly-flavoured, purple-brown olives, similar in appearance and taste to Niçoise olives; they are grown extensively on Crete. Use whenever a mildly flavoured olive is called for.

Khourmades   Named for their shape and appearance, *khourmades* ("dates") are large, dark brown, and attractively wrinkled. Some of the best come from the island of Chios where they take pride of place on the *meze* table.

Ionian Green   Grown on the Ionian islands, picked young, and cured in a light brine. Lovely mild, mellow olives to serve just as they are. Or sprinkle with lemon juice, olive oil, and a little finely chopped preserved lemon and parsley.

Kalamata   Probably the most famous Greek olives and a favourite the world over: Large and glossy, purple-black, almond-shaped, and with a distinctive flavour from the red wine vinegar used in the curing. Good Kalamatas are meaty and firm, at their best 4-5 months after curing, but can be kept longer. Named for the town of Kalamata (at the entrance to the Messenia Valley in the western Peloponnese), they are the perfect olive for many salads, and especially good marinated.

To use these olives in cooking, first blanch them for 5 seconds in boiling water.

Nafplion   Grown in the eastern Peloponnese and picked in September when young and under-ripe. Their mild and slightly nutty flavour is good in salads and Nafplion is the traditional olive to serve with *taramosalata*. Occasionally I like to mix them with a little finely chopped preserved lemon, olive oil, and crushed coriander seeds.

Thasos* or *Throumbes Grown on the island of Thasos in the northern Aegean, these olives are salt-cured (a process that produces a wrinkled skin and concentrated flavour), then stored in olive oil. They are excellent with *myzithra* cheese.

Volos Smooth, round brown olives of varying size from the province of Thessaly in central Greece. Their unusual colour and appearance make them an ideal *meze* olive and they are especially good with the strong country flavours of sausages and offal meats, or *kephalotyri* cheese.

When buying olives be guided by your nose! Regardless of the curing method used, good olives smell fresh and intriguingly complex, never overwhelmingly salty. Unfortunately, it is now legal to lye-cure (steep in caustic soda) and dye olives in Greece, as it is in every other European Union country; lye-curing means that the one- to four-month natural fermentation period can be completed in a few hours. Avoid flavourless lye-cured or dyed olives by buying only those labelled "naturally cured" or "naturally fermented", and without the additive, ferrous gluconate (or iron gluconate).

Left in the storage solution, olives can be kept for months, although all are best eaten as soon as possible after buying.

Olive Oil / *Elaiolatho*

Three significant factors influence the quality of olive oil: the growing conditions, the timing of the harvest, and, probably the most important, the way they are harvested – the olives should be picked, sorted, and pressed with care and precision, preserving as much of the fine natural flavour as possible.

Cold-pressed olive oil is made by spreading olive pulp on mats that fit in layers into a wooden press. A weight is placed on the top mat and the pressure releases the oil into a vat below. This exquisite oil, unfortunately, is becoming hard to find, even in Greece, for it is time-consuming to prepare. Extra virgin olive oil (defined by its low acidity, less than 1 percent) is made from the pulp of just-ripe olives and has the best flavour for salads. The pressed oil, standard cold-pressed or extra virgin, is left to settle for a few days to a week, then decanted into crocks, ready for the kitchen.

There have, of course, been modern advances in olive production – picking and oil extraction is now mechanized and there are chemicals available to "persuade" the olives to ripen and fall. But a machine cannot distinguish between ripe, just-ripe, and under-ripe olives nor strip trees on rocky hillsides where the best-tasting olives grow. Nor can mass production, relying on chemicals to accelerate filtering, "improve" flavour, and lengthen shelf life, yield an oil with anything approaching the rich quality, beautiful green-gold colour, and fruity flavour of oils produced by traditional methods.

Olive oil of the highest quality can be expensive, but there is no substitute for it in good cooking. When buying olive oil, use the same discernment as you would when buying wine. Look for a young oil, with a fruity, immediately recognizable, aroma and taste and a good balance of flavour, and buy only a small quantity at first. Although the best village oil does have a distinctive green-gold colour, it is a mistake to use only the colour criterion when buying – unscrupulous producers have been known to alter the colour with additives.

Greek olive oils are finally achieving the recognition they have long deserved. Greece, the third largest olive oil producing country in the world (making about 18% of total production), produces 75% of the world's extra virgin olive oil, and Greeks consume more olive oil than anyone else (about 20 kilos per person a year). The unique, richly-flavoured olive oils of Crete and the Peloponnese, in particular, are worth searching for here. The ancient Greeks considered the best olive oil to be from slightly under-ripe olives, and both these regions of antiquity produce a special olive oil (*agourelaio*) from green olives, picked in the late autumn, at the start of the harvest. Buy olive oil only from shops where there is a high turnover and where the oil has been carefully stored in airtight containers, away from heat or sunlight. In your own kitchen, store olive oil in a dark cool place – it does not require refrigeration.

Greeks appreciate fine olive oil and demand high standards from commercial brands. If economy in the kitchen is an issue, it's worth keeping both extra virgin and virgin olive oil on hand. Use the extra virgin olive oil in salads and in dishes requiring a last-minute addition of oil; use the less expensive virgin olive oil in cooked dishes or for deep-fat frying (virgin olive oil has none of the "debris" left in extra virgin oils).

Sea Salt / *Alati tis Thalassas*

Salt was important in the ancient world, both to enliven frugal diets and as a preservative, but in recent years we have become more aware of the health risks associated with too much salt. However, it is possible to use salt to gain maximum taste advantage without endangering health. For example, adding lemon juice to salt strengthens its flavour, so you can use less salt but retain the taste, and relatively small quantities of strongly salted foods (such as olives) satisfy the body's natural requirements for this important mineral.

Sea salt, the type commonly used in Greece, is a wonderful flavour-enhancer, and it also contains other trace minerals beneficial to health. When a villager explains how to make a dish, salt is never far from the top of his or her list of ingredients. It is considered a digestive, an appetizer, and has an ability to balance and mellow flavours. It also deepens colour and aroma and has the effect of drawing out liquid – which is why villagers always add salt to grilled food after cooking, not before.

Sea salt is more expensive than other types but you use less of it. It's a good idea to keep two varieties of sea salt in your kitchen – fine-grain for most cooking, and coarse-grain for some dishes and for the table.

Vinegar / *Xsithi*

Only wine vinegar, mainly that made from red wine, is used in the Greek kitchen and it's a commodity that's taken seriously. As much care is taken over vinegar making as wine making and often the village winemaker has a dual role as the local supplier of good vinegar. In one old village house I once occupied, a huge earthenware pot stood in a corner of the courtyard – this contained the village vinegar supply and during the day villagers would stop by for a ladleful of vinegar, sometimes bringing a little wine to top up the pot.

One of the first "food additives," vinegar is a digestive, a preservative, and a versatile flavouring agent. There is an enormous difference in flavour between good- and poor-quality wine vinegars, and it is an important distinction since the quality of the vinegar affects the quality of the dishes and sauces made with it. The quality depends primarily on the quality of the wine converted or soured by the vinegar "mother" – a self-perpetuating colony of harmless

bacteria that float around in the wine while slowly acidifying it.

To make your own wine vinegar Stand a large glazed earthenware crock on a shelf or in a corner, and add leftover red wine whenever you have any available. When you have about 600 ml/1 pint, add 4 tablespoons good-quality red wine vinegar, loosely cover the crock to keep it dust-free but open to the air, and leave undisturbed for a week or two. A "mother" will form. Continue adding red wine, tasting occasionally to see if you are satisfied with the vinegar. Once you are, decant most of it into bottles and seal. Add more red wine to the "mother," which will continue to grow – eventually you will need to break it up and donate bits to your friends!

If you cannot find aged red wine vinegar imported from Greece, or make your own, substitute Italian balsamic vinegar, but use less than is called for in the recipe.

Wine in Cooking / *Krasi sti Magiriki*

Wine does not feature in Greek recipes as often as you might expect. As an old winemaker on the island of Santorini once told me, wine is made to drink! However, red wine's ability to tenderize tough cuts of meat is used to full effect in casseroles, and traditional nectar-sweet wines are used to flavour sweet dishes. Madeira can be used in place of sweet Greek wines such as Samos or Mavrodaphne, which can sometimes be difficult to find.

Yogurt / *Yiaourti*

Fresh milk, a controlled temperature, and the help of two friendly bacteria (*lactobacillus bulgaricus* and *streptococcus thermophilus*) are the essential requirements for making yogurt. A rich source of minerals and vitamins, especially vitamin B, yogurt can also taste wonderful. The best deliciously thick and creamy versions have a refreshing taste and luxurious texture, totally different from the thin and lustreless product that too often passes as yogurt on our supermarket shelves.

Yogurt is used throughout the Balkan region and the Middle East as a tenderizer, to enrich stews, to make sauces, and in salads, desserts, and cakes. And the food-curious visitor to Greece very soon discovers what I consider to be the best snack in the world – a plate of thick white sheep's milk yogurt covered with fragrant Hymettus honey.

The best yogurt I have ever tasted was made in the small Cretan village of Vrisses. It was sold in unglazed flat-bottomed bowls for which each customer paid a deposit; if you brought back the bowl all you had to pay for next time was the yogurt. That memorable yogurt was made from sheep's milk but village yogurt is also made from goat's milk which gives a different, less creamy, sharper flavour.

The easiest way to ensure that you have a good supply of flavourful yogurt is to make it yourself. Despite the complicated instructions often given for yogurt making, it's really very simple. All you need is good-quality fresh milk, a few tablespoons of live yogurt starter, and a fairly warm (about 24-26C/75-80F) draught-free spot.

Live yogurt starter can be bought in Greek or health food shops. Once you have made your first batch, you save some of it to use as a starter for the second batch, and so on. The taste of your finished yogurt depends largely on this starter; 1- to 2-day-old starter will produce a

mildly sweet version, 5- to 6-day-old starter a sharper, tarter one. Every month or two you will need a new starter (the bacteria gradually lose their potency). Taste is also affected by the length of time yogurt is incubated – the longer you leave it, the stronger the result.

Both the texture and flavour of Greek yogurt is difficult to reproduce outside the countries of the Near East. I find that Channel Island milk gives a similar smooth, thick, and creamy consistency, but this may not appeal to dieters. Experiment with the milk you have available to find what works best for you. Yogurt added to cooked dishes or salads must be thick; thin yogurt can be strained for a few hours to remove excess water. Left longer to strain, it becomes a delicious creamy cheese.

To make your own yogurt
Makes 1 litre/1³/₄ pints

1 litre/1³/₄ pints Channel Island milk or milk of choice
3 tablespoons live yogurt

Heat the milk to just under a boil and pour into a glass, china, or earthenware bowl. Let cool, uncovered, to about 43C/110F (you should be able to comfortably leave your finger in the milk for a count of 5). A skin will have formed on the surface (this makes a special treat later, with honey). To retain the skin, push a little of it to one side and spoon the yogurt into the milk. For yogurt with a textured crust, cover the bowl loosely, if at all; for yogurt without a crust, cover the bowl with a plate. Set aside for 10-12 hours in a warm draught-free spot, such as an oven with a pilot light, until thick and creamy. Cover and refrigerate for up to 4 days. (Remember to make another batch of yogurt before finishing the bowl.)

Do not be put off if your first few attempts are disappointing. Your yogurt may not set – in which case make sure that the incubating spot is warm enough and the temperature is constant; if your yogurt still does not set, you need to begin again with a new starter. Or it may curdle – the most common causes of curdling are incubating yogurt in a place that is too warm or for too long a period.

Strained Yogurt Line a sieve with two layers of muslin and set over a bowl. Pour in 1 litre/1³/₄ pints yogurt, pull up the sides of the muslin, and tie together to make a bag. Hang the bag over the bowl in a cool place and let drain for 3 hours. Do not drain the yogurt in the refrigerator or it will set firm rather than just thickening. Give the bag an occasional squeeze to remove as much water (whey) as possible. (You can use the whey in a soup or casserole.) Refrigerate in an airtight container for up to five days. (Makes about 700 ml/1¹/₄ pints.)

Yogurt Cheese Strain 1 litre/1³/₄ pints yogurt and return the bag to the sieve. Open the muslin and stir in ¹/₄-¹/₂ teaspoon fine-grain sea salt if liked. Fold the muslin over the yogurt, place in a heavily weighted plate on top, and set aside for 2 hours. Transfer to the refrigerator and leave another 2 hours.

Dry the muslin bag with paper towels and, leaving the muslin in place, refrigerate the yogurt cheese in an airtight container for up to 4 days.

For breakfast, serve with honey, fresh fruit, and crusty bread. For lunch, sprinkle with extra virgin olive oil, a little freshly ground pepper, and/or finely chopped fresh herbs such as parsley and oregano. (Makes about 275 g/10 oz.)

Cheeses / *Tyria*

Greece produces relatively few types of traditional cheese but each has a distinctive flavour. In the villages cheese is made according to local practices that determine its unique character. For this reason, Greek cheeses are rarely named: to a villager, cheese is cheese! Some of the finest Greek cheeses come from the island of Crete, where sheep and goats graze on herb-covered foothills and where cool mountain temperatures provide an ideal environment for storing and ripening cheese to perfection.

The best-known Greek cheese, *feta*, suffers from an unfortunate form of flattery – it is now made in several northern European countries. This *feta*, usually made from cow's milk and in an industrialized environment, bears no comparison to the true *feta* of the Greek countryside.

Below is a short guide to the traditional cheeses referred to in this book, as well as the ones a visitor to Greece is most likely to find. Most are available here from Greek or Middle Eastern shops, and some are available from our better supermarkets:

Anthotyro A soft, delicate, very pale yellow cheese, made from goat's milk – a speciality of the island of Crete. Its name means 'blossom cheese' in Greek, because the curds 'bloom' as they rise to the surface on stirring. Soured or aged *anthotyro* is the cheese that gives Cretan pies their unique flavour. You can make a decent substitute by adding finely grated *feta* to drained and sieved cottage cheese (use 1 part *feta* to 4 parts cottage cheese).

Batsos A white, semi-hard brine cheese made from sheep or goat's milk, *batsos* is not exported. But if you visit the wine-producing area of Naoussa, in the Peloponnese, try *batsos* with the local olives and a glass of Naoussa wine.

Feta The most famous Greek cheese, sometimes known in Greece as farmhouse cheese. Made from sheep's milk, *feta* is white and crumbly with a slightly sour, salty flavour – a pleasant, moderately priced table cheese. In isolated villages it is still made traditionally by pouring fresh unpasteurized sheep's milk into large leather pouches that are left hanging through the heat of the day. This process quickly curdles the milk, separating it into curds and whey. The curds are scooped out and packed into small baskets, the whey combined with salt to make brine, and the cheese is then stored in this brine for a week or two.

Although cheese-makers throughout Greece use the same basic method to make *feta*, there are marked regional variations. A good *feta* has a flaky texture and a mildly salty, fresh flavour. When you buy *feta* ask for some of the brine in which it is stored – the cheese can be refrigerated in this for up to 2 weeks longer, but without it your *feta* will only last a few days. Buy only Greek *feta*; many other countries now make this cheese but do not always use the distinctively flavoured sheep's milk and the result is a vastly inferior product. *Feta* is best eaten young (ripened for a month or two); if ripened longer it becomes unpleasantly salty. Enjoy *feta* just as it is or sprinkle it with a little olive oil and dried *rigani* or fresh oregano and serve it as a *meze* or with grilled dishes. With the exception of Prawns in a Pot with Feta Cheese (page 115) and Baked Aubergines with Tomatoes and Feta Cheese (page 199), I do not recommend using *feta* in cooked dishes, as cooking dissipates its fresh flavour.

Galotyri A distinctive soft and creamy cheese made from ewe's milk in late summer. The best is said to come from the mountain villages of Epirus in central Greece. *Galotyri* ("milk-cheese") is naturally fermented in crocks, goatskins or barrels for up to two months, and rich with the flavours of the local flora. A thick smooth texture (similar to that of yogurt) and tart flavour makes *galotyria* a deliciously refreshing snack or dessert; serve with figs, or other ripe fruits, and honey.

Graviera   A mild-tasting, slightly salted cheese made from sheep's or cow's milk. Similar in both texture and flavour to gruyère cheese, *graviera* is used mostly in sauces (page 156 and page 240). The best *graviera* is produced in the Cretan mountains, and this is served as a traditional and delicious accompaniment to fresh or poached fruits (pages 287 and 288).

Halloumi   A soft or semi-hard creamy-white cheese from Cyprus. This salty goat's milk cheese is often flavoured with coriander or mint. It is very good grilled and sprinkled with lemon juice as a *meze*.

Kasseri   *Kephalotyri*'s milder and creamier cousin, known to Greeks as "factory cheese" since it is reconstituted from the curds of *kephalotyri*. However, it is often a perfectly acceptable, good-tasting cheese – always taste before buying.

Kaskavali   A ewe's milk cheese made in the north of Greece, and in the Balkans. Its distinctive flavour is derived from the curds being heated before salting and pressing. With its thin rind, pale yellow colour and herbal flavour, *kaskavali* is a very pleasant *meze* cheese.

Kephalotyri   Named for its head-like shape, *kephalotyri* is a hard, pale yellow cheese made from unpasteurized sheep's or goat's milk. The curds are rubbed with salt, then returned to the mould for 3 days for a rind to form. Young *kephalotyri* is a good table cheese; one around 8 months old or more makes excellent Fried Cheese (page 38), and aged *kephalotyri* is perfect for grating over *macaronia* dishes.

Kopanisti   This cheese is ripened in earthenware crocks called *kopanisti* – hence the name. It is a blue cheese, made only on the islands. Freshly made curds are cut and wrapped in cloth, then left to dry to develop a bluish-green mould. This mould, along with salt, is kneaded into the curds and left to ripen. With a light peppery flavour, *kopanisti* is a perfect *meze* cheese, a wonderful complement to Thasos olives.

Lathotyri   One of Greece's best-known regional cheeses, *lathotyri* is produced only on the islands of Lesbos and Zakynthos. Each cheese is made in the shape of a miniature barrel and stored for 1-3 months in olive oil, hence its Greek name, "oil-cheese". True *lathotyri* is delicious, but there are many inferior imitations on the market.

Manouri   A fresh *manouri* cheese, made in the spring by Cretan shepherds, is one of the great flavours of the Greek kitchen. *Manouri* is sweet, creamy-white, with a buttery, slightly 'earthy' flavour – it is the perfect dessert cheese. Serve with rich, aromatic Greek honey and fresh figs or other seasonal fruit, or enjoy the cheese for breakfast with currant bread (page 262) and fresh fruit.

Metsovo   Also excellent for the *meze* table are two cheeses made in the Pindus mountain village of Metsovo. One type of *metsovo* is a light flaky goat's milk cheese flavoured with whole black peppercorns, the other an unusual smoked sheep's milk cheese.

Megithra *Megithra*, made only on the Cycladic islands, is one of the few Greek cheeses that has anything added to the curds. When the curds are cut for the first time, herbs, usually oregano or thyme, are mixed in, and the curds are pressed into a goatskin and left to mature for 4 months or more.

Myzithra Made from the whey from *feta* or *kephalotyri*. Fresh sheep's or goat's milk is added to the whey, then the curds are separated and poured into muslin-lined baskets, with light weights placed on top. After one or two days this young fresh *myzithra*, sometimes known as *anari*, is ready to enjoy. During the autumn, winter, and early spring these flavourful unsalted cheeses, still displaying the indentations of the baskets, are sold in every Greek market. Unfortunately, young *myzithra* is not exported, but fresh ricotta is a reasonable substitute – or you can make your own (recipe follows). The *myzithra* widely available here is a pale yellow semi-hard cheese with a mildly nutty, almost buttery flavour. This is aged *myzithra*, about three months old, and a perfect grating cheese for *macaronia* dishes.

Toulomotyri Matured for three months encased in animal hide, *toulomotyri* ("skin-cheese") does not look like the most appetizing cheese in the world. But if you visit Greece and are offered a chance to sample this glorious cheese, please do. It's a cheese with an ancient pedigree – a pure white sheep's curd cheese, semi-soft, a little sour, even strangely musty, and truly delicious with sweet wine and fruit. The whey left over from making *toulomotyri* is used to make a tangy version of *manouri* (see above).

Fresh Cheese
Myzithra
Makes about 225 g/8 oz

2 litres/3¹/₂ pints Channel Island or organic full-fat milk or other milk of choice
Juice of 1 small lemon, strained

Line a sieve with 2 layers of muslin and set over a bowl. Bring the milk to a boil in a stainless steel saucepan. Immediately remove from the heat, add the lemon juice, and stir with a wooden spoon until the curds separate from the whey. If they do not separate, return the saucepan to very low heat and stir until they do. Pour slowly through the muslin and set aside for 15 minutes to drain. Refrigerate the whey for later use in soups or casseroles. Fold the muslin over the curds, place a weighted plate on top, and let drain for 1 hour. For a firmer cheese, refrigerate overnight with the weight in place. Dry the muslin bag with paper towels and refrigerate it in an airtight container. For the freshest flavour, use within 2 days but it can be kept for up to 5 days.

Serve with honey, fresh fruit, and crusty bread. Or sprinkle with extra virgin olive oil, *rigani* (page 14), a little fine-grain sea salt, and cracked black pepper, and serve with olives and bread.

Butter / *Voutiro*

In the hot Greek climate fresh sweet butter is a rare commodity. But when you do find it, made from sheep's or goat's milk and rather like clotted cream in texture, it tastes wonderful. According to some Greeks, goat's milk butter, which quickly develops a rather "high" aroma and flavour, is an essential flavouring for *macaronia* (page 235).

In Greek cooking butter does not generally play an important flavouring role, except in pastries. Unsalted butter can be used but clarified butter is the traditional choice and produces the finer flavour. Butter can be clarified in large quantities and, once processed, it keeps for several months in the refrigerator.

To clarify butter   Melt 900 g/2 lb butter in a heavy saucepan over low heat. When it begins to foam, gently stir in 4 tablespoons cracked wheat. Cook over low heat until the butter no longer steams (this indicates that all the water is expelled), remove from the heat, and set aside for 30 minutes. Carefully decant into a container, leaving the salt and other residues on the bottom of the saucepan with the cracked wheat. You can also clarify butter by straining it through 3 layers of muslin, but decanting produces the clearest, most satisfactory, result.

Herbs and Spices / *Votana ke Aromata*

It would be difficult to imagine Greek food without the characteristic aromatic pungency of a wide range of fresh herbs and spices. Parsley, coriander, and mint, fresh from the kitchen garden, are used in large quantities; wild herbs (*rigani*, marjoram, thyme, sage, and fennel), with a fresh concentrated strength, are gathered from the dry rocky hillsides.

Listed below you will find information on the herbs and spices most commonly used in the Greek kitchen and in these recipes.

Various factors, such as climate, soil, time of year, and length of storage, all affect the pungency of any herb or spice you use. Thus, I have given guidance on seasonings for each dish but feel free to adjust the amounts specified – let your own taste be the final judge.

Dill / *Anithos*   Quickly glancing at bunches of fresh herbs in a Greek market, it is easy to mistake the gentle fronds of dill for fennel; their seasons overlap. But dill is earlier and a darker green. In early spring dill is a favourite flavouring in soups or dishes made with *avgolemono* sauce.

Bay Laurel / *Dafni*   An indispensable flavouring in both savoury and sweet dishes, bay laurel is pungent and strong. Its Greek name is a legacy from myth – Daphne had the misfortune to be turned into a bay laurel tree by the sun god Apollo!

Rosemary / *Dendrolivano* or *Arismari*   Rosemary grows wild throughout Greece and the best aromatic rosemary, with beautiful tiny purple-blue flowers, is said to grow on the dry hills close to the sea. Rosemary is used in Greek cooking mainly to aromatize roasts and grilled meats and fish – a few sprigs of fresh rosemary make a perfect basting brush.

Anise / *Glykaniso*   The seeds of the anise bush, a member of the hemlock family, are used to flavour ouzo, breads, biscuits, and cakes. Anise is available in Greek and Middle Eastern shops; buy only in small quantities as it quickly loses its flavour.

Cumin / *Kimino* Cumin is a member of the same botanical family as fennel, dill, and coriander. For the sweetest, most pungent flavour, buy the dried seeds whole, and grind them when needed. In Greek cooking cumin gives a very special character to roast pork and lentil dishes.

Coriander / *Koriandron* Coriander has been cultivated in Greece since antiquity. Fresh coriander leaves are a stimulating aromatic in dried bean dishes and vegetables cooked *à la grècque* (pages 190 to 192); the pulverized dried seeds are a popular flavouring for pork (pages 170, 171 and 173). Ground coriander quickly loses its perfumed pungency, so store the seeds whole and pulverize them only when needed. The ancients believed a cordial of fresh coriander, garlic, and wine to be an effective aphrodisiac. Dried coriander seeds are also used to preserve meat (*pastourmas*, page 348) and to flavour sausages (pages 176, 178).

Parsley / *Maidanos* or *Petroselino* Few savoury Greek dishes do not require parsley. Flat leaf parsley, which is measured by the handful in Greek cooking, has a more delicate appearance and milder flavour than the more common curly-leaf variety. Greeks regard parsley as a true tonic (it contains iron, minerals, and vitamins A and C) and consider it a natural deodorizer, absorbing the smell of other strong flavours such as wine, garlic, and vinegar. Take a minute or two to strip the leaves from the parsley stalks before use to prevent any trace of bitterness in your finished dish.

Marjoram / *Mandzurana* Pot marjoram (*origanum onites*) is the type most commonly used in Greek cooking. It is a smaller, more delicate herb than its botanical cousin, sweet or "garden" marjoram (*origanum hortensis*), which has a markedly different flavour. There can be confusion over the two so be sure to check which one you are buying if you wish to avoid disappointment in your finished dish. Marjoram is the essential flavouring in many lamb dishes and in *loukoumia* (known to us as turkish delight).

Fennel / *Marathon* In spring, new shoots of fennel flavour an exquisite bread (page 256). Later, the silky fronds are added to salads, wild greens, pies, and beetroot dishes. During early autumn the seeds are collected and dried, to be used in fish dishes, sweet breads, and pork dishes all through the year. The flavour is similar to liquorice.

Mastic / *Mastiha* The resin collected from the bark of a small bush, mastic is a flavouring unique to the Eastern Mediterranean. It is sold as small hard granules – pulverize them in a clean coffee grinder or mortar, with double the quantity of sugar, before using. Mastic flavours biscuits (page 281), breads (page 258), drinks (page 334) and rice pudding (page 299).

Oregano / *Rigani* Greek oregano is a stronger sharper version of the familiar imported Italian herb. The word *oregano* is from the Greek, meaning "joy of the mountains", and *oreganum heracleoticum*, the herb known to the ancient Greeks, covers the hills and mountain slopes of Greece and perfumes the air. You can find large bunches of dried *rigani* in Greek shops; it is worth seeking out to give an authentic flavour to these recipes. Use the leaves on salads, on grilled foods, and in casseroles, and throw the twigs on a barbecue fire. Italian oregano (*oreganum vulgare*) can be substituted but will not provide the characteristic pungency associated with *rigani*.

Celery / *Selino*   Celery is a very popular flavouring in meat and fish casseroles, soups, and pickles. The celery available to the Greek cook is wild celery; its natural habitat is marshland near the sea but in Greece it is semicultivated. The leaves, similar in appearance to flat leaf parsley, are a beautiful shade of dark green; they have a mild, almost sweet, flavour, without any trace of the slightly bitter aftertaste of the pale leaves of large cultivated celery. During spring and summer Greek and Chinese shops stock wild celery; if unavailable, use the darkest leaves of rib celery, but first blanch them in boiling water.

Mint / *Thiosmos or Mentha*   Several varieties of this deliciously refreshing herb are popular in Greece. Water mint is the type most commonly used in cooking dishes such as stuffed tomatoes. Peppermint, spearmint, lemon mint, and corn mint are all used to make fragrant herbal teas. Our nearest equivalent for cooking is fresh garden mint (use only the young tender leaves). Dried spearmint is delicious in *tsatsiki* (page 54).

Savory / *Throumbi*   There are two types of this fragrant herb. Winter savory (*satureia hortensis*) is a favourite herb for flavouring grilled dishes, especially lamb and pork. Delicate summer savory (*satureia thymbra*) is rarely used in Greek cooking but it makes a soothing and popular tea.

Thyme / *Thymari*   The thyme most widely available in Greece, the type that covers the dry limestone hills and is the source of the wonderful fragrance and flavour of Hymettus honey, is too strong to be used in cooking. But in the hillside villages, a gentler, sweeter version grows and this is used a great deal in the kitchen. It flavours game and pork as no other herb can.

Basil / *Vasilikos*   Pots of sweetly fragrant basil, believed to keep flies away, are a common sight in Greece, but this herb is rarely used in cooking except in cakes and breads celebrating important religious events. The reasons for this are lost in folklore and myth, although basil's Greek name, meaning "kingly," may give us a clue; but it is also known as the "devil plant" and is associated with misfortune.

The herbs detailed above are all grown in Greece, but it was trade in other aromatics that helped create the wealth on which classical Greece thrived. These were mainly spices, some introduced through trade with Egypt, others brought back from eastern military campaigns by Alexander the Great.

Cinnamon / *Kanella*   Produced from the bark of the cinnamon tree this heady spice is used to maximum advantage in the Greek kitchen. A favourite flavouring in lamb dishes (it is essential for magnificent *moussakas*), it also lends a delectable fragrance to cakes, syrups, biscuits, and pies. Whole cinnamon sticks can be stored almost indefinitely; ground cinnamon is easier to use but be sure to buy only small quantities at a time since it quickly loses its pungency.

Nutmeg and Mace / *Moskhokario*   Deep-yellow nutmegs are the hard seeds of soft fruit; mace is nutmeg's lacy reddish-orange natural covering. Nutmeg, rich and pungent, is best stored whole and grated as needed; mace has a milder, less acrid flavour, and ground mace is fine for cooking. Both impart a lovely fragrance to sauces and casseroles.

Cloves / *Moskokarfi* Spicy cloves, the unopened flower buds of the clove tree, have a powerful fragrance. Whole cloves are used to perfume syrups, decorate biscuits, and impart an unforgettable fragrance to beef casseroles; ground cloves add a delicious flavour to biscuits.

Pepper / *Piperi* Pungent black pepper is generally preferred to the stronger, less subtle white. Invest in a good-quality pepper mill – ready-ground pepper is no substitute for freshly ground. I find it useful to have three pepper mills: one for black pepper, one for white, and one for a mixture of the two.

Vanilla / *Vanillia* Vanilla, the dried pod of a tropical orchid, is a relative newcomer to the Greek kitchen (used only since the medieval period) but is an essential flavouring in many cakes and pastries. Buy only good-quality pure vanilla extract. You can also make vanilla sugar by keeping a vanilla bean in a jar of granulated or caster sugar.

Carob / *Xsilokerata* Carob is now better known as "health-food chocolate," a substitute for the real thing. But at other times in its long history, it had considerable economic importance (its seeds were the original carat measurement used by jewellers). In antiquity, carob was a favourite flavouring in confections. On Crete, the world's largest exporter of carob, it is now mostly used in wine production or to make syrup.

In addition to these aromatic flavourings, such spices as caraway seeds, paprika, aniseed, allspice, cayenne pepper, mustard seeds, and dry mustard appear in many Greek dishes.

With the exception of cinnamon, all spices should be bought whole if possible and ground in a spice grinder or electric coffee grinder as required. Buy in small quantities and store in airtight jars away from the light to minimize loss of the spice's oil. It is this oil that aromatizes and flavours food.

Capers / *Kapari*

In the spring, the small tender leaves of the spindly wall-hugging caper bush, a native of the eastern Mediterranean, are picked; in early summer the tight flower buds, varying in size from tiny currants to small olives, are gathered. Leaves and buds are thoroughly cleaned and dried, then pickled in white wine vinegar aromatized with bruised fennel seeds. The capers can be eaten after one month or stored in the pickling liquid for up to a year. Capers give incomparable zest and character to grilled foods (especially lamb), beef casseroles, and fish dishes. Sprinkled with a little olive oil they can also be served as part of a *meze* table. Caper leaves make a pretty and edible garnish or flavouring. Buy small capers packed by a reputable supplier; some of the larger ones on the market are actually nasturtium buds.

Nuts / *Karythia*

Almonds (*amigdala*) have probably been cultivated in Greece for as long as the grape, the fig, and the olive and they feature in many ancient and traditional recipes. Eaten instead of meat and dairy products during religious fasts they are also symbols of long life and happiness. For festive sugar-coated almonds – and to flavour preserves – the Jordan, or "bitter," almond is used. For all other purposes the "sweet" almond is the type of choice.

Almonds are the central ingredient in rich Greek cakes (page 270), in Garlic Almond Sauce (page 314), and a soft marzipan sweetmeat called *amigdalota*. Pounded with sugar to a sweet paste, they are used to make *soumada*, a delicious syrupy drink. On Crete almonds are believed to prevent a hangover and are eaten in large handfuls before any serious raki drinking begins. These nuts are sold on every street corner, either salted or coated with honey.

Karythia is the Greek word for nuts but it is also the name for the walnut, popular throughout Greece. During autumn newly ripe walnuts are everywhere – served with ouzo or raki, made into cakes, sprinkled over desserts, and pounded into a creamy sauce (page 317). Very young walnuts are preserved for the winter – either in salt and vinegar to serve as a *meze* or in honey to nibble with coffee.

Waxy white pine nuts (*koukounaria*), from the cones of the stone pine, are a delicate and essential ingredient in a favourite *pilafi* (page 227) and make a delicious sauce (page 318). Since the stone pine bears fruit only every three years and the nuts have to be extracted from their tough outer covering by hand, pine nuts are expensive even in Greece.

Hazelnuts (*foundouki*), sold by every street vendor, are used to make wonderful biscuits. On the vendor's tray there are also purple-skinned, green-fleshed pistachio nuts (*fistikia*); their delicate sweet perfume scents elegant creamy desserts (page 303) and often replaces sesame seeds in *pasteli*, a popular sweet.

Shop-bought ground nuts are, of course, easy for the cook. But in terms of moistness and flavour it is worth shelling, skinning, and grinding nuts yourself. The skins are easily removed after dipping the nuts into boiling water, and a food processor or blender makes short work of grinding (use a clean coffee grinder for small quantities or treat yourself to an antique nut grinder).

Honey / *Meli*

According to legend, honey was literally a lifesaver for Zeus, the king of the ancient Greek gods. His father, Cronos, had a nasty habit of murdering his male offspring to prevent them threatening his omnipotence and power. Keeping the baby Zeus quiet, therefore, was vital; spoonfuls of sweet and fragrant honey did the trick! Perhaps this is why honey-candied fruits were once a favourite sacrificial offering to the gods.

For Greeks the best honey comes from Mount Hymettus; clear and thick, it is perfumed with the thyme blossom that covers the mountain slopes. Most Greek honeys have a herbal bouquet although a few hint at the more floral notes of almond or citrus blossom. Honey contains natural minerals and trace elements beneficial to health and its aroma and pungency are so satisfying that only small amounts are needed. So, for a variety of reasons, honey is a healthier sweetener than sugar.

Honey and bread is a quick, nutritious snack; add honey to yogurt and you have a meal fit for the gods. Pungent blends of honey and vinegar are traditional flavourings for Greek casseroles, vegetables, and fish, and what would filo pastry be without its luscious drenching of honey syrup?

You can now find Hymettus honey in Greek and Middle Eastern shops, health food shops, and our better supermarkets, but if this proves difficult, unfiltered herb or orange blossom honey are good substitutes.

Lemons / *Lemonia*

The clear sharp tang of lemon was unknown to the ancient Greeks; this pretty fruit made its first appearance in Greece at the time of the thirteenth-century Crusades. But it would be difficult now to imagine Greece without its profusion of lemon trees, or a Greek meal without the colour and piquant flavour lemons bring.

Lemon juice is an essential ingredient in many marinades and sauces, and it is the perfect complement to rich fruity olive oil. A small bunch of lemon leaves makes an exquisitely perfumed basting brush for grilled foods, and lemon zest and juice give a refreshing pungency to syrups and savoury dishes. And what would a platter of tiny fried fish, *kephtedes*, or *souvlakia* be without their garnish of bright lemon wedges? Oil extracted from lemon zest is also a fragrant flavouring in sweet pies and cakes, and pretty rolled strips of peel make a luscious sweetmeat.

To make the most of versatile lemons it's a good idea to invest in three inexpensive kitchen implements – a zester (to remove tiny strips of zest), a wooden reamer (to quickly juice a lemon), and a stripper (to remove small sections of zest for flavouring or garnish). Empty lemon halves, pierced with a skewer and dipped into olive oil, make perfect natural basters for grilled fish and other dishes.

From every Greek lemon harvest some fruit is set aside to be preserved. Lightly treated with salt and stored in olive oil, lemons acquire a lively and distinctive flavour, perfect as a last-minute addition to casseroles, beans, and liver and fish dishes. Save the olive oil used as a preservative – it adds a delicious flavouring to salads and grilled dishes.

Preserved Lemons

5 large lemons (unsprayed if possible)
5 tablespoons coarse-grain sea salt or kosher salt
Extra virgin olive oil, to cover the lemons
Sprigs of dried *rigani* (page 14), marjoram, or thyme or large bay leaves

If you have unsprayed lemons you need only to rinse them well. Otherwise, cover the lemons with boiling water and set aside to cool. Drain, then cover with cold water. Set aside for 2 days, changing the water 3 or 4 times. Dry the lemons, cut off a thin slice from each end, and cut lemon into 6 mm/$1/4$ inch slices. Remove any seeds with the point of a small knife, spread the slices on a plate, and sprinkle with the salt. Cover and refrigerate 24 hours.

Layer the slices in glass or earthenware jars and pour over any of the brine (salt water) left on the plate. Place the herb sprigs or bay leaves on top of the lemons, wedging them under the rims of the jars, and pour over enough oil to cover. The sprigs keep the slices immersed and flavour the olive oil. Cover tightly with cling film and let sit at room temperature for at least 2 weeks. Refrigerate after opening, and use within 3 months.

Oranges / *Portokalia*

Navel and Seville are the types of oranges generally found in Greek kitchens. Navel oranges, large juicy, sweetly perfumed, and thick-skinned, are on every dining table during their season. The skins are made into sweetmeats (Candies, below) or a spoon sweet (page 298), or the zest (orange rind) dried to flavour cakes and casseroles. To dry the zest, remove the orange part of the skin in long strips and dry in a very low oven or in the sun. Hang the strips in the kitchen – they will add a lovely scent to the room – and break off pieces as you need them. (Treat lemon zest the same way.)

Seville oranges have a bitter flavour so cannot be eaten straight from the tree. Tiny ones, however, are preserved whole in a thick honey or sugar syrup as a delicious spoon sweet. The juice from larger oranges is used in dishes such as Pork in Aspic (page 36).

The blood orange, not widely popular on the Greek mainland, is more appreciated on the islands. Similar to a navel orange in taste, the flesh of a blood orange is a startling deep blood red. Its juice makes an unusual mayonnaise and a vibrantly coloured drink.

Orange extract is used to flavour biscuits and cakes; orange blossom infused to make a headily perfumed essence or "water" to flavour syrups, and also made into an exquisite spoon sweet (page 298). There is no substitute for orange extract or orange flower water; the best brands are available in speciality shops.

Candies / *Zakharota*

Candies, or sweetmeats, are a legacy of antiquity. The word is derived from *Candia*, the ancient name for Crete, where it was considered that the best honey and honeyed fruits originated. The candies so beloved by the ancients were sweet and fragrant, and many of these are still made in Greece in exactly the same way. The most popular are *pasteli* (Honey Sesame Sweetmeats, page 308), Moustalevria Sweetmeats, flavoured with cinnamon (page 306) sugared almonds, *loukoumia* (known here as turkish delight), and a sweet paste made from the quince. A more modern sweetmeat, very simple and economical to produce at home, can be made from the peel of oranges, lemons, or grapefruit.

Candied Citrus Peel / *Portokalofloutho glyko*

Cut oranges into 8 or 10 lengthways segments, lemons into 6, and grapefruit into 12. Remove the flesh with a small paring knife. Weigh the peels and measure out an equal quantity of sugar; set aside.

Place the peels in a large saucepan, cover with cold water, and bring to a boil. Drain and repeat the process 3 times. Drain, cover with cold water, and set aside for 2 hours. Drain, and thoroughly dry with paper towels.

Thread a trussing or other large needle with thin kitchen string and tie a large knot at the end. Roll each piece of peel into a spiral and thread onto the string, passing the needle through the roll so it will not unravel. Thread no more than 18 rolls onto each length of string, and tie the two ends together.

Place the sugar and half its volume of water in a large heavy saucepan. Slowly bring to the boil, stirring until the sugar is dissolved. Simmer 5 minutes, then add the strings of peel. Simmer uncovered for 30 minutes or until a needle will easily pierce the rolls. Remove from the syrup and let cool.

Carefully pull out the string. The rolls will be left intact. Boil the syrup until it just reaches the light thread stage (112C/230F) on a sugar thermometer. Stir in the juice of 1 small lemon and pour this syrup over the rolls. Store the syrup in a covered container for up to 1 month.

To serve, remove the rolls from the syrup and coat each one with honey, preferably Hymettus, or granulated sugar.

Ingredients at Home

In some recipes here I use ingredients that consumers and consumer groups today may rightly question on health grounds. I find that if I know the source of my ingredients, I feel secure in using them. I buy meat only when I can be assured of the standards of the farm where it was raised; vegetables and greens I cannot grow myself I buy from smallholdings nearby or from the organic section in my local supermarket; I've found a source of organic milk and grains and I make my own yogurt and bread; a local farm, where the chickens appear as happy as I would imagine chickens were able to be, provides my eggs and poultry. I enjoy best of all ingredients grown or produced close to home for I know I am not only eating fresh food, but also food which has not suffered all the manhandling entailed in our modern packaging/storing methods.

pots, pans, and kitchen tools
tsoukalia, tigania ke ergalia kouzinas

The most important, and most frequently used, tool in the Greek kitchen is the mortar and pestle. Greek cooks like to have three – a large walnut mortar in which to pound and blend *salates,* a large marble mortar and pestle for pulverizing nuts and spices, and a small brass or wooden mortar and pestle for bruising herbs. A food processor or blender could do this work quickly and easily, but these machines cannot produce the fine flavour that traditional equipment seems to be able to. I find too that the delectable aromas released into the air when herbs and spices are pounded with oils are wonderfully satisfying.

Your repertoire of pots and pans should include the following:

An enamelled cast-iron casserole with a tight-fitting lid, for long slow oven baking. The best is called a *doufeu*. It has an indented lid that can be filled with water to keep the food moist during slow baking. Without the water, the *doufeu* can be used as an ordinary heavy casserole.

Heavy cast-iron sauté pans, the plainer and heavier the better. (Fancy surfaces soon wear out and also prevent meat from browning properly.) You need one medium-sized and one large one.

A cast-iron omelette pan. In Greece a traditional shallow cast-iron pan is preferred as it can be taken straight to the table.
Also useful is a **round aluminium baking dish (*tapsi*),** about 5-7 cm/2-3 inches deep and 37 cm/15 inches in diameter, available in Greek and Middle Eastern shops.

For cooking and serving traditional dishes, nothing can beat **earthenware pots**. They should be glazed on the inside. If kitchen space is limited choose one deep casserole with a lid and one oval or round baking dish. If you can store more, add a deep bean pot (similar to a *cassoulet* pot), a rectangular dish (for baked *macaronia* dishes), and an unglazed clay pot (which I find produces a wonderful flavour in potatoes and beetroot).

Pickles and vinegar are best stored in stoneware jars. Stoneware is not, in fact available in Greek villages but it is a much better material for long-term storage than porous earthenware. Small stoneware or glazed earthenware jars with tight-fitting stoppers are the most effective containers for dried herbs and spices. You may also like to collect special storage jars for specific ingredients, such as salt-glazed containers for sea salt or a jar with a tap at the base for vinegar.

Three good knives should be a minimum requirement in any serious cook's kitchen: a large chopping knife, a flexible filleting knife, and a paring knife.

The utensil I would least like to be without is the moulis-légumes. Unlike a food processor or blender, a moulis-légumes produces a delicious texture in soups and vegetable dishes and it can process larger quantities at one time.

A hinged double grill saves work too, making the grilling of small fish and pieces of meat simple.
And a few more:
A balloon whisk and small sauce whisk
A colander and several sizes of sieve
A wide pastry brush, for filo
Heavy baking trays

Coffee-making equipment

Briki long-handled, small brass coffee pot; the 4- or 6-cup size is the most useful.

Flintzani tiny coffee cups

Milos tou kafe a magnificent coffee grinder, usually brass, but older ones are often made of copper.

There are other kitchen tools, dishes, and storage pots in common use in Greek village kitchens of interest to serious cooks elsewhere. All have their origins in antiquity but are in daily use in the village. If you enjoy exploring markets you may like to look for a few of the following:

Bread-making equipment

Skafi a wooden trough for mixing and kneading the dough, usually about 90 cm/3 feet long and 60 cm/ 2 feet wide

Koskino a large shallow sieve, for sifting flour

Petromilos a large millstone with a wooden handle, for grinding flour

Tipari a carved wooden seal about 15 cm/6 inches in diameter, used to imprint "offering" bread for the church

Casseroles

Kapamas or lopas a glazed earthenware casserole with sloping sides and a conical lid; it gives its name to the dish *kapamas* (page 124)

Pithos a beautiful tall earthenware bean pot

Tsentsero a deep earthenware casserole with an elegant lid

Tsouka a round earthenware baking dish without a lid, for baking foods in the *fournos*

Tsoukali a smaller version of the *tsouka*, but with a lid and sometimes a handle

Grilling equipment

Souvles 30- to 45-cm/12- to 18-inch long skewers, often with elaborate cast metal animals at one end, for *souvlakia*

Foufou a beautiful little clay brazier, based on a design used by the Minoans and still to be found in Cretan villages; for grilling small birds and fish

Mangali a deep metal tray on legs, standing about 60 cm/2 feet high, for *souvlakia*. The ends of the skewers (*souvles*) rest on the sides of the *mangali*, so no metal grill is needed

Cheese-making equipment

Trikon a deep basket with slightly sloping sides, made in many sizes – the smallest holds a ¹/₄-kilo cheese, the largest, a cheese weighing several kilos; lined with muslin, the *trikon* is then filled with curds and left on a tray to drain

Kopanaki wooden paddle for kneading and shaping the curds

And in village courtyards you may be lucky enough to find:

Kazani (colloquial Arabic name) or **lebes** (Greek) the ubiquitous iron cooking pot, used on a tripod over an open fire

Pitharia unglazed storage pots, some standing 1.2 m/4 feet high, and decorated with simple but beautiful designs dating from antiquity

Stamnos a gorgeous squat pot with two handles at the neck, for storing liquids such as vinegar or wine

Souratha similar to the *stamnos*, but with a spout on one side of the neck for easier pouring; with a *souratha* you do not need to master the difficult trick of tilting the large *stamnos* over your shoulder

Amourghi an earthenware cooking pot with cups attached on both sides, to hold the ingredients to be added to the pot in the cooking

Hydria a large earthenware jar with three handles, for carrying and storing water

Kakave a three-legged pot, which gives its name to the dish *kakavia* (fish soup)

Skoupa the appropriately named brush for sweeping the courtyard

My neighbour on the island of Crete, Irina, keeps a traditional kitchen, still using many of these ancient cooking tools. The entrance to her house is through a pretty paved courtyard that serves as an extension of both kitchen and sitting room; on warm days a large dining table is set up here, shaded from the fierce midday sun by a beautiful trellised vine.

Built in to the far side of the courtyard wall is a beehive-shaped oven (*fournos*) where all the family baking is done. Nearby are propped a long handled wooden rake and paddle, used for removing baking trays and red-hot embers, and in one corner is a pile of kindling (the rest of the wood, mostly olive, is neatly stacked on the roof). In the corner a small blackened alcove encloses a fireplace and metal tripod supporting a large encrusted black cauldron with a gleaming interior, and a grill rests against the stones surrounding the fire. A small opening in the wall leads to a small stone building where the grape press, olive press, and huge storage jars (*pitharia*) for wine, olive oil, olives, vinegar, and pickles are kept.

Inside the small kitchen, a double burner (fuelled by bottled gas) occupies one shelf; this is used mainly to make coffee – a concession to progress that most villagers have made. Four small wall cupboards hold bowls and kitchen tools; casseroles and saucepans are stored outside. Three mortars of varying sizes stand against one wall. A tiny pantry extends beyond the kitchen where preserves, preserved meats, pickles, yogurt, and cheeses are stored, and bunches of herbs and smoked sausages dangle from the ceiling.

A short walk from the house brings you to the delightful kitchen garden where Irina grows the herbs and all the vegetables she needs. Caper bushes cover the surrounding low stone walls and the lush greenery of asparagus and artichoke plants contrasts vividly with the barren hills beyond. In one corner of the garden is a well, tapping a natural spring, and beyond the garden is a small field where Irina's father grows wheat. Along the hillside, beyond the wheat field, are the vines and olive trees that have provided Irina's family with their basic necessities for centuries.

For me the simplicity of Irina's traditional kitchen was a revelation. I quickly discovered that I could produce superb food with very little sophisticated equipment and that there is wonderful satisfaction in working with traditional tools in an atmosphere of calm, tranquillity, and order.

About the Recipes

There is a marked gender bias in the preparation and serving of food in Greece. This does not, of course, affect the flavour of the food but it does influence any selection of recipes. The oral tradition in the kitchen, passing recipes from mother to daughter, is still very strong, but men also take a keen interest in food and have their own oral tradition, passing on knowledge and skill in spit roasting, grilling, and oven (*fournos*) baking from father to son. In hotels, restaurants, and tavernas most chefs are male and, while they have a broad overview of their country's food, their knowledge is often confined to the professional, rather than the domestic, kitchen.

My experience of food and cooking in Greece falls somewhere between all these categories. I learned a great deal about grilling and roasting, for example, from good male cooks in the village where I lived. Through their experience and knowledge I also began to appreciate the particular culinary skills of Greek hunters and fishermen.

And since I lived in a village, I was always welcome in family kitchens – traditionally the woman's domain and a place where men are rarely seen. Here I learned just how pleasurable and creative food preparation can be, and how skilled Greek women cooks are at a range of remarkable vegetable cookery and at bread and pastry making.

Occasionally Athens would lure me. In this cosmopolitan city I enjoyed the company of urban Greek friends, many from families returned from Asia Minor. They too have their food preferences and particular flavouring skills in the kitchen. And I have to thank the chefs, on the mainland and on the beautiful islands, who shared with me their professional secrets and taught me much about the Greek attitude to food, to cooking, and to flavour. These combined experiences, city and country, domestic and professional, provided me with the inspiration and information for this selection of recipes.

I have tried to be completely scrupulous in crediting the recipes, but it has not been an easy task! Few people, especially villagers, could be persuaded to give me a recipe I could actually write down, preferring instead to give me an idea (albeit lovingly descriptive) of the "essence" of a dish. Or they would give me a list of ingredients calling for "a little of this, more of that," until the flavour was "just right". Details about traditional dishes such as *stifado* (page 166) or *fassolada* (page 66) tended to follow these lines – how on earth could anyone not know the best way to make and flavour these familiar dishes?

My recipes are the result of tasting and more tasting, until I was satisfied I had reproduced an authentic Greek flavour. Most of the recipes have been adapted to a greater or lesser degree to suit our kitchens and tastes. Where I have used a recipe exactly as it was given to me, or stressed a technique or ingredient in the way it was stressed to me, I have said so and credited the cook who passed the recipe on to me. These were usually the recipes of the chefs, who understood my need for a concise explanation. However, even they tended to answer the question "Why?" with the response, "Because that is the way it has always been done."

Appetizers and First Courses

mezedes ke orektika

Philosophers the ancient Greeks may have been, but they were practical too. They knew, for example, that drinking wine on an empty stomach is not a sensible idea. With characteristic creative logic they made it impossible in Greek society to indulge in such a barbaric practice – by the simple expedient of making delectable mouthfuls of solid food available wherever and whenever drinks were served. From this practical precaution stems the tradition and culture of the *meze*, now, as then, an integral part of the fabric of Greek social life.

Mezedes is usually translated as "appetizers" and, of course, these tempting little dishes are served with drinks as hors d'oeuvre and many make imaginative first courses. But the translation hardly does justice to the sheer range, ingenuity, and delight of *mezedes* nor to their fundamental place in Greek tradition.

Mezedes are available in cafés at any time; for many Greeks meeting friends to enjoy a refreshing drink and a *meze* platter makes a relaxing break in the busy working day. In Greek homes *mezedes* are automatically offered to all visitors, whether friends or strangers.

Guests are expected to help themselves to as much as they like from the *meze* platter and it's the host's duty to make sure empty dishes are replenished with more, or different, *mezedes* as necessary. This is not just politeness but an important social ritual. By providing food, drink, stimulating conversation, and an easy relaxed atmosphere the host demonstrates his/her ability to satisfy both the physical and spiritual needs of the guests. At the *meze* table the food is colourful, intensely aromatic, and highly flavoured and the conversation is similarly exuberant, dramatic, and high-spirited.

In his writings, the philosopher Plato gives us a good idea of the range of tastes and texture offered by a well-balanced *meze* table. Laid out before the guests, he says, were platters of radishes, olives, beans, green vegetables, figs, cheese, fresh chickpeas, and myrtle. Here are foods both sweet and savoury, fresh and preserved, crunchy and tender, and flavours subtle and strident. The same principle of contrasts is evident in good *meze* platters today – fresh

and preserved vegetables, crunchy nuts, soft creamy *salates*, pickles, tiny savoury pies and miniature meat patties, crumbly cheese, morsels of fried fish, octopus, or smoked eel, and fresh or dried fruit – the list is practically endless.

Mezedes are perfect for buffets and picnics, make unusual first courses, and are ideal as light lunches. A traditional *meze* table might comprise twenty-five dishes or more but for our purposes twelve to sixteen will create a spectacular display. It does take time to organise and cook a good variety of *mezedes*, but the pickled and preserved dishes can be prepared months ahead and many others one or two days before serving. You need provide only a small quantity of each *meze*, but do make sure each is decorated with an attractive edible garnish that enhances both its flavour and appearance.

Mezedes are served everywhere in Greece, from the tiniest bar to the smartest hotel, and are one of the most enjoyable features of Greek life. Some of the best *mezedes* I've tasted were in one of the crowded *meze* cafés in the back streets of Athens, around the ancient Athinas market. These high-ceilinged, marble-floored cafés ring with the buzz and bustle of humanity, all chaos and confusion. With an attractive *meze* table, ouzo, raki, or wine to drink, and the stimulating company of good friends, you can create something of the atmosphere of those vibrant cafés.

mezedakia
Small appetizers

Mezedakia
Serves 8

At the sight of a tray of *mezedakia* – small *mezedes* – tastebuds tingle and eyes light up in anticipation. The bite-size morsels, in a seductive array of colours, textures, and flavours, are titbits par excellence and Greek cooks assemble *mezedes* platters with consummate artistry and skill. On a well-balanced platter you'll find something crunchy (peppery radishes, perhaps, or fresh walnuts), something refreshing (tiny fingers of cucumber or melon or juicy tomato wedges), something salty (olives, capers, pickled aubergines), savouries such as crumbly fresh cheese or tiny fried fish, and sweet treats like dried figs or tiny plump currants.

2 large ripe tomatoes
Large pinch of sugar
Sea salt to taste
1 cucumber, peeled
12 olives, Amfissa, Thasos, or cracked green
12 Marinated Olives (page 29) or Kalamata olives
225 g/8 oz feta cheese, cut into slices or cubes

12 radishes, stems trimmed to 2.5 cm/1 inch, a few small leaves left in place

And 2 or more of the following:
24 Salted Almonds (page 30)
4–8 Peppered Dried Figs (page 30)
8 Pickled Tiny Aubergines (page 327)
8 toursi peppers (page 327)
24 capers, drained
8 salted anchovy fillets, rinsed and patted dry or small sardines packed in
olive oil (page 349)
8 slices smoked ham or sausage (page 178)

A few minutes before serving, core the tomatoes, cut each into 6 or 8 wedges, and sprinkle with sugar and salt. Cut the cucumber in half lengthways, then into 1 cm/¹/₂ inch slices to make half-moons.

Keeping each ingredient separate, arrange the *mezedakia* on a large platter, either in concentric circles or as triangular wedges.

Marinated Olives
Elies Marinata

A small barrel of these glistening aromatic olives is a familiar sight in Greek homes. They are easy to prepare and the pungent herbs used in the marinade make the fleshy Kalamata olives irresistible. After the olives are eaten, use the olive oil in salad dressings.

450 g/1 lb Kalamata olives
4 tablespoons dried *rigani* (page 14)
1 tablespoon dried rosemary
¹/₂ tablespoon dried thyme
1 teaspoon dried marjoram
5 cm/2 inch strip of orange zest
3 sprigs of dried *rigani* or thyme, each about 7 cm/3 inches long
Extra virgin olive oil, to cover the olives

Spread the olives between layers of paper towels and blot dry to remove most of the brine. Mix together the olives, dried herbs, and orange zest in a bowl. Pack loosely into a glass jar, lay the herb sprigs on top, and add olive oil to cover. Cover tightly and store for 2 days to 1 week.

Salted Almonds
Amigdala Alatismena

Traditional Greek wisdom says that eating salted almonds when you take a drink (or several!) will keep you sober. I have not put this tip to serious test myself so cannot vouch for its success, but I do know that once you've tasted the delicious sweet-sour flavour of these almonds you'll be in no hurry to buy commercially prepared ones again.

350 g/12 oz almonds, with brown skins intact
Juice of 2 lemons
3 tablespoons coarse-grain sea salt

Heat the oven to 160C/325F/gas mark 3. Combine the almonds and lemon juice in non-reactive bowl and set aside for 10 minutes; stir the almonds with a wooden spoon occasionally so they are evenly coated.

Arrange the almonds on a baking tray in a single layer and sprinkle with the salt. Bake 20 minutes or until lightly browned, stirring once or twice. Let cool and serve, or store in small airtight containers for up to 1 month.

Peppered Dried Figs
Sika Piperata

If possible, use fleshy, juicy organic figs imported from southern Greece for this simple *meze*, and prepare three days ahead for the richest flavour.

24 good-quality, moist dried figs
4 tablespoons cracked black pepper
12–18 bay leaves

Trim the fig stems. Gently roll each fig in the pepper to lightly coat.

Cover the bottom of a glass jar with a few of the bay leaves, or make an overlapping circle of leaves on 2 layers of cling film. Then make alternate layers of figs and bay leaves, finishing with a layer of leaves. Gently press down on the leaves with the palm of your hand, then tightly cover the jar or pull the edges of the cling film together into an airtight packet. Store at room temperature for up to 1 month.

Serve the figs on a bed of bay leaves.

Smoked Fish Salad
Tsirosalata
Serves 6 to 8

There is a long tradition of preserving fish in Greece and markets display a variety of brightly coloured smoked fish, stacked in decorative layers in wooden crates and barrels. On these market stalls you will also find whole anchovies packed in salt, fish roe in beeswax, sardines in olive oil, bonito in brine, or young mackerel or octopus dried in the sun. Look for preserved fish in Greek stores or delicatessens; this recipe is for smoked fish but you could substitute good-quality tuna, bonito, sardines or anchovies.

1 large smoked mackerel or herring or 2 small smoked mackerel (about 350 g/12 oz)
2 tablespoons aged red wine vinegar

For serving
1 tablespoon capers, drained
1 tablespoon extra virgin olive oil, or to taste
Coarsely ground black pepper to taste
2 tablespoons snipped fresh dill or chervil or 1 tablespoon coarsely chopped flat leaf parsley
Elitses or Niçoise olives, drained

Hold the mackerel by its tail above an open flame until the skin blisters and breaks. (Or place under a hot grill until the skin blisters.) Peel off the skin and discard the head and tail. With a thin-bladed knife, make a slit along the underside of the fish, open it like a book and, with your palm, press firmly to flatten it. Discard the backbone and skeleton. Place the fillets in a bowl, add 1 1/2 tablespoons of the vinegar, and cover with cold water. Set aside for 10 minutes.

Remove the fillets, discarding the liquid, thoroughly dry with paper towels, and cut into thin strips or bite-size pieces. Arrange on a serving plate and sprinkle with the capers, olive oil, pepper, dill, olives, and the remaining vinegar.

Tiny Fried Fish
Marithes Tiganites
Serves 6 to 8

Frugal Greek cooks let nothing go to waste. The tiniest fish of the catch are not worth sending to the market, so a taverna or café close to the harbour is the place to try this mouth-watering *meze*. Tiny fish, freshly caught and crisply fried in olive oil, are piled high on a platter, surrounded with lemon wedges, and served with ouzo or wine. In Greece, delicate little pickerel or anchovies, or the tiniest sardines, are the fish of choice for this dish; for us, whitebait are far easier to find and they make a good substitute. It's important to choose glossy-looking very fresh fish since the whole whitebait is eaten, including the bones and head.

450 g / 1 lb tiny whitebait
50 g / 2 oz plain flour
1 tablespoon chickpea flour
$^{1}/_{2}$ tablespoon coarse-grain sea salt, or more to taste
1 tablespoon cracked black pepper, or to taste
Extra virgin olive oil, for frying

For serving
2 large lemons cut into wedges

Rinse the fish, drain between layers of paper towels, and blot dry. Combine the two flours, salt, and pepper in a bowl, add the fish, and toss to coat.

Pour a 1 cm/$^{1}/_{2}$ inch layer of olive oil into a large heavy sauté pan set over low heat. When hot but not smoking, raise the heat to medium-low and add enough fish to fill the pan without overcrowding. Fry until golden brown, turning once, and drain on paper towels. Repeat with the remaining fish.

To serve, pile on a warm platter, surround with the lemon wedges, and sprinkle with more salt and pepper if desired.

Kephtedakia
Makes approximately 4 dozen *kephtedakia* or 3 dozen *kephtedes*

Kephtedakia – small, highly flavoured meat croquettes or patties, traditionally made with lamb or pork and fried or baked in good olive oil – are popular on *meze* tables whatever the occasion. Delicious warm or cold, tiny *kephtedakia* (about the size of marbles) are the perfect titbit to serve with ouzo. Make them egg-sized instead and they become *kephtedes*, which, served with a green salad, make an enjoyable and economical main course.

2 medium onions, finely chopped
450 g / 1 lb lean lamb or beef or a mixture of both, finely minced
1 large potato, peeled and grated
50 g / 2 oz fresh breadcrumbs
2 eggs, lightly beaten
1 tablespoon aged red wine vinegar, or more to taste
4 tablespoons finely chopped flat leaf parsley
Sea salt and freshly ground black pepper to taste
1 tablespoon ground cumin or 1 $^{1}/_{2}$ tablespoons ground coriander or $^{1}/_{2}$ tablespoon ground cinnamon or 2 tablespoons finely grated *kasseri* or parmesan cheese
Plain flour, for dredging
Extra virgin olive oil, for frying or baking

For serving
Juice of 1 large lemon

Combine the onion and 115 ml/4 fl oz water in a small saucepan, bring to a boil and simmer until the liquid has evaporated, about 6 minutes. Combine the onion, meat, potato, breadcrumbs, beaten egg, vinegar, parsley and a generous amount of salt and pepper in a large bowl and add one of the spices or the cheese. With a wooden spoon or your hand, mix until well blended. Add additional vinegar, salt and/or pepper to taste; the mixture should be highly flavoured. Cover and refrigerate for 1 hour.

Moisten your hands with cold water and pat them barely dry. Form the meat mixture into 2 cm/3/4 inch patties (or 4 cm/1¹/2 inch patties for *kephtedes*), flattening each slightly between your palms, and lightly dredge with flour.

To fry, pour a 6 mm/¹/4 inch layer of olive oil into a heavy frying pan set over medium-low heat. When the oil is hot but not smoking, add just enough *kephtedakia* (or *kephtedes*) to fit comfortably in a single layer. Fry until golden brown on both sides and drain between 2 layers of paper towels. Repeat with the remainder.

To bake, heat the oven to 160C/325F/gas mark 3 and warm 2 or more baking trays. Brush with olive oil and arrange the *kephtedakia* 2.5 cm/1 inch apart on the trays. Lightly brush with olive oil and bake 20-25 minutes (25-30 minutes for *kephtedes*), turning once to brown on both sides. Drain between layers of paper towels.

To serve, arrange on a platter and sprinkle with lemon juice.

Note For a buffet or first course, form the meat mixture into 2.5 cm/ 1 inch patties and cook as directed. To serve, combine the following:

1 small head of Cos lettuce, rinsed and cut into thin ribbons (chiffonade)
just before serving
6 spring onions, trimmed, the best green parts left intact, and thinly sliced
5 tablespoons coarsely chopped flat leaf parsley
1 tablespoon dried *rigani* (page 14)

Arrange this salad on a platter. Sprinkle with the strained juice of 1 lemon and extra virgin olive oil, salt, and pepper to taste. Pile the *kephtedakia* on top.

Potato Kephtedakia
Patatokephtedakia
Makes approximately 30 *kephtedakia* or 24 *kephtedes*

In the Cretan port of Aghios Nikolaos there was once a café where, along with the local backgammon players, you would also find a mouth-watering variety of traditional Cretan *mezedes*; the great speciality were these delicious *kephtedakia*. Potato *kephtedakia* may not be sophisticated eating, but the taste is superlative. Serve with a variety of other *mezedes* and *khorta* (page 220) for a traditional meal, or include them in a buffet or picnic. Larger potato *kephtedes* and a salad of wild greens (page 221) make an unusual light lunch.

450 g/1 lb boiling potatoes
3 tablespoons fresh mint leaves or chopped fresh dill
25 g/1 oz unsalted butter, melted
1 egg yolk
4 spring onions, trimmed and finely chopped
2 tablespoons finely chopped flat leaf parsley
1 tablespoon fresh lemon juice
Sea salt *and* freshly ground white pepper to taste
40 g/1^1/$_2$ oz fine bulgur, *optional*
Plain flour, for dredging
About 4 tablespoons extra virgin olive oil, for baking

Scrub the potatoes and cut larger ones in half or into quarters. Place in a saucepan with cold salted water to cover and bring to a boil. Cover, and simmer 15 minutes or until just cooked. Drain, and as soon as the potatoes are cool enough to handle, peel them. Pass through a moulis-légumes (food mill) fitted with the fine disc into a large bowl. Or mash with a potato masher or fork, then push through a sieve into a large bowl. Tear the mint leaves into small pieces. Combine the melted butter and the egg yolk and add to the potatoes, with the mint, spring onions, parsley, lemon juice, and salt and pepper. Lightly mix with a fork, and refrigerate.

If using the bulgur, combine it with 2 tablespoons flour in a food processor and process until the mixture has a sand-like consistency. Spread the mixture, or plain flour, on a plate. Heat the oven to 190C/375F/gas mark 5 and place 2 baking trays in the oven to heat. Moisten your hands with cold water and pat barely dry. Shape spoonfuls of the potato mixture into 2 cm/3/4 inch balls for *kephtedakia*, or a little larger for *kephtedes*. Flatten slightly between your palms and lightly dredge with the bulgur mixture or flour. Brush the hot baking trays with olive oil and arrange the *kephtedakia* 2.5 cm/1 inch apart on them. Lightly brush with olive oil and bake 15-20 minutes, turning once to brown on both sides. Drain between layers of paper towels.

Pile on a platter and serve hot or warm.

Potato Kephtedakia with Cheese
Polpetes

On Crete, two favourite cheeses are used to flavour potato *kephtedakia*: either aged *myzithra* cheese or the fresh, slightly sour-tasting, *anthotyro*. Anthotyro is available only in Greece, but *feta* makes a good substitute.

Omit the parsley and use dill rather than mint. Add 40 g/1^1/$_2$ oz finely grated aged *myzithra* cheese, or 2 tablespoons finely grated *feta* cheese and 50 g/2 oz well-drained cottage cheese, passed through a sieve, to the potato mixture. Chill, shape into *kephtedakia* or *kephtedes*, and bake and serve as above.

Potato Kephtedakia with Tomatoes
Polpetes me Domates

Make these beautiful little *kephtedakia* when tomatoes are in season. Core, skin, and seed 2 large ripe tomatoes. Cut into dice, place in a sieve set over a bowl, and sprinkle with a large pinch of sugar and a small pinch of salt. Set aside for at least 30 minutes, then press the tomatoes gently but firmly against the sides of the sieve to remove as much juice as possible. Combine the tomato with the potato or potato-cheese mixture just before shaping.

Potato and Vegetable Kephtedakia
Polpetes Lakhanika

Add a purée of spinach, cauliflower or fresh broad beans to either the potato mixture or the potato-cheese mixture. For each 225 g/8 oz potato mixture, add 115 g/4 oz vegetable purée.

Note To fry *kephtedakia*, use a light olive oil. To deep-fry, form the mixture into small round patties no more than 2.5 cm/1 inch in diameter. Heat the olive oil until hot but not smoking, and fry the *kephtedakia*, a few at a time, until golden brown. Drain between layers of paper towels.

To pan-fry, pour a 6 mm/$^1/_4$ inch layer of olive oil into a heavy frying pan set over medium-low heat. Heat until hot but not smoking, and fry the slightly flattened *kephtedakia* in batches until golden brown on both sides. Drain between layers of paper towels and serve hot or warm.

Lamb's Liver with Lemon Juice and Rigani
Sikotakia Tikhanita
Serves 10

Thin squares of tender lamb's liver, lightly fried in a well-flavoured olive oil, are a classic of Greek cuisine. Justly so, since that treatment lifts humble liver into the realms of the sublime. If lamb's liver is unavailable, you can substitute calf's liver, although the dish will be less authentic.

450 g/1 lb lamb's or calf's liver
Plain flour, for dredging
5 tablespoons extra virgin olive oil
1 teaspoon paprika

Coarse-grain sea salt *and* cracked black pepper to taste
Strained juice of 1 large lemon

For serving
2 tablespoons dried *rigani* (page 14), briefly pounded in a small mortar
1 small bunch of flat leaf parsley, leaves coarsely chopped
1 small red or mild onion, cut into thin rings

Trim off any membrane from the liver, cut it into thin slices, and cut the slices into 5 cm/2 inch squares. Lightly dust with flour and shake off the excess.

Heat 4 tablespoons of the olive oil in a large heavy frying pan and fry the liver over medium-low heat until light brown and slightly crusty on both sides, about 4 minutes. (It should still be moist in the centre.) Sprinkle with the paprika, salt and pepper, and half the lemon juice. Reduce the heat to low and cook 1 minute longer.

Transfer to a warm platter and sprinkle with the remaining olive oil and the lemon juice, salt and pepper to taste, and the *rigani*, parsley and onion. Serve immediately.

Pork in Aspic
Pikti
Serves 12 to 14 as a first course, 8 as a light lunch

A common sight in village kitchens in autumn and winter is a sturdy tripod supporting a well-used blackened pot from which steams the most tantalizing spicy aroma. In the pot, pork and pig's feet simmer gently with herbs and spices. A good *pikti* takes time to prepare, but it is an important traditional dish and will repay your effort. Prepare it at least four hours before serving so it will have time to set. It makes a beautiful buffet centrepiece, garnished with olives, radishes, cucumber and tiny tomatoes. It can also be served as an elegant first course, accompanied by toasted wholemeal bread and black olives or Black Olives and Lentil Salata (page 39). For a satisfying lunch, serve it with Beetroot Salad with Allspice (page 184), black olives and crusty bread.

2 pig's trotters, cut into pieces by the butcher
900 g/2 lb lean pork on-the-bone (any cut), trimmed of fat
12 black peppercorns
1 tablespoon sea salt
4 bay leaves
3 cloves
$^1/_2$ teaspoon dried red pepper flakes
1 tablespoon dried rosemary *or* sage leaves
115-225 g/4-8 oz lean mild ham, *optional*
3-5 tablespoons white wine vinegar
2 egg whites
1 small bunch of flat leaf parsley, leaves finely chopped

Rinse the pig's trotters and pork, place in a stockpot, and add water to cover. Bring to a boil and remove any surface froth with a slotted spoon. Add the peppercorns, salt, bay leaves, cloves, red pepper flakes, and rosemary. Reduce the heat, cover, and simmer 1 hour.

Add the ham, cover, and simmer 2-3 hours longer, or until the meat is falling off the bones. Strain, and set aside the meat and bones to cool; discard the seasonings. Strain the stock through 2 layers of muslin into a bowl, set aside to cool, and refrigerate, uncovered, until cold.

Remove and discard the surface layer of hardened fat. Heat the stock until it has just liquefied, then measure it. You should have 1 litre/1 3/4 pints; if necessary, reduce by rapid boiling. When cool, add 3 tablespoons of the vinegar and the egg whites, and stir with a wooden spoon. Bring to a boil over medium-low heat, stirring constantly, until the egg whites set and become stringy. Simmer a few minutes longer.

Set a fine-meshed sieve lined with 2 layers of muslin over a bowl and strain the stock. You should have about 425 ml/3/4 pint of clear straw-coloured aspic. Taste, add more vinegar if desired; the aspic should be quite tangy. Loosely cover and refrigerate.

Remove the meat from the bones and discard the fat, sinew and bones. Cut the ham and the meat from the pig's trotters into tiny dice and the remaining meat into 6 mm/1/4 inch dice. Once the aspic has begun to thicken and stick to the sides of the bowl, stir in the meat and parsley. Transfer the mixture to an oiled 1 litre/13/4 pint mould, cover, and refrigerate until set, or for up to 3 days.

To serve, dip the mould in a bowl of boiling water for 5 seconds. Invert a serving plate on top and, holding the plate firmly in place, turn upside down to remove from the mould.

Note You can substitute 50 ml/2 fl oz Seville orange juice and the juice of 1 lemon for the vinegar to make a slightly different version of this traditional dish.

Snails in Vinegar
Salingaria me Xsithi
Serves 4

This rather startling *meze* is a speciality of the island of Crete. The islanders enjoy it with plenty of crusty bread and copious quantities of robust local red wine, together with two or three other *mezedes* such as olives, marinated vegetables and *khorta* (page 220) to complement the taste and texture of the snails.

2 tablespoons coarse-grain sea salt
24 cleaned snails in their shells, boiled 15 minutes and their protective
skins removed (page 350)
2 tablespoons extra virgin olive oil
Boiling water, to cover the snails
115 ml/4 fl oz aged red wine vinegar

For serving
1 small bunch of flat leaf parsley, leaves coarsely chopped

Spread the salt on a plate, press the rim of each snail into it, and set aside.

Add the olive oil to a large heavy sauté pan that will hold all the snails in a single layer and heat it over low heat. Add the snails and gently roll them around with a wooden spoon so they heat through. Add enough boiling water to barely cover the snails and simmer until the water has evaporated, about 12 minutes. Take care not to let the snails burn. Add the vinegar, cover, and cook over very low heat for 5 minutes or until reduced by half, occasionally shaking the pan.

Transfer the snails to a warm platter or individual plates, spoon over the sauce, sprinkle with the parsley, and serve.

Fried Cheese
Saganaki
Serves 6

Saganaki means "two-handled frying pan", and this savoury *meze* is named after the dish in which it was originally cooked. Serve bubbling hot, and have ready some olives, *kephtedakia* (page 32), and one or two *salates* – then bring on your *saganaki* centrepiece with a flourish.

225 g/8 oz kephalotyri or kasseri cheese (page 10)
Plain flour, for dredging
Extra virgin olive oil, for frying

For serving
Strained juice of 1 large lemon
Finely chopped flat leaf parsley
Cracked black pepper to taste

Cut the cheese into 6 mm/$1/4$ inch slices with a thin-bladed knife or cheese wire, and cut each slice into rectangles approximately 4 x 5 cm/$1^1/_2$ x 2 inches. Dredge with flour, shaking off any excess, and set aside.

Cover the bottom of a heavy frying pan with a thin layer of olive oil and heat over medium-low heat just until the oil sizzles when you drop in a crumb of cheese; don't allow the oil to reach smoking temperature. Fry the cheese slices, a few at a time, on both sides until golden brown and crusty, about 6 minutes. Drain between layers of paper towels and keep warm in a low oven until all the slices are fried.

Transfer to a warm platter, sprinkle with the lemon juice, parsley and pepper, and serve immediately.

salates

Greek *salates* bear little resemblance to what we know as salads. Most are purées made from fresh or dried vegetables, blended with herbs, spices and olive oil. Sometimes nuts are substituted for vegetables; the popular *taramosalata* is made from the puréed roe of the mullet fish. With a culinary history stretching back into antiquity, *salates* are attractive additions to a buffet table and offer a variety of interesting flavours and textures. The best *salates* are still made in the traditional way, using a large walnut mortar, which imparts its own special flavour. Blenders and food processors make speedy and simple work of them but tend to mash the ingredients into a smoother, blander texture than that of the traditional. Serve two or three *salates* on a *meze* table, accompanied by warm pitta or crusty bread and fresh or preserved *mezedakia* such as cucumbers and olives.

Salates are appealing to busy cooks, as many can be made ahead of time, giving the flavours time to mellow and deepen. They are also versatile – Broad Bean Salata (page 40), for example, can be served as an unusual first course. Or, to serve with drinks, spread one or two contrasting *salates* on toast for quick and simple canapés.

Black Olives and Lentil Salata
Elaiosalata
Serves 10 to 12 as a *meze*, 8 as a first course

All over Greece olives appear in an infinite variety of guises. In this attractive *salata*, the magnificent flavour of oil-cured black olives is at its powerful best. Ideal as a spread for canapés, it's especially good with savoury appetizers and Tiny Cracked Potatoes (page 55).

175 g/6 oz green lentils, picked over, rinsed, and soaked for 30 minutes in cold water to cover
75 g/3 oz oil-cured black olives, pitted
2 tablespoons capers, rinsed and patted dry
2 small anchovy fillets (page 343), rinsed and patted dry
2 tablespoons dried *rigani* (page 14)
1 large clove garlic, finely chopped
Juice of 1 large lemon
4 tablespoons extra virgin olive oil, or more to taste

For serving
Oil-cured olives
1 teaspoon dried *rigani*, briefly pounded in a small mortar
Coarsely chopped flat leaf parsley

Drain the lentils and place in a large saucepan with cold water to cover by 7 cm/3 inches. Bring to a boil, cover, and simmer 30 minutes, or until they are soft but not disintegrating. Drain, and set aside to cool; shake the colander once or twice to make sure all the lentils are dry.

Place the olives, caper, anchovies, *rigani*, garlic, and lentils in a food processor or blender container. With the machine running, add half the lemon juice, then add the olive oil in a thin steady stream. Add more lemon juice or olive oil to taste and process just until the mixture is thick and creamy.

Spread on a platter and place the olives in the centre. Sprinkle with the *rigani* and parsley, and serve.

To make the traditional way Fit a moulis-légumes (food mill) with the fine disc and press all the ingredients through into a large wooden mortar. Pound for 5 minutes, or until well mixed. Add half the lemon juice and then add the olive oil drop by drop, pounding constantly, until you have a thick, creamy purée. The more olive oil you use, the better the flavour. Add more lemon juice to taste.

Note To store, refrigerate for up to 24 hours in an airtight container or store for up to 6 months in small sterilized jars, with a thin layer of olive oil on top of the purée to "seal" it. Before serving, stir in the olive oil.

Broad Bean Salata
Fava
(serves 8 as a *meze*, 4 as a vegetable dish)

There is no doubt that shelling and skinning broad beans is labour-intensive, but don't let that stop you from making this wonderful classic dish. The earthiness of the beans is sharpened by the lemon juice and yogurt, olive oil gives a creamy texture, and fragrant dill lends pungency. The combination produces a *meze* of surprisingly fine flavour and texture. Or try it as a side dish for roast or grilled pork or lamb.

1.4 kg/3 lb broad beans in the pod
6 spring onions, trimmed, with 5 cm/2 inches of green left intact
5-6 tablespoons extra virgin olive oil
2 tablespoons finely chopped fresh dill
Sea salt and freshly ground black pepper to taste
Strained juice of 1 small lemon
4 tablespoons Strained Yogurt (page 8)

For serving
Fresh dill sprigs
4-8 Elitses or Niçoise olives

Shell the beans, remove their skins, and set aside. Coarsely chop the spring onions, then finely chop 2 tablespoons and set aside for garnish.

Heat 2 tablespoons of the olive oil in a large heavy frying pan over low heat and sauté the spring onions for 5 minutes, or until soft. Add the beans, cover, and cook 5 minutes longer, shaking the pan occasionally.

Transfer the beans and spring onions to a food processor or blender container and add the dill, salt, and pepper. With the machine running, add most of the lemon juice and yogurt, and 2 tablespoons of the remaining olive oil, and process to a purée. If the purée seems too thick, add a few tablespoons of water. Add lemon juice, yogurt, or olive oil for a sharper, lighter, or deeper flavour (in that order).

Spread on a plate and sprinkle with the reserved spring onions and the remaining olive oil and lemon juice. Garnish with dill sprigs and olives and serve at room temperature.

To make the traditional way Prepare the beans in the same way, but finely chop the spring onions before sautéing with the beans and dill. Pound the sautéed bean mixture in a large wooden mortar for 10 minutes before adding the remaining ingredients. To obtain a creamier purée, double the quantity of olive oil.

Fava Bean Salata
Fava

Serves 8 to 10 as a *meze*, 6 as a vegetable dish

The success of this traditional country *salata* depends on the quality of the olive oil you use – the better the oil, the richer the flavour. The base is a melting mixture of finely diced carrot, celery, onions, garlic and bay leaf, sweetened by long slow cooking in the olive oil. It's a distinctive dish that never fails to please, and it improves in flavour if made a day or two ahead. Serve as a *meze*, with bowls of yogurt and *khorta* (page 220), or as a side dish for roast or grilled meats. If using dried fava beans seems too time-consuming, you can substitute tinned or dried butter beans, although the dish will lose some authenticity of flavour.

275 g/10 oz dried fava or butter beans, soaked overnight in water to cover, or
2 x 400 g/14 oz tins butter beans, rinsed
6 tablespoons extra virgin olive oil
1 medium onion, finely chopped
1 clove garlic, finely chopped
1 medium carrot, finely diced
$^1/_2$ stick of celery, finely diced
2 bay leaves, crumbled
3 tablespoons finely chopped flat leaf parsley
Sea salt and freshly ground black pepper to taste
1 thick slice coarse-grain white or wholemeal bread, crust removed, and soaked for 5
minutes in 1-3 tablespoons extra virgin olive oil (to taste)
Juice of 1 small lemon

For serving
Large pinch of paprika

Drain the dried beans and place in a large saucepan with cold water to cover. Bring slowly to a boil, reduce the heat, cover, and simmer 5 minutes; drain and rinse the beans. Rinse out the saucepan, return the beans to the pan, and add cold water to cover by 7 cm/3 inches. Bring to a boil, reduce the heat, cover, and gently simmer 20-25 minutes, or until soft. Drain, reserving 115 ml/4 fl oz of the cooking liquid. Remove the fava bean skins with your fingers and spread the beans between layers of paper towels to dry. (This step is unnecessary if using butter beans.)

Heat half the olive oil in a large heavy pan. Sauté the onion, carrot, garlic, celery and bay leaves over medium-low heat for 15-20 minutes, or until dark golden brown, stirring occasionally with a wooden spoon.

Stir in 2 tablespoons of the parsley, the salt, pepper, beans, and reserved cooking liquid. (If using tinned beans, add 115 ml/4 fl oz water.) Cook for 2-3 minutes, or until the liquid has evaporated.

Transfer to a food processor or blender container and add the bread. With the machine running, add about two thirds of the lemon juice and most of the remaining olive oil, and process until thick and smooth. Add a few drops of water if the purée seems too thick, and add salt, pepper, olive oil, and/or lemon juice to taste.

Serve on a platter, sprinkled with the remaining parsley and olive oil and the paprika.

To make the traditional way Pound the cooked vegetable-bean mixture and the bread in a large wooden mortar for 5 minutes. Slowly add about two thirds of the lemon juice and then 4 tablespoons of the olive oil. Pound for 5 minutes longer, and add salt, pepper, olive oil, and/or lemon juice to taste.

Chickpea and Garlic Salata
Revithosalata
Serves 10

The best *revithosalata* has a thick creamy consistency, a spicy coriander tang, and a pleasing mustard colour. The flavours of garlic and olive oil, although not over-powering, should be detectable. Serve with *mezedakia*, vegetable appetizers, a bowl of yogurt, and warm pitta bread.

350 g/12 oz chickpeas, soaked overnight in water to cover
2 large cloves garlic, chopped
1 teaspoon ground coriander or $^1/_2$ teaspoon ground cumin
1 teaspoon sea salt, or more to taste
$^1/_2$ teaspoon freshly ground black pepper, or more to taste
5 tablespoons extra virgin olive oil
Strained juice of 2 lemons, or to taste

For serving
Finely chopped flat leaf parsley
1 tablespoon dried *rigani* (page 14), crumbled
1 teaspoon paprika

Drain the chickpeas and place in a large saucepan with cold water to cover. Bring slowly to a boil, drain, and rinse. Rinse out the saucepan, return the chickpeas to the pan, and add cold water to cover by 7 cm/3 inches. Bring to a boil, reduce the heat, cover, and gently simmer for 50 minutes or until soft. Drain, reserving 115 ml/4 fl oz of the cooking liquid and a few whole chickpeas for garnish.

Place the chickpeas, garlic, coriander, salt, and pepper in a food processor or blender container. With the machine running gradually add 4 tablespoons of the olive oil and most of the lemon juice. Add more salt and pepper and the remaining lemon juice if desired and process until smooth and creamy. For a thinner consistency, gradually add some or all of the reserved cooking liquid. (If you plan to store the *salata*, add all the reserved liquid – it will thicken on standing.)

Spread on a platter and sprinkle with the parsley, *rigani*, and reserved whole chickpeas. Combine the paprika and remaining olive oil and sprinkle over the *salata*.

Note To store, refrigerate in an airtight container for up to 2 days.

Salt-Dried Fish Roe Salata
Taramosalata
Serves 10 to 12 as a *meze*, 8 as a first course

The ancient Greeks were very fond of this smooth sharp fish pâté and it's just as popular in Greece today. Barrels of salted dried mullet roe, the basic ingredient of *taramosalata*, are a familiar sight in busy fish markets. For Greeks *taramosalata* is a winter dish, especially popular during the Lenten fast when no meat or dairy products are eaten. For us, with jars of *tarama* readily available in Greek and Middle Eastern shops, it can be a year-round treat. Versions vary from region to region, even from cook to cook – some favour the use of just bread, others use potatoes instead, others both. Experiment until you find your favourite combination of ingredients, texture, and flavour. Best made just before serving, *taramosalata* is an attractive buffet dish; served on small plates, garnished with radishes, olives, and cucumber, it makes an elegant first course or a dinner party.

275 g/10 oz *tarama*
1/2 medium onion, finely grated
175-225 g/6-8 oz fresh breadcrumbs (made from good white bread, crusts removed)
Juice of 1 1/2 lemons
115 ml/4 fl oz extra virgin olive oil, or more to taste

For *serving*
12 Nafplion olives or other Greek green olives (page 2)
Finely chopped flat leaf parsley

Place the *tarama* in a bowl, cover with cold water, and break up any lumps with your fingers. Set aside for 30 minutes.

Line a sieve with 2 layers of muslin and drain the *tarama* over a bowl. Gently squeeze the muslin "bag" to remove as much of the salty water as possible; discard the water. Place the *tarama*, onion and 275 g/10 oz of the breadcrumbs in a food processor or blender container. With the machine running, add the juice of 1 lemon, and then add the olive oil in a thin steady stream and process until the *taramosalata* has the consistency and texture of thick cream. Add a little cold water if it is too thick, or additional breadcrumbs if too thin. If you prefer a sharper flavour, add some or all of the remaining lemon juice; for a more mellow taste, add more olive oil.

Serve on a platter, surrounded with the olives and sprinkled with the parsley.

To make the traditional way With a large wooden mortar and pestle, pound the *tarama*, most of the breadcrumbs, and the onion for 5 minutes, or until well-mixed. Slowly add the lemon juice and 150 ml/5 fl oz olive oil, and pound for 5 minutes longer. Add a little cold water if the mixture seems too thick, or additional breadcrumbs if too thin.

Note You can substitute 450 g/1 lb mashed potato for the breadcrumbs or use a mixture of potatoes and breadcrumbs. Use a mortar and pestle – potatoes lose their firm texture if processed.

Grilled Aubergine Salata
Melitzanosalata
Serves 10 to 12

For this *salata*, aubergines are first grilled, then the soft cooked flesh is scooped from the shells and mixed with an aromatic blend of tomato, *rigani*, onion, garlic, lemon juice, and seasoning. A food processor will make fast work of this unusual dish – but a smoky flavour is essential so the aubergines must be grilled, not baked.

1 large ripe tomato, skinned, seeded, and diced
3 or 4 large unblemished aubergines (about 1.4 kg/3 lb)
1 tablespoon dried *rigani* (page 14)
2 tablespoons finely chopped mild onion
1-2 cloves garlic, crushed
Sea salt *and* freshly ground white pepper to taste
Juice of 1 small lemon
4 tablespoons Strained Yogurt (page 8)
4 tablespoons coarsely chopped flat leaf parsley
4 tablespoons extra virgin olive oil

For serving
6 small capers, drained and rinsed
Large pinch of paprika

Heat the grill. Drain the diced tomato in a sieve.

Trim the stem ends from the aubergines, make 6 small slits in each aubergine, and place on the grill tray 5-7 cm/2-3 inches from the heat source. Grill for about 15 minutes, until the skins scorch, turning them carefully so they brown evenly on all sides. Test by inserting the point of a knife into the centre of each aubergine – they should be very soft. Set aside to cool.

When the aubergines are cool enough to handle, carefully scrape out the flesh from the skins and, with a teaspoon, remove and discard as many of the seeds as possible (there's no need to be too fussy). Gently squeeze the flesh between paper towels to remove excess moisture.

Place the *rigani*, onion, garlic, salt and pepper, and lemon juice in a food processor or blender container and process a few seconds, until well-mixed and finely chopped but not pulverized. Add the tomato, aubergines, and 3 tablespoons each of the yogurt and parsley, and pulse 2 or 3 times to mix. Add the olive oil in a thin steady stream, continuing to pulse – but stop before the mixture is smooth. Add salt and pepper, lemon juice, and/or olive oil to taste. Transfer to a serving bowl, cover tightly, and chill for at least 1 hour.

To serve, spoon the remaining yogurt on top of the *salata* and sprinkle with the capers, paprika, and the remaining parsley.

To make the traditional way Grill the aubergines over the embers of a wood fire. Leave to cool, then remove the flesh and seeds, and cut the flesh into tiny dice. Pound the onion, garlic, and salt and pepper in a large wooden mortar for 5 minutes. Add the aubergines, tomato, *rigani*, lemon juice, yogurt, and parsley. Pound 5 minutes longer, or until well pulverized. Add the olive oil in a thin steady stream, still pounding, until the mixture is thick and well combined. Although the quantities of the other ingredients remain the same, 2 or 3 tablespoons more olive oil are needed to obtain the right consistency – this is one reason why traditionally made *melitzanosalata* has a deeper, more interesting, flavour.

Sweet and Spicy Tomato Salata
Domatosalata
Serves 6

Anastasia, a friend on the island of Khios, taught me how to make this appetising *salata*. The dish has a charm all its own, especially when served in a shallow bowl with a swirl of creamy white yogurt and a sprinkling of glossy fresh parsley or coriander leaves for garnish. You can also use the *salata* as a rich tomato sauce, perfect with baked or grilled fish, meat *pilafi* and *macaronia* dishes.

4 tablespoons extra virgin olive oil
1 large onion, finely chopped
1.4 kg/3 lb firm ripe tomatoes, skinned and diced, juices reserved
1 tablespoon tomato purée diluted with 2 tablespoons water
1 1/2 teaspoons ground cinnamon, or to taste
1 large clove garlic, finely chopped
Sea salt to taste

¹/₂ teaspoon freshly ground black pepper, or more to taste

Pinch of cayenne pepper

2 tablespoons aromatic honey, such as Hymettus

1-2 tablespoons aged red wine vinegar *or* 1 tablespoon light balsamic vinegar

For serving

2 tablespoons Strained Yogurt (page 8), *optional*

Finely chopped flat leaf parsley *or* a few fresh coriander leaves

Heat the olive oil in a large heavy frying pan and sauté the onion over medium-low heat for 10 minutes or until soft; do not let it brown. Add the tomatoes and their juices, tomato purée, cinnamon, garlic, cayenne pepper, salt, and pepper. Raise the heat and boil uncovered 30-40 minutes, or until most of the liquid has evaporated, stirring occasionally with a wooden spoon. The purée should be thick enough to remain separated for a few seconds when you draw the spoon across the bottom of the pan. Add the honey, reduce the heat, and cook, stirring occasionally, for 10 minutes longer, or until thick and slightly syrupy. Be careful not to let it burn. Remove from the heat and set aside to cool.

Stir in half the vinegar, taste, and add more cinnamon, salt, pepper, cayenne and/or vinegar if desired.

Transfer to a shallow bowl, add a swirl of the yogurt in the centre, sprinkle with the parsley, and serve.

Note To store, refrigerate for up to 1 week in an airtight container or store for up to 3 months in small sterilized jars "sealed" with a thin layer of olive oil. Use this oil in salad dressings or other dishes, or stir into the *salata* before serving.

aubergine and other vegetable appetizers

Aubergine Appetizers / *Melitzanes Mezedes*

Aubergines are such a characteristic ingredient of Mediterranean cuisines that it may be a surprise to learn that they are not native to the region but instead originated in tropical Asia. In Greece, aubergines form the basis of an infinite variety of simply prepared delicacies – baked, they lend a subtle earthy flavour and richness to casseroles and other dishes; stuffed with aromatic or spicy fillings, they become satisfying main courses; and puréed into delicate creamy *salates* they have pride of place on a good *meze* table. For simple snacks aubergine slices can be fried plain in olive oil or dipped in fritter batter and fried.

Visit any Greek market in early summer and displayed before you is the abundance, variety and splendour of the exotic aubergine: skilfully stacked in huge geometric piles, glossy skins gleaming in the sun, small round aubergines nestle next to thin elongated varieties and bulbous pear shapes. Their variegated colours create a feast for the eye, ranging from pure pearly white and white streaked with green to the deepest velvet purple and black.

Reject any aubergines with bruised or wrinkled skins and check that the stem end looks fresh and the prickly calyx firm and bright. Fresh aubergines feel heavy in your hand and the skins should be glossy and tight. Size and shape do not affect flavour, so choose according to the requirements of your recipe.

Aubergines contain a bitter juice that must be removed before cooking. Cut the vegetable in half or into slices or dice, sprinkle the cut surfaces with salt, and let drain in a colander for about one hour. The cut surfaces will then be covered by droplets of pale brown liquid, which you can remove by patting the pieces with paper towels. Remove as much moisture as you can. This salting and drying process not only seasons the aubergine but also prevents it from absorbing too much olive oil during cooking. Aubergines and olive oil are, however, natural partners so do not be tempted to skimp on the amounts called for in these recipes. A Greek friend says that olive oil helps the "shy" aubergine to discover its "true talkative personality" – and I agree with him.

Grilled Aubergines
Melitzanes Skharas

An informal supper that always pleases friends is simplicity itself to prepare: grilled aubergines, a tasty fish *meze*, juicy olives, *feta* cheese, plenty of bread, and a glass or two of ouzo. Each guest receives a whole aubergine and, according to taste, adds a dressing of olive oil, lemon juice, and seasonings to the aubergine's delicious smoky-flavoured flesh.

One 10-12 cm/4-5 inch long aubergine per person

For serving
A small jug of extra virgin olive oil
Lemon wedges
Coarse-grain sea salt *and* freshly ground black pepper

Heat the grill.

Trim the ends from each aubergine and make 6 small slits in the skin to allow moisture to drain during grilling. Place on a grilling tray 5-7 cm/2-3 inches from the heat source and grill, using tongs to turn carefully, until lightly charred and blistered on all sides, about 10 minutes. Drain briefly on paper towels.

Slit open each aubergine from one end to the other, taking care not to let any charred pieces of skin fall inside, and press the ends to open them slightly.

Arrange on a platter or individual plates and serve immediately. Pass around the olive oil, lemon wedges, salt, and pepper grinder.

Fragrant Aubergines with Olives
Melitzanes Aromatikes
Serves 4

Turning everyday ingredients into special treats is a traditional Greek skill, as this popular *meze* demonstrates. Aubergine slices are simply fried or grilled, but the last-minute addition of good red wine vinegar, succulent olives, bright green parsley and perfumed *rigani* creates a colourful dish with a highly unusual flavour. Serve with thick yogurt in which to dip the aubergine slices.

3 medium aubergines (about 550 g/1¼ lb), each around 5 cm/2 inches in diameter
Sea salt to taste
Extra virgin olive oil, for frying or grilling

For serving
3 tablespoons aged red wine vinegar, or to taste
1 dozen Elitses or Niçoise olives, drained
2 tablespoons finely chopped flat leaf parsley
1 tablespoon dried *rigani* (page 14), briefly pounded in a small mortar
Cracked black pepper to taste

Trim off the ends from the aubergines and cut into 6 mm/¼ inch slices. Sprinkle with salt and set aside for 1 hour to "sweat".

To grill, arrange a grill rack about 7 cm/3 inches above hot coals, or heat an overhead grill. Thoroughly dry the aubergine slices with paper towels and brush on both sides with olive oil. Grill 2.5-5 cm/1-2 inches from the heat source until dark golden brown on both sides; don't worry if they blacken in places.

To fry, cover the bottom of 1 or 2 large heavy frying pans with a thin layer of olive oil and heat over medium-low heat. Fry the aubergine slices, a few at a time, until golden brown on both sides. Drain between layers of paper towels.

Arrange the slices in an attractive pile on a platter. Just before serving, sprinkle with the vinegar, olives, parsley, *rigani*, and salt and pepper. Serve hot, warm, or at room temperature (within 1 hour of cooking).

Aubergines with Courgettes and Artichoke Hearts
Tiganita Lakhanika
Serves 12 as a *meze*, 6 as a light lunch

In early summer, when courgettes and artichokes are at their crunchy best, these delectable vegetable fritters appear on taverna tables throughout Greece, as part of a *meze* table, or as a simple lunch. Garlic adds the finishing touch – these fritters are traditionally served with a powerful garlicky sauce.

3 medium aubergines, about 450 g/1 lb
Sea salt
450 g/1 lb medium courgettes
12 small or 6 medium artichokes
1 lemon, cut in half
Plain flour, for dredging
115 g/4 oz fresh fine breadcrumbs
3 eggs
Freshly ground black pepper to taste
Extra virgin olive oil, for frying

For serving
5 tablespoons coarsely chopped flat leaf parsley
1 tablespoon dried *rigani* (page 14)
Finely grated zest of $^1/_2$ lemon
Juice of 1 large lemon
1 dozen Elitses or Niçoise olives, drained
Garlic Almond Sauce (page 314) or Potato Skordalia (page 315)

Trim off the stem ends of the aubergines and cut into 6 mm/$^1/_4$ inch lengthways slices. Cut these crosswise in half or into quarters, sprinkle with 1 tablespoon salt, and set aside for 45 minutes to "sweat". Wipe the courgettes and cut into 6 mm/$^1/_4$ inch crosswise slices. Sprinkle with 1 tablespoon salt and set aside.

Prepare a large bowl of iced water. Trim the stalks of the artichokes and remove the tough outer leaves. With a sharp knife, slice off the top third of each artichoke to expose the choke. Scoop out the fuzzy part with a small spoon and trim off any remaining leaves from the heat. Cut large hearts in half or into quarters. Rub all the cut surfaces with a half-lemon, place in the bowl of iced water, and add the lemon halves to the bowl.

Spread the flour on one plate and the breadcrumbs on another. Break the eggs into a small bowl, add salt and pepper to taste, and lightly beat together with a fork. Place 2 large heavy frying pans over low heat and add olive oil to make a thin layer. With paper towels, dry enough aubergine slices to make a single layer in the frying pans. Lightly dust with flour and shake off any excess. Dip the slices first in the egg mixture, then in the breadcrumbs, to coat on both sides. When the oil is hot but not smoking, fry the aubergine slices until light golden brown on both sides, about 6 minutes. Drain between layers of paper towels, and repeat with the remaining aubergines and the courgette slices.

Add enough olive oil to one of the frying pans to make a 6 mm/¹/₄ inch layer. When the oil is hot, fry the artichoke hearts until light golden brown on all sides. Drain between layers of paper towels. Chop the parsley, *rigani*, and lemon zest together until well mixed.

To serve, arrange the vegetables on a platter and sprinkle with the lemon juice, olives, and the parsley mixture. Serve hot, warm, or at room temperature, with the garlic sauce.

Note For greater speed, you can deep-fry the vegetables in olive oil but be sure to keep the temperature of the oil just below smoking.

Island Aubergines
Nisiotikes Melitzanes
Serves 8 to 10 as a first course, 6 as a vegetable dish

This hearty aubergine dish from the Greek islands, with its combination of robust contrasting flavours, reflects the Turkish occupations of medieval times. Serve cold as an elegant appetizer or buffet dish or warm as an unusual accompaniment to grilled meats and egg dishes. If possible, make a day ahead to give the flavours time to mellow.

675 g/1¹/₂ lb medium round aubergines
Sea salt
6 sticks of celery, rinsed and tough strings removed
2 red bell peppers, roasted and skinned (page 343)
115 ml/4 fl oz extra virgin olive oil, or to taste
2 large onions, quartered and thinly sliced
1 large clove garlic, minced, *optional*
6 large ripe tomatoes, skinned and diced, juices reserved
1 teaspoon honey
1 tablespoon tomato purée diluted with 2 tablespoons water
3 tablespoons dried *rigani* (page 14)
¹/₂ teaspoon freshly ground black pepper, or more to taste
450 g/1 lb tiny potatoes, baked in a clay pot (page 205) or boiled until
barely tender, *optional*
1 small bunch of flat leaf parsley, leaves finely chopped
2 dozen Elitses *or* Niçoise olives, rinsed and pitted
2–3 tablespoons capers, rinsed and coarsely chopped (to taste)
4 salted anchovy fillets, rinsed and finely chopped

For serving
Juice of 1 large lemon

Trim the ends from the aubergines and cut into 2 cm/3/4 inch cubes. Sprinkle the cut surfaces with 1 tablespoon salt and set aside in a colander for 45 minutes to "sweat". Cut the celery into large julienne (matchsticks) and blanch in boiling water for 1 minute. Drain under cold running water and set aside. Remove the cores and seeds from the peppers and wipe with paper towels to remove any remaining seeds. Slice lengthways into strips.

Heat half the olive oil in a large sauté pan and sauté the onions over low heat for 10 minutes or until soft. Add the garlic, tomatoes and their juices, honey, tomato purée, *rigani*, and salt and pepper. Raise the heat and lightly boil for 20-30 minutes, or until reduced by half. The sauce should remain separated for a second or two when a wooden spoon is drawn across the bottom of the pan.

Meanwhile, in another large sauté or frying pan, heat most of the remaining olive oil over medium heat. Thoroughly dry the aubergines with paper towels and fry 10-15 minutes or until golden brown on all sides. Drain between layers of paper towels and set aside.

Add the celery, peppers, potatoes, parsley, olives, capers, anchovies, and aubergines to the tomato sauce. Stir gently just to combine and cook over very low heat for 5 minutes. Add salt, pepper, and/or the remaining olive oil to taste.

To serve, arrange on a platter or individual plates and sprinkle with the lemon juice.

Note If you intend to reheat the dish, don't add extra salt until just before serving; the salty olives, anchovies, and capers will flavour the other ingredients.

Aromatic Giant Beans
Fassolia Gigantes
Serves 10 to 12 as a *meze*, 4 as a light lunch

This is one of my favourite Greek dishes and one I always associate with impromptu village gatherings in cool courtyards. Whatever the occasion, these beans are always present! Long slow cooking in olive oil sweetens and mellows the vegetables and the dish has a very special nutty flavour.

275 g/10 oz dried fava beans or butter beans, soaked and cooked (page 40) or
2 x 400 g/14 oz tins butter beans, drained and rinsed
5 tablespoons extra virgin olive oil
1 large onion, cut in quarters and thinly sliced
1 stick of celery, finely diced
2 medium carrots, peeled or scrubbed, and finely diced
450 g/1 lb ripe tomatoes, skinned and diced, juices reserved
1 teaspoon honey
1 tablespoon ground coriander
2 tablespoons dried *rigani* (page 14)
1 large clove garlic, finely chopped
Sea salt and freshly ground pepper to taste

For serving
Juice of 1/2 small lemon, or to taste

Heat half the olive oil in a large heavy pan. Sauté the onion, celery, and carrot over medium-low heat for 20 minutes, or until light golden brown, stirring occasionally with a wooden spoon. Add the tomatoes and tomato juices, honey, coriander, *rigani*, and garlic, and stir well. Simmer until the sauce becomes thick and syrupy and stays separated for a few seconds when the spoon is drawn across the bottom of the pan. Gently stir in the beans, salt (tinned beans may not need added salt), and a generous sprinkling of pepper. Cover and simmer 5 minutes longer.

Transfer to a shallow bowl, sprinkle with the lemon juice and the remaining olive oil, and serve hot, warm, or cold.

Meze Salad Medley
Lakhanika Diafora Marianata
Serves 10 as a *meze*, 5 to 6 as a light lunch

This enticing trio of vegetable salads captures all the unmistakable fragrance and flavours of the eastern Mediterranean. Serve with plenty of crusty bread to mop up the delicious sauces.

900 g/2 lb young broad beans in the pod
1 small bunch of flat leaf parsley, leaves coarsely chopped, stalks removed and
tied in a bundle
Strained juice of 3 lemons, or to taste
Coarse-grain sea salt *and* cracked black pepper to taste
Large pinch of powdered mustard
225 ml/8 fl oz extra virgin olive oil or to taste
2 tablespoons snipped fresh chervil, *optional*
4 medium artichoke hearts, lightly boiled until tender and cut into quarters
350 g/12 oz slender asparagus, steamed or lightly boiled (page 182)
2 tablespoons coarsely chopped fresh oregano or 1 tablespoon dried *rigani* (page 14)

For serving
1 red bell pepper, roasted and skinned (page 343), seeded, and cut into thin strips

Fill a large saucepan with lightly salted water and bring to a boil. Shell the beans, reserving 2 pods. Add the pods and parsley stalks to the boiling water and boil for 5 minutes. Add the beans and boil for 2 minutes longer. Drain, discarding the pods and parsley stalks. While the beans are still warm, remove the skins. Drain between layers of paper towels and pat dry.

Divide the lemon juice between 3 non-reactive bowls; add salt and a generous amount of pepper to each. Add the mustard to one of the bowls, divide the olive oil between the bowls, and add the chervil (or 1 tablespoon of the parsley) and artichokes to the bowl with the mustard. Add the (remaining) parsley and asparagus to the second bowl, and the oregano and broad beans to the third. Gently stir each mixture, tightly cover, and set aside for 1 hour.

To serve, taste each sauce and add lemon juice, salt and/or pepper if necessary; the sauces should be highly seasoned. Arrange the vegetables attractively on a flat platter or on individual plates, keeping them separate. Garnish the broad beans with strips of bell pepper.

Yogurt and Cucumber Salad
Tsatsiki
Serves 8 as a *meze*, 4 as a salad

Variations of this crisp refreshing salad are popular throughout an area stretching from northern India to the Balkans and Greece. In the Greek version, large amounts of garlic and flat leaf parsley are used or, better still, fresh mint which gives a light fragrant flavour. Serve *tsatsiki* as soon as possible after preparing or it will become watery. Delicious as part of a *meze* table, *tsatsiki* also nicely complements *kephtedes*, *souvlakia*, grilled meats and fried liver (page 35).

1 large cucumber, peeled
¹/₂ tablespoon sea salt, or more to taste
300 ml/¹/₂ pint Strained Yogurt (page 8)
2 tablespoons extra virgin olive oil
1 tablespoon fresh lemon juice
Freshly ground white pepper to taste
2 large cloves garlic, finely chopped (to taste)
5 tablespoons fresh mint leaves or coarsely chopped flat leaf parsley or
2 tablespoons dried mint, crushed

Using a knife, food processor, or mandoline, slice the cumber into julienne (matchsticks). Sprinkle with salt and set aside in a colander for 1 hour to drain.

Combine the yogurt, olive oil, lemon juice, pepper, and garlic in a large bowl. Cover, and refrigerate.

Just before serving, beat the yogurt sauce with a wooden spoon until smooth. Tear the mint leaves into small pieces. Dry the cucumber by gently squeezing it between paper towels; don't worry if the cucumber bruises – it is more important to avoid a watery salad. Combine with the yogurt mixture and mint, add salt and pepper to taste, and serve.

Leeks the Classic Way
Klassika Prassa
Serves 12 as a *meze*, 6 as a first course

This simple dish features traditional ingredients of the ancient Greek cuisine – spicy coriander, perfumed bay leaves, sweet honey, pungent vinegar, and rich olive oil. A popular *meze* since the days of Homer, it looks beautiful and has an unusual sweet-sour flavour.

12 slender leeks, 1 cm/¹/₂ inch in diameter
75-115 ml/3-4 fl oz extra virgin olive oil (to taste)
1¹/₂ tablespoons whole coriander seeds, crushed
3 bay leaves

1 teaspoon cracked black pepper
2 tablespoons aromatic honey, such as Hymettus
4 tablespoons aged red wine vinegar
75 g/3 oz currants or small seedless raisins
Coarse-grain sea salt to taste

For serving
2 tablespoons finely chopped flat leaf parsley

Slice off the roots and green tops of the leeks. Cut a slit lengthways halfway through each leek, keeping the original shape intact. Hold upright under running water and gently pull the layers apart, one at a time, to wash out any grit or dirt. Shake off any excess water, drain between layers of paper towels, and blot dry.

Place a heavy sauté pan large enough to hold the leeks in a single layer over low heat, and add 75 ml/3 fl oz of the olive oil, the coriander seeds, bay leaves, and pepper. Cook for 1 minute or until the coriander is aromatic. Add the leeks, turning to coat with the oil and spices.

Combine the honey and vinegar and add to the leeks along with the currants. Cover and bring just to a boil; reduce the heat to very low and simmer 10-15 minutes, or until the leeks are tender but still firm in the centre.

Transfer to a serving dish and set aside to cool. Add salt to taste and the remaining olive oil if desired. Sprinkle with the parsley and serve warm or at room temperature.

Note Twelve tender sticks of celery can be substituted for the leeks. Remove the tough strings with a paring knife and cut wide sticks lengthways in half. Cut into 12 cm/ 5 inch pieces. Boil for 1 minute in lightly salted water, drain, and add to the aromatic olive oil.

Tiny Cracked Potatoes
Patates Antinaktes
Serves 8 to 10 as a *meze*, 4 as a vegetable dish

This simple but superbly aromatic dish is a perfect *meze* with yogurt, *khorta* (page 220), *kephtedakia* (page 32), and Fried Cheese (page 38), or serve it with grilled meats and chicken.

675 g/1 ½ lb tiny new potatoes
4 tablespoons extra virgin olive oil
5 tablespoons aged red wine vinegar
4 tablespoons coriander seeds, lightly crushed
Sea salt *and* cracked black pepper to taste
4 tablespoons coarsely chopped flat leaf parsley
1 tablespoon small capers, rinsed and patted dry
1 tablespoon finely grated lemon zest

Scrub the potatoes and pat dry. With a heavy kitchen mallet or meat pounder, firmly tap each potato to crack it slightly, taking care not to break it apart.

Heat the olive oil in a large sauté pan with a tight-fitting lid. Add the potatoes in a single layer, cover, and cook for 1 minute over low heat, or until light golden brown, shaking the pan frequently.

Drain off most of the oil from the pan. Add the vinegar, coriander, salt, and a generous amount of pepper to the potatoes, cover, and cook over very low heat for 15 minutes, or until the potatoes are tender. Take care not to let the potatoes burn. Chop the parsley, capers, and lemon zest together to mix.

Transfer the potatoes to a warm serving dish and sprinkle with the parsley mixture. Serve hot, warm, or at room temperature.

meze pies

Fried Cheese Pies
Tyropittes Tighanites
Makes 1¹/₂ to 2 dozen pies: Serves 8 as a *meze*, 4 to 6 as a light lunch

These tiny fried pies are a real taste of Greece. Made with an orange-flavoured pastry, they conceal a sweet cheese filling, perfumed with fresh mint. Whenever I serve them to guests, either as a *meze* or light lunch, they disappear very quickly. Fry them in olive oil for the most authentic flavour, or, if you prefer, bake them.

Pastry
225 g/8 oz unbleached plain flour
1 teaspoon sea salt, or to taste
¹/₂ teaspoon caster sugar
2 tablespoons virgin olive oil
1 egg white, lightly beaten
4–5 tablespoons strained fresh orange juice, as needed

Filling
5 tablespoons fresh mint leaves
350 g/12 oz fresh *myzithra* cheese (page 11), crumbled, or small-curd cottage cheese,
drained and pressed through a fine sieve
50 g/2 oz finely grated *feta* cheese
1 whole egg *plus* 1 egg yolk, lightly beaten
2 tablespoons honey
25 g/1 oz unsalted butter, melted
¹/₂–1 teaspoon ground cinnamon (to taste)
Olive oil, for frying

For serving
Sifted icing sugar
Ground cinnamon

To make the pastry, combine the flour, salt, sugar, olive oil, egg white, and 3 tablespoons of the orange juice in a large bowl. Knead for 5 minutes, adding more orange juice if needed to make a smooth and elastic dough. Tightly wrap in cling film and refrigerate for 1 hour.

To make the filling, finely chop the mint leaves and mash together all the filling ingredients with a wooden spoon until well mixed but not smooth.

Divide the dough in half, rewrap 1 portion, and return to the refrigerator. Roll out the pastry on a lightly floured surface and cut out circles with a 5 cm/2 inch- or 10 cm/4 inch-round cutter; or cut into 5 x 10 cm/2 x 4 inch rectangles. Place 1 heaped tablespoon of filling in the centres of half the 5 cm/2 inch circles, or all the large circles or rectangles. Brush the edges of the pastry with the remaining orange juice. Cover the 5 cm/2 inch circles with the remaining small circles, or fold the 10 cm/4 inch ones in half to make half-moons; fold rectangles in half to make 5 cm/2 inch squares. Crimp the edges with a fork to seal. Repeat with the remaining pastry and filling.

Pour a 1 cm/1/2 inch layer of olive oil into a large heavy sauté pan, or heat olive oil in a deep-fat fryer. When the olive oil is hot but not smoking, fry the pastries over medium heat until deep golden brown on both sides; or deep-fry until golden. Drain on paper towels, arrange on a warm platter, sprinkle liberally with the icing sugar and cinnamon, and serve hot or warm.

Note To bake, heat the oven to 180C/350F/gas mark 4. Arrange the pastries 5 cm/2 inches apart on lightly oiled baking trays and bake for 15 minutes. Lightly beat 2 egg yolks with 2 tablespoons olive oil and brush the pastries with this glaze; bake 10 minutes longer, or until deep golden brown. Or you can make squares or circles with a little of the filling exposed in the centre (page 274) and bake these.

Baked Cheese and Spinach Pies
Spanakopittes me Tyri
Makes 1 1/2 to 2 dozen pies

These little pastries, filled with a creamy nutmeg-spiced spinach mixture, are perfect picnic food. You can make them with either pastry dough or with filo and they freeze beautifully (freeze before cooking).

1 recipe Pastry (above) or 450 g/1 lb packet of filo pastry (page 266), thawed if frozen

Filling
675 g/1 1/2 lb fresh spinach
115 ml/4 fl oz extra virgin olive oil
5 spring onions, trimmed, the best green parts left intact, and thinly sliced
1/4 teaspoon grated nutmeg

Sea salt to taste
1 teaspoon cracked black pepper, or to taste
175 g/6 oz small-curd cottage cheese, drained and pressed through a fine sieve
115 g/4 oz crumbled *feta* cheese
1 small bunch of flat leaf parsley, leaves coarsely chopped
2 egg yolks, lightly beaten (for pastry pies), or 50 g/2 oz unsalted butter, melted (for filo pies)

If using filo, remove the packet from the refrigerator and set aside unopened.

Rinse the spinach in several changes of cold water, discard the stalks and any bruised or tough leaves, and place in a heavy saucepan. Cover and cook, with just the water that clings to the leaves, for 1 minute, or until wilted and barely soft. Drain, pressing the greens against the sides of the colander to remove as much liquid as possible. Finely chop the spinach and set aside.

Warm half the olive oil in a heavy sauté pan and sauté the spring onions over low heat until soft, about 5 minutes. Stir in the spinach, nutmeg, salt, and pepper and cook 2 minutes. Remove from the heat and drain off any liquid. Add the cottage cheese, *feta* cheese, and parsley, and gently mash together with a fork. Season to taste with salt and pepper.

Heat the oven to 180C/350F/gas mark 4. Make the pies with the pastry as directed on page 57 or with the filo as directed on page 266. Arrange 5 cm/2 inches apart on lightly oiled baking trays. Brush pastry pies with the remaining olive oil, filo pies with a mixture of the olive oil and melted butter. Bake pastry pies for 15 minutes, brush with the beaten egg yolks, and bake 10 minutes longer, or until deep golden brown. Bake filo pies 15-20 minutes, or until deep golden brown. Serve hot or warm.

Note If tender young beetroot greens or chard are available, try the country version of these pies. Substitute 900 g/2 lb greens for the spinach; discard all tough stalks and bruised or blemished leaves. Prepare as the spinach but cook 3 minutes or until just soft.

Sesame Spinach Pies
Spanakopittes
Makes 1½ to 2 dozen pies: Serves 8 as a *meze*, 4 to 6 as a lunch dish

These delicious sesame-topped miniature pies and some good fresh cheese are the perfect nibbles to accompany a glass of wine. Or serve them the Cretan way, as a side dish with roast or grilled pork. Wild greens provide the most authentic country flavour, but you can substitute beetroot greens, chard or spinach.

1 recipe Pastry (page 57)

Filling
1.4 kg/3 lb young water spinach (*vlita*, page 220) or beetroot greens or ruby chard or
900 g/2 lb young fresh spinach
115 ml/4 fl oz extra virgin olive oil
2 medium onions, quartered and thinly sliced

1 teaspoon ground cumin
1 small bunch of fresh dill or fennel, coarsely chopped
1 teaspoon sea salt, or to taste
1 teaspoon cracked black pepper, or to taste
Juice of 1 small lemon
2 egg yolks, lightly beaten
150 g/5 oz sesame seeds

Rinse the greens in several changes of cold water and discard the stalks and any tough or discoloured leaves. Boil the water spinach, covered, in 1 cm/¹/₂ inch water for 5 minutes, or until barely tender. (Boil beetroot greens or ruby chard in 115 ml/4 fl oz water for 2 minutes, spinach in a few tablespoons water for 1 minute.) Drain, and press the greens firmly against the side of the colander to remove excess water.

Heat 6 tablespoons of the olive oil in a heavy sauté pan and sauté the onion over low heat until soft, about 10 minutes. Stir in the cumin. Finely chop the greens, and add to the onions with the dill. Cook 2 minutes longer, and add the salt, pepper, and lemon juice; the mixture should be highly seasoned.

Heat the oven to 180C/350F/gas mark 4. Make the pies as directed on page 57 and arrange them 5 cm/2 inches apart on lightly oiled baking trays. Brush with the remaining olive oil and bake 15 minutes. Brush with the beaten egg yolks, liberally sprinkle with the sesame seeds, and bake 8 minutes longer, or until deep golden brown. Serve hot or warm.

Variations
Add 50 g/2 oz rice, cooked, and 40 g/1¹/₂ oz currants to the filling.

Add 50 g/2 oz drained small-curd cottage cheese, pressed through a sieve, and 25 g/1 oz toasted pine nuts to the filling.

Increase the amount of dill or fennel to 1 large bunch and use 1.2 kg/2¹/₂ lb water spinach or beetroot greens.

Note To freeze, spread uncooked pies in a single layer on a baking tray and freeze. Remove from the baking tray and store in freezer bags. Defrost before baking.

Tiny Vegetable Pies
Bourekakia Lakhanika
Makes 1¹/₂ to 2 dozen pies

Serve these little delicacies as the glorious centrepiece to a *meze* table. Aubergines, courgettes, leeks, onions, or bell peppers can all be used in the filling; next time you grill or bake vegetables, cook a few extra, and cut down on your preparation time the next day. You can make *bourekakia* with either pastry dough or with filo.

1 recipe Pastry (page 57) or 450 g/1 lb packet of filo pastry (page 266), thawed if frozen

Filling
1 large aubergine
Coarse-grain sea salt to taste
6 tablespoons extra virgin olive oil
1 teaspoon cracked black pepper, or to taste
150 g/5 oz small-curd cottage cheese, drained and pressed through a fine sieve
75 g/3 oz crumbled *feta* cheese
2 eggs, beaten
1 teaspoon *rigani* (page 14), briefly pounded in a mortar
1 small bunch of flat leaf parsley, leaves coarsely chopped
3 egg yolks, lightly beaten (for pastry pies), or 50 g/2 oz unsalted butter,
melted (for filo pies)

If using filo, remove the packet of dough from the refrigerator and set aside unopened.

Trim the aubergines and cut into 2.5 cm/1 inch dice. Sprinkle with 1 tablespoon salt and set aside in a colander to drain.

Warm 4 tablespoons of the olive oil in a heavy sauté pan. Wipe the aubergine dice with paper towels and sauté over low heat, turning occasionally, until deep golden brown, about 15 minutes. Drain on paper towels and transfer to a bowl.

Mash the aubergine to a pulp with a fork or potato masher and add salt and pepper to taste, the cottage cheese, *feta* cheese, eggs, *rigani*, and parsley. Continue gently mashing with a fork until well-mixed. Taste, and add salt and pepper if necessary; the mixture should be highly seasoned.

Heat the oven to 180C/350F/gas mark 4. Make the pies with the pastry as directed on page 57 or with the filo as directed on page 266. Arrange 5 cm/2 inches apart on lightly oiled baking trays. Brush pastry pies with the remaining olive oil, filo pies with a mixture of the olive oil and melted butter. Bake pastry pies for 15 minutes, brush with the beaten egg yolks, and bake 10 minutes longer, or until deep golden brown. Bake filo pies 15-20 minutes, or until deep golden brown. Serve hot or warm.

Variations

Substitute 3 medium courgettes, baked (page 204), grilled or sautéed in olive oil, or 2 medium leeks, thoroughly cleaned, thinly sliced, and lightly sautéed in olive oil, for the aubergine. Take care to drain the courgettes properly to ensure a firm filling and mash as described. Use a small handful of fresh dill instead of parsley and omit the *rigani*.

Substitute 2 medium onions, each one cut in half and slow-roasted or grilled with olive oil, or sliced and gently sautéed until deep golden brown, or 3 medium bell peppers, any colour, cut in half, seeds discarded, and roasted or grilled, or sliced and sautéed in olive oil, for the aubergine. Roughly chop the vegetables, and drain on paper towels, before mashing with the cheese.

Substitute 50 g/2 oz cooked long-grain rice for the cottage cheese, use only 50 g/2 oz *feta* cheese, and add 2 tablespoons toasted pine nuts and 2 tablespoons currants to the filling.

Marjoram Meat Pies
Kreatopittes
Makes 1½ to 2 dozen pies: Serves 8 as a *meze*, 4 to 6 as a lunch dish

These spicy pastry parcels are a treat, especially good in late spring when lamb has a delicate succulent flavour and marjoram leaves are at their most fragrant. If you have the patience, you'll achieve the best texture and flavour if you chop the meat by hand.

Pastry
225 g/8 oz unbleached plain flour
1 teaspoon sea salt
2 tablespoons extra virgin olive oil
1 egg, lightly beaten
3 tablespoons red wine vinegar or yogurt, preferably home-made (page 8)
3-4 tablespoons cold water

Filling
115 ml/4 fl oz extra virgin olive oil
2 large onions, chopped
675 g/1½ lb lean lamb or beef or a mixture of both, finely chopped or minced
115 ml/4 fl oz dry red wine or 2 tablespoons red wine vinegar
½ teaspoon coarse-grain sea salt, or to taste
1 teaspoon cracked black pepper, or to taste
1 teaspoon ground cinnamon
¼ teaspoon ground cloves
1 small bunch of flat leaf parsley, leaves finely chopped
2 tablespoons fresh marjoram, chopped, or 1 tablespoon dried *rigani* (page 14), crumbled
65 g/2½ oz lightly toasted pine nuts
2 egg yolks beaten with 1 tablespoon water
65 g/2½ oz sesame seeds, *optional*

To make the pastry, sift the flour into a large bowl and add the salt, olive oil, egg, and vinegar. Knead for 5 minutes, adding enough of the old water if needed to make a smooth and elastic dough. Tightly wrap in cling film and refrigerate for 1 hour.

To make the filling, heat 3 tablespoons of the olive oil in a large heavy sauté pan and sauté the onion over medium-low heat until golden brown, about 15 minutes, stirring continuously. Add the meat and cook until lightly browned, breaking up any lumps with a wooden spoon. Add the wine and boil until almost evaporated. Stir in the salt, pepper, cinnamon, and cloves, cover, and simmer 15 minutes over very low heat. Add 1 or 2 tablespoons water if the mixture starts to dry out; or, if there is still liquid remaining in the pan, uncover for the last few minutes to let it evaporate. Add the parsley, marjoram, and pine nuts. Season to taste and set aside to cool.

Heat the oven to 180C/350F/gas mark 4. Roll out the pastry on a lightly floured surface, and cut out circles with a 10 cm/4 inch-round cutter or cut into 5 x 10 cm/2 x 4 inch rectangles. Place 2 scant tablespoons of filling in the centre of each shape and brush the edges of the pastry with water. Fold the circles in half to make half-moons or fold the rectangles in half to make 5 cm/2 inch squares. Crimp the edges with a fork to seal.

Arrange the pies 5 cm/2 inches apart on a lightly oiled baking tray and brush with the remaining olive oil. Bake 10 minutes, then brush with the egg yolks and lightly sprinkle with the sesame seeds. Bake 15 minutes longer, or until deep golden brown. Serve hot or warm, or cool to room temperature on racks.

Note These can be made with filo pastry, but the filling must be moister. Add 2 skinned and diced tomatoes to the meat along with the spices, or add 175 g/6 oz drained cottage cheese, pressed through a sieve, with the pine nuts. Shape into triangles, rolls, or rectangles as directed on page 272 or into 1 large pie as directed on page 94, and bake as directed in each recipe.

Soups

Soupes

For Greeks an ideal one-dish meal is a large bowl of aromatic and hearty soup, accompanied by crusty bread, plenty of local wine, juicy olives, peppery radishes, and soft crumbly cheese. From classical time Greeks have believed in the fortifying powers of good soups and they have a particular reverence for bean soups, which they believe develop physical and mental stamina. These substantial winter soups are especially popular during the Lenten fast.

At the other extreme, the Greek cook is also adept at creating a variety of delicate broths which make light and elegant first courses. These are usually laced with *avgolemono*, giving them a beautiful pale lemon colour.

The most exquisitely flavoured soup of this type is *mayeritsa*, the Easter soup made from the offal of the Paschal lamb and flavoured with fresh dill and *avgolemono*. Served at the midnight breakfast of Easter morning and at Easter Sunday lunch, *mayeritsa* is a treat not to be missed. It's difficult to reproduce with complete success outside Greece, but if you are in Greece at Easter, don't miss the opportunity to sample it.

An introduction to Greek soups is not complete without some reference to fish soups, staple food on Greek tables, especially on the islands. The most popular of these is *kakavia*, almost certainly the original of *bouillabaise* and introduced into France by occupying Greeks of classical times. You will not, however, find a recipe for this soup in my selection. This is not an oversight but a recognition of the fact that it is almost impossible to reproduce *kakavia* with any kind of authenticity outside Greece since the requisite variety of fish is not available. But if you visit Greece be sure to seek out *kakavia* and discover its delights for yourself.

Bean and Vegetable Soup
Fassolada
Serves 6 to 8

For the Greeks of antiquity *fassolada* was the staple winter food – not only delicious and aromatic, but nourishing, filling, and easy to make with ingredients to hand. It's still the most popular winter soup in Greece today and it is served in large shallow bowls, accompanied by *feta*, olives, a green salad, crusty bread, and a robust red wine. For best results use top-quality olive oil – it's essential for an authentic flavour.

350 g/12 oz dried cannellini or small white beans or black-eyed peas, soaked for 4 hours
in water to cover
115 ml/4 fl oz extra virgin olive oil, or to taste
2 medium onions, finely chopped
4 medium carrots, finely diced
2 celery sticks, finely diced
4 sprigs of celery leaves (page 15), lightly chopped, *optional*
2 large cloves garlic, finely chopped
2 tablespoons dried thyme or *rigani* (page 14) or a mixture of both
1 medium bunch of flat leaf parsley, leaves coarsely chopped
Sea salt *and* cracked black pepper to taste
2 litres/3½ pints water or Light Meat Stock (page 347) or a mixture of both
3 large ripe tomatoes, skinned and diced, juices reserved
1 tablespoon tomato purée diluted with 3 tablespoons water

For serving
Aged red wine vinegar *or* lemon juice, *optional*

Drain the beans and place in a large saucepan. Add cold water to cover by 7 cm/3 inches, bring slowly to a boil, drain, and rinse. Set aside.

Rinse out the saucepan and set over medium-low heat. Heat 6 tablespoons of the oil and add the onion, carrot, and celery. Sauté for 30 minutes or until pale gold, stirring occasionally with a wooden spoon. Add the celery leaves, if using, the garlic, thyme, half the parsley, the pepper, beans, and water. Bring to a boil, cover, and simmer for 1 hour, or until the beans are soft but not disintegrating. Meanwhile, sprinkle the tomatoes with salt and set aside for 15 minutes.

Stir the tomato purée and tomatoes into the soup, season with salt and pepper, and simmer for 5 more minutes. Stir in the remaining parsley, olive oil, and vinegar if desired. Serve hot.

Bean and Vegetable Soup with Spinach
Fassolada me Spanaki

Thoroughly wash 225 g/8 oz young spinach leaves, discard the tough stalks, and slice the leaves into chiffonade (thin ribbons). Add to the soup with the tomatoes. Sprinkle 1 tablespoon aged red wine vinegar over each bowl of soup when serving, and provide each guest with a small bowl of crôutons (page 344).

Green Lentil Soup with Sorrel
Fakes Soupa
Serves 6

Lentil and onion soup does not sound exotic – but add the richness of honey-sweetened ripe tomatoes, the strong sharp tang of sorrel, and a swirl of yogurt and you have a soup in an entirely different class. The trick of adding wild greens to bean soups is a common village practice and works well in softening the texture of lentils and improving their flavour.

4 tablespoons extra virgin olive oil
1 large mild onion, finely chopped
225 g/8 oz green lentils, picked over, rinsed, and soaked for 10 minutes in cold water
to cover
1.1 litres/2 pints light stock (chicken, meat, or vegetable, pages 344, 347 and 351)
or water
2 large ripe tomatoes, skinned, and cut into small dice
$^1/_2$ teaspoon honey
Sea salt and cracked black pepper to taste
225 g/8 oz fresh sorrel

For serving
115 ml/4 fl oz Strained Yogurt (page 8)

Heat the olive oil in a heavy saucepan and sauté the onion over low heat for 10 minutes. Drain the lentils and add to the saucepan with the stock. Bring slowly to a boil, cover, and simmer 40 minutes, or until the lentils are soft. (Keeping the heat low prevents an unattractive froth from forming.)

Meanwhile, place the tomatoes in a colander set over a bowl, sprinkle with the honey and salt, and set aside to drain. Wash the sorrel in several changes of cold water, strip the leaves from the stalks, and discard any bruised or discoloured parts of the leaves.

Drain the lentils over a bowl and set aside the cooking liquid. Transfer the lentils to a food processor or blender container, in batches if necessary, and pulse, adding enough reserved cooking liquid (and water if needed) to make a light soup. Return the soup to the rinsed-out saucepan.

Slice the sorrel into chiffonade (thin ribbons) and reserve a few choice strips for garnish. Add the sorrel and the tomatoes to the soup and season with pepper. Simmer 2 minutes, or just until the sorrel is soft. Add salt and pepper to taste.

Serve in individual bowls with a spoonful of yogurt in the centre of each, and sprinkle with the reserved sorrel.

Aromatic Yellow Split Pea Soup
Aromatiki Soupa
Serves 4

This savoury cumin-flavoured soup looks elegant, comforts on cold days, and yet is surprisingly refreshing in cold weather.

175 g/6 oz yellow split peas, picked over and rinsed
4 tablespoons extra virgin olive oil
1 medium onion, finely chopped
1 medium carrot, finely diced
1 small celery stick, finely diced
$1/_2$–1 tablespoon cumin seeds (to taste), gently heated in a small clean frying pan
until their aroma rises, and pulverized in a clean coffee grinder or mortar
850 ml/$1^1/_2$ pints Chicken Stock (page 344) or water
Sea salt *and* freshly ground white pepper to taste

For serving
4 tablespoons Strained Yogurt (page 8)
Juice of 1 small lemon
Coarsely chopped flat leaf parsley

Cover the split peas with cold water and set aside. Heat the olive oil in a large heavy saucepan and sauté the onion, carrot and celery over medium heat until golden brown, about 20 minutes, stirring occasionally with a wooden spoon. Stir in the cumin and cook 1 minute longer. Drain the split peas and add with the stock. Bring to a boil, cover, and gently simmer 40 minutes or until the peas are soft.

Purée the soup in a food processor or blender or push through the medium disc of a moulis-légumes (food mill). Add water if necessary to make a light soup. Return to the rinsed-out saucepan, add salt and pepper, and heat slowly. Add more cumin if desired (you should be able to taste the cumin but its flavour should not be overpowering).

Divide the soup between warm individual bowls and place a spoonful of yogurt in the centre of each. Sprinkle with lemon juice and parsley and serve hot or warm.

Variations

Add 2 skinned and diced ripe tomatoes to the puréed soup and simmer 5 minutes. Omit the lemon juice.

Serve with golden-brown crôutons (page 344) rather than yogurt, and sprinkle each serving with the parsley and lemon juice and 1 teaspoon finely chopped Preserved Lemon (page 18).

Country Tomato Soup
Soupa Domata
Serves 4

The gentle slow cooking of chopped onion, celery, and carrot, perfumed with thyme, creates a fragrant base for this colourful country soup. Make it when tomatoes are at their sweetest and serve with olives, *feta* cheese, crusty bread, and a green salad.

2 tablespoons extra virgin olive oil
1 large onion, finely chopped
$^1/_2$ small celery stick, finely diced
1 small carrot, finely diced
1 tablespoon dried thyme
675 g/1$^1/_2$ lb ripe tomatoes, skinned and diced, juices reserved
1 teaspoon honey
Sea salt *and* cracked black pepper to taste
1 litre/1$^3/_4$ pints Chicken Stock (page 344) or water
50 g/2 oz small *kritharaki* (tiny pasta, page 244) or 4 tablespoons medium-grain bulgur
(available from Greek or Middle Eastern shops, see *Note*)
1 bunch of watercress, leaves only, rinsed and coarsely chopped
2 tablespoons finely chopped flat leaf parsley

For serving
Finely grated kasseri, kephalotyri, or parmesan cheese

Warm the olive oil in a large heavy saucepan set over low heat and sauté the onion, celery, carrot, and thyme until pale golden brown, about 25 minutes; stir occasionally with a wooden spoon. Stir in the tomatoes and their juices, honey, and salt and pepper, and simmer 4 minutes, or until the tomatoes are soft. Add the stock and bring to a boil. Add the *kritharaki* and simmer 4 minutes, or until the *kritharaki* is almost cooked. Add the watercress and simmer 1 minute longer. Stir in the parsley and serve immediately, with small bowls of grated cheese.

Note If using the bulgur, bring a small saucepan of water to a boil over medium heat. Add the bulgur, boil 1 minute, drain, and rinse under cold running water. Set aside.

Chicken Avgolemono Soup
Avgolemono Soupa
Serves 6 to 8

A traditional favourite in Greek homes and tavernas, *avgolemono* soup has its origins back in antiquity. It's a most delicious and refreshing soup – light, nourishing, and elegant enough to serve at a dinner party. My version is based on a rich chicken stock enhanced with saffron, which gives a delicate but distinctive flavour. The addition of rice makes a more substantial soup.

1.6 litres/2¾ pints Rich Chicken Stock (page 344)
50 g/2 oz short-grain rice, *optional*
4 eggs, separated
Juice of 2 large lemons
Sea salt *and* freshly ground white pepper to taste

For serving
2 tablespoons finely-chopped flat leaf parsley

Bring the stock to a boil in a large saucepan. (If using rice, add to the stock, cover, and simmer 15 minutes, or until the rice is cooked.)

Five minutes before you are ready to serve the soup, whisk the egg whites in a large bowl with a wire whisk or electric mixer until stiff. Whisk in the egg yolks, add the lemon juice, and whisk 1 minute longer. Hold a ladleful of the hot soup broth about 30 cm/12 inches above the bowl and slowly add it to the eggs and lemon juice, whisking constantly. (This trick helps prevent curdling the egg mixture, because by the time the broth reaches the bowl it is hot but not boiling.) Off the heat, whisk the egg and lemon juice sauce into the soup. Do not return the soup to the heat. Add salt and pepper to taste, sprinkle with the parsley, and serve at once.

Note Once the egg and lemon juice flavouring is added, the soup must not be reheated.

Avgolemono Soup with Kephtedes
Avgolemono Soupa me Kephtedes
Serves 8

This delicate and delicious soup is satisfying without being heavy – ideal for a light lunch. For convenience both the soup broth and the tiny crisp *kephtedes* can be made in advance, but do not combine them until 10 minutes before serving.

225 g/8 oz lean lamb, finely minced
1 egg yolk, lightly beaten
1 small onion, finely grated

2 tablespoons finely chopped flat leaf parsley
25 g/1 oz fresh fine breadcrumbs, soaked for 5 minutes in 1 tablespoon milk
½ tablespoon aged red wine vinegar
Sea salt and freshly ground black pepper to taste
1 tablespoon olive oil, or more to taste
2 litres/3½ pints Light Meat Stock (page 347)
2 egg yolks
Juice of 2 lemons

For serving
Finely chopped flat leaf parsley

Heat the oven to 190C/375F/gas mark 5.

Combine the lamb, lightly beaten egg yolk, onion, parsley, breadcrumbs, vinegar, and salt and pepper, and mix until thoroughly blended. Moisten your hands with cold water and pat barely dry. Shape the meat mixture into small balls the size of your thumbnail; you should have about 3 dozen.

Lightly brush a baking tray with olive oil and place in the oven for 2 minutes to heat. Arrange the *kephtedes* on the baking tray and bake 15-20 minutes or until golden brown. Drain between layers of paper towels.

Bring the stock to a boil in a large saucepan. Add the *kephtedes*, reduce the heat, cover, and gently simmer 10 minutes; do not let the soup broth boil. Whisk the egg yolks in a large bowl until pale and frothy, add the lemon juice, and whisk 1 minute longer. Hold a ladleful of the hot broth about 30 cm/12 inches above the bowl and slowly add it to the eggs, whisking constantly.

With a slotted spoon, transfer the *kephtedes* to a warm soup tureen or divide among warm individual bowls. Off the heat, lightly whisk the egg and lemon juice mixture into the soup. Add salt and pepper to taste, stir in the parsley, ladle the soup over the *kephtedes*, and serve.

The Monks' Onion Soup
Monarcho Soupa
Serves 4 to 6

Staple fare in Byzantine monasteries, this soup is based on the humblest ingredients. It was served to the monks to remind them of the virtues of the simple religious life, removed from worldly extravagance. Although it is simple, and easy to prepare, this onion soup has a delicious flavour and makes a warming winter meal.

2 tablespoons unsalted butter
4 tablespoons extra virgin olive oil
3 large onions, quartered and thinly sliced
Sea salt and freshly ground black pepper, to taste

2 thick slices wholemeal bread, crusts removed, and cut into 1 cm/$\frac{1}{2}$ inch dice
3 egg yolks
3 tablespoons aged red wine vinegar or 1 tablespoon balsamic vinegar

For serving
Finely chopped flat leaf parsley
Ground cinnamon to taste

Heat the butter and 1 tablespoon of the olive oil in a large, preferably enamel-lined, saucepan and sauté the onions over low heat for 20 minutes; stir occasionally with a wooden spoon and don't let the onions colour. Cover, reduce the heat, and cook 50 minutes longer, stirring once or twice. If the onions begin to stick, sprinkle with 1 or 2 tablespoons of water. They will reduce almost to a purée, but should remain very pale. Add 1 litre/1^3/$_4$ pints water, salt, and pepper, and bring to a boil over medium heat. Cover, reduce the heat, and simmer for 15 minutes.

Heat the remaining olive oil in a heavy frying pan and fry the diced bread over medium-low heat until golden brown on all sides. Drain these crôutons between layers of paper towels.

Just before serving, whisk the egg yolks with the vinegar in a large bowl. Hold a ladleful of the hot soup about 30 cm/12 inches above the bowl and slowly add it to the eggs, whisking constantly; whisk 10 seconds longer. Off the heat, stir the egg mixture into the soup. Add salt and pepper to taste.

Divide the soup between warm individual bowls and sprinkle with the crôutons, parsley, and cinnamon. Serve at once.

Note For a more substantial soup, substitute Chicken or Light Meat Stock (pages 344 and 347) for some or all of the water.

Light Meals

yevmata ellafra

Greek cooks have a special talent for creating quick and appetizing snacks and light meals. Often the clue to their enchantment is the sheer simplicity of their preparation and the perfect freshness of the ingredients used.

The satisfying Greek egg dishes are a good example of this skill. I have been delighted by an unpretentious platter of creamy eggs on a laden taverna table, a frittata of courgettes in the cool shade of a perfumed summer garden, and, at a country café buzzing with local gossip, a fragrant herbed omelette enveloping tiny browned diced potatoes.

In summer a colourful variety of stuffed vegetables are served as light meals, and tavernas display tempting trays of vegetable shells bulging with spicy rice or meat fillings. In the villages stuffed vegetables with an olive oil and lemon juice or tomato sauce are slowly baked to a moist mellowness in the baker's oven, producing a wonderful richness of flavour. The amount of olive oil used in the following stuffed vegetable recipes may seem high. But the pungency of good-quality olive oil is essential to flavour both vegetable and filling – without it you will not achieve the richness and depth of taste that's characteristic of these aromatic country meals.

Savoury pies, made with crumbly pastry or filo, are favourite snacks and light meals too. Every bus or train station and every town square has its pie shop, selling tiny pastries concealing mouthfuls of spicy meat, cheese, chicken, or wild greens. Honeyed nuts or sweet custard fillings are popular too.

Many of the following recipes can be prepared in advance and reheated or served cold, and several, notably the pies, freeze very well (but freeze *before* cooking). Remember too that many *mezedes* and vegetable dishes can also be served as light meals or tasty snacks.

egg dishes

A Villager's Eggs
Avga Khoriatiki
Serves 2

An omelette made with just-laid eggs and a handful of pungent fresh wild herbs is a favourite country snack. Villagers are especially fond of wild asparagus, mallow, wild chervil, purslane, wild leeks, courgette flowers, and wild artichokes in their omelettes and we can enjoy some of these country flavours too. I have found wild chervil in Chinese markets, purslane in a potato field, and mallow alongside country footpaths.

225 g/8 oz wild asparagus or slender young asparagus
2 tablespoons extra virgin olive oil
1 tablespoon fresh lemon juice
Coarse-grain sea salt and cracked black pepper to taste
4 eggs, lightly beaten

For serving
Coarsely chopped flat leaf parsley
Lemon wedges

Break off the tough ends of the asparagus stalks at the point where they snap easily and discard. Blanch the asparagus in boiling water for 5 seconds, rinse under cold running water, drain between layers of paper towels, and blot dry. Cut into 5 cm/2 inch pieces.

Warm the olive oil in a seasoned 23 cm/9 inch omelette pan or heavy frying pan and sauté the asparagus over medium-low heat until barely tender. Sprinkle with the lemon juice and salt and pepper. Pour the eggs over the asparagus and tilt the pan to distribute evenly. Reduce the heat to low.

When the omelette is lightly set, lift one edge with a palette knife to allow any still-liquid egg to flow underneath. Slide out onto a plate, invert the pan over the plate, and, firmly holding both, invert once more so the omelette is upside down in the pan. Cook 20 seconds longer, or until set, and invert onto a warm serving platter. Sprinkle with the parsley and serve at once, with the lemon wedges.

Note To season an omelette pan, sprinkle 2 tablespoons salt over the bottom of the pan and set it over low heat for 5 minutes. The salt will turn light brown as it absorbs all the extraneous substances that inevitably stick to the surface of kitchen utensils. Discard the salt and thoroughly wipe out the pan with paper towels.

Cheese Omelette
Omeleta Tyri
Serves 2

In this tasty dish garlic is used to flavour the cooking oil, giving a robust character to the omelette; the crunchy oven-dried breadcrumbs add an unusual nutty texture. Serve with a tomato or bean salad or Beetroot Salad with Allspice (page 184).

2 tablespoons extra virgin olive oil
1 clove garlic, cut into 3 pieces
3 tablespoons dried fine breadcrumbs
50 g/2 oz *feta* cheese, crumbled, or aged *myzithra*, grated
4 eggs
Freshly ground black pepper to taste

For serving
1 tablespoon finely chopped flat leaf parsley
1 spring onion, trimmed, and thinly sliced
2 teaspoons fresh oregano, chopped, or 1 teaspoon dried *rigani* (page 14), crumbled
6 Elitses or Niçoise olives
Lemon wedges

Heat the olive oil in a seasoned 23 cm/9 inch omelette pan or heavy frying pan (page 74). Sauté the garlic for a minute or two over medium-low heat and discard. Add the breadcrumbs to the pan and fry until pale golden brown, stirring occasionally. Lightly whisk together the cheese, eggs, and pepper and pour over the breadcrumbs, tilting the pan to distribute evenly.

When the omelette is lightly set, lift one edge with a palette knife to allow any still-liquid egg to flow underneath. Slide the omelette out onto a warm plate, invert the pan over the plate, and, firmly holding both, invert once more so the omelette is upside down in the pan. Cook 20 seconds longer, or until set, and invert onto a warm serving platter.

Chop the parsley, spring onion, and oregano together just to mix and sprinkle the mixture over the omelette, along with the olives. Serve immediately, with the lemon wedges.

Sausage and Potato Omelette
Omeleta me Loukhanika ke Patates
Serves 2

Make this substantial and spicy omelette with *pastourmas* sausages (page 176) or Country Sausages (page 178) and whatever fresh herbs are available. Serve with a salad of wild greens (page 221) and Shepherd's Bread (page 250) or Olive Bread (page 253).

3 tablespoons extra virgin olive oil
Two 10-12 cm/4-5 inch sausages, casings discarded, cut into
1 cm/$^1/_2$ inch slices
2 medium boiling potatoes, peeled if desired, cooked and cut into
1 cm/$^1/_2$ inch dice
5 eggs, lightly beaten
Cracked black pepper to taste

For serving
2 tablespoons coarsely chopped flat leaf parsley or fresh coriander
or fresh dill
Large pinch of ground paprika
Lemon wedges

Heat half the olive oil in a seasoned 23 cm/9 inch omelette pan or heavy frying pan (page 74) and sauté the sausages until lightly browned on both sides. Drain between layers of paper towels and wipe the pan clean.

Heat the remaining olive oil in the pan and sauté the potato dice over medium-low heat until golden brown on all sides, about 6 minutes. Add the sausages and lightly stir to mix. Pour in the eggs, reduce the heat to low, and tilt the pan to distribute the eggs evenly. Season with pepper (the sausages are salty). When lightly set, lift one edge with a palette knife to allow any still-liquid egg to flow underneath. Slide the omelette onto a warm plate, invert the pan over the plate, and firmly holding both, invert once more so the omelette is upside down in the pan. Cook 20 seconds longer, or until set, and invert onto a warm serving platter.

Sprinkle with the parsley and paprika and serve immediately, with the lemon wedges.

Variations
Add 1 roasted, seeded, and skinned red bell pepper (page 343), cut into strips, or 1 medium aubergine or courgette, cut into small dice and fried, or 1 leek, thinly sliced and sautéed, to the pan with the potatoes.

Saffron Eggs with Lamb's Kidneys
Avga me Nefra apo Arnaki
Serves 2

I first came across this surprising dish one Easter in a village on the island of Paxos. This was the speciality of the village café and I must say I had my reservations about sampling it, but it tasted superb. It is an unusual dish with a bold conjunction of distinctive flavours; it's well worth trying. With crusty bread and a wild greens salad (page 221), purslane salad (page 219), or green salad, it's an ideal lunch or supper when you want a meal that's quick and easy but out-of-the-ordinary.

2 or 3 small lamb's kidneys
Sea salt
3 tablespoons aged red wine vinegar
4 tablespoons extra virgin olive oil
6 large flat mushrooms, preferably wild, trimmed and cut into
6 mm / $^1/_4$ inch slices
$^1/_4$ teaspoon saffron threads
1 tablespoon hot water
1 teaspoon fresh thyme or oregano, finely chopped
1 teaspoon whole coriander seeds, pulverized
$^1/_2$ teaspoon freshly ground black pepper
1 teaspoon honey
4 eggs

For serving
1 tablespoon finely chopped parsley
1 tablespoon finely chopped chives

Slice each kidney horizontally in half to expose the centre. Cut out the valves and discard. Cut the kidneys lengthways into 6 mm/$^1/_4$ inch slices and place in a bowl with $^1/_2$ teaspoon salt, half the vinegar, and water to cover. Set aside for 30 minutes.

Heat 1 tablespoon of the olive oil in a heavy frying pan and sauté the mushrooms over medium-low heat for a minute or two. Once they have released some of their water, raise the heat to medium and cook, stirring occasionally, until most of the liquid has evaporated. Set aside.

Heat the saffron in a small dry frying pan until aromatic, crumble into the hot water, and set aside. Drain the kidneys and rinse in several changes of cold water until the water runs clear; thoroughly dry with paper towels.

Heat 1 tablespoon of the remaining olive oil in a heavy frying pan and sauté the kidneys over medium heat for about 3 minutes, or until lightly browned. Sprinkle with the thyme, coriander, salt, and pepper. Combine the honey and remaining vinegar and add with the mushrooms. Cover, shake gently to mix, and cook for 1 minute, or until most of the liquid has disappeared. Set aside and keep warm.

Strain the saffron water, discarding the saffron and reserving the liquid. Lightly beat the eggs and add the strained saffron water, salt, and pepper. Add the remaining olive oil to a seasoned 23 cm/9 inch omelette pan or heavy frying pan (page 74) set over medium-low heat. Pour in the eggs and cook, stirring with a fork, until lightly set. Reduce the heat and spoon the warm kidney and mushroom mixture over the eggs.

Sprinkle with the parsley and chives and serve immediately.

Country Vegetable Omelette
Sfongata
Serves 2

A fragrant dish of vegetables and eggs flavoured with Mediterranean cheese, a *sfongata* is essentially a frittata. You can use aubergines, potatoes, grilled bell peppers, onions, beans, leeks or courgettes – whatever you have available. If you include tomatoes your *sfongata* will have a soft and creamy texture. A *sfongata* made without tomatoes, which is easier to manoeuvre, is usually turned over to brown on both sides. Garnish with tiny olives and parsley and serve with country bread, slices of *feta* or *myzithra* cheese, and a salad of wild greens (page 22).

5 small firm courgettes (about 450 g/1 lb)
Coarse-grain sea salt
6 tablespoons extra virgin olive oil
1 shallot, finely chopped
1 small clove garlic, minced
2 large ripe tomatoes, skinned, seeded, and diced
Pinch of sugar, optional
5 eggs
2 tablespoons finely grated *kephalotyri* or parmesan cheese
Freshly ground black pepper to taste
1 teaspoon fresh oregano or marjoram, finely chopped

For serving
2 tablespoons coarsely chopped flat leaf parsley
6 Elitses or Niçoise olives, drained

Trim the courgettes and cut into large julienne (matchsticks). Sprinkle with 1 teaspoon of salt and set aside for 30 minutes to drain.

Heat half the olive oil in a seasoned 23 cm/9 inch omelette pan or heavy frying pan (page 74). Dry the courgettes with paper towels and sauté over medium-low heat for about 8 minutes, or until light golden brown. Drain on paper towels. Wipe out the pan and set aside.

Heat 1 tablespoon of the remaining olive oil in a heavy frying pan and cook the shallot and garlic over low heat until soft. Add the tomatoes, sugar, and a pinch of salt and gently boil 1 minute. Set aside.

Whisk together the eggs, cheese, and pepper. Heat the remaining olive oil in the omelette pan over low heat and spread the courgettes over the bottom of the pan. Sprinkle with the oregano, pour the egg mixture over the courgettes, and cook until the eggs are lightly set. Using a slotted spoon, spoon the tomato mixture over the eggs, and season to taste.

Sprinkle with the parsley and olives and serve.

stuffed vegetables

Tiny Stuffed Vegetables
Mikra Yemista Lakhanika
Serves 12 to 15 as a *meze*, 8 as a first course

These tiny stuffed vegetables are miniature works of art, masterpieces of the Greek kitchen. The vegetables used may be tomatoes, aubergines, peppers, onions, artichokes, courgettes, or squash. The main criteria for selection are that they add splashes of brilliant colour to the *meze* table (see pages 28-29) and are the best available.

For a large gathering, buffet, or picnic these vegetables are a gift. They look spectacular and they're very long suffering – staying fresh and delicious even in hot sunshine and after the first wave of guests has descended on the table. Although the preparation is fairly time consuming, most of it can be done ahead of time. Any of the meatless fillings for stuffed vegetables given on pages 85 and 87 can be used but my own favourite is the following recipe. Its tantalizing herbal aroma reminds me of villages in the rugged Greek mountains where these highly flavoured tiny treats are a speciality.

2 firm round aubergines, no more than 7 cm/3 inches long
Sea salt
2 courgettes, 5-7 cm/2-3 inches long
3 small squash suitable for stuffing, about 5 cm/2 inches in diameter or
2 courgettes, 5-7 cm/2-3 inches long
3 small bell peppers, green, red, or yellow *or* a combination of all three
6 boiling onions, about 4 cm/1¹/₂ inches in diameter
4 small tomatoes
¹/₂ teaspoon sugar
115-175 ml/4-6 fl oz extra virgin olive oil
1 small onion, finely grated
1 large clove garlic, finely chopped
1¹/₂ teaspoons ground cinnamon *or* 1 tablespoon ground coriander
Freshly ground black pepper to taste
150 g/5 oz long-grain rice, cooked
4 tablespoons finely chopped flat leaf parsley

2 tablespoons dried *rigani* (page 14), briefly pounded in a small mortar
75 g/3 oz currants or small dark seedless raisins, optional
Juice of 1 lemon

For serving
Lemon wedges

Slice off the stem ends of the aubergines, cut lengthways in half, and sprinkle the cut sides with 2 teaspoons salt. Set aside for 30 minutes to "sweat".

Fill a large saucepan with water and bring to a boil. Meanwhile, rinse the courgettes and other squash and rub with a tea towel to remove any fuzz. Slice off the stem ends of the courgettes and squash and remove a thin slice from the base of each squash so that they stand upright. Add the courgettes and other squash to the boiling water and lightly boil for 5 minutes, or until barely soft. Drain on paper towels and retain the boiling water for the next stage.

Slice off the tops of the peppers, remove the cores and seeds, and rinse the tops and peppers. Peel the onions, slicing off the root and stem ends. Add the peppers, pepper tops and onions to the boiling water. Lightly boil the peppers for 5 minutes or until slightly softened, the onions 3 or 4 minutes longer, or until just soft, and drain.

Slice off the tops of the tomatoes and set aside. With a small spoon, scoop out the seeds, sprinkle the insides with the sugar and a pinch of salt, and invert on paper towels to drain. With the point of a small paring knife, push out the centres of the boiled onions, leaving shells of 2 layers. Finely chop the centres.

Heat the oven to 160C/325F/gas mark 3. Place a heavy frying pan over medium-low heat and add 3 tablespoons of the olive oil. Dry the aubergines with paper towels and fry until the cut sides are golden brown and the skins are dark and wrinkled, about 12 minutes. Drain on paper towels.

Cut the courgettes lengthways in half and carefully scoop out the flesh, leaving 6 mm/¼ inch shells. Scoop out the flesh of the aubergines and squash. Discard the aubergine seeds and finely dice all the flesh.

Heat 2 tablespoons of the remaining olive oil in a heavy sauté or frying pan. Add the chopped onion, grated onion, and garlic, and sauté over low heat until soft. Add the tomato dice, aubergine pulp, courgette and squash pulp, cinnamon, and pepper, stir with a wooden spoon and cook for 1 to 2 minutes. Add the rice, parsley, *rigani*, currants, and half the lemon juice, and gently stir to mix. Add salt and pepper, cinnamon and/or lemon juice to taste; the mixture should be highly flavoured.

Arrange all the vegetable shells in a single layer in a large shallow baking dish. Loosely fill with the rice mixture, taking care not to split the shells. Replace the tops of the tomatoes and peppers and sprinkle all the vegetables with the remaining lemon juice and olive oil to taste. Add 225 ml/8 fl oz water to the dish and bake uncovered for 1 hour, or until the vegetables are soft; reduce the oven temperature to 150C/300F/gas mark 2 if the vegetables start to brown. If necessary, add a little more water to the dish.

Let the vegetables cool in the baking dish, then transfer to a serving plate. Surround with lemon wedges and sprinkle with pan juices and olive oil to taste. Serve at room temperature.

Note If you prefer to use less olive oil, the aubergines can be cut in half and added to the boiling water with the courgettes. Boil 5 minutes and drain on paper towels. Because this dish has an overall mellowness, the rich flavour of aubergines prepared in olive oil is not essential to its success.

Baked Aubergines to Make the Sultan Swoon
Imam Bayildi
Serves 12 as a first course, 6 as a vegetable dish

Imam Bayildi is of Turkish origin, and there are many stories about how the dish acquired its name. Some say the sultan fainted in blissful pleasure at his first taste of this rich and spicy aubergine dish, others that he was overcome by the beauty of the young woman who served it to him. Whatever its origins, it is delectable. *Imam Bayildi* is ideal for a large party since it is best made a day ahead to give the flavours time to mellow and deepen. Serve warm for a first course, hot as a side dish for grilled meats, or cold as part of a buffet.

12 slender aubergines, about 10 cm/4 inches long, or 6 medium aubergines (about 1.2 kg/2^1/$_2$ lb)
Coarse-grain sea salt to taste
175-225 ml/6-8 fl oz extra virgin olive oil (to taste)
675 g/1^1/$_2$ lb onions, quartered and thinly sliced
2 large cloves garlic, finely chopped
675 g/1^1/$_2$ lb ripe tomatoes, skinned and diced, juices reserved
75 g/3 oz currants or small dark seedless raisins
1 tablespoon ground allspice
1 small bunch of flat leaf parley, leaves finely chopped
Freshly ground black pepper to taste
1 tablespoon honey
Juice of 2 lemons
2 tablespoons dried *rigani* (page 14)

Slice off the ends of the aubergines and cut lengthways in half. Sprinkle the cut sides with salt and set aside for 30 minutes to "sweat".

Heat 4 tablespoons of the olive oil in a heavy sauté pan and sauté the onions over low heat until soft and pale golden brown, about 15 minutes; stir occasionally. Add the garlic and tomatoes with their juices and boil until most of the liquid has evaporated, about 10 minutes. Stir in the currants, allspice, most of the parsley, and salt and pepper to taste, and set aside.

Heat the oven to 160C/325F/gas mark 3. Thoroughly dry the aubergines with paper towels. Place a large heavy frying pan over medium-low heat, add 3 tablespoons of the remaining olive oil, and fry half the aubergines until the cut sides are a deep golden brown and the skins are dark and wrinkled, about 10 minutes. Drain between layers of paper towels. Add 2 tablespoons of the remaining olive oil to the frying pan, fry the remaining aubergines, and drain on paper towels. With a small spoon, scoop out the aubergine centres, leaving 6 mm/^{1}/$_4$ inch-thick shells. Discard most of the seeds, finely dice the flesh, and stir into the onion and tomato mixture.

Arrange the aubergine shells in a heavy baking dish just large enough to hold them. Divide the filling between them, heaping it a little in the centre for an attractive appearance. Combine the honey, lemon juice, and olive oil to taste and drizzle over the aubergines. Sprinkle with the *rigani*, salt, and pepper. Pour 115 ml/4 fl oz water into the dish and bake uncovered for 45 minutes. Add a little more water to the dish if it appears to be drying out.

Arrange the aubergines on a platter or on individual plates, spoon over any cooking liquid, and sprinkle with olive oil to taste and the remaining parsley.

Note To serve as a main course use large round aubergines, 12-15 cm/5-6 inches long and increase the filling by half. Or add 115 g/4 oz cooked rice (Perfect Pilaf, page 226) or lightly browned, finely minced, lean lamb, or a mixture of both, to the filling, adding more currants and allspice to taste; place 1 thin tomato slice on top of each aubergine, to prevent the rice from drying out during baking. Bake uncovered at 160C/325F/gas mark 3 for 1 hour.

Imam Bayildi in Vine Leaves
Imam Bayildi me Ambelofila

Using 12 small slender aubergines, fry the aubergines and prepare the filling as directed above. Line a heavy baking dish, just large enough to hold the aubergines in a single layer, with fresh or brine-preserved vine leaves that have been blanched in boiling water (3 seconds for preserved leaves, 5 seconds for fresh), glossy sides facing down. (You will need about 12 large leaves or 18 medium leaves.) Divide the filling between the aubergines and arrange them in the baking dish. Cover with a second layer of blanched vine leave, glossy sides facing up. Pour the lemon juice, honey, and olive oil mixture over the aubergines; omit the *rigani*. Add 115 ml/ 4 fl oz water to the dish and bake uncovered at 160C/325F/gas mark 3 for 1 hour. Add a little more water to the dish if necessary.

To serve, discard the top layer of vine leaves and carefully transfer the aubergines to a platter or individual plates. Serve with lemon wedges.

Stuffed Aubergines with Cinnamon Tomato Sauce
Yemistes Melitzanes
Serves 4

These subtly spiced stuffed aubergines are easy to make. If possible, prepare and bake them a day ahead and gently reheat before serving. This gives the rich flavours a chance to deepen and brings out all the pungent fragrance of herbs and spices. Bell peppers can be substituted for aubergines – in that variation cumin becomes the dominant spice.

2 large or 4 medium aubergines (about 675 g/1 1/2 lb)
Sea salt
175 ml/6 fl oz extra virgin olive oil, or to taste

1 medium onion, finely chopped
225 g/8 oz lean lamb, finely minced
1 1/2 teaspoons ground cinnamon (to taste)
175 g/6 oz long-grain rice
350 ml/12 fl oz Chicken or Light Meat Stock (page 344 or 347) or water
50 g/2 oz small dark seedless raisins
1 small bunch of flat leaf parsley, leaves finely chopped
1 large ripe tomato, skinned and cut into 8 slices
1 teaspoon sugar
Cracked black pepper to taste
225 ml/8 fl oz Tomato Sauce (page 321), made with cinnamon and parsley, *and*
115 ml/4 fl oz water *or* 4 tablespoons tomato purée diluted with 300 ml/1/2 pint water

For serving
Juice of 1 lemon

Slice off the ends of the aubergines and cut lengthways in half. Dust the cut sides with salt and set aside for 30 minutes to "sweat".

Heat 3 tablespoons of the olive oil in a heavy saucepan and sauté the onion over low heat until pale golden, about 12 minutes; stir occasionally. Add the lamb, raise the heat, and cook until lightly browned, breaking up any lumps with a wooden spoon. Stir in the cinnamon, salt to taste, and the rice. Add the stock, bring to a boil, cover, reduce the heat, and simmer until the liquid has disappeared from the surface, about 15 minutes. Set aside.

Heat the oven to 160C/325F/gas mark 3. Thoroughly dry the aubergines with paper towels. Warm 4 tablespoons of the remaining olive oil in a heavy frying pan and fry the aubergines over medium-low heat until the cut sides are golden brown and the skins are dark and wrinkled, about 10 minutes. Drain between layers of paper towels. With a small spoon, scoop out the flesh, leaving 6 mm/1/4 inch-thick shells. Discard most of the seeds and finely dice the flesh. Stir the aubergine dice, raisins, and half the parsley into the rice mixture.

Arrange the aubergine shells in a heavy baking dish, just large enough to hold them. Divide the filling between the shells. Place a tomato slice on top of each, sprinkle with the sugar, salt, a generous amount of pepper, and the remaining olive oil. Pour the tomato sauce and water into the dish and bake, uncovered, for 1 hour, basting occasionally with the sauce. Add more water if the dish is in danger of drying out.

To serve, remove the aubergines from the dish with a slotted spoon and set aside. Pour the sauce onto a warm platter, arrange the aubergines on top, and sprinkle with lemon juice and the remaining parsley. Serve hot or warm.

Stuffed Bell Peppers with Tomato Cumin Sauce
Yemistes Strongiles Piperies

Substitute 8 medium green and/or yellow bell peppers for the aubergines, cumin for the cinnamon, and 6 sprigs of celery leaves (page 351), coarsely chopped, for the raisins. Slice off the tops of the peppers, discard the cores and seeds, and rinse out to remove any remaining seeds. Blanch the tops and shells in boiling water for 5 minutes, and drain well. Fill the peppers and replace the tops. Arrange them in a heavy baking dish just large enough to hold them. Sprinkle with the sugar, salt and pepper, and olive oil, and add the sauce and water. Cover and bake for 1 hour, basting the peppers occasionally with the sauce.

Serve sprinkled with the lemon juice and parsley.

Note The peppers can also be simmered in a heavy saucepan on top of the stove. Bring the sauce to a boil, reduce the heat, and simmer for 45 minutes to 1 hour, until tender.

Stuffed Aubergines with Green Grape Sauce
Yemistes Melitzanes me Agouritha
Serves 6

This Cretan version of stuffed aubergines is one of my favourite dishes – substantial enough to feed the hungriest family, yet impressive enough for an elegant dinner. The rice filling is spiced with cloves, sharpened by the sauce made from under-ripe green grapes, and exotically coloured and aromatized with saffron. The vine leaves protect the aubergines from drying out in the oven and, of course, impart a subtle flavour to the dish. Serve with bowls of Strained Yogurt (page 8), radishes, tiny black Elitses olives, and a salad of wild greens (page 221).

3 large or 6 medium aubergines (about 900 g/2 lb)
Sea salt
150 g/6 oz yellow split peas, picked over, rinsed, and soaked for 3 hours in water to cover
225 ml/8 fl oz extra virgin olive oil, or to taste
1 medium onion, grated
225 g/8 oz lean lamb, finely minced
1 teaspoon saffron threads
1/2 teaspoon ground cloves
1 teaspoon cracked black pepper, or to taste
115 g/4 oz long-grain rice
300 ml/1/2 pint Chicken or Light Meat Stock (page 344 or 347) or water
5 tablespoons finely chopped chives or the best green parts of spring onions

6 tablespoons Green Grape Sauce (page 320) or the juice of 1 large lime
1 bunch of flat leaf parsley, leaves finely chopped
50 g/2 oz brown sugar
Juice of 1 large lemon
16 fresh or brine-preserved vine leaves, blanched in boiling water
(3 seconds for preserved leaves, 5 seconds for fresh) and drained

Slice off the ends of the aubergines and cut lengthways in half. Sprinkle the cut sides with salt and set aside for 30 minutes to "sweat".

Drain the split peas, place in a medium saucepan with water to cover by 5 cm/2 inches, and bring to a simmer over medium heat. Reduce the heat and simmer 20 minutes, or until just tender. Drain and set aside.

Meanwhile, heat 3 tablespoons of the olive oil in a heavy saucepan and sauté the onion over medium heat until golden brown, about 12 minutes. Add the meat, raise the heat, and cook until lightly browned, breaking up any lumps with a wooden spoon. Gently heat the saffron in a small dry frying pan until aromatic, and crumble it into the lamb mixture. Stir in the cloves, pepper, salt to taste, and the rice. Add the stock and bring to a boil, without stirring. Cover, reduce the heat to low, and cook 15-20 minutes, or until all the liquid has been absorbed by the rice.

Heat the oven to 160C/325F/gas mark 3. Thoroughly dry the aubergines with paper towels. Place a large heavy frying pan over medium-low heat, add 3 tablespoons of the remaining olive oil, and fry the aubergines until the cut sides are dark golden brown and the skins are dark and wrinkled, about 10 minutes. (Fry in 2 batches if necessary, adding 2 tablespoons olive oil before frying the second batch.) Drain between layers of paper towels. Scoop out the flesh with a small spoon, leaving 6 mm/¼ inch-thick shells. Discard most of the seeds and cut the flesh into small dice. Combine the aubergine dice, split peas, chives, Green Grape Sauce, three-quarters of the parsley, and the lamb and rice mixture. Season to taste with salt and pepper.

Arrange the aubergine shells in a heavy baking dish just large enough to hold them. Divide the filling between the aubergine shells, heaping the filling in the centres. Combine the sugar, lemon juice, and 225 ml/8 fl oz water, and pour into the baking dish. Add more water if necessary to come halfway up the sides of the aubergine shells. Sprinkle the remaining olive oil over the aubergines and cover with the vine leaves, glossy sides facing down.

Bake uncovered for 50 minutes to 1 hour, or until the vine leaves are dry and wrinkled, basting frequently with the liquid in the dish. Add a little more water if the dish is in danger of drying out.

To serve, discard the vine leaves, arrange the aubergines on a warm platter, pour over the pan juices, and sprinkle with the remaining parsley. Serve hot or warm.

Stuffed Onions
with Green Grape Sauce
Yemista Kremithia me Agouritha

Served in ancient Greece, this spicy dish is still popular today. Substitute 4 large onions for the aubergines. Peel them, slice off the root and stem ends, and cook in boiling water for 10 minutes; drain. Push out the centres to leave shells of 3 layers, and separate these to make 12 shells. Finely chop 1 of the centres and add it to the rice mixture. (Reserve the remaining centres for another use.)

Arrange the onion shells in a heavy baking dish and divide the filling between them. Pour the sugar-lemon juice mixture over the onions and sprinkle with the olive oil; omit the vine leaves. Bake uncovered until the filling is golden brown, about 1 hour, basting frequently with the liquid in the dish. Serve hot or warm, with the syrupy pan juices poured over.

Serve 2 or 3 per person as a main course or, for an unusual vegetable to accompany grilled meats, omit the lamb, and serve 2 to each person.

Stuffed Bell Peppers
with Green Grape Sauce
Yemistes Strongiles Piperies me Agouritha

Substitute 12 small to medium red, yellow, and/or green bell peppers for the aubergines. Slice off the tops, discard the cores and seeds, and rinse out to remove any remaining seeds. Blanch the tops and shells in boiling water for 5 minutes and drain. Divide the filling between the peppers and replace the tops. Add the sugar-lemon juice mixture and sprinkle with the olive oil; cover with vine leaves if desired. Bake uncovered 1 hour, basting frequently with the liquid in the dish. Serve hot or warm, with the pan juices.

Stuffed Bell Peppers Avgolemono
Yemistes Strongiles Piperies Avgolemono

In this recipe a perfumed rice filling is enhanced with *avgolemono* to produce a dish that's both sweetly aromatic and exquisitely beautiful. Choose small bell peppers for a first course, medium-sized ones for a main course – or substitute courgettes or onions if you prefer.

115 ml/4 fl oz extra virgin olive oil
25 g/1 oz unsalted butter
3 shallots, finely chopped, or 6 spring onions, white part only, finely chopped
350 g/12 oz long-grain rice
1 teaspoon saffron threads
1.1 litres/2 pints Chicken Stock (page 344) or water
1 teaspoon sea salt, or to taste
16 small *or* 10 medium yellow, green, *and/or* red bell peppers
115 g/4 oz small dark seedless raisins
75 g/3 oz lightly toasted pine nuts
1 tablespoon dried *rigani* (page 14)
1 small bunch of flat leaf parsley, leaves finely chopped
3 tablespoons finely chopped Preserved Lemon (page 18) or the strained juice of 1 lemon
Freshly ground black pepper to taste
3 eggs
Strained juice of 2 large lemons

Heat 2 tablespoons of the olive oil and the butter in a heavy saucepan and sauté the shallot over low heat until soft, about 5 minutes. Add the rice and cook for 1 minute, stirring with a wooden spoon, until opaque. Heat the saffron in a small dry frying pan until aromatic and crumble it into 225 ml/8 fl oz of the stock. Add the saffron stock, 450 ml/16 fl oz of the remaining stock, and the salt to the rice. Raise the heat and boil uncovered for 8 minutes, or until the liquid has disappeared and holes appear in the surface of the rice. Remove from the heat, cover with 2 layers of paper towels and a tight-fitting lid, and set aside for 30 minutes in a warm place such as the back of the stove.

Fill a large saucepan with water and bring to a boil. Slice the tops off the peppers, discard the cores, and rinse off the seeds from both tops and shells. Add to the boiling water, cover, and boil 5 minutes. Drain and set aside.

With a fork, lightly mix the raisins, pine nuts, *rigani,* most of the parsley, the Preserved Lemon, and pepper into the rice. Add salt and lemon juice to taste. Loosely fill the pepper shells with this mixture and replace the tops. Arrange upright in a heavy saucepan just large enough to hold them, pour the remaining olive oil and stock over, and bring to a boil. Cover, reduce the heat, and simmer 40 minutes to 1 hour, until the peppers are soft, adding water if the liquid in the saucepan reduces to less than 225 ml/8 fl oz.

Ten minutes before serving, whisk the eggs in a large bowl for 2 minutes, or until pale and frothy. Slowly add the lemon juice and whisk for 1 minute longer. Remove the peppers from the saucepan, reserving the cooking liquid, and keep warm. Add 225 ml/8 fl oz of the reserved liquid to the egg mixture in a slow steady stream, whisking constantly. Transfer the sauce to a small heavy saucepan or the top of a double boiler set over hot water. Stir over low heat until the sauce thickens enough to coat the back of the spoon; do not allow to boil.

Arrange the peppers on a warm platter or individual plates and pour over the sauce. Sprinkle with the remaining parsley and serve immediately.

Stuffed Courgettes Avgolemono
Yemista Kolokithia Avgolemono

Substitute 5 medium courgettes, 10-12 cm/4-5 inches long (to serve as a main course), or 8 small courgettes, 7 cm/3 inches long (to serve as a first course), for the peppers, and make half the amount of filling. Trim the ends of the courgettes and rub them with a tea towel to remove any fuzz. Blanch in boiling water (5 minutes for large courgettes, 3 minutes for small), and drain. Cut lengthways in half, scoop out the centres with a small spoon, and arrange in a baking dish. Finely chop the flesh and add it to the rice mixture. Add salt, pepper, and lemon juice to taste. Fill the courgettes, pour over the remaining olive oil and stock, and bake uncovered in a preheated oven at 180C/350F/gas mark 4 until tender, about 40 minutes; add water if liquid in the dish reduces to less than 225 ml/8 fl oz. Make the sauce and serve immediately.

Stuffed Onions Avgolemono
Yemista Kremithia Avgolemono

Substitute 5 large onions (to serve as a main course) or 16 small onions (to serve as a first course) for the peppers. Peel, and slice off both ends. Blanch in boiling water (10 minutes for large onions, 5 minutes for small), drain, and let cool slightly. Push out the onion centres, leaving shells of 2 layers. If using large onions separate the layers to make 10 shells. Arrange the shells in a heavy baking dish. Fill the shells with the rice mixture, piling it high. Pour over the remaining olive oil and stock, and bake uncovered in a preheated oven at 180C/350F/gas mark 4 until tender, about 40 minutes for small onions, 1 hour for large, occasionally basting with the stock. Make sure there is always at least 225 ml/8 fl oz cooking liquid in the dish; add water if necessary. Make the sauce and serve hot.

Note For a meat filling sauté 350 g/12 oz finely minced lean lamb in 2 tablespoons olive oil until lightly browned. Drain on paper towels and sprinkle with a little salt and lemon juice. Stir into the cooked rice mixture with a fork.

Baked Stuffed Tomatoes and Peppers
Yemistes Domates ke Piperies
Serves 8 as a first course, 4 as a main course

Huge shallow trays of beautiful stuffed vegetables – tomatoes and multi-coloured peppers, courgettes, aubergines, and onions – await the hungry visitor to any taverna. In this recipe either chickpeas or pine nuts can be used to provide an unusual texture. Currants or raisins add a gentle sweetness and fresh mint or *rigani,* a hillside fragrance. Although the vegetables take some time to prepare, they can be baked ahead of time. Serve cold with yogurt, olives, and lemon wedges for a perfect summer lunch.

8 small or 4 large ripe tomatoes
$^1/_2$ tablespoon sugar
Sea salt
8 small or 4 medium green bell peppers, roasted, seeded, and skinned (page 343)
115 ml/4 fl oz extra virgin olive oil, or more to taste
1 medium onion, grated
1 teaspoon ground allspice
150 g/5 oz long-grain rice, cooked
50 g/2 oz crumbled cooked chickpeas or lightly toasted pine nuts
5 tablespoons fresh mint leaves, torn into small pieces at the last minute, *or*
1$^1/_2$ tablespoons dried *rigani* (page 14), crumbled
75 g/3 oz currants or small dark seedless raisins
1 small bunch of flat leaf parsley, leaves finely chopped
Juice of 1 lemon
50 g/2 oz fresh wholemeal breadcrumbs

Heat the oven to 160C/325F/gas mark 3. Slice off the tops of the tomatoes and set aside. Scoop out the pulp with a small spoon, discard the seeds, and dice the pulp. Set aside with the juices. Sprinkle the sugar and salt into the tomato shells, invert onto paper towels, and set aside to drain.

Slice off the tops of the peppers, discard the cores, and wipe the seeds off the tops and shells. Drain on paper towels.

Warm 4 tablespoons of the olive oil in a heavy saucepan and sauté the onion over low heat until golden brown, about 12 minutes; stir occasionally. Add the tomato dice and juices, allspice, pepper, and salt to taste, and cook 5 minutes, or until most of the liquid has evaporated. With a fork, stir in the rice, chickpeas, mint, currants, and half the parsley. Season to taste. Loosely fill the tomatoes and peppers, replace their tops, and arrange them in a heavy baking dish. Sprinkle with the lemon juice and the remaining olive oil; sprinkle the breadcrumbs over the tomatoes. Add 225 ml/8 fl oz water to the dish and bake uncovered for 40 minutes to 1 hour, until the vegetables are soft and slightly darkened, basting occasionally with the liquid in the dish. Add a little more water to the dish if it appears to be drying out. Let the vegetables cool in the dish.

To serve, arrange the vegetables on a platter and sprinkle with the cooking liquid, olive oil if desired, and the remaining parsley.

Baked Stuffed Aubergines, Tomatoes, and Peppers
Diafora Parayemista

Choose slightly smaller tomatoes and peppers, and add 4 round aubergines, about 10 cm/4 inches long. Trim off the stems of the aubergines, cut lengthways in half, and fry in 3 tablespoons olive oil until the cut sides are golden brown and the skin is dark and wrinkled. Scoop out the flesh with a small spoon, discard the seeds, and dice the pulp. Add the aubergine dice and an additional 50 g/2 oz cooked rice, 25 g/1 oz pine nuts or crumbled cooked chickpeas, and salt and pepper to taste, to the filling. Arrange the vegetables in a heavy baking dish, divide the filling between them, and replace the tomato and pepper tops. Sprinkle with the lemon juice and olive oil if desired. Sprinkle the breadcrumbs over the tomatoes. Add 225 ml/8 fl oz water to the dish and bake uncovered for 1 hour, basting frequently with the liquid in the dish. Let the vegetables cool in the dish.

Arrange on a large platter or individual plates, pour over the pan juices, and serve with lemon wedges.

Stuffed Cabbage Leaves in Tomato Sauce
Lakhanodolmades me Saltsa Domatas
Serves 4

In the winter months cabbages, cheap and at their best, are used for a variety of salads and family meals, and this is one of the most popular dishes. The Greek affection for cabbage has a long history: Hippocrates is said to have prescribed it as a cure for colic and Pythagoras to have composed a eulogy on this humble vegetable! Serve with Perfect Pilaf (page 226) or Pilaf with Green Lentils (page 229).

One 675-900 g/1¹/₂-2 lb firm white or pale green cabbage
4 tablespoons extra virgin olive oil
1 small onion, finely chopped
225 g/8 oz lean pork or beef, finely minced
1 teaspoon ground allspice, or to taste
3 tablespoons lightly toasted pine nuts
4 tablespoons currants
115 g/4 oz long-grain rice, cooked
Sea salt *and* freshly ground black pepper to taste
2 tablespoons fresh mint leaves, or to taste
4 tablespoons finely chopped flat leaf parsley
Juice of 1 lemon *or* 2 tablespoons white wine vinegar
350 ml/12 fl oz Tomato Sauce (page 321), made with parsley and bay leaves

Discard any torn or discoloured outer cabbage leaves and, with a sharp paring knife, cut out as much of the core as possible. Cook, covered, in boiling water for 5 minutes, drain and set aside.

Heat half the olive oil in a heavy saucepan and sauté the onion over low heat until soft, about 6 minutes. Raise the heat, add the meat, and sauté until lightly browned, breaking up any lumps with a wooden spoon. Add the allspice, pine nuts, currants, rice, and salt and pepper. Chop the mint and half the parsley together and add to the meat along with the lemon juice. Stir with a fork until well mixed. Add allspice, salt, pepper, and/or mint if desired; the mixture should be highly flavoured.

Turn the cabbage upside down. Separate 16 to 20 leaves from the core with a paring knife by pulling each one down and off. Trim and discard any thick spine and lay the leaves flat between layers of paper towels to dry.

Lay a cabbage leaf on your palm (or on a flat surface), spine side up, and place 1 heaped tablespoon of filling on the bottom third of the leaf. Fold over both sides and, keeping the filling in place with your thumb, firmly roll up from the leaf base to tip; repeat with the remaining leaves and filling. As you finish each stuffed leaf, place it seam side down in a heavy sauté pan large enough to hold all the *dolmades* in a single layer, pressing the rolls tightly against each other.

Pour over the Tomato Sauce and add enough water to come barely to the top of the *dolmades*. Place a heat-resistant plate slightly smaller than the pan on top and set a weight (such as a large tin of fruit) on top of the plate. Slowly bring to a boil, reduce the heat, and simmer gently for 1 hour. Add a little more water if the liquid begins to disappear from the surface. Remove from the heat and set aside for 5 minutes with the weight still in place.

Transfer the *dolmades* to a warm platter and pour over the sauce and the rest of the olive oil. Sprinkle with the remaining parsley and serve hot or warm.

savoury pies

Spinach Pie
Spanakopitta
Serves 8-10

One of the finest examples of Greek home-cooking, *spanakopitta* is a colourful centrepiece on any table, from a family picnic to an elegant supper. For a flavour closer to that of the village kitchens, make the pie with beetroot greens or other *khorta* (page 220). Serve with olives and a jug of rosé wine (page 340).

Filling
900 g/2 lb fresh spinach
115 ml/4 fl oz extra virgin olive oil
8 spring onions, trimmed, the best green parts left intact, and thinly sliced or 2 leeks, trimmed, thoroughly rinsed and thinly sliced

6 sprigs of fresh dill, coarsely chopped
$^1/_4$ teaspoon grated nutmeg
1 teaspoon cracked black pepper, or to taste
115 g/4 oz small-curd cottage cheese, drained and pressed through a fine sieve
175 g/6 oz crumbled *feta* cheese
4 eggs, beaten
1 small bunch of flat leaf parsley, leaves coarsely chopped
Sea salt to taste
350 g/12 oz filo pastry, thawed if frozen
50 g/2 oz unsalted butter, melted

Rinse the spinach in several changes of cold water, discard the stalks and any bruised or tough leaves, and place in a heavy saucepan. Cover and cook, with just the water that clings to the leaves, for 1 minute, or until wilted and barely soft. Drain, pressing the greens against the sides of the colander to remove as much liquid as possible. Finely chop the spinach and set aside.

Warm half the olive oil in a heavy sauté pan and sauté the spring onions over low heat until soft, about 3 minutes (leeks will take a few minutes longer). Stir in the dill, spinach, nutmeg, and pepper and cook 1 minute; remove from the heat. Add the cottage cheese, *feta* cheese, eggs, and parsley, and mash together with a fork. Check the seasonings and add salt and pepper to taste.

Heat the oven to 180C/350F/gas mark 4. Remove the filo from the refrigerator and set aside.

In a bowl, combine the melted butter with the remaining olive oil. Divide the filo sheets into 2 portions, tightly rewrap one, and refrigerate. Lightly brush a 25 cm/10 inch square or round baking tin, at least 5 cm/2 inches deep, with the oil/butter mixture. Line with 1 filo sheet, gently pressing it into the sides of the tin, and brush the sheet with the oil/butter. Repeat with the remaining unrefrigerated sheets of pastry, but do not brush the last sheet. Turn a round tin 60° each time you add a sheet, a square tin 90°. Gently spread the filling over the filo and lightly smooth it flat. Fold the edges of the filo over the filling and brush with the oil/butter.

Remove the second portion of filo from the refrigerator. Lay 1 sheet over the filling, letting the edges hang over the sides of the tin. Lightly brush with the oil/butter mixture, and layer until all the sheets are used; do not brush the last sheet.

Carefully ease your fingers down between the edge of the pie and the sides of the tin, pull the bottom edges of the pie towards the centre, and tuck the top sheets in around the bottom of the pie. Liberally brush the top sheet with the remaining oil/butter mixture and, with a sharp knife, score the top 2 sheets of filo into rectangles or diamond shapes for serving. Do not score a round pie – this would make it impossible to remove from the tin. Bake 45-50 minutes, or until deep golden brown.

When the pie is cooked, immediately cut through the score marks to the bottom of the tin. Serve from the tin or arrange the pieces on a dish. Transfer a round pie to a serving platter: Invert a large plate over the baking tin, turn upside down, remove the tin, and invert a serving platter over the bottom of the pie. Hold firmly and turn right side up.

Serve hot, warm, or cold.

Variation

Substitute young beetroot greens, ruby chard, or water spinach (page 220) for the spinach, and cook 3 minutes, or until barely soft, before mixing with the rest of the ingredients. Use leeks instead of spring onions.

Aromatic Lamb Filo Rolls
Arnaki Tiligmeno me Filo
Serves 6

There are several versions of this delicious and versatile dish. It can be made as small rolls for a buffet or lunch, or as one large round or rectangular pie. It's composed of an aromatic meat layer topped with a spicy cheese mixture, and wrapped in filo to make a neat package for baking. Although it sounds complicated it's not really too difficult to make, and you can prepare the filling a day ahead and refrigerate overnight if you prefer. I like even more exotic versions, with an extra layer of *pilafi,* spinach, or rice or, perhaps, sautéed diced aubergines. Serve with a salad of wild greens (page 221) or a green salad.

6 tablespoons extra virgin olive oil
75 g/3 oz unsalted butter
1 large onion, finely chopped
675 g/1 1/2 lb lean lamb, finely minced
2 large ripe tomatoes, skinned and diced
1 teaspoon honey
1 tablespoon ground cinnamon, or to taste
1/2 teaspoon sea salt, or to taste
1 teaspoon cracked black pepper, or to taste
4 tablespoons reduced Meat Stock (page 347) or robust red wine
1 1/2 tablespoons chopped fresh marjoram or 2 1/2 tablespoons dried *rigani* (page 14), crumbled
4 tablespoons finely chopped flat leaf parsley
175 g/6 oz fresh myzithra or small-curd cottage cheese, drained
50 g/2 oz finely grated *feta* cheese
1/2 teaspoon grated nutmeg
2 egg yolks
12 sheets filo (from a 450 g/1 lb packet, page 266)

For serving
Icing sugar
Ground cinnamon

Warm 1 tablespoon of the olive oil and 25 g/1 oz of the butter in a heavy sauté pan and sauté the onion over low heat until soft, about 8 minutes. Raise the heat, add the meat, and sauté until lightly browned, breaking up any lumps with a wooden spoon. Add the tomatoes, honey, cinnamon, salt, and 1/2 teaspoon of the pepper, and bring to a boil. Add the stock, bring to a boil, reduce the heat, and simmer 15 minutes, or until almost all the liquid has evaporated. Add the marjoram and parsley, and additional cinnamon, marjoram, and pepper to taste (do not add salt at this point, as the cheese mixture is salty). Set aside, or refrigerate for up to 24 hours.

Heat the oven to 190C/375F/gas mark 5. Press the *myzithra* through a sieve into a bowl. Combine with the *feta,* nutmeg, remaining 1/2 teaspoon of pepper, and the egg yolks. Cover and set aside.

Combine the remaining butter and olive oil in a small saucepan, and melt over very low heat. Brush a heavy baking tray with some of this mixture. Lay the filo sheets one on top of another and cut in half crosswise to make 24 sheets. Tightly rewrap half the sheets and refrigerate. Lay 1 of the remaining sheets on a clean work surface with a long end facing you, and brush lightly with the butter mixture. Lay a second sheet on top, brush it with the mixture, and repeat with a third sheet. Lay another sheet on top. Divide the mixture into 6 portions. Place 1 portion on the bottom third of the top filo sheet and shape it into a sausage about 20 cm/8 inches long. Divide the cheese filling into 6 portions and spread 1 portion over the meat. Fold the bottom edges of the filo layers over the filling, then fold over the 2 sides and roll up to make a firm neat parcel. Place on the baking tray and repeat with the remaining filo and filling.

Brush the rolls with the remaining butter mixture and bake for 25-30 minutes, or until deep golden brown. Drain on paper towels, sprinkle liberally with the icing sugar and cinnamon, and transfer to a warm platter.

Note To make one large round or rectangular pie, use a 450 g/1 lb packet of filo and additional melted butter and olive oil as needed for brushing the sheets. Assemble the pie as directed on page 97. Bake for 35-40 minutes, or until deep golden brown. Sprinkle liberally with the icing sugar and cinnamon and serve warm.

Cretan Chicken Pie
Tzoulamas
Serves 10 to 12

At a wedding feast high in a remote mountain village on Crete, this pie was the magnificent centrepiece to the wedding buffet table laid out in the village square. Around us were the snow-capped mountain peaks, in the distance a brilliant blue sea sparkling in the sunlight. No wonder the *tzoulamas* tasted wonderful! But it tastes almost as good in less romantic settings, can be prepared ahead, and even freezes well (freeze before baking), so don't miss out on it.

A traditional *tzoulamas* is made with layers of crisp pastry (fried in olive oil before the pie is assembled), mildly spiced chicken and rice, fresh mountain cheese, and hot goat's butter. My version replaces the fried pastry with filo, the *anthotyro* cheese with *feta* and cottage cheese, and the goat's butter with unsalted butter and lemon juice. Begin the meal with *mezedes* such as Grilled Aubergine Salata (page 44) or *taramosalata* (page 43).

One 2.3-2.7 kg/5-6 lb chicken, cut into serving pieces, skin and fat removed and giblets reserved
1 large onion, chopped
2 carrots, scrubbed, and cut into thick slices
1 large bunch of flat leaf parsley, stalks removed and tied in a bundle, leaves finely chopped
Chicken Stock (page 344) or water to cover the chicken
Sea salt and freshly ground white pepper to taste
5 tablespoons extra virgin olive oil
4 shallots, finely chopped

1 tablespoon ground cumin
225 g/8 oz long-grain rice
6 bay leaves
Juice of 2 lemons
4 tablespoons finely chopped Preserved Lemon (page 18) or the finely grated zest of 1 lemon
1 large clove garlic, finely chopped
4 tablespoons capers, rinsed
One 450 g/1 lb packet of filo pastry, thawed if frozen
225 g/8 oz unsalted butter
50 g/2 oz grated *feta* cheese
350 g/12 oz small-curd cottage cheese, drained
200 g/7 oz small dark seedless raisins
115 g/4 oz lightly toasted pine nuts

Place the chicken pieces, giblets, onion, carrot, parsley stalks, stock, and salt and pepper in a large saucepan. Bring slowly to a boil, cover, reduce the heat, and simmer 40 minutes, or until the chicken is cooked. Strain over a bowl, and strain the cooking liquid once more through muslin. Set aside 450 ml/16 fl oz of the liquid (and refrigerate or freeze the rest for another use). Discard the vegetables and all the giblets except the liver.

Warm 4 tablespoons of the olive oil in a heavy saucepan and sauté the shallots over low heat for 10 minutes, or until soft. Add the cumin and cook 1 minute, or until aromatic. Stir in the rice, reserved stock, the bay leaves, and salt to taste, and bring to a boil without stirring. Cook uncovered for 8 minutes, or until holes appear in the surface of the rice and the liquid has evaporated. Remove from the heat, cover with 2 layers of paper towels and a tight-fitting lid, and set aside for 30 minutes in a warm place.

Remove the chicken from the bones and cut the meat into almond-sized pieces. Cut the liver into tiny dice. Place the chicken and liver in a bowl and sprinkle with half the lemon juice and pepper to taste. Set aside 2 tablespoons of the parsley and add all but 1 tablespoon of the Preserved Lemon, the garlic, 3 tablespoons of the capers, and a pinch of salt to the remaining parsley. Chop to mix. Combine with the chicken, using your fingers to make sure each piece is coated. Cover and set aside. (The chicken can be prepared ahead and refrigerated overnight.)

Heat the oven to 190C/375F/gas mark 5. Remove the packet of filo from the refrigerator and set aside unopened. (If you have refrigerated the filling, remove that too.) With a fork, mash the *feta* and cottage cheeses together in a small bowl. Melt 175 g/6 oz of the butter over very low heat and add the remaining olive oil.

Divide the filo sheets into 2 portions, tightly rewrap one, and refrigerate. Lightly brush a 25 cm/10 inch square or round baking tin with the butter mixture. Line with 1 filo sheet, gently pressing it into the sides of the tin, and brush the sheet with the butter mixture. Repeat with the remaining unrefrigerated sheets of pastry, but do not brush the last sheet. Turn a round tin 60° each time you add a sheet, a square tin 90°. Spread the rice mixture over the filo and then spread with the chicken and parsley mixture. Scatter the cheese mixture over the chicken as evenly as possible, then sprinkle the raisins and pine nuts over the cheese. Sprinkle with a few tablespoons of the chicken stock if the filling seems dry. Fold the edges of the filo over the filling and brush with the butter mixture.

Remove the second portion of filo from the refrigerator. Lay 1 sheet over the filling, letting the edges hang over the sides of the tin. Lightly brush with the butter mixture, and layer until all the sheets are used; do not butter the last sheet.

Carefully ease your fingers down between the edge of the pie and the sides of the tin, pull the bottom edges of the pie towards the centre, and tuck the top sheets in around the bottom of the pie. Liberally butter the top sheet and, with a sharp knife, score the top 2 sheets of filo into rectangles or diamond shapes for serving. Do not score a round pie – this would make it impossible to remove from the tin. Bake 35-40 minutes, or until deep golden brown.

While the pie is baking, heat the remaining butter in a small saucepan over very low heat for 10 minutes, or until foamy and nutty brown; don't let it burn. Strain through muslin into a small bowl, add the remaining lemon juice and set aside in a warm place. Chop the reserved parsley and remaining capers and Preserved Lemon together.

When the pie is cooked, immediately cut through the score marks to the bottom of the tin. Serve from the tin or arrange the pieces on a dish. Transfer a round pie to a serving platter. Invert a large plate over the baking tin, turn upside down, remove the tin, and invert a serving platter over the bottom of the pie. Hold firmly and turn right side up. Carefully make a small hole in the centre of the pie, pour over the brown butter, and sprinkle with the parsley mixture. Serve at once.

Fish and Seafood

psaria ke psarika thalassina

For me any mention of Greek fish dishes immediately conjures up images of waterfront tavernas by a sparkling azure sea on a day shimmering with heat and brilliant sunlight. Seated at a rickety table under the welcome shade of a pine tree, you choose the fish that takes your fancy, then relax with an ouzo and *mezedes* while it's prepared. Your anticipation of the treat ahead mounts as a bewildering array of fish dishes, their mouth-watering aromas filling the air, are served to tables around you.

The sheer variety of fish readily available in Greece is amazing. The Greek cook has the choice of over thirty different kinds of fish, plus shellfish and the cephalopods such as octopus and squid, and makes good use of them all. Situated in the warmest part of the Mediterranean, Greece and her islands have enjoyed a wonderfully rich sea harvest since ancient times.

Methods of preparation and presentation have changed remarkably little over the centuries. Fish is always served complete with its head – to Greeks this is the tastiest and most nutritious part. They also prefer many fish dishes to be served warm rather than hot, a practice that many visitors to Greece are not used to.

Most of the dishes included here are very simple to prepare. And, although we may not have the Greek cook's wide choice of fish, in many of these dishes almost any kind of fish steak or whole fish can be substituted.

Crusty Baked Fish
Psaria Plaki sto Fourno
Serves 4

This gloriously aromatic dish is a concoction of olive oil, parsley, tomatoes, and garlic with a crunchy crusty top. Village cooks say *psaria plaki* should be made only with John Dory but almost any firm-fleshed fish can be baked this way, using whole fish, steaks, or fillets. You can make a lighter version by substituting white wine or fish or chicken stock for some of the olive oil. Serve with lemon wedges.

2 firm-fleshed white fish such as John Dory (page 346), sea bream, or bass, about 550 g/1¼ lb each, cleaned and scaled (page 345) *or* 4 fillets, 175-225 g/6-8 oz each

Coarse-grain sea salt *and* cracked black pepper to taste

Juice of 1 lemon

225 ml/8 fl oz extra virgin olive oil *or* 5 tablespoons extra virgin olive oil *and* 150 ml/5 fl oz Light Fish or Chicken Stock (pages 345 and 344) *or* dry white wine

3 tablespoons finely chopped fresh oregano or thyme *or* 2 tablespoons dried *rigani* (page 14), crumbled

2 medium onions, cut in half and thinly sliced

1 large clove garlic, finely chopped

550 g/1¼ lb boiling potatoes, peeled and cut into thin slices (boiled 10 minutes if fillets are used)

6 large ripe tomatoes, skinned and cut into slices

3 bay leaves, broken in half

12 Elitses or Niçoise olives, rinsed and pitted

For serving
1 dozen sprigs of flat leaf parsley, leaves coarsely chopped
Lemon wedges

Dry the fish with paper towels. Make 2 deep parallel incisions on either side of the whole fish. Rub whole fish inside and out, fillets on both sides, with salt and pepper, half the lemon juice, and 1 tablespoon of the olive oil. Sprinkle the cavities of the whole fish, or both sides of the fillets, with 2 tablespoons of the oregano, cover, and set aside for 30 minutes to marinate.

Heat 3 tablespoons of the remaining olive oil in a heavy frying pan and sauté the onions over low heat until pale golden, about 12 minutes. Stir in the garlic, cook 1 minute longer, and set aside.

Heat the oven to 180C/350F/gas mark 4. Brush a heavy deep baking dish with 1 tablespoon of the remaining olive oil. Dry the potato slices with paper towels and arrange about two thirds of them in the bottom of the baking dish. Cover with the onion slices and lay the fish on top. Cover with the tomato slices and sprinkle with any remaining marinade, the bay leaves, and salt and pepper. Arrange the remaining sliced potatoes on top, leaving the tomato slices partially exposed.

Pour the remaining lemon juice and olive oil (or olive oil and stock) over the potatoes, cover, and bake 30 minutes. Reduce the oven temperature to 160C/325F/gas mark 3, uncover,

and bake 20-30 minutes longer, or until golden brown and crusty. Gently press the olives into the potato-onion crust and bake 5 minutes longer.

Sprinkle with the parsley and the remaining oregano and serve at once.

Corfiot Baked Fish
Bourtheto
Serves 4

This Corfu island speciality is one of the few hot and spicy dishes in Greek cuisine. The Corfiots use small, bony fish, the cheapest in the market. For our taste, fillets of any firm-fleshed white fish such as bass, sea bream, or halibut are probably a better choice – and easier to eat. Or try a popular island alternative – *bourtheto* made with octopus. This colourful country food, traditionally cooked in a shallow earthenware dish, is easy to make and perfect for a leisurely summer lunch.

4 firm-fleshed white fish, about 400 g/14 oz each, cleaned and scaled
(page 345) or 4 fillets, 175-200 g/6-7 oz each
Juice of 1 small lemon
Sea salt *and* freshly ground black pepper to taste
1 large bunch of flat leaf parsley, stalks reserved, leaves finely chopped
115-175 ml/4-6 fl oz extra virgin olive oil (to taste)
3 large mild onions, quartered and thinly sliced
1 large clove garlic, finely chopped
4 tablespoons aged red wine vinegar
1 tablespoon honey
6 tablespoons dry red wine
1 teaspoon cayenne pepper, or to taste
4 large ripe tomatoes, skinned, seeded, and diced
3 bay leaves
1 teaspoon fresh thyme

For serving
24 Elitses or 12 Niçoise olives, rinsed and pitted

Dry the fish with paper towels. Rub whole fish inside and out, fillets on both sides, with the lemon juice and salt and pepper. Place in a shallow dish along with the parsley stalks, pour 4 tablespoons of the olive oil over, cover, and set aside for 1 hour to marinate.

Heat 3 tablespoons of the remaining olive oil in a large heavy sauté pan and cook the onions, covered, over low heat until very soft, about 30 minutes; reduce the heat if the onions begin to brown.

Heat the oven to 180C/350F/gas mark 4. Stir the garlic into the onions. Combine the vinegar and honey, add to the pan, and boil until syrupy. Add the wine and boil 1 minute longer. Stir in the cayenne pepper, tomatoes, bay leaves, thyme and half the parsley, and pour into a baking dish. Remove the fish from the marinade, discarding the parsley stalks, and lay the fish on top of the onions. Sprinkle with the remaining olive oil, cover, and bake 20 minutes (fillets) to 30 minutes (whole fish), or until the fish is an even white all the way through.

Sprinkle with the olives and remaining parsley and serve hot.

Baked Fish with Garlic and Vinegar
Psari sto Fourno me Xsithi
Serves 4

This is a popular way of cooking a plump whole fish, especially for a small dinner party. The ingredients produce an interestingly sweet but mildly piquant flavour, and the finished dish is elegant and polished. Whole cloves of garlic and sprigs of herbs support the fish in the baking dish and impart fragrance and flavour. The only other requirements are a salad, wine, and plenty of bread to mop up the delicious sauce and roasted garlic.

One 1.4-1.7 kg/3-3¹/₂ lb sea bass or other firm-fleshed white fish, cleaned and scaled, scored (page 345)
1¹/₂ tablespoons coarse-grain sea salt, or to taste
1 tablespoon cracked black pepper
2 bay leaves
275 ml/10 fl oz extra virgin olive oil
24 cloves garlic (unpeeled), feathery skin rubbed off and stem ends trimmed
6 sprigs of dried rosemary or thyme or *rigani* (page 14)
5 tablespoons aged red wine vinegar

For serving
Coarsely chopped flat leaf parsley
Thasos or Kalamata olives

Dry the fish with paper towels and rub inside and out with half the salt and pepper. Place the bay leaves inside the cavity, cover, and set aside for 1 hour.

Heat the oven to 160C/325F/gas mark 3. Liberally brush a heavy baking dish, just large enough to hold the fish, with some of the olive oil. Lay the garlic cloves in the baking dish in a single layer, brush with olive oil, and bake, uncovered, for 20 minutes. Lay the rosemary sprigs over the garlic and lay the fish on top. Whisk together the vinegar and remaining olive oil. Pour half this mixture over the fish and sprinkle with the remaining salt and pepper. Add 4 tablespoons of water to the baking dish, cover loosely with aluminium foil, and bake 15 minutes. Remove the foil and bake 30-40 minutes longer, until the fish is an even white all the way through. Baste the fish and garlic frequently with the remaining vinegar and olive oil mixture, and add a little more water to the dish if the garlic is in danger of burning.

Transfer the fish to a warm platter and surround with the garlic. Spoon over the pan juices and any remaining oil and vinegar sauce, sprinkle with the parsley, and serve the olives in bowls.

Baked Sole in Vine Leaves
Glosses Fournou se Ambelofila
Serves 4

Dover sole is a favourite choice for this dish but other flat fish or slender fillets of bass make fine substitutes. John Dory fillets (page 346) or whole sardines are also delicious cooked this way. The layers of vine leaves keep the delicate fish moist and infuse the dish with their subtle and unique fragrance

8 fillets of sole, 115-150 g/4-5 oz each or 4 large fish fillets
Juice of 1 lemon
Sea salt *and* freshly ground black pepper to taste
75-115 ml/3-4 fl oz extra virgin olive oil (to taste)
Fresh *or* brine-preserved vine leaves, to make 2 layers in the baking dish, blanched in boiling water (3 seconds for preserved leaves, 5 seconds for fresh) and drained

For serving
Finely chopped flat leaf parsley
12 Elitses or Niçoise olives, rinsed and pitted, *optional*
Lemon wedges

Dry the fillets with paper towels. Sprinkle both sides with half the lemon juice and salt and pepper, and set aside for 30 minutes.

Heat the oven to 160C/325F/gas mark 3. Brush a shallow earthenware or enamel-lined cast-iron baking dish, just large enough to hold the fillets in a single layer, with some of the olive oil, and cover the bottom of the dish with half the vine leaves, glossy sides up. Brush the leaves with olive oil, lay the fillets on top, and sprinkle with the remaining lemon juice and olive oil. Cover with the rest of the vine leaves, glossy sides down, and sprinkle with 2 tablespoons water. Bake, uncovered, for 20 minutes, or until the fillets are an even milky white all the way through.

Discard the top layer of vine leaves. Spoon the pan juices over the fish, sprinkle with the parsley, olives, and pepper, and serve with the lemon wedges.

Fish Spetsai-Style
Psari Spetsiotiko
Serves 4

From the charming island of Spetsai, famous for its fragrant pinewoods, comes this good country dish. The fish is smothered in an aromatic tomato sauce flavoured with cinnamon, cloves and garlic, topped with a layer of breadcrumbs, and baked until golden and crisp. It can be served hot or cold. Fried or grilled aubergines are a good accompaniment, and resin-flavoured retsina is the perfect wine to complement the fish.

Two 675 g/1¹/₂ lb sea bream, cleaned and scaled, scored (page 345) or
4 fillets of white-fleshed fish such as bass, about 200 g/7 oz each
Juice of ¹/₂ lemon
Coarse-grain sea salt *and* cracked black pepper to taste
115 ml/4 fl oz extra virgin olive oil
1 small onion, finely chopped
2-4 cloves garlic, finely chopped
8 large tomatoes, skinned and diced, juices reserved
1 teaspoon honey
One 7 cm/3 inch cinnamon stick, broken in half *or* 1 teaspoon ground cinnamon
3 cloves *or* ¹/₄ teaspoon ground cloves
4 tablespoons coarsely chopped flat leaf parsley
115 ml/4 fl oz dry white wine
40 g/1¹/₂ oz dried coarse breadcrumbs
1 teaspoon dried *rigani* (page 14)

Dry the fish with paper towels. Rub whole fish inside and out, fillets on both sides, with the lemon juice, salt and pepper, and 2 tablespoons of the olive oil. Cover and set aside.

In a heavy sauté pan heat 2 tablespoons of the remaining olive oil over low heat and sauté the onion until soft, about 6 minutes. Add the garlic, tomatoes with their juices, honey, cinnamon, cloves and half the parsley. Raise the heat to medium-low and simmer until the cooking liquid is reduced by half. Add the wine and boil for 1 minute. Strain the sauce through a coarse sieve into a large bowl, pressing on the solids to extract as much liquid as possible. Measure, and add water if necessary to make 700 ml/1¹/₄ pints. Season to taste with salt and pepper. Place the fish in the sauce, turn once or twice to coat, and set aside for 30 minutes.

Heat the oven to 160C/325F/gas mark 3. Brush a baking dish, just large enough to hold the fish, with some of the remaining olive oil, place the fish in it, and pour over the sauce. Sprinkle with olive oil and bake, uncovered, for 20 minutes. Baste the fish with the sauce and sprinkle with the breadcrumbs and the rest of the olive oil. Bake 15 minutes longer, or until the fish is an even white all the way through and the sauce is thick and syrupy.

Sprinkle with the *rigani* and the remaining parsley, and serve hot or warm.

Sea Bass with Vinegar and Rosemary
Lavrakia Marinata

Serves 4

Sea bass is a favourite taverna dish – best eaten, say the Greeks, at an open-air restaurant close by the sea. The fish, glistening and plump, looks beautiful, while sweet rosemary lends a subtle fragrance. Here the dusting of flour keeps the fish from splitting and flaking during frying and cuts down fish odours in the kitchen. Chickpea flour, available in Greek, Middle Eastern and health food shops, gives just the right traditional nutty flavour.

Four 450-550 g/1-1¼ lb sea bass, cleaned and scaled (page 345) or 4 fillets, about 200 g/7 oz each
Juice of ½ lemon
1 teaspoon coarse-grain sea salt, or to taste
½ tablespoon cracked black pepper, or to taste
4 tablespoons chickpea flour *and* 2 tablespoons plain flour *or* 6 tablespoons plain flour
175-225 ml/6-8 fl oz extra virgin olive oil (to taste)
1 large clove garlic, cut into slivers, *optional*
5 tablespoons aged red wine vinegar
2 tablespoons hot water
2 tablespoons fresh rosemary
4 bay leaves

For serving
Small sprigs of fresh rosemary
Elitses or Niçoise olives

Wipe the fish with a damp cloth and rub whole fish inside and out, fillets on both sides, with the lemon juice and half the salt and pepper. Dust with 2 tablespoons of the flour, cover, and set aside for 30 minutes.

Place a large heavy sauté pan over medium-low heat and add half the olive oil. Dust the fish again with half the remaining flour and shake off any excess. When the olive oil is hot but not smoking, fry the fish on both sides until pale golden, about 15 minutes for whole fish, 10-12 minutes for fillets. The fish is cooked if it flakes easily when you insert a thin knife blade into the thickest part of the fish; it should be an even white all the way through. Drain between layers of paper towels. Strain the frying oil through 2 layers of muslin to remove any residue and set aside.

Wipe out the pan with paper towels and return to low heat. Sprinkle the remaining flour over the bottom of the sauté pan and stir a minute or two with a wooden spoon until deep golden brown. Whisk in the reserved frying oil and the remaining olive oil. Add the garlic and cook, stirring, 1 minute longer, or until the flour is a deep nutty brown. The flour and oil will not blend together, but the flour will flavour and colour the oil. Add the vinegar, water, rosemary, bay leaves and remaining salt and pepper. Whisk to mix, and simmer for 3 minutes.

Return the fish to the sauté pan, cover, and heat through. Transfer to a warm dish, pour over the sauce, and surround with the rosemary sprigs. Serve hot or warm, with black olives.

Note To serve cold, add 115 ml/4 fl oz dry white wine or 225 ml/8 fl oz strained Tomato Sauce (page 321, made with parsley and bay leaves) along with the vinegar. Let the sauce cool, then transfer the fish and sauce to a shallow glass or china dish, add olive oil to cover, tightly cover the dish, and refrigerate overnight or for up to 3 days before serving. Turn the fish in the marinade once or twice. Serve as a *meze* or lunch dish.

Red Mullet in Savoury Sauce
Barbounia me Saltsa Savori
Serves 4

Red mullet has always been highly prized in Greece. One ancient manuscript lists a two-pound mullet at the same price as two dozen slaves. Nowadays large red mullet are popular and therefore more expensive, but it is the smaller fish that have the sweeter flavour. In Greece the liver and cheeks are considered a delicacy – I prefer to do without the liver unless the fish is very fresh. This dish tastes equally delicious hot or cold; the piquant sauce also marries well with fillets or steaks of bass, halibut, or sea bream.

8 red mullet, 225-275 g/8-10 oz each, cleaned and scaled (page 345) or
4 fillets of bass or sea bream, about 200 g/7 oz each
1 teaspoon coarse-grain sea salt, or to taste
1/2 tablespoon cracked black pepper, or to taste
115 ml/4 fl oz extra virgin olive oil
1 large clove garlic, cut into slivers
5 tablespoons aged red wine vinegar
1 teaspoon honey
6 large ripe tomatoes, skinned, seeded, diced, and drained in a colander for 30 minutes
1/4 teaspoon ground cinnamon
5 tablespoons currants or small dark seedless raisins, soaked for 30 minutes in 1 tablespoon hot water
4 bay leaves
1 tablespoon fresh thyme, finely chopped or 1/2 tablespoon dried thyme, crumbled

For serving
4 tablespoons coarsely chopped flat leaf parsley
2 salted anchovy fillets (page 343), rinsed, patted dry, and finely chopped

Wipe the fish with a damp cloth and rub whole fish inside and out, fillets on both sides, with half the salt and pepper. Cover and set aside for 30 minutes.

Place a large heavy sauté pan over medium-low heat, add half the olive oil, and heat until hot but not smoking. Fry the fish on both sides until pale golden, about 15 minutes for whole fish, 10-12 minutes for fillets. The fish is cooked if it flakes easily when you insert a thin knife blade into the thickest part; it should be an even white all the way through. Drain between layers of paper towels.

Drain off the olive oil and wipe out the sauté pan with paper towels. Add half the remaining olive oil and sauté the garlic over low heat just until fragrant; don't let it colour. Combine the vinegar and honey and add to the pan, raise the heat, and boil until reduced to about 3 tablespoons. Add the tomatoes, cinnamon, currants, bay leaves, thyme, and remaining salt and pepper, lower the heat, and simmer 3 minutes. Return the fish to the pan, cover, and heat through.

Transfer to a warm platter, pour over the sauce and remaining olive oil, and sprinkle with the parsley and chopped anchovies. Serve hot or warm.

Note To serve cold, add 115 ml/4 fl oz dry white wine to the sauté pan once the vinegar is reduced, boil 1 minute, and then add the tomatoes and remaining ingredients. Let the sauce cool, transfer the fish and sauce to a glass or china dish, and add olive oil to cover. Tightly cover the dish, and refrigerate overnight or for up to 3 days. Turn the fish in the marinade once or twice. Serve as a *meze* or light lunch dish.

Grilled Fish
Psaria Skharas
Serves 4

Few treats can equal the splendour of a freshly-caught fish grilled over an aromatic charcoal fire and served with a scattering of fresh herbs. Walk along any Greek harbourside and you'll find tavernas whose speciality is the daily creation of this culinary masterpiece.

For grilling, Greeks choose a variety of fish and seafood, including red mullet, the colourful members of the bream family, bonito, tuna, and swordfish, delicious little sardines, and lobster, prawns, octopus, cuttlefish, and squid. Before grilling, fish is often steeped in a well-flavoured marinade.

The charcoal should be produced from hardwood (olive wood and vine clippings make the best); it should be moderately hot and have reached what the Greeks call the "digested stage", i.e., lightly covered with grey ash.

Herbs, both fresh and dried, are a fundamental way of flavouring grilled fish, but how you use them is more important than which herbs you choose. Don't be tempted to just throw a handful of bay leaves onto the fire – the acrid smoke they produce will not enhance the flavour or the fish! Sprigs of fresh herbs such as thyme, rosemary or oregano are used as basting brushes, in marinades, and in sauces; dried *rigani* is used in marinades and at serving time.

The most common problems with grilled fish are drying up and breaking. Guard against this by choosing plump and succulent fish of at least 675 g/1¹⁄₂ lb in weight (smaller fish are better fried), brush both fish and grill liberally with olive oil before grilling, and take special care over cooking times (this depends on the thickness of the fish, not its length).

Two 800 g–1 kg/1³⁄₄–2¹⁄₄ lb or one 1.7 kg/3¹⁄₂ lb firm-fleshed fish, cleaned and scaled (page 345) or 4 fish steaks, at least 1 cm/¹⁄₂ inch thick (about 225 g/8 oz each)
Juice of 1 lemon (reserve 1 juiced lemon half)

Sea salt *and* freshly ground pepper to taste
4–6 tablespoons extra virgin olive oil (to taste)
6 sprigs of fresh oregano
3 bay leaves

For serving
Purslane Salad (page 220) or watercress sprigs

Dry the fish with paper towels and score fish larger than 900 g/2 lb so they cook evenly. With a sharp knife, make two or three deep 5 cm/2 inch parallel diagonal incisions on each side of the fish. (The heads are always left intact on fish prepared for the grill – the cheeks taste particularly good.) Rub whole fish inside and out, steaks on both sides, with half the lemon juice, salt, and pepper, and 1½ tablespoons of the olive oil. Scatter the oregano and bay leaves over the fish and set aside while you prepare the fire.

Set a grill rack 10-12 cm/4-5 inches above hot coals and brush with olive oil, or brush a hinged double grill with olive oil. Brush the fish with some of the remaining olive oil. Combine the remaining lemon juice and olive oil to make a basting sauce. Pierce the lemon half with a skewer and use it as a 'baster', dipping it in the sauce. Grill the fish on both sides until cooked through, about 10 minutes for steaks, up to 15 minutes for smaller whole fish and 25 minutes for larger fish, basting liberally with the sauce.

Spread the Purslane Salad over a warm platter and arrange the fish on top. Sprinkle with the remaining basting sauce, salt, and pepper and serve immediately.

Grilled Marinated Fish
Psari Marinata tis Skhara
Serves 4

Traditionally used by village cooks to preserve freshly caught fish, aromatic marinades inspired by a variety of ingredients continue to add a delightful flavour to grilled fish. Swordfish steaks are particularly good with the marinades given here. Either will give any grilled fish an authentic Greek taste, whether you serve it simply garnished with fresh herbs or accompanied by one of the suggested sauces, along with a salad of wild greens (page 221) and Olive Bread (page 253).

Two 900 g–1 kg/2–2¼ lb or one 1.7 kg/3½ lb firm-fleshed fish, cleaned and scaled, scored
(page 345) or 4 fish steaks, at least 1 cm/½ inch thick (about 225 g/8 oz each)
Juice of 1 small lemon (see Note)
Sea salt *and* freshly ground black pepper to taste
115 ml/4 fl oz extra virgin olive oil

Marinade 1
1 large mild onion, thinly sliced

2 tablespoons aged red wine vinegar
Pinch of cayenne pepper

For serving
Coarsely chopped fresh coriander or flat leaf parsley
Black Olives and Lentil Salata (page 39) or Anchovy Sauce (page 325)

Marinade 2
3 shallots, finely chopped
4 sprigs of parsley
2 sprigs of fresh thyme
Juice of $^1/_2$ lemon
2 bay leaves

For serving
Finely chopped flat leaf parsley
Peloponnese Honey Sauce (page 324) or latholemono sauce (4 parts extra virgin
olive oil to 1 part fresh lemon juice, whisked together, with finely chopped fresh
thyme or parsley to taste)

Dry the fish with paper towels. Rub whole fish inside and out, steaks on both sides, with the lemon juice and salt and pepper. Place in a shallow china or glass dish and add all the ingredients for either of the marinades and half the olive oil. Cover and set aside for 1 hour.

Prepare the fire and set a grill rack 10-12 cm/4-5 inches above the coals. Brush the grill, or a hinged double grill, with olive oil. Remove the fish from the marinade, strain the marinade, and combine with the remaining olive oil. Remove any onions or herbs sticking to the fish and grill on both sides until cooked through, about 10 minutes for steaks, up to 15 minutes for smaller whole fish and 25 minutes for larger whole fish. Baste occasionally with the marinade.

Transfer to a warm platter, sprinkle with the coriander or parsley, and drizzle with the remaining marinade mixture. Serve immediately and pass the *salata* or sauce separately.

Note Reserve 1 of the juiced lemon halves for a 'baster' (pierce it with a skewer and dip it in the marinade) or use sprigs of dried *rigani* or fresh thyme as a basting brush.

Pan-Seared Tuna with Beetroot Greens
Thonnos Psiti me Khorta
Serves 4

For centuries Greeks have enjoyed this ancient dish, which brings land and sea together in perfect harmony: from the sea, the rich strongly flavoured oily fish and from the land, the earthy country tones of beetroot greens. The combination creates a colourful succulent dish

that looks enticingly exotic, but is very easy to prepare. Surprising as it may sound, a good dry red wine complements the flavours in this dish best.

4 tuna, bonito or swordfish steaks, about 225 g/8 oz each
Coarse-grain sea salt to taste
1 tablespoon cracked black pepper, or to taste
4-6 tablespoons aged red wine vinegar (to taste)
4 bay leaves
2 sprigs of fresh or dried thyme
$^1/_2$ teaspoon ground paprika
75-115 ml/3-4 fl oz extra virgin olive oil (to taste)
450 g/1 lb beetroot greens
1 large clove garlic, cut into slivers

For serving
1 tablespoon small capers, rinsed

Wipe the fish steaks and rub with salt, half the pepper, and 1 tablespoon of the vinegar. Place in a shallow china or glass dish with the bay leaves and thyme, and sprinkle with half the paprika and 1 tablespoon of the olive oil. Cover and set aside 1 hour to marinate.

If the beetroot greens are young and tender, with bright green leaves, just strip the leaves from the stalks. If the greens are older, with dark green leaves, remove the tough stalks. Blanch the leaves in boiling water for 3 minutes and drain in a colander, pressing out excess moisture.

Heat a heavy cast-iron frying pan or sauté pan over medium-low heat, and add 2 tablespoons olive oil. Remove the fish from the marinade, discarding the bay leaves and thyme, and sear on both sides until the fish is an even colour all the way through, about 8-10 minutes. Transfer to a warm platter, cover, and keep warm.

Wipe out the pan with paper towels, return to low heat, and add 1 tablespoon olive oil. Sauté the garlic until golden. Add 3 tablespoons of vinegar to deglaze the pan; it will reduce by half almost immediately. Slice the fresh greens into thin ribbons or coarsely chop the cooked greens and add to the pan with salt and the remaining pepper. Stir with a wooden spoon until tender greens are just cooked or cooked greens are hot.

Transfer to a platter and arrange the fish on top. Sprinkle with the capers, remaining paprika and vinegar, and olive oil to taste. Serve immediately.

shellfish and crustaceans
ostraka ke ostrakithi

Greeks revel in subtle and innovative blends of taste and texture, but they also know when to leave well enough alone – and the shellfish and crustaceans available to them, deliciously fresh from the sea, need very little help from the cook.

Cockles and scallops are eaten raw as *mezedes* or made into *pilafi* or soup. Mussels are removed from their shells, coated with egg and breadcrumbs, and deep-fried, to be served as a *meze*, with *macaronia*, or in a *pilafi*.

Prawns are popular throughout Greece and her islands. The fishermen baste them with lemon juice, olive oil, and coarse-grain sea salt and grill them – nothing could be more delicious.

Lobster is the prize catch of the Mediterranean and many Greeks prefer their lobster simply boiled and served with a good mayonnaise or a light *latholemono* sauce – but charcoal-grilled lobster is popular too.

Langouste with Latholemono Sauce
Astakos me Latholemono
Serves 4

The small langouste, or spiny lobster, is the most common lobster in Greek waters and many Greeks prefer its flavour to that of the larger lobster (*karavida* [Greek] or *homard*). In homes and tavernas lobster is always presented very simply, with olive oil, lemon juice, and a scattering of fresh parsley or oregano – an especially lovely treat on a warm summer's day.

4 tablespoons wine vinegar
1 tablespoon sea salt
2 live langoustes or small lobsters, 450-550 g/1-1¼ lb each
Juice of 1 lemon
Large pinch of dry mustard
Sea salt *and* freshly ground black pepper to taste
115 ml/4 fl oz extra virgin olive oil

For serving
Finely chopped fresh oregano or flat leaf parsley

Fill a large saucepan with water and bring it to a boil over high heat; add the vinegar and salt. Add the langoustes, bring back to a boil, reduce the heat slightly, and cook 6 minutes longer. Drain and blot dry.

De-vein the langoustes and discard the small sac beneath the heads. Cut in half along the length of the body. Take out the olive-green livers and, if there is any, the bright orange coral. Mash the coral (and liver, if liked) to a paste with half the lemon juice, the mustard, and salt and pepper. Whisk in the olive oil to make a creamy sauce, and add the remaining lemon juice to taste.

Remove the meat from the tails and chop it into small pieces. Toss with 2 tablespoons of the sauce and replace in the shells. If using small lobsters, crack the claws (only the tail meat of the langouste is eaten). Arrange the langoustes attractively on a platter and sprinkle with the oregano. Serve the sauce separately.

Grilled Lobster
Astakos tis Skhara
Serves 4

Small lobsters are the best choice for grilling; their meat stays moist and sweet. If you can prepare your fire using woody rosemary bush branches or olive hardwood you will enjoy grilled lobster with a very special flavour. Better still, have some branches of rosemary ready to throw on the fire just before grilling the lobsters and use several sprigs of rosemary tied together as a basting brush.

Coarse-grain sea salt
6 tablespoons wine vinegar
4 live small lobsters or langoustes
175-225 ml/6-8 fl oz extra virgin olive oil (to taste)
1 teaspoon honey
$^1/_2$ teaspoon ground coriander
Crushed black peppercorns to taste
Juice of 1 lemon

Fill a large saucepan with water and bring to a boil over high heat; add 1 tablespoon salt and 4 tablespoons of the vinegar. Add the lobsters, bring back to a boil, reduce the heat slightly, and boil 3 minutes longer. Drain and blot dry.

Set a grill rack 7 cm/3 inches above charcoal and brush it with olive oil.

Combine the remaining vinegar, 5 tablespoons of the olive oil, honey, coriander, and salt and pepper and brush the lobsters liberally with this sauce. Grill 20-30 minutes, basting and turning frequently, until the shell can be easily separated from the flesh. Leave the shells in place, but de-vein each lobster, and discard the small sacs beneath the heads. Remove the orange coral, if there is any, and mash to a paste with the lemon juice and remaining olive oil.

Arrange the lobsters on a serving platter. Serve the remaining sauce separately, and have plenty of napkins on the table.

Prawns in a Pot with Feta Cheese
Garithes Youvetsi
Serves 4

This is a pretty – and convenient – dish for a dinner party. It can be prepared a few hours ahead of time and baked at the last minute. Serve in individual earthenware dishes for a beautiful presentation and have plenty of country bread on the table for your guests to mop up the delicious sauce.

675 g/1^1/$_2$ lb prawns in the shell
115 ml/4 fl oz extra virgin olive oil
2 onions, quartered and thinly sliced
1 large clove garlic, finely chopped
7 medium ripe tomatoes, 4 of them skinned, seeded, and diced, the remaining 3 skinned, cored, and cut in thin slices
^{1}/$_2$ teaspoon honey
^{1}/$_4$ teaspoon cayenne pepper, optional
^{1}/$_2$ teaspoon ground cumin
1 tablespoon dried rigani (page 14), crumbled
1 small bunch of flat leaf parsley, leaves coarsely chopped
225 ml/8 fl oz dry white wine
Coarse-grain sea salt to taste
^{1}/$_2$ tablespoon cracked black pepper, or to taste
350 g/12 oz feta cheese, cut into 8 slices

For serving
Lemon wedges

Remove the legs from the prawns and de-vein (but do not remove from the shell). Rinse and dry between layers of paper towels. Heat 2 tablespoons of the olive oil in a heavy sauté pan, add the prawns, cover, and cook 4 minutes over medium-low heat, occasionally giving the pan a vigorous shake. Transfer the prawns and oil to a bowl, tightly cover, and refrigerate. Wipe out the pan.

Heat the oven to 180C/350F/gas mark 4. Heat half the remaining olive oil in the sauté pan and cook the onions over low heat until soft, about 8 minutes. Add the garlic, diced tomatoes, honey, cayenne pepper, and cumin, raise the heat to medium, and simmer 10 minutes, or until most of the liquid has evaporated. Add the rigani, most of the parsley, the wine, salt, and pepper. Cook, stirring occasionally, for about 8 minutes; the sauce should remain separated for a few seconds when a wooden spoon is drawn across the bottom of the pan.

Divide the sauce between 4 individual ovenproof dishes. Peel the prawns, catching any juices in the bowl. Arrange the prawns on top of the sauce and sprinkle with the juices. Cover with the tomato and feta cheese slices, sprinkle with the remaining olive oil, and bake 15 minutes, or until heated through.

Sprinkle with the rest of the parsley and serve hot, with the lemon wedges.

Sea Urchins
Achini
Serves 4

Until recently any cookbook mention of sea urchins would have been of purely academic interest. Now that these fascinating sea creatures are in greater demand, they are far more widely available here.

Greeks have enjoyed eating sea urchins since before the time of Homer. They gather only the females since it is the females that yield the distinctive coral (roe) and gather sea urchins only at around the time of the full moon, when, for some mysterious reason, they contain the greatest number of eggs.

Serve sea urchins in the shell so guests can scoop out the coral for themselves, or gently detach the coral from the sides of each shell and serve it on small dishes, and offer ouzo, raki, or a jug of chilled dry white wine to drink.

4 dozen very fresh sea urchins (page 349)

For serving
Lemon wedges or aged red wine vinegar

To prepare a sea urchin, wrap one of your hands in a heavy cloth and grip the spike-covered shell, soft side facing upwards. Insert a blunt-ended knife into the mouth in the centre of this soft side and, with a circular motion, gently scoop out the mouth and the top third of the shell; the shell cracks easily, so care is needed. As you finish preparing each sea urchin, rinse it in a bowl of water; the loose inner grey mass should float out, leaving the roe adhering to the inside of the shell. Check that no spikes have found their way into the shell, and set aside; or scoop the roe out onto a small platter.

Serve immediately, or tightly cover and refrigerate for no more than an hour or two. Serve with lemon wedges.

octopus, squid, and cuttlefish
khtapothi, kalamaria, ke soupia

Octopus, squid, and cuttlefish (the cephalopods) are everyday food in Greece. Inexpensive and nutritious, they appear on taverna menus everywhere, especially on the islands.

Small squid and cuttlefish are the tastiest and the most tender. As a *meze*, these tiny creatures are fried whole to crisp perfection and served just with a little lemon juice and salt. For a main course, squid may be slowly simmered in an aromatic wine or ink sauce.

Larger squid are usually stuffed – popular in Greece are stuffings made with rice, shallots, spinach, and tomatoes; breadcrumbs, olives, pine nuts, and currants; or rice, parsley, currants, and pine nuts – and simmered until they are tender and the flavours have blended beautifully. Cuttlefish can also be stuffed, but it is easier to cut it into pieces before cooking. It's from cuttlefish ink that the pigment sepia is extracted (the Greek name for cuttlefish is *soupia)*.

Perhaps the best way to try octopus for the first time is grilled (page 118). In Greece not only the octopus itself but also the ink sacs are considered *meze* delicacies. Large ink sacs are fried; small ones roasted in an aubergine or onion shell in the embers of a fire. Check the glossary for more information on mastering the art of cleaning and preparing these traditional delicacies.

Octopus in Red Wine
Khtapothi Krasato
Serves 6

Remnants of Minoan and Classical Greek pottery adorned with strange and beautiful octopus-inspired motifs have been found on island and mainland archaeological sites, and they testify to a Greek fascination with the octopus stretching back to antiquity.

The traditional way to kill an octopus is for the fisherman to bite through the nerve centre which passes behind the octopus' eyes. Traditionally too he tenderizes the octopus by beating it against a rock – 40 times, say some fishermen, as many times as you can stand it, say others! Octopus is usually sold cleaned, and tenderized (tenderizing must be done when the octopus is killed, so don't waste your time trying to pound a tough one to tenderness). Octopus must also be skinned but this is an easy job if you let the cooking do some of the work for you. In this recipe the octopus first braises in its own juices until the moisture has evaporated, at which point it will be almost cooked and the skin will peel off easily. Serve Octopus in Red Wine with other strong flavours of the Greek countryside – *khorta* (page 220), tiny sweet Elitses olives (page 2), slices of *feta* or *kephalotyri* cheese, and Country Bread (page 249).

One 2.2–3.4 kg/5–7 lb tenderized octopus, with eyes, mouth, and inside of head discarded (page 118)
350 ml/12 fl oz dry red wine
6 tablespoons extra virgin olive oil
450 g/1 lb small boiling onions, about 2.5 cm/1 inch in diameter, peeled (page 132)
6 large ripe tomatoes, skinned, diced, and juices reserved
1 teaspoon honey
4 bay leaves
Freshly ground black pepper to taste
4 sprigs of dried thyme *or rigani* (page 14)

For serving
1 small bunch of flat leaf parsley, leaves coarsely chopped
1 tablespoon dried thyme *or rigani*
Sea salt to taste (see Note)

Heat the oven to 150C/300F/gas mark 2. Rinse the octopus well in several changes of water, place in a heavy baking dish with 4 tablespoons red wine, cover tightly, and bake 1 hour. Check once or twice, and add a few tablespoons of water if necessary. Thoroughly rinse, cover tightly, and refrigerate until cold.

Heat half the olive oil over low heat in a large heavy casserole. Add the onions and gently roll them in the oil for 5 minutes. Meanwhile, cut up the octopus: sever the legs from the body; cut the body (head) lengthways in quarters; and peel off the skin to expose the pale pink flesh – the suckers come off easily with the skin. Cut into 4 cm/1½ inch pieces and add to the casserole. Add the tomatoes and their juices, honey, bay leaves, pepper, and the remaining olive oil and red wine. Tie the thyme sprigs into a bundle with kitchen string and add to the casserole. Bring to a gentle boil, cover tightly, and simmer over very low heat for 2 hours. Stir occasionally; by the end of the cooking time the sauce should be reduced by half.

Discard the thyme sprigs. Chop together the parsley, thyme, and salt, and sprinkle over the octopus. Serve hot.

Note Never rub octopus with salt or add salt to the pot before it is almost cooked, or it will toughen beyond redemption.

Grilled Octopus
Khtapothi sti Skhara
Serves 6

The taste of octopus grilled over the embers of a wood fire always reminds me of beach parties in Greece on balmy star-lit nights. Guests are greeted with a glass of ouzo or raki and while they chat the charcoal burns down to just the right dull glow and the octopus marinates in olive oil, lemon juice, and *rigani*. Grilling takes just a few minutes and the octopus, cut into small pieces, is served as a *meze,* accompanied by bowls of olives and cheese. Or serve it as a main course with pilaf and Beetroot Island-Style (page 182), or *khorta* (page 220).

One 2.2-3.4 kg/5-7 lb octopus, tenderized (page 116)
450 ml/16 fl oz dry white wine or water
300 ml/½ pint extra virgin olive oil
Juice of 2 lemons
12 sprigs of fresh oregano or rosemary, leaves stripped from the stems, and stems reserved or 4 tablespoons dried *rigani* (page 14)
1 tablespoon coarse-grain sea salt, or to taste
1 tablespoon cracked black pepper

For serving
Lemon wedges
1 large bunch of flat leaf parsley, leaves coarsely chopped

Start preparing the dish one day ahead of serving. First, remove the eyes, mouth, and inside of the head of the octopus if it has not been done already. To remove the head, cut below the eyes at the spot where the tentacles meet; to remove the eyes and mouth, turn the pouch-like head inside out, discard the innards, and cut out the eyes and mouth. Rinse well in several changes of water and place in a large saucepan with the wine, adding water, if necessary, to cover. Bring slowly to a boil, cover, reduce the heat, and simmer 1¹/₄ hours (for a 2.2 kg/5 lb octopus) to 1³/₄ hours (for a 3.4 kg/7 lb octopus). Drain, thoroughly rinse, cover tightly, and refrigerate overnight.

Prepare the fire. Meanwhile, cut up the octopus: sever the legs from the body and leave whole; cut the body (head) lengthways in quarters; and peel off the skin to expose the pale pink flesh – the suckers come off easily with the skin.

Whisk together 225 ml/8 fl oz of the olive oil, the lemon juice, and *rigani* in a shallow bowl. Add the octopus pieces and turn to coat with the marinade. Set aside.

Set a grill rack 10 cm/4 inches above hot coals, and brush with olive oil. Throw the herb stems on the fire. Remove the octopus pieces from the marinade, sprinkle with the salt and pepper, and grill a few minutes on either side, or until browned, brushing once or twice with the marinade. Arrange on a warm serving plate and surround with the lemon wedges. Sprinkle with the parsley.

Cuttlefish in Ink Sauce
Soupia me Saltsa Melanis
Serves 4

At any time of year Crete's largest city, Heraklion, boasts a lively market, vibrant with colour, bustling with noise, and overflowing with produce from the surrounding villages. In spring and autumn Greek cooks head first for the fishermen's stalls, which are piled high with towers of gleaming cuttlefish. Bargaining with stall-holders, they reject the large cuttlefish and choose instead the small ones. Cuttlefish are the most tender and easily prepared of all cephalopods and a favourite food on the islands, especially when cooked with this creamy inky sauce.

1.5 kg/3 lb cuttlefish, preferably small, of a similar size
5 tablespoons extra virgin olive oil
2 large mild onions, quartered and thinly sliced
115 ml/4 fl oz dry white wine
3 tablespoons finely chopped flat leaf parsley
¹/₂ tablespoon fresh oregano finely chopped, or dried *rigani* (page 14), crumbled
Coarse-grain sea salt *and* cracked black pepper to taste

For serving
1 tablespoon finely chopped Preserved Lemon (page 18), *optional*
Lemon wedges

Rinse the cuttlefish. Small ones (10-12 cm/4-5 inches) can be left whole. Prepare larger ones as follows: gently pull off the head with the tentacles still attached, then carefully slash the centre front of the body with a sharp knife. Remove the 2 small black ink sacs, and check to make sure they contain no sand – try to avoid rinsing them, or they will lose too much ink. Set aside 8 sacs, and discard the rest. Rinse off any ink from the cuttlefish. Remove the single bone, discard everything else from inside the body, and rub off the brownish outer skin. Rinse again, cut into long 2.5 cm/1 inch-wide strips, and place in a colander to drain.

Slice off and discard the part of the head that contains the eyes, and rinse the head. Slice it open so it unfolds into a strip, with the tentacles on one side. Discard the beak, and thoroughly rinse and rub the tentacles to remove any sand. Cut into 2.5 cm/1 inch pieces and add to the colander.

Heat 4 tablespoons of the olive oil in a large heavy frying pan and sauté the onion over low heat until soft, about 6 minutes. Add the cuttlefish and cook, stirring occasionally, until any liquid has evaporated and the cuttlefish and onion begin to colour, about 15 minutes. Put the ink sacs and 115 ml/4 fl oz water into a small bowl and gently rub the sacs to expel all the ink. Strain through a fine strainer into the pan, add the wine, and raise the heat to medium-low. Cook, stirring frequently, until all the liquid has evaporated and the cuttlefish are coated with a creamy sauce, about 15 minutes. Stir in most of the parsley, season with salt and a generous amount of pepper, and cook 1 minute longer.

Chop the Preserved Lemon, remaining parsley, and a large pinch of salt and pepper together to mix. Transfer the cuttlefish to a warm platter, or serve directly from the pan, sprinkled with the lemon mixture and the rest of the olive oil. Serve at once, with the lemon wedges.

Chicken and Game

kotopoula ke kinigi

Sizzling on spits, scented with lemon and fruity olive oil, glistening and golden-roasted – that's how Greeks like chicken best. That's also how the traveller to Greece most often remembers chicken – the pungent aroma of mountain herbs as chicken spit-roasts assail the senses and set the taste buds racing. Greek chickens may not be as plump as our own but they are invariably free range and have a superb flavour and texture.

But Greeks also enjoy a variety of chicken casseroles and baked dishes. These traditional dishes are meant to be baked in the village oven, but they are easily adapted to our ovens and slow cookers. Greek ways to flavour chickens may come as a surprise: many feature the strong use of eastern spices – Chicken in a Pot (page 124), for example, includes cloves and cinnamon, and just the aroma of this heartening dish envelops you in a comforting warmth of gastronomic expectation. Also spiced, with cumin, allspice, and cloves, is Baked Chicken and Okra (page 125), a colourful dish to make in early summer when this vegetable is at its best. Other chicken dishes are tied to seasonal change – in spring, the clear lemony fragrance of a poached Chicken in Avgolemono Sauce (page 127) and, in autumn, the creamy coriander-and-walnut flavoured sauce enrobing a braised chicken (page 126) are delights.

For us chicken is commonplace: for Greeks in rural communities rabbit, hare, and game birds in season are everyday fare. Simple spit-roast rabbit or game birds are popular at village feasts and the spicy *stifado,* made with rabbit, hare, or even snails, and sweetened with large quantities of onions, is a favourite winter meal. Greece lies on the migratory path between northern Europe and Africa and from September to November Greek skies are darkened with flocks of birds on their way to the sun. At this time of year "hunter's pot" (page 136) may contain quail, woodcock, partridge, or pigeon, gently braised under a covering of vine leaves and fragrant with herbs. Duck, particularly wild duckling from the Macedonian lakes, is a popular spring food – cooked Thessalia-style (page 139), scented with juniper berries, cloves, and orange zest, it's a dish fit for the gods.

Roast Chicken with Rigani and Garlic
Kotopoulo Riganato

Serves 4 to 6

Pungent *rigani* grows in wild abundance on the mountain slopes of Greece. The Greek cook's favourite herb, it's in strong evidence in this aromatic roast chicken. This is a dish for garlic lovers too – the amount used is generous! Cook the chicken whole for elegance, or cut into serving pieces for speed and convenience.

One 1.8-2.3 kg/4-5 lb chicken, whole or cut into serving pieces, skin and excess fat removed
Juice of 1¹/₂ lemons
75-115 ml/3-4 fl oz extra virgin olive oil (to taste)
¹/₂ tablespoon coarse-grain sea salt, or to taste
900 g/2 lb roasting potatoes, cut lengthways into quarters
6 cloves garlic (unpeeled), lightly crushed
4 tablespoons dried *rigani* (page 14), crumbled
Cracked black pepper to taste
6 bay leaves
1 tablespoon unsalted butter
400 ml/14 fl oz Chicken Stock (page 344)
¹/₂ teaspoon Dijon mustard
1 teaspoon honey

For serving
1 small bunch of flat leaf parsley, leaves coarsely chopped

Heat the oven to 190C/375F/gas mark 5. Rub the chicken with the juice of 1 lemon, 3 tablespoons of the olive oil, and the salt. Place the chicken in a deep heavy baking dish and surround with the potatoes and garlic in a single layer.

Sprinkle the chicken with the *rigani,* pepper, bay leaves, and the remaining olive oil and dot with the butter. Add half the stock, and roast, uncovered, 15 minutes. Reduce the oven temperature to 180C/350F/gas mark 4 and continue roasting until tender – about 1 hour longer for a whole chicken, 40 minutes longer for chicken pieces. Baste the chicken and potatoes frequently, adding more stock to the dish if necessary.

Transfer the chicken, potatoes, and garlic to a serving platter and keep warm. Strain the pan juices into a small saucepan, remove the fat with a spoon, and add any remaining stock. If there is more than about 350 ml/12 fl oz of liquid, reduce it by rapid boiling. Combine the mustard, honey, and half the remaining lemon juice and stir into the sauce. Add the salt, pepper, and lemon juice to taste, and heat to warm.

Pour sauce over the chicken and potatoes just to moisten, and sprinkle with the parsley. Serve the remaining sauce separately.

Chicken in a Pot
Kapama Kotopoulo
Serves 4 to 5

On a morning stroll through a traditional Greek village visitors are often welcomed by the warm, comforting aromas of *kapamas* wafting from private kitchens or the baker's oven. These are no ordinary stews: they are rich and colourful creations cooked slowly so that flavours blend and the meat becomes so tender that you could eat it with a spoon. *Kapama kotopoulo,* a classic country dish, is flavoured with cloves and cinnamon, marjoram and bay leaves, tomatoes, onions, and honey; you can use this recipe to make glorious casseroles of lamb or hare, too. The real secret of these wonderful stews is that the ingredients are packed in closely together and a tight-fitting lid locks in the spicy flavour during baking. Serve with fried aubergine slices, *pilafi* and grated *kasseri* cheese.

One 1.8-2.3 kg/4-5 lb chicken, cut into serving pieces, skin and excess fat removed and giblets reserved
2 tablespoons extra virgin olive oil
1 tablespoon unsalted butter
1 large onion, chopped
8 ripe tomatoes, skinned and diced
1 teaspoon honey
3 bay leaves, broken into pieces
1 tablespoon dried marjoram or rosemary, crumbled
4 cloves
One 7 cm/3 inch cinnamon stick or 1 teaspoon ground cinnamon
115-225 ml/4-8 fl oz chicken stock (page 344) or water
1 teaspoon cracked black pepper, or to taste
4 tablespoons plain flour
1 clove garlic, finely chopped
1 teaspoon coarse-grain sea salt, or to taste
40 g/1 $^1/_2$ oz pine nuts
3 tablespoons finely chopped flat leaf parsley
12 Amfissa or Niçoise olives

Heat the oven to 160C/325F/gas mark 3. Discard the chicken liver. Rinse the remaining giblets and trim off the membranes. Heat the olive oil and butter in a heavy frying pan and sauté the chicken and giblets over medium-low heat until lightly browned. Drain between layers of paper towels and transfer to a heavy casserole.

Drain off most of the fat from the pan, add the onions and sauté until soft, about 5 minutes. Add the tomatoes, honey, bay leaves, marjoram, cloves, cinnamon, 115 ml/4 fl oz of the stock, and pepper, and simmer 5 minutes. Pour over the chicken.

Mix the flour with a little water to make a thick paste and spread it over the top rim of the casserole and inner rim of the lid. Place the lid in position, smooth the paste to make a good seal, and bake 15 minutes. Reduce the oven temperature to 150C/300F/gas mark 2 and bake 2$^1/_2$ hours longer.

Meanwhile, pound the garlic and salt together in a mortar or bowl until blended. Add the pine nuts and half the parsley, pound until well-mixed, and set aside. (You can use a food processor, but process only until the nuts are chopped, not ground.)

Lift off the casserole lid, using a blunt-ended knife to break the seal, and wipe the rim. Transfer the chicken pieces to a serving bowl and keep warm. Strain the sauce into a saucepan, pressing against the solids with a wooden spoon to extract as much liquid as possible; discard the solids. Add stock or water to the sauce if needed to make 450 ml/16 fl oz. Bring to a simmer, add the parsley mixture and olives, and season to taste; the sauce should be highly flavoured.

Pour the sauce over the chicken, sprinkle with the remaining parsley, and serve.

Baked Chicken and Okra
Kotopoulo me Bamies
Serves 4 to 6

In early summer when okra is at its best, this intriguing dish appears on taverna menus all over Greece. The colourful combination of golden chicken and onions, pale green okra, and vivid red tomatoes, spiced with cumin, cloves, and allspice, makes this a perfect party dish. Adding the okra at the end of cooking time keeps it whole and deliciously juicy. If okra is unavailable, you can substitute green beans, leeks, or artichokes. Potatoes in a Clay Pot (page 205) makes a good side dish.

675 g/1 1/2 lb okra, trimmed and rinsed
Juice of 2 large lemons
1 tablespoon coarse-grain sea salt
One 1.8-2.3 kg/4-5 lb chicken, cut into serving pieces and skin and excess fat removed
or 3 whole chicken breasts, skinned and split in half
115-175 ml/4-6 fl oz extra virgin olive oil (to taste)
2 large onions, thinly sliced
1 teaspoon ground allspice
1/2 tablespoon ground cumin
6 cloves
6 large ripe tomatoes, skinned, seeded, and diced
1 teaspoon honey
1 1/2 tablespoons dried thyme, crumbled
225 ml/8 fl oz Chicken Stock (page 344) or dry white wine or water
1 tablespoon cracked black pepper, or to taste
1 small bunch of flat leaf parsley, leaves coarsely chopped

Spread the okra on a baking tray in a single layer, sprinkle with half the lemon juice and 2 teaspoons of the salt, and set aside for 1 hour.

Heat the oven to 190C/375F/gas mark 5. Heat 3 tablespoons of the olive oil in a large heavy frying pan and sauté the chicken over medium-low heat until lightly browned on all sides. Drain between layers of paper towels and transfer to a baking dish.

Drain off most of the oil from the pan, reduce the heat to low, and sauté the onion 10 minutes, or until soft. Stir in the allspice, cumin, cloves, and tomatoes. Raise the heat to medium, bring to a boil, and boil until the liquid is reduced by one third. Add the honey, thyme, stock, a pinch of salt, and 1/2 tablespoon of the pepper. Simmer a few minutes longer and pour over the chicken. Cover and bake chicken pieces 35 minutes, chicken breasts 20 minutes.

Meanwhile, rinse the okra and dry with paper towels. Heat 3 tablespoons of the remaining olive oil in a large heavy sauté pan and sauté the okra over low heat until it begins to change colour, rolling it gently around the pan with a wooden spoon. Drain between layers of paper towels.

Add the okra to the baking dish; firmly but carefully shake the dish to combine the ingredients. Bake, uncovered, 15 minutes longer.

Add some or all of the remaining lemon juice to the baking dish; its flavour should be quite distinct. Add the remaining salt, pepper, olive oil to taste, and the parsley. Shake gently to mix all the ingredients together and serve at once.

Chicken with Walnut and Coriander Sauce
Kotopoulo me Saltsa Karythion
Serves 4 to 6

I first tasted this unusual dish in a tiny taverna in the mountains of northern Greece, as all around me the villagers gathered the autumn harvest from the ancient walnut trees in the village square.

Freshly gathered walnuts give the best flavour but plump older walnuts (blanched to remove any bitterness) can be substituted. I like the creamy sauce with a slightly coarse nutty texture, but use a food processor to produce a smooth version if you prefer. Serve with *pilafi* and a courgette dish.

115 ml/4 fl oz extra virgin olive oil
One 1.8-2.3 kg/4-5 lb chicken, cut into serving pieces and skin and excess fat removed
225 ml/8 fl oz dry white wine
3 bay leaves
350 ml/12 fl oz hot Chicken Stock (page 344) or water
Sea salt *and* freshly ground black pepper to taste
115 g/4 oz walnut halves or pieces (if not freshly gathered, blanch in boiling water for 1 minute)
2 tablespoons coriander seeds, crushed or 1/2 tablespoon ground coriander
1 large clove garlic, finely chopped
Pinch of cayenne pepper
Juice of 2 lemons, or to taste
3 large eggs

For serving
5 tablespoons coarsely chopped flat leaf parsley

Heat the oven to 180C/350F/gas mark 4. Heat half the olive oil in a heavy sauté pan and lightly brown the chicken pieces on all sides. Drain between layers of paper towels and transfer to a heavy casserole.

Drain off the oil from the pan, add the wine, and boil 1 minute, stirring in the browned bits from the bottom of the pan. Pour over the chicken, and add the bay leaves, stock, and salt and pepper. Cover and bake 45 minutes or until tender.

Meanwhile, in a large wooden mortar or bowl, pound the walnuts, coriander, garlic, and cayenne pepper to a fairly smooth paste. Add the remaining olive oil and half the lemon juice, drop by drop, pounding constantly, until well mixed. (Or you can do this in a food processor, using the pulse switch; do not over-process.) Season to taste and set aside.

Transfer the chicken to a serving platter and keep warm. Strain the liquid from the casserole, measure 350 ml/12 fl oz, and combine it with the walnut sauce. Set aside.

Whisk the eggs in a large bowl with a whisk or an electric mixer until pale and frothy. Gradually add the remaining lemon juice, beating constantly. Stir in the walnut sauce. Transfer to a heavy saucepan and heat slowly, stirring with a wooden spoon, until creamy and a little thickened, about 5 minutes; don't let it boil.

Pour the sauce over the chicken and sprinkle with the parsley. Serve at once.

Chicken in Avgolemono Sauce
Kotopoulo Avgolemono
Serves 4

The taste of this classic springtime dish is fresh and clean, the flavours light and fragrant: zesty lemon, delicate dill, and mild, vitamin-rich lettuce. Serve with Potatoes in a Clay Pot (page 205) or boiled new potatoes, and a dry white wine to enhance the subtle flavour. As a variation try *arnaki fricassé,* a popular version made with boned lamb instead of chicken.

One 1.6 kg/3¹/₂ lb chicken, cut into serving pieces, skin and excess fat removed
450 ml/16 fl oz Chicken Stock (page 344) or water
2 carrots, cut into large pieces
1 stick of celery, cut into large pieces
3 bay leaves
6 black peppercorns
6 spring onions, trimmed, with 5 cm/2 inches of green left intact
2 tablespoons extra virgin olive oil
2 heads of Cos or endive lettuce, trimmed of outer leaves and tough stems and cut into 6 mm/¹/₄ inch-wide ribbons
1 small bunch of fresh dill, coarsely chopped
Sea salt *and* freshly ground white pepper to taste
Juice of 2 large lemons
3 eggs, separated

Combine the chicken, stock, carrots, celery, bay leaves and peppercorns in a large heavy saucepan. Slowly bring to a boil, cover, reduce the heat, and simmer 40 minutes or until the chicken is tender.

Meanwhile, slice the spring onions lengthways in half and cut into 2.5 cm/1 inch-long pieces. Warm the olive oil in a heavy sauté pan and cook the spring onions over low heat until soft, about 2 minutes. Add the lettuce, cover, and cook, stirring once or twice, until wilted, about 2 minutes. Stir in the dill, salt and pepper, and half the lemon juice. Add the cooked chicken to the pan and set aside.

Strain the cooking broth into a bowl. Whisk the egg whites in a large bowl with a whisk or an electric mixer until they hold soft peaks. Add the yolks and whisk 1 minute longer. Slowly add the remaining lemon juice and the broth, whisking constantly. Transfer to a medium saucepan and gently heat over low heat, stirring constantly with a wooden spoon, until creamy and slightly thickened, about 5 minutes; don't let the sauce boil.

Pour the sauce over the chicken, place the sauté pan over low heat, and heat to warm through – do not boil. Season to taste, transfer to a warm serving dish, and serve at once.

Marinated Chicken with Tiny Onions and Vinegar
Kotopoulo Marinato me Xsithi
Serves 4

This ancient recipe brings together traditional ingredients favoured by Greek cooks for centuries. Honey and vinegar blend to produce a sweet-and-sour sauce and the piquant theme is repeated in the garnish of capers, parsley, and lemon zest. This delicious dish makes for easy entertaining too – much of the work can be done ahead of time. Serve with Pilaf with Green Lentils (page 229).

One 1.4–1.8 kg/3–4 lb chicken, cut into serving pieces, skin and excess fat removed
2 tablespoons extra virgin olive oil
1 tablespoon fresh lemon juice
1 teaspoon coarse-grain sea salt, or to taste
1 teaspoon freshly ground black pepper, or to taste
2 bay leaves
1 sprig of fresh thyme or rosemary
2 tablespoons unsalted butter
450 g/1 lb tiny boiling onions, peeled (page 132)
3 tablespoons aged red wine vinegar
1 teaspoon honey diluted with 1 tablespoon hot water
4 large ripe tomatoes, skinned, seeded, and diced
4 tablespoons small dark seedless raisins, soaked in 2 tablespoons hot water for 30 minutes

Rub the chicken with the olive oil, lemon juice, and most of the salt and pepper, and place in a bowl with the bay leaves and thyme. Cover and let marinate for 2 hours in the refrigerator.

Melt the butter in a heavy saucepan and add the chicken, marinade, including the herbs, and onions. Turn the chicken and onions to coat with the butter, cover tightly, and cook 40 minutes over low heat, or until the chicken is tender; add 2 tablespoons water if the butter begins to brown. Transfer the chicken to a warm platter, cover, and keep warm.

Pour off the pan juices, remove the fat with a spoon, and reserve; discard the bay leaves and thyme. Add the vinegar to the saucepan, raise the heat to medium high, and reduce to a syrup by rapid boiling. Add the honey and tomatoes and boil gently for 1 minute. Add the raisins, reserved pan juices, and remaining pepper, and reduce the heat.

Chop the parsley, capers, lemon zest, and remaining salt together. Spoon the onions and tomatoes around the chicken, sprinkle with the parsley mixture, and serve.

Bay-Scented Chicken with Figs
Kotopoulo me Dafni ke Sika
Serves 4

Bay trees and bushes flourish in Greece and the leaves are widely used in Greek cooking – a dozen leaves impart a pungent perfume to this dish. The chicken and figs are cooked separately so that their individual flavours remain distinct. Serve with Pilaf with Currants and Pine Nuts (page 227).

One 1.4-1.8 kg/3-4 lb chicken, cut into serving pieces, skin and excess fat removed
2 tablespoons extra virgin olive oil
1 teaspoon coarse-grain sea salt, or to taste
1 teaspoon freshly ground black pepper, or to taste
1 tablespoon unsalted butter
12 bay leaves
4 ripe figs, rinsed or 4 dried figs, soaked in 115 ml/4 fl oz dry red wine or water for 30 minutes
1¹/₂ tablespoons aged red wine vinegar
1 teaspoon honey
4 tablespoons dry red wine
115 ml/4 fl oz Chicken Stock (page 344) or water
24 Elitses or Niçoise olives, rinsed and pitted

For serving
Sprigs of watercress

Rub the chicken with the olive oil and half the salt and pepper and place in a bowl. Sprinkle with the bay leaves, cover, and refrigerate for 2-4 hours.

Heat the oven to 160C/325F/gas mark 3. Melt the butter in a flameproof baking dish over low heat. Add the chicken, bay leaves, and 2 tablespoons water. Cover and simmer 2-3 minutes. Transfer to the oven and bake 30-40 minutes, basting occasionally, until the chicken is cooked; if the butter begins to brown, add 2 tablespoons water.

Meanwhile, trim the stems from the figs, cut lengthways in half, and arrange in a baking dish, cut sides up. Add 3 tablespoons water (or the liquid remaining from soaking dried figs) and bake fresh figs 20 minutes, dried figs 10 minutes.

Transfer the chicken to a platter and keep warm. Discard the bay leaves. Add the vinegar to the dish and reduce the cooking liquid by rapid boiling to 2 tablespoons. Add the honey, wine, and stock, and reduce to 115 ml/4 fl oz. Add the olives and heat to warm.

Spoon the sauce over the chicken, and surround it with the figs and watercress sprigs.

Spit-Roasted Chicken
Kotopoulo tis Souvla
Serves 4

Homer relates that Odysseus enjoyed a spit roast or two on his homeward journey after the Trojan War. Modern Greeks have certainly inherited his love of them. Turn a corner in any Greek city and you'll meet with the enticing smell and sight of a turning spit threaded with sizzling golden-brown chickens. For a successful spit roast you need a plump young chicken, a patient cook to baste it constantly, and a good hardwood fire to sear the skin but keep the meat juicy.

Two 1.2-1.4 kg/2½-3 lb chickens, excess fat removed
Juice of 1 large lemon
115 ml/4 fl oz extra virgin olive oil
1 teaspoon sea salt
1 teaspoon freshly ground black pepper
1 tablespoon finely chopped fresh oregano or flat leaf parsley

For serving
1 large bunch of watercress, sprigs only
Lemon wedges
24 Elitses or 12 Amfissa or Niçoise olives
Kephalotyri or mild *feta* cheese, cut into slices

Rub the chickens with the lemon juice and half the olive oil. Set aside for 1 hour. Prepare the fire.

Fasten the wing tips over the chicken breasts with short metal or wooden skewers. Insert the spit into each chicken to dissect the wishbone and tie the drumsticks and tail together; the chickens will now revolve with the spit.

Brush the chickens with the remaining olive oil, and place the spit about 30-38 cm/12-15 inches above the hot coals. Roast 10 minutes, frequently turning the spit, catching the juices in a pan held under the chickens.

Raise the spit 5-7 cm/2-3 inches and roast 30-45 minutes longer, turning the spit and basting with the juices, until deep golden brown. The juices will gradually darken and become very aromatic; to prevent them from burning, add a few tablespoons water to the pan. Check if the meat is cooked by piercing the thickest point of one chicken thigh with a skewer or knife; the juices should run clear. Sprinkle the chickens with salt and pepper.

Strain the pan juices into a small saucepan. Heat to warm and stir in the oregano. Carve the chicken into serving pieces.

Line a platter with the watercress, place the chickens on top, and surround with the lemon wedges. Serve the sauce, olives, and cheese separately.

Spit-Roasted Mountain Rabbit
Kounelli tou Vounou
Serves 4-5

Mountain villagers in Greece are practised in the art of creating memorable feasts from simple foods. Spit-roasted rabbit, a variety of salads, olives, cheese, country bread, and wild pears, all washed down with fiery raki, make for splendid – and lively – village celebrations. Aubergine dishes are particularly good with spit-roasted rabbit. If raki is not to your taste, choose a full-bodied red wine.

One fresh 2.3 kg/5 lb rabbit, prepared by the butcher (see Note)
1 tablespoon wine vinegar
Juice of 1 lemon
3 sprigs of fresh thyme
2 bay leaves, broken in pieces
2 shallots, thinly sliced
4 juniper berries, lightly crushed
5 tablespoons extra virgin olive oil
115 ml/4 fl oz Chicken Stock (page 344) or white wine
1 tablespoon Dijon mustard
1 teaspoon cracked black pepper, or to taste
Sea salt to taste
2 tablespoons finely chopped flat leaf parsley

Rub the rabbit all over with the vinegar, then rinse it and dry with paper towels. Place in a glass or china dish with the lemon juice, thyme, bay leaves, shallots, juniper berries, and olive oil. Tightly cover and marinate for 12-48 hours in the refrigerator.

Prepare the fire.

Secure the rabbit to the spit and set it 30-38 cm/12-15 inches above medium fire. Set a pan on a rack underneath to catch the juices. Add the stock to the marinade and baste the rabbit with this mixture. Roast, turning and basting, until the rabbit is cooked, about 50 minutes. Check if the meat is cooked by piercing the thickest part of one thigh with a skewer or knife; the juices should run clear.

Strain the pan juices and any remaining marinade into a small saucepan. Add the mustard, pepper, salt, and parsley, and heat to warm. Cut the rabbit into serving pieces, arrange on a warm platter, and pour over just enough sauce to moisten. Serve the remaining sauce separately.

Note This recipe can also be made with rabbit pieces rather than a whole rabbit. Use a hinged grill to hold the pieces and grill over medium-low fire for 15-20 minutes, basting frequently and turning occasionally.

Rabbit Stifado
Kounelli Stifado
Serves 6

Stifado is a favourite family casserole in winter: rich and sustaining, spiced with cumin, cloves, and cinnamon, it's a dish full of character. Although it's traditionally made with wild rabbit, I have made delicious versions with chicken, beef, and pork, and a neighbour on Crete makes a remarkable snail *Stifado*. The most important ingredient, however, is onions – large quantities are essential to produce the characteristic rich sweet sauce. Like most stews, *Stifado* can be made ahead of time and it tastes even better when reheated.

1.4 kg/3 lb small boiling onions, about 2-2.5 cm/³/₄-1 inch in diameter
One 2.3 kg/5 lb rabbit, cut into 8 serving pieces and excess fat removed
Plain flour, for dredging
175 ml/6 fl oz extra virgin olive oil, or to taste
115 ml/4 fl oz aged red wine vinegar
2 cloves garlic, finely chopped
6 large tomatoes, skinned, seeded, and diced
1 teaspoon honey
One 5 cm/2 inch cinnamon stick
1¹/₂ tablespoons ground cumin
8 cloves
1 teaspoon ground allspice
4 bay leaves
Zest of 1 orange, removed in large strips and tied together with kitchen string
2 tablespoons tomato purée diluted with 115 ml/4 fl oz water
225 ml/8 fl oz red wine

Sea salt to taste
$^1/_2$ tablespoon cracked black pepper, or to taste

For serving
4 tablespoons finely chopped flat leaf parsley

Slice the root end off each onion and remove the feathery outside layer of skin. Blanch the onions in boiling water for 5 minutes, drain, and peel. Set aside.

Heat the oven to 180C/350F/gas mark 4. Rinse the rabbit pieces and pat dry with paper towels. Lightly dredge with flour. Heat 4 tablespoons of the olive oil in a large heavy sauté pan and lightly brown the meat on all sides. Drain between layers of paper towels and transfer to an earthenware or enamel-lined cast-iron casserole.

Add the onions to the pan and sauté 10 minutes, or until lightly browned. Transfer to the casserole.

Drain off the oil from the pan and add the vinegar. Boil 1 minute, scraping up the browned bits from the bottom and sides with a wooden spoon. Add the garlic, tomatoes, honey, cinnamon, cumin, cloves, allspice, bay leaves, and orange zest, and boil 1 minute. Stir in the tomato purée, red wine, and remaining olive oil and season with salt and pepper. Pour over the meat, cover tightly, and bake 20 minutes. Reduce the oven temperature to 150C/300F/gas mark 2 and bake 1$^1/_2$ hours longer; if the liquid in the casserole reduces to less than 450 ml/16 fl oz, add hot water as necessary.

Discard the orange zest and season to taste. Sprinkle with the parsley and serve hot.

Marinated Hare with Juniper Berries
Lagos Stifado
Serves 6-8

This is a wonderful cold-weather dish, strongly spiced and rich in flavour. The marinade can also be used with great success for other meats, such as beef. Serve with a *pilafi* or *macaronia* dish and *khorta* (page 220) or a green salad.

One 3.2–3.6 kg/7–8 lb hare, skinned, cut into 12–14 serving pieces
(page 346), trimmed, and excess fat removed
350 ml/12 fl oz aged red wine vinegar
6 cloves garlic
6 juniper berries, lightly crushed
6 whole allspice berries
3 cloves
12 black peppercorns
One 7 cm/3 inch cinnamon stick, broken into pieces
8 bay leaves

115 ml/4 fl oz extra virgin olive oil, or to taste
900 g/2 lb ripe tomatoes, skinned, seeded, and diced
1 tablespoon honey
$^1/_2$ tablespoon cracked black pepper, or more to taste
1 tablespoon paprika
2 tablespoons ground coriander
1.8 kg/4 lb small boiling onions, peeled (see previous recipe)
225 ml/8 fl oz robust red wine
1 tablespoon dried thyme or winter savory (page 15)
Sea salt to taste

For serving
Coarsely chopped fresh coriander

Rinse the meat and pat dry with paper towels. Place in a china or glass bowl and add the vinegar, garlic, juniper berries, allspice, cloves, peppercorns, cinnamon, and 4 of the bay leaves. Tightly cover and refrigerate for 1-2 days, occasionally turning the meat in the marinade.

Heat the oven to 180C/350F/gas mark 4. Transfer the meat to an earthenware or enamel-lined cast-iron casserole.

Pour the marinade (and spices) into a small saucepan and reduce to about 175 ml/6 fl oz by rapid boiling over high heat; strain over the meat and discard the solids. Add half the olive oil, the tomatoes, honey, pepper, paprika, coriander, onions, red wine, and remaining bay leaves to the meat. Cover and bake 20 minutes.

Reduce the oven temperature to 150C/300F/gas mark 2 and bake 2$^1/_2$ hours longer; add hot water as necessary if there appears to be less than 600 ml/1 pint of liquid in the casserole.

Add the thyme, salt, and remaining olive oil and bake 15 minutes longer. Season to taste, sprinkle with the fresh coriander, and serve hot.

Pheasant over a Fire
Fasianos sti Skhara
Serves 4 to 6

In Hania on the island of Crete, there is a tiny taverna set into the rock, and the focal point of its one cave-like room is a huge open fire over which plump pheasants are often slowly roasting. The birds are stuffed with a country mixture of bacon, mushrooms, and pine nuts and wrapped in blackberry leaves and pork fat, and the whole room fills with their heavenly aroma.

4 young pheasants, giblets reserved
Sea salt and freshly ground black pepper to taste
115 ml/4 fl oz extra virgin olive oil
2 tablespoons unsalted butter
115 g/4 oz lean bacon, cut into tiny dice

450 g/1 lb mushrooms, trimmed and cut into small dice
50 g/2 oz pine nuts, chopped
4 tablespoons port or sweet red wine
8 thin slices streaky bacon
8 slices wholemeal bread, crusts removed
1 clove garlic, cut into 3 or 4 pieces
2 tablespoons hot water

Prepare the fire. Rub each pheasant inside and out with salt and pepper, half the olive oil, and 1½ tablespoons of the butter. Set aside. Trim and finely chop the giblets.

Heat the remaining butter and 1 tablespoon olive oil in a heavy saucepan and sauté the giblets and bacon dice 2 minutes over low heat, stirring constantly. Add the mushrooms, pine nuts, and pepper and cook 2 minutes longer. Stir in the port and remove from the heat.

Stuff the pheasants with the mushroom mixture and sew up the openings or fasten with small skewers. Cover the breasts and legs with the streaky bacon, securing it with toothpicks.

Secure the pheasants to the spit and set the spit 60 cm/2 feet above medium-hot coals. Baste with olive oil, catching the juices in a pan held under the pheasants. Roast, turning the spit and basting with the pan juices, until cooked, about 50 minutes. Remove the streaky bacon 10 minutes before the pheasants are done, to let them brown. Check if the meat is cooked by piercing the thickest part of one pheasant thigh with a skewer or knife; the juices should run clear.

Meanwhile, heat the remaining olive oil in a large sauté pan and sauté the garlic until it is pale golden and the oil is aromatic. Discard the garlic. Fry the bread until golden on both sides and drain on paper towels. Cut into triangles and keep warm.

Remove the stuffing from the pheasants with a spoon and keep warm. Pour off any juices from the cavities of the pheasants into the pan of roasting juices and add the hot water. Heat over medium-low heat, stir in the browned bits from the bottom and sides of the pan with a wooden spoon, and strain the sauce into a pitcher or gravy boat.

Carve the pheasants and arrange on a warm serving platter. Spread the stuffing on the slices of fried bread and arrange around the pheasants. Serve the sauce separately.

Hunter's Pot
Tsoukali Kinigou
Serves 4

This rich and herb-scented dish is traditionally made with partridge, pigeon, or guinea fowl – the spoils of a day's hunting in ancient times. I have made highly successful versions with game hens and chicken. It is a sweet and fragrant casserole that will fill your kitchen with a warm homely aroma to create a wonderful welcome for family and friends. Serve with Potatoes in a Clay Pot (page 205), fried aubergines and a robust red wine.

2 large partridges or 4 pigeons, giblets reserved
Juice of 1/2 lemon
7 tablespoons extra virgin olive oil
Sea salt *and* freshly ground black pepper to taste
115 g/4 oz lean bacon, finely diced
1 tablespoon unsalted butter
2 medium carrots, finely diced
1 small onion, finely chopped
3 bay leaves
1 tablespoon fresh rosemary, crumbled
1 tablespoon dried thyme, crumbled
4 cloves garlic
3 tablespoons finely chopped parsley
350 ml/12 fl oz dry white wine or Chicken Stock (page 344) or a mixture of both
8 fresh or brine-preserved vine leaves, rinsed, blanched in boiling water for 5 seconds if fresh, 3 seconds if preserved, and drained
25 g/1 oz fresh coarse wholemeal breadcrumbs
20 Elitses or 10 Niçoise olives, rinsed, pitted, and coarsely chopped

Rub the partridges inside and out with the lemon juice, 3 tablespoons of the olive oil, and salt and pepper. Set aside for 1 hour.

Trim the giblets. Heat 1 tablespoon of the remaining olive oil in a heavy sauté pan and lightly brown the bacon and giblets. With a slotted spoon, transfer to a heavy casserole. Add the butter to the pan, lightly brown the partridges on all sides over medium-low heat, and transfer to the casserole.

Heat the oven to 190C/375F/gas mark 5. Add the carrots, onion, bay leaves, rosemary, thyme, garlic, and half the parsley to the pan and reduce the heat to low. Sauté 15-20 minutes, or until golden brown, stirring occasionally with a wooden spoon. Transfer to the casserole.

Add the wine to the pan and bring to a boil, scraping up the browned bits from the bottom and sides of the pan with a wooden spoon. Pour into the casserole, cover the partridges with the vine leaves, and tightly cover the casserole. Reduce the oven temperature to 160C/325F/gas mark 3 and bake 40-50 minutes.

Meanwhile, heat the remaining 3 tablespoons olive oil in a frying pan. Add the breadcrumbs and fry, stirring occasionally, until golden brown. Drain on paper towels.

Transfer the partridges to a warm platter, discarding the vine leaves and giblets, and keep warm. Pour the liquid from the casserole into a shallow saucepan and reduce by rapid boiling over high heat to 175 ml/6 fl oz; add any juices that have accumulated around the partridges. Add the breadcrumbs, olives, and remaining parsley to the vegetables in the casserole, stir just to mix, and return to the oven to heat through. Strain the sauce. Spoon the vegetables around the partridges, pour over the sauce, and serve at once.

Note You can substitute 4 whole game hens or one 1.6 kg/3 1/2 lb chicken, cut into serving pieces and skin and excess fat removed, for the partridges.

Grilled Quail
Ortikia tis Skhara
Serves 4

Quail is a popular autumn dish in Greece and, in some country tavernas, it is still cooked in a traditional way. Rubbed with olive oil and herbs, the quail is wrapped in red clay and baked until the clay hardens – at the table the pot is cracked open with a dramatic flourish to reveal a perfectly cooked bird. The nearest modern equivalent is baking in parchment or in a pot tightly sealed with a flour-and-water paste. Or try this recipe, which gives the tiny birds an exquisite delicate flavour; game hens can be substituted if quail is not available.

4 quail, livers reserved
Juice of 1 large lemon
1 teaspoon freshly ground black pepper, or more to taste
1 onion, sliced
6 sprigs of parsley
6 bay leaves
3 sprigs of dried *rigani* (page 14) or fresh oregano or marjoram
6 tablespoons extra virgin olive oil
4 slices wholemeal bread, crusts removed and cut into triangles
$^1/_2$ tablespoon aromatic honey, such as Hymettus
1 teaspoon Dijon mustard
Fine-grain sea salt to taste

For serving
Sprigs of watercress
Lemon wedges

Using poultry shears or a sharp knife, split the quail along their breastbones, turn over, and flatten by gently pressing on the backbones with the palm of your hand. Combine half the lemon juice, the pepper, and 3 tablespoons of the olive oil in a bowl. Place the quail in this marinade and set aside for 1-2 hours, turning the quail occasionally.

Prepare the fire.

Arrange a grill rack over medium-hot coals and brush the grill with olive oil. Remove the quail from the marinade, leaving all the herbs in the bowl. Grill until lightly browned on both sides, about 15 minutes.

Meanwhile, heat the remaining olive oil and fry the breadcrumbs over medium-low heat until golden on both sides. Dip the livers in the marinade and fry them. Mash gently, spread on the fried bread, and keep warm.

Strain the marinade. Combine the honey, mustard, and remaining lemon juice in a saucepan, add the marinade, and heat to warm.

Arrange the quail on a warm platter, season with salt and pepper, pour over the sauce, and surround with the fried bread, watercress, and lemon wedges.

Duckling Thessalia-Style
Papaki Thessalias
Serves 4

Highly perfumed lemons are the secret of this sweet roasted duckling. Lemon juice is rubbed inside the duckling, and it is also used in the roasting dish so that the meat absorbs its fragrance throughout the slow cooking. Serve with Beetroot Island-Style (page 182) or Turnips and Grapes in Aromatic Sauce (page 188).

One 1.4 kg/3 lb duckling, excess fat removed and giblets reserved
1 carrot, scrubbed, and cut into large pieces
1 onion, sliced
3 bay leaves
2 sprigs of fresh thyme
Sea salt *and* freshly ground black pepper to taste
Juice of 1 large lemon
4 tablespoons extra virgin olive oil
4 juniper berries
3 cloves
Zest of $^1/_2$ orange, removed in thin strips
50 g/2 oz fresh coarse wholemeal breadcrumbs
3 tablespoons finely chopped flat leaf parsley
50 g/2 oz lightly toasted pine nuts
24 Elitses or 12 Niçoise olives, soaked in hot water for 5 seconds, drained, pitted, and coarsely chopped

For serving
Sprigs of watercress
Lemon wedges

Place all the giblets except the liver in a small saucepan, and add the carrot, onion, 1 bay leaf, 1 sprig of thyme, salt and pepper, and 350 ml/12 fl oz water. Bring to a boil, cover, reduce the heat, and simmer 40 minutes. Strain the broth into a bowl and set aside; discard the solids.

Rub the duckling inside and out with half the lemon juice, the olive oil, and salt and pepper. Set aside.

Heat the oven to 190C/375F/gas mark 5.

Place the remaining 2 bay leaves, 1 sprig of thyme, the juniper berries, cloves, and orange zest in the duckling's cavity and sew up the opening or fasten with small skewers. Lay the duckling on its side in a heavy baking dish and add 4 tablespoons water to the dish. Roast, uncovered, for 20 minutes. Remove the fat with a spoon and set aside. Add the remaining lemon juice to the dish and stir in the browned bits (residue) from the bottom and sides of the dish with a wooden spoon. Roast 5 minutes longer to caramelize the juices. Pour the pan juices into a measuring cup and add enough reserved fat to make about 4 tablespoons. Set aside.

Turn the duckling onto its other side, pour over 175 ml/6 fl oz of the reserved broth, and roast 20 minutes longer, basting occasionally. Turn the duckling breast upwards and roast until deep golden brown, about 10 minutes.

Meanwhile, heat the reserved pan juices in a heavy frying pan. Add the breadcrumbs and cook over low heat until lightly browned and most of the liquid has been absorbed. Stir in the parsley, pine nuts, and olives and heat through. Keep warm.

Pour off the pan juices from the baking dish and remove the fat with a spoon. Add the spices and any juices from the cavity of the duckling and strain the sauce into a warm serving bowl or gravy boat.

Carve the duckling. Spread the breadcrumb mixture on a warm serving plate, arrange the duckling pieces on top, surround with the watercress and lemon wedges, and coat with a little sauce. Serve the remaining sauce separately.

Meats

kreata

According to Greek mythology, the god Prometheus made mankind from clay and, in opposition to Zeus, the king of the gods, stole fire for his new creation from the forge of the fire god Hephaestus. Fitting, then, that many of the best Greek meat dishes are readily associated with this gift of the ancient gods, with the crackling brilliance of living flame and the soft, lambent glow of red embers.

Spit roasting and grilling over an open fire has been an integral part of Greek life for centuries, and equipment for long-ago barbecues has been found on Minoan archaeological sites. Its popularity is undiminished today, and for anyone who has visited Greece or the islands, the sizzling aroma of herb-perfumed meat roasting outdoors and the scented haze of wispy wood smoke inevitably conjures up myriad images of the country.

Tradition, custom, and experience dictate the preferred aromatics and flavourings for different meats and the types of wood used for the fire. Pine is said to give an authentic traditional taste, grapevine clippings bring out the fine flavour of game, and hardwoods such as olive, apple, pear, or cherry make perfect embers over which to grill meat to tender succulence. Charcoal, of course, is more convenient; the type made from softwoods like cedar or pine makes a perfect fire for the meats in this chapter, or you can just use charcoal briquettes.

Easter, the most important date in the Greek Orthodox calendar, is marked not by a dish of amazing intricacy and complexity, but by a splendidly simple aromatic spit-roasted tender young lamb. Lamb, kid, and suckling pig are all favourites for spit roasting, and for these meats aromatic marinades are important; many of those used today are traditional recipes based on vinegar, wine, yogurt, pomegranate juice, and onion juice. An infinite variety of other meat delicacies also acquire a unique flavour when marinated and grilled, most notably *souvlakia* – small pieces of deliciously tender meat, speared on skewers, and grilled over charcoal – and *sheftalia* – highly-seasoned sausage. All over Greece *souvlakia* (from the Greek word, *souvla*, for spit or skewer), *sheftalia*, and a variety of other sausage snacks are sold from *souvlaki* stands – covered stalls or tiny cafés boasting a fierce grill, a makeshift counter, and, perhaps, a rickety table or two. These stands are everywhere and are never short of customers, day or night.

The Greek repertoire also includes versatile oven-baked meat dishes. In the country these dishes are still cooked in the traditional wood-burning *fournos*, and *fournos* cooking does produce a truly delectable and unique flavour, especially if clay pots are used. The meat simmers gently in its own juices, enhanced with herbs, spices and vegetables; the result is meltingly tender meat covered with a thick aromatic sauce. While the open-air spit roasts and grilled dishes of Greece are inspired by the delicate fragrance of hillside and mountain herbs, the flavours of these oven-baked dishes are stronger and more pungent. They are characterized by heady Eastern spices and a generous use of strong flavourings. The oven-baked dishes in this chapter are traditional recipes adapted for use with modern ovens and enamel-lined cast-iron pots, but if you do possess a partly glazed clay pot, so much the better.

The Paschal Lamb
Arnaki Paskalino
Serves 10 to 12

After the dark austerity of the Lenten fast comes the abundance and joy of the season of rebirth. All over Greece the centrepiece of the celebratory meal, traditionally cooked by men, is spit-roasted milk-fed lamb. As early as sunrise on Easter Day coils of fragrant smoke begin to rise from pinewood fires in preparation for the midday feast. All morning the whole lamb turns on a long spit and the cooks, using brushes made from rosemary sprigs, lemon leaves, or branches of thyme, baste the meat with olive oil. My memories of this splendid celebration always explode with brilliant colour – the burning red of spring poppies, the ecclesiastical purple of wild irises, the paint-box blue skies – and above all, an atmosphere of happiness and rejoicing. Only the finest accompaniments are fit for the Paschal Lamb – spring vegetables, especially young asparagus and broad beans, a salad of Cos lettuce, and, of course, the special Easter Bread (page 259). For this roast you will need a spit around 1.8 metres/6 feet long to pass through the whole length of the lamb; for smaller parties this recipe works equally well with a leg of lamb.

1 milk-fed lamb, about 10 kg/22 lb
Juice of 2 lemons
Lemon wedges

Prepare the fire.

Rub the lamb inside and out with the juice of 1 lemon and sew up the stomach using a larding needle. Pierce the skin in a dozen or so places with the point of a sharp knife, and baste liberally with the olive oil.

Secure the lamb to the spit and place it about 60 cm/2 feet above the glowing embers. Roast 2-2½ hours, slowly moving the spit closer to the embers until the lamb is only 15 cm/6 inches from the heat, and catching the juices in a pan. Baste liberally at frequent intervals with the pan juices and remaining olive oil; near the end of the roasting time, add the juice of the second lemon to the pan.

To make the sauce, add a few tablespoons of water to the pan juices and stir to mix. Strain into a small saucepan and gently heat to warm. Carve the lamb, arrange on a large warm platter, and sprinkle with salt and pepper. Pour some of the sauce over and surround with the lemon wedges. Serve the remaining sauce separately.

Spit-Roasted Leg of Lamb
Arnaki tis Souvla
Serves 6

For really tender meat and a rich country flavour let the lamb marinate overnight and be sure to baste it frequently as it roasts. The marinade given here is also very good with kid (page 146); for a different flavour try the marinade on thta same page.

One 2.3–2.8 kg/5–6 lb leg of lamb
Red wine vinegar, to rub over the lamb
3 tablespoons coriander seeds, crushed
2 tablespoons fresh rosemary, chopped
$^1/_2$ tablespoon freshly ground black pepper
Sea salt to taste
Juice of 2 small lemons (reserve 1 juiced lemon half)
115 ml/4 fl oz extra virgin olive oil
50–115 ml/2–4 fl oz dry red wine or water (to taste)

For serving
Sprigs of fresh rosemary

Trim off any excess fat or tough skin from the lamb and pierce the meat in a dozen places with the point of a sharp knife. Moisten a cloth with the vinegar and wipe the lamb all over to remove any gamy flavour. Combine the coriander, rosemary, pepper, salt, and lemon juice in a bowl, and whisk in the olive oil. Rub this marinade over the lamb, cover loosely, and set aside for 4 to 6 hours at room temperature, or refrigerate overnight.

Prepare the fire.

Run the spit lengthways through the leg and arrange it so the lamb is about 30 cm/12 inches above medium-hot coals. Roast 45 minutes to 1 hour, slowly moving the spit closer to the coals, until the lamb is only 15 cm/6 inches from the heat; pierce the lemon half with a skewer and use it to baste the lamb liberally at frequent intervals with the marinade, catching the juices in a pan.

Strain the pan juices and any remaining marinade into a small saucepan. Add the wine to the pan that held the pan juices, stir in any browned bits from the bottom of the pan, and strain into the saucepan. Heat to warm.

Slice the lamb, arrange on a warm platter, pour over some of the sauce, and garnish with the rosemary sprigs. Serve the remaining sauce separately.

Spit-Roasted Easter Sausages
Kokoretsia
Serves 8 to 10

Kokoretsia, made from the offal of the Paschal Lamb, are an integral part of the Easter Day feast, eaten as either a mid-morning snack or a *meze*. The diced offal is marinated in herbs and spices, garlic, and lemon juice, wrapped in the lamb's intestine, and roasted over glowing charcoal. The 'sausages' are then cut into thick slices and sprinkled with sliced onion, salt, and parsley. *Kokoretsia* are served with lemon wedges, olives, and radishes as a *meze*.

225 g/8 oz lamb's liver
4 lamb's kidneys
2 small lamb's hearts
2 lamb's sweetbreads
Other lamb's offal, *optional*
Sea salt
1 tablespoon wine vinegar
Juice of 1 large lemon
$1/2$ teaspoon ground cumin
1 teaspoon dried thyme, crumbled
1 tablespoon dried *rigani* (page 14), crumbled
$1/2$ tablespoon cracked black pepper
75–115 ml/3–4 fl oz extra virgin olive oil (to taste)
4 bay leaves
1 large clove garlic, lightly crushed, *optional*
1 small bunch of flat leaf parsley, leaves finely chopped
About 225 g/8 oz prepared sheep's intestine or sausage casings (page 349)
About 175 g/6 oz pork caul fat (page 349)

For serving
1 small red or mild onion, thinly sliced

Trim off and discard all the fat sinew, valves and membranes from the offal. Dissolve 1 tablespoon of salt and the vinegar in a bowl of water, and soak the meats for 30 minutes.

Drain and pat dry with paper towels. Chop the liver, kidneys and heart into 6 mm/$1/4$ inch dice and the other offal into smaller dice.

Combine the lemon juice, cumin, thyme, *rigani*, pepper, 1 teaspoon of salt and 4 tablespoons of the olive oil in a large bowl. Add the meats, bay leaves and garlic, and mix together with your hands. Cover and set aside for 1 hour.

Prepare the fire.

Discard the bay leaves and garlic, and add half the parsley to the meats; mix well. Stuff the intestine or sausage casing to make 1 large or 2 small sausages, and tie at both ends. Carefully spread out 1 or 2 sheets of caul fat and wrap the sausage(s) in it. Insert a skewer the length of the sausage(s).

Add the remaining olive oil to any marinade remaining in the bowl and baste the sausages liberally with this.

Arrange the skewer(s) 30 cm/12 inches above medium-hot coals. Slowly roast thin sausages 45 minutes, plump sausages 1-1^1/$_4$ hours, turning and basting frequently, until browned on all sides.

Cut into 1 cm/^{1}/$_2$ inch slices, sprinkle with the onion, salt, and the remaining parsley, and serve immediately.

Spit-Roasted Kid
Katsiki tis Souvla
Serves 8 to 10

Spit roasting is the best way to cook young kid, and a long marinating time produces the most tender, flavoursome meat. The strong marinade in this mountain recipe includes garlic, herbs, bay leaves, orange zest, peppercorns, and juniper berries, and the meat rests in this heady mixture for 36 hours. The finishing touch is the clear sharp flavour of a sauce made from blueberries. Fresh blueberries are occasionally available in our better supermarkets and greengrocers; blueberries preserved in light syrup are available year-round. Greeks begin a festive meal like this with *mezedes* of olives, cheese, aubergines, and beans; with the kid they enjoy Potatoes in a Clay Pot (page 205), country bread, and a green salad. A full-bodied red wine such as Naoussa is the perfect accompaniment.

One 2.8–3.3 kg/6–7 lb leg of kid, prepared by the butcher
4 tablespoons wine vinegar

Marinade
2 onions, sliced
3 carrots, scrubbed, and cut into large pieces
2 cloves garlic, lightly crushed
2 sprigs each of fresh thyme *and* rosemary
3 sprigs of fresh summer savory, (page 15, *optional*)
6 bay leaves
1 tablespoon chopped dried orange zest (page 348)
24 black peppercorns
8 juniper berries, lightly crushed
Dry red wine, to cover the meat

225 ml/8 fl oz extra virgin olive oil
115 g/4 oz bacon, cut into small dice
1 tablespoon plain flour
450 ml/16 fl oz Light Meat Stock or Meat Stock (page 347)

5 tablespoons fresh blueberries or 4 tablespoons strained preserved blueberries (see Note)

$^1/_2$ tablespoon cracked black pepper, or to taste

Sea salt to taste

For serving

Watercress sprigs

Soak a cloth with the vinegar and rub the meat all over to remove any stall. Rinse and pat dry. Place all the marinade ingredients in a large glass or china bowl, add the meat, cover, and set aside for 36 hours at room temperature.

Remove the meat, onion, and carrots from the marinade and pat dry with paper towels. Trim the meat of all fat and skin, and cut these trimmings into 2.5 cm/1 inch pieces. Dice the onion and carrot. Set aside.

Bring the marinade, including all the herbs and spices, to the boil in a large heavy saucepan and reduce to 600 ml/1 pint by rapid boiling. Strain and set aside.

Prepare the fire.

Run the spit lengthways through the legs and arrange it so the kid is about 30 cm/12 inches above medium-hot coals. Roast 2-2$^1/_2$ hours (20 minutes per 450 g/1 lb), basting frequently with the reduced marinade and olive oil and catching the juices in a pan.

Meanwhile, add 2 tablespoons of the olive oil to a heavy saucepan and sauté the bacon and meat trimmings over low heat until browned. Add the diced onion and carrot and lightly brown, stirring frequently. Sprinkle with the flour, stir to mix, and cook 1 minute. Add 300 ml/10 fl oz of the reduced marinade and the stock, reduce the heat, and simmer until reduced to 450 ml/16 fl oz. Strain into another saucepan, add the syrup, pepper, and salt, and set aside.

Skim the excess fat from the pan juices and stir the juices into the sauce. Season to taste.

Slice the meat, arrange on a warm platter, surround with the watercress, and spoon over enough sauce to moisten. Serve the remaining sauce separately.

Note To make blueberry syrup, combine 275 g/10 oz fresh berries and 2 tablespoons water in a non-reactive saucepan and simmer for 10 minutes. Press through a sieve, preferably plastic, measure the juice, and return to the saucepan. Add an equal amount of sugar and simmer for 10 minutes. Strain and store in airtight jars or bottles for up to 1 month. Preserved blueberries need only to be drained and pressed through a sieve.

The Villagers' Grilled Lamb
Arni Skharas Khoriatiko

Serves 4

Fresh and fragrant country herbs, perfumed lemons, and tender lean meat are the essence of this simple classic dish. Since the cooking is fast, the lamb benefits from the tenderizing and flavouring of a sharp marinade of lemon juice, pepper, and pungent bay leaves. The flavourful pan juices, to which a liberal amount of *rigani* is added, make a delicious sauce and aubergine or bean dishes are the perfect accompaniment.

8 small loin or rib lamb chops
Juice of 1 large lemon (reserve 1 juiced lemon half)
Cracked black pepper to taste
4 bay leaves
4-6 tablespoons extra virgin olive oil, to taste
Coarse-grain sea salt
2 tablespoons dried *rigani* (page 14), briefly pounded in a mortar or
1 tablespoon dried thyme or rosemary, crumbled

For serving
Lemon wedges

Trim off most of the fat from the chops and carefully wipe them to remove any bone splinters. Place in a glass or china bowl. Sprinkle with the lemon juice, pepper, and the bay leaves, cover, and set aside for 3-4 hours, turning the chops occasionally.

Prepare the fire.

Set a grill rack 10 cm/4 inches above hot coals. Lightly brush the grill and the chops with the olive oil, and add the remaining oil to any marinade left in the bowl. Discard the bay leaves. Pierce the lemon half with a skewer and use this as a 'baster'.

Grill the lamb until browned on both sides, basting frequently with the marinade and catching the juices in a pan. Raise the grill 5 cm/2 inches and grill about 5 minutes longer for rare meat, 15 minutes longer for well done. A few minutes before the chops are done, add salt, pepper, and half the *rigani* to the marinade, and baste the chops several times.

Add 2 or 3 tablespoons water to the pan juices, stir to mix, and heat; strain this sauce. Arrange the chops on a warm platter and pour over enough sauce to moisten. Sprinkle with salt, pepper, and the remaining *rigani* and surround with the lemon wedges. Serve the remaining sauce separately.

Marinated Lamb Souvlakia with Pilaf
Arni Souvlakia me Pilafi
Serves 6

This is wonderful party food – preparation can be done well ahead of time and then it takes only minutes to produce succulent *souvlakia*, grilled to a dark crust outside, tender and juicy within. To keep the meat tender, serve *souvlakia* immediately they're ready – with bowls of radishes, olives, *feta* cheese, *khorta* (page 220), and a fresh bean or green salad.

1.2 kg/2¹/₂ lb lean leg of lamb
Juice of 2 lemons
115 ml/4 fl oz extra virgin olive oil

Coarse-grain sea salt *and* cracked black pepper to taste
24 (dry) bay leaves
2 tablespoons dried *rigani* (page 14)
1 teaspoon dried thyme

Pilaf
50 g/2 oz unsalted butter
50 g/2 oz crushed (broken into small pieces) vermicelli
350 g/12 oz long-grain rice
1 teaspoon ground allspice
1 teaspoon sea salt
850 ml/1¹/₂ pints Light Lamb Stock (page 347) or water

For serving
1 small bunch of flat leaf parsley, leaves coarsely chopped
Finely grated zest of 1 small lemon or 1 tablespoon finely chopped Preserved
Lemon (page 18)
2 small red or mild onions, cut into thin rings
3 lemons, cut into wedges

Cut the meat into 2.5 cm/1 inch cubes and trim off any fat or sinew. (Reserve the bones to make stock.)

Combine the juice of 1¹/₂ lemons, 5 tablespoons of the olive oil, and salt and pepper in a glass or china bowl. Add the lamb, mix together with your hands, cover tightly, and refrigerate for 4 hours or overnight.

One hour before grilling, remove the bowl from the refrigerator.

Melt the butter in a heavy saucepan and cook the vermicelli 10 minutes over medium-low heat, or until the butter is dark nutty brown. Add the rice and allspice and cook 1 minute, stirring constantly. Add the salt and stock, raise the heat, and boil 8 minutes, or until holes appear in the surface of the rice. Turn off the heat, place 2 layers of paper towels over the top of the saucepan, and cover with the lid. Set aside for 30 minutes in a warm place such as the back of the stove.

Meanwhile, prepare the fire.

Remove the meat from the marinade and thread onto 6 lightly oiled skewers, occasionally alternating the pieces with the bay leaves. Brush liberally with the marinade.

Set the grill rack 7 cm/3 inches above the hot coals and lightly brush with olive oil. Grill the *souvlakia* until browned on all sides, basting frequently with the marinade. Raise the grill 5 cm/2 inches and grill 8-10 minutes longer, basting, until the meat is dark and crusty outside, juicy and tender inside.

Pound the *rigani* and thyme together in a small mortar until aromatic and add to the remaining marinade along with olive oil to taste. Continue basting the *souvlakia* with this mixture.

Chop the parsley and lemon zest together until mixed, and combine with the onion, remaining lemon juice, and salt and pepper.

Spread the *pilafi* on a warm platter. Using a fork, push the *souvlakia* off the skewers onto the rice. Sprinkle with the onions, remaining marinade, and salt and pepper, and surround with the lemon wedges.

Yogurt Lamb Souvlakia with Saffron Rice

Arni Souvlakia Yiaourti

Serves 6

The saffron crocus produces a deep purple flower with feathery red stamens that yield a rich yellow colouring and strong, aromatic flavour. For centuries saffron has been a highly prized commodity; the early Minoan civilisation on Crete prospered through the cultivation and export of this sought-after spice. Proof of its importance to the Minoans can still be seen at the reconstructed Cretan Palace of Knossos where a fresco depicts saffron gatherers at work. Greeks now use Macedonian saffron, which has a pungent aroma; here Spanish saffron, which has an excellent flavour and strong colour, is the most widely available. Accompanied by Beetroot Salad with Allspice (page 184) or Beetroot Island-Style (page 182), this delicious dish is ideal for informal dinner parties.

1.2 kg/2$^1/_2$ lb lean leg of lamb
Juice of 1 large onion (page 348), about 5 tablespoons
350 ml/12 fl oz Strained Yogurt (page 8)
1-3 cloves garlic to taste, finely chopped
12 bay leaves
Coarse-grain sea salt, to taste
Extra virgin olive oil, for basting
Cracked black pepper, to taste

Saffron Rice
1 teaspoon saffron threads
700 ml/1$^1/_4$ pints Light Lamb Stock (page 347) or water
4 tablespoons extra virgin olive oil
350 g/12 oz long-grain rice
1 teaspoon sea salt

For serving
1 large bunch of watercress, sprigs only or a handful of rocket, small fresh leaves only, torn in pieces
24 Elitses or Niçoise olives, drained
4 tablespoons finely chopped flat leaf parsley
3 lemons, cut into wedge

Cut the lamb into 2.5 cm/1 inch cubes and trim off any fat or tendons. (Reserve the bones to make stock.)

Combine the onion juice, yogurt, garlic, bay leaves, and salt in a glass or china bowl. Add the lamb and mix with your hands. Cover tightly and refrigerate for at least 12 hours, turning the lamb in the marinade 2 or 3 times.

One hour before grilling, remove the bowl from the refrigerator.

Heat the saffron in a small dry frying pan over low heat until aromatic. Crumble the threads into the stock. Heat the olive oil in a heavy saucepan over medium-low heat, add the rice, and cook, stirring, 1 minute. Add the salt and the saffron broth, raise the heat, and boil 8 minutes, or until holes appear in the surface of the rice. Turn off the heat, place 2 layers of paper towels over the top of the saucepan, and cover with the lid. Set aside for 30 minutes in a warm place such as the back of the stove.

Meanwhile, prepare the fire.

Remove the meat from the marinade and thread on to 6 lightly oiled skewers. Baste with the marinade, brush liberally with olive oil and dust with the pepper.

Set the grill rack 7 cm/3 inches above the hot coals and lightly brush with olive oil. Grill the *souvlakia* on all sides until crusty, basting frequently with the marinade and olive oil. Raise the grill 5 cm/2 inches and grill 8-10 minutes longer, basting, until the meat is dark and crusty outside, juicy and tender inside.

Spread the saffron rice in the centre of a warm platter and surround with the watercress. Using a fork, push the *souvlakia* off the skewers onto the rice. Sprinkle olive oil over the salad greens and the olives and parsley over the *souvlakia*, season with salt and pepper, and surround with the lemon wedges. Serve immediately.

The Baker's Lamb
Arni me Fassolia
Serves 6

In the morning quiet of a Greek village traditionally clad women may be seen hurrying to the village baker with huge covered trays; at midday they return to pay the baker a few drachmas and to collect the now succulent stews that have been simmering in the baker's oven. This aromatic dish of new lamb and young broad beans, cooked with tomatoes and onions and spiced with cumin and *rigani*, is the spring version of a popular Greek dish that is made year-round in an infinite variety of meat, vegetable, and spice combinations. In summer and autumn chicken may be substituted for the lamb; in winter a pork and dried beans version warms and sustains. For best results, make sure the cooking is slow and steady, so that the pungent flavours of the herbs and spices can penetrate the meat and vegetables and develop a rich and highly seasoned sauce.

6 lean lamb chops
5–8 tablespoons extra virgin olive oil (to taste)
2 large onions, quartered and thinly sliced
900 g/2 lb ripe tomatoes, skinned and diced, juices reserved
1 teaspoon honey
Sea salt
1 teaspoon cracked black pepper, or to taste
1 tablespoon tomato purée diluted with 2 tablespoons water
115 ml/4 fl oz Meat Stock (page 347) or water
2 tablespoons ground cumin

3 tablespoons dried *rigani* (page 14)
900 g/2 lb green beans such as young broad beans (page 344) or fine beans, trimmed,
strings removed, and cut into 5-7 cm/2-3 inch lengths (see Note)
1 large bunch of flat leaf parsley, leaves coarsely chopped
Juice of 1 large lemon, or to taste

For serving
2 tablespoons finely chopped Preserved Lemon (page 18) or finely grated lemon zest,
blanched in boiling water for 5 seconds
1 large clove garlic, finely chopped

Heat the oven to 160C/325F/gas mark 3. Trim off all fat and sinew from the lamb and carefully wipe the meat to remove any bone splinters.

Heat 3 tablespoons of the olive oil in a large heavy sauté pan and lightly brown the lamb over medium heat. Drain on paper towels and transfer to a deep glazed clay or enamel-lined cast-iron casserole at least 10 cm/4 inches deep. Reduce the heat to low and sauté the onion 10 minutes or until soft. Add the tomatoes, honey, salt, and pepper, raise the heat, and boil 3 minutes or until reduced by one third. Add the tomato purée, stock, cumin, and *rigani*, stir to mix, and pour over the meat. Cover, and bake 50 minutes.

Blanch the beans in slightly salted boiling water for 1 minute. Drain and add to the casserole with the remaining olive oil. Shake gently to mix, cover, and bake 30 minutes longer. There should be about 350 ml/12 fl oz sauce – if there is more, uncover the dish; if less, add a few tablespoons water and cover – bake 15 minutes longer. Reserve 2 tablespoons of the parsley, and stir in the rest. Set aside in a warm place for 5 minutes.

Chop the Preserved Lemon, garlic, reserved parsley, and a large pinch of salt to mix.

Add salt, pepper, and the lemon juice to taste to the casserole; the sauce should be highly seasoned. Serve straight from the casserole, or transfer to a warm serving dish. Sprinkle with the parsley mixture and serve.

Note Unless you can find very tender young broad beans, shell them before using.

Variations
Substitute 6 lean bone-in beef steaks for the lamb, and use allspice instead of the cumin, dried thyme instead of the *rigani*.

Substitute lamb shanks for the lamb chops. Popular in eastern Mediterranean countries, lamb shanks produce a rich gelatinous sauce. Have the butcher cut 4 medium shanks into 2 or 3 thick slices each. Substitute 1^1/2 tablespoons ground cinnamon for the cumin if desired.

Substitute chicken for the lamb. Cut 1 large chicken into 8 serving pieces and remove the skin and excess fat. Lightly brown the pieces in olive oil and bake only 15 minutes before adding the beans.

Substitute large cubes of aubergines, cauliflower florets, small potatoes, baby courgettes, artichoke hearts, slender leeks, or cooked dried beans for the green beans. Fry the aubergine dice in olive oil until golden brown on all sides before adding to the meat; blanch the fresh vegetables in boiling water for 1 minute before adding. Cooked dried beans need no additional advance preparation.

Cinnamon Lamb with Aubergines
Arni Kanellas
Serves 6

Sweet raisins and honey, spicy perfumed cinnamon, and pungent vinegar and capers – the combination of flavours in this recipe evokes the tastes of medieval Byzantine cooking. Ideal for a lunch or dinner party, this casserole tastes even better if made a day ahead to allow the strong flavours a chance to mellow.

3 large aubergines (about 675 g/1^1/$_2$ lb)
Sea salt
65 g/2^1/$_2$ oz small dark seedless raisins
5 tablespoons aged red wine vinegar or 2 tablespoons balsamic vinegar diluted with 2 tablespoons water
1.6 kg/3^1/$_2$ lb very lean lamb, preferably from the leg
115 ml/4 fl oz extra virgin olive oil
2 large onions, quartered and thinly sliced
2 large cloves garlic, finely chopped
1 kg/2^1/$_4$ lb ripe tomatoes, skinned and diced, juices reserved
1 tablespoon honey
Cracked black pepper to taste
1 tablespoon ground cinnamon, or to taste

For serving
1 bunch of flat leaf parsley, leaves coarsely chopped
1 tablespoon small capers, rinsed, *optional*

Trim off the ends of the aubergines and cut into 4 cm/1^1/$_2$ inch cubes. Sprinkle with 2 tablespoons salt and set aside for 30 minutes to "sweat".

Combine the raisins and vinegar in a glass or china bowl and set aside. Trim off all fat and sinew from the lamb and cut into 4 cm/1^1/$_2$ inch cubes.

Heat the oven to 180C/350F/gas mark 4.

Heat half the olive oil in a large heavy sauté pan and lightly brown half the lamb over medium heat. With a slotted spoon, transfer to a heavy casserole. Repeat with the remaining lamb.

Reduce the heat under the pan to low and sauté the onion until soft, about 10 minutes. Add the garlic, stir well, and transfer to the casserole.

Dry the aubergines thoroughly with paper towels. Wipe out the pan, set it over medium-low heat, and add half the remaining olive oil. Add half the aubergines and fry until deep golden brown on all sides, about 12 minutes. Drain on paper towels and add to the casserole. Repeat with the remaining olive oil and aubergines.

Add the tomatoes and their juices, honey, salt, pepper, 1 tablespoon of the cinnamon, and the raisins and vinegar to the casserole. Add 4 tablespoons water, cover, and bake 1 hour.

Season the sauce with salt, pepper, and additional cinnamon to taste. There should be about 350 ml/12 fl oz of sauce – if there is more, leave the casserole uncovered; if less, add a few tablespoons water and cover – bake 30 minutes longer.

Chop the parsley and capers together just to mix. Serve the lamb hot or warm, piled high in a shallow serving bowl, with the parsley mixture sprinkled on top.

Variations

Substitute 1 tablespoon ground allspice for the cinnamon.

Substitute ground cumin for cinnamon, and 6 tablespoons Meat Stock (page 347) for the vinegar and raisins. To serve, sprinkle with a mixture of 3 tablespoons coarsely chopped fresh mint, 1 small bunch of flat leaf parsley, leaves coarsely chopped, and 2 tablespoons finely chopped Preserved Lemon (page 18).

Spring Lamb with Mountain Herbs
Arni me Votana
Serves 6

On spring Sundays the fragrance of this immensely satisfying dish floats on the morning air of many Greek villages. My particular memory of it takes me back to the mountain village of Milia where, on trestle tables set up in a cool whitewashed courtyard, crusty bread, bowls of crisp green salad, and jugs of local rosé wine awaited a gathering of family, friends, and neighbours. At midday our hostess brought out large shallow bowls of this aromatic soup-cum-stew – a complete Sunday lunch in one pot. No haute cuisine meal, I decided, could taste more wonderful at that moment.

1.4 kg/3 lb small lamb shoulder chops
115 ml/4 fl oz extra virgin olive oil
450 g/1 lb small boiling onions, peeled (page 132)
2 tablespoons plain flour
115 ml/4 fl oz dry red wine, *optional*
225-350 ml/8-12 fl oz Meat Stock (page 347)
6 large tomatoes, skinned and diced, juices reserved
1 tablespoon tomato purée diluted with 2 tablespoons water
1 teaspoon honey
2 tablespoons fresh rosemary, chopped, *or* 3 tablespoons dried rosemary, crumbled
2 tablespoons dried *rigani* (page 14), crumbled
1 tablespoon dried thyme, crumbled
6 bay leaves
2 large cloves garlic, finely chopped
Coarse-grain sea salt *and* cracked black pepper to taste
450 g/1 lb young carrots, cut into 5 cm/2 inch lengths
450 g/1 lb small new potatoes, peeled if desired, and cut in half

6 small young turnips, peeled and cut in half
350 g/12 oz green beans such as fine beans, trimmed and cut into 4 cm/
1 ¹/₂ inch lengths

For serving
1 small bunch of flat leaf parsley, leaves coarsely chopped

Trim off all the fat from the meat and wipe it to remove any bone splinters. Heat half the olive oil in a large sauté pan and brown half the lamb over medium heat. Transfer to a large heavy saucepan, and repeat with the remaining lamb.

Reduce the heat under the sauté pan, add the remaining olive oil, and cook the onions until lightly browned on all sides, about 10 minutes. Drain between layers of paper towels and transfer to the saucepan.

Drain off most of the olive oil from the sauté pan and sprinkle the pan with the flour. Stir any browned bits into the flour with a wooden spoon and gradually add the wine, stirring vigorously. Bring to a boil, simmer 1 minute, and stir in 225 ml/8 fl oz of the stock. Stir in the tomatoes and their juices, tomato purée, honey, rosemary, *rigani*, thyme, bay leaves, garlic, and salt and pepper. Transfer to the saucepan and bring to a boil over medium heat. Cover, reduce the heat, and slowly simmer 1 hour.

Fill a large saucepan with lightly salted water and bring to a boil. Add the carrots and potatoes and lightly boil 4 minutes. Add the turnips and boil 1 minute longer. Drain and add to the lamb. Add more stock or water if necessary to make about 450 ml/16 fl oz sauce. Cover, bring to a boil, and simmer 15 minutes longer.

Bring a small saucepan of water to a boil, add the beans, cook 1 minute, and drain. Add the beans to the casserole and shake gently to combine; don't stir or the vegetables may break up. Simmer 15 minutes longer, or until the vegetables are just done. Season to taste with salt and pepper.

Sprinkle with the parsley and serve.

Lamb Klephtiko
Arni Klephtiko
Serves 6

In this classic dish thick slices of lamb, larded with slivers of garlic and seasoned with oregano, lemon juice, and olive oil, cook gently in a tight paper parcel from which no juices or tantalizing aromas can escape. The dish probably has as many origins as there are storytellers. Village women have told me that the cooking method was devised to protect food from the hungry marauding bandits who had an unpleasant habit of turning up at mealtimes. Village men say that the meat would be left cooking gently in paper while courageous villagers went off to rout out the bandits. On their return their supper would be tender, aromatic, and cooked to perfection! Traditionally only lamb, goat, and fish are cooked this way but this wonderfully flavourful method can also be used very successfully with vegetables.

One 2.4–2.8 kg/5–6 lb leg of lamb cut (by the butcher) into 4 cm/1¹/₂ inch slices across the
bone *or* 1 boned leg of lamb cut into 4 cm/1¹/₂ inch slices *or* six 2.5 cm–/1 inch-thick
lean lamb chops
115 ml/4 fl oz extra virgin olive oil, or to taste
2 large cloves garlic, cut into large slivers
Sea salt *and* cracked black pepper to taste
3 tablespoons coarsely chopped fresh oregano *or* rosemary *or*
2 tablespoons dried *rigani* (page 14), crumbled
Juice of 1 large lemon

Trim off any fat from the meat; wipe lamb on-the-bone to remove any tiny bone splinters. Tie
a piece of kitchen string around each slice of boned lamb to keep it in shape.

Heat 3 tablespoons of the olive oil in a large sauté pan and brown half the meat over
medium-low heat. Drain on paper towels. Repeat with the remaining meat.

Heat the oven to 200C/400F/gas mark 6. Cut out six 30 cm/12 inch squares of parchment
paper. Fold each piece in half and trim the two outer corners to make 6 folded ovals. Open up
the papers and divide the meat between them, placing it in the centre of the bottom half of the
paper. (Remove the string from the boneless lamb.) Push the garlic into creases in the meat,
season generously with salt and pepper, and sprinkle with the oregano, lemon juice, and
remaining olive oil. Fold the top halves of the papers over the meat and roll up the edges tightly
to make neat parcels that will not leak. Arrange on a large baking tray and bake 10 minutes.

Reduce the oven temperature to 180C/350F/gas mark 4 and bake boneless lamb 20
minutes longer, lamb on-the-bone 35–40 minutes longer.

Place the parcels on warm dinner plates. Carefully open each one by cutting the four corners
with scissors and pulling back the edges of the paper.

Moussaka
Moussakas
Serves 8 to 10

One of the best-known Greek dishes, *moussakas* remains a popular favourite all over Greece
and her islands. In tavernas it's usually made in large shallow baking dishes; in a private home
you may be presented with *papoutsakia*, "little shoes" of aubergine shells filled with meat
sauce and cheese custard, or your own individual *moussaka* cooked in a clay pot. An authentic
moussakas does take time, but it can be made a day ahead, and it also freezes well.

4 large aubergines (about 1 kg/2¹/₄ lb)
Sea salt
175 ml/6 fl oz extra virgin olive oil
2 large onions, finely chopped
900 g/2 lb lean lamb *or* 450 g/1 lb each of lamb *and* beef, finely minced
225 ml/8 fl oz red wine, *optional*

6 large ripe tomatoes, skinned and diced, juices reserved
1 teaspoon honey
1 bunch of flat leaf parsley, leaves finely chopped
225 ml/8 fl oz Meat Stock (page 347)
4 tablespoons dried *rigani* (page 14), crumbled
2 tablespoons ground cinnamon, or to taste
1 teaspoon ground allspice, or to taste
Freshly ground black pepper to taste
450 ml/16 fl oz milk
50 g/2 oz unsalted butter
4 tablespoons plain flour
115 g/4 oz small-curd cottage cheese, drained
50 g/2 oz *feta* cheese, grated
115 g/4 oz *graviera* or gruyère cheese, grated
1 teaspoon grated nutmeg
5 large eggs
50 g/2 oz *kephalotyri* or parmesan cheese, grated
40 g/1^1/$_2$ oz fresh fine breadcrumbs

Trim off the ends of the aubergines and cut into 6 mm/^{1}/$_4$ inch slices. Sprinkle with 2 tablespoons salt and set aside in a colander for 1 hour to "sweat".

Heat 3 tablespoons of the olive oil in a large deep sauté pan and cook the onion over medium-low heat until soft, about 6 minutes. Raise the heat, add the meat, and sauté until lightly browned, breaking up any lumps with a wooden spoon and stirring occasionally to prevent sticking. Add the wine and boil until reduced by half. Add the tomatoes with their juices and the honey, lower the heat, and simmer 10 minutes. Set aside 1 tablespoon of the parsley, and stir in the rest with the stock, *rigani*, cinnamon, allspice, and 1 teaspoon each of salt and pepper. Simmer 30 minutes, or until almost all the liquid has evaporated. Season to taste with salt, pepper, and cinnamon. Cover and set aside (or refrigerate overnight).

Heat 3 tablespoons of the remaining olive oil in a large frying pan (or use 2 frying pans for extra speed). Thoroughly dry the aubergine slices with paper towels. Add just enough slices to make a single layer in the pan and fry over medium heat until dark golden brown on both sides. Drain between layers of paper towels. Add 1 tablespoon olive oil to the frying pan and fry another batch of aubergine slices; repeat with the remaining slices. Set aside.

Melt the butter in a heavy saucepan, add the flour, and stir with a wooden spoon until smooth. Cook, stirring, over low heat, 1-2 minutes, until the roux turns pale golden brown. Gradually add the milk, 115 ml/4 fl oz at a time, stirring until smooth after each addition. Bring to a boil, stirring, and remove from the heat.

Combine the cottage *feta, graviera*, and nutmeg, and stir into the white sauce. With a wire whisk or electric mixer, beat the eggs until pale and frothy. Thoroughly stir one third of the beaten eggs into the cheese mixture, then add the remainder all at once. Season to taste and set aside.

Heat the oven to 180C/350F/gas mark 4. Arrange about one quarter of the aubergine slices in the bottom of a large 7-10 cm/3-4 inch-deep baking dish, cover with one third of the meat sauce, then lightly smooth about 4 tablespoons of the cheese mixture over it. Make 2 more layers of aubergines, meat sauce, and cheese, and top with the remaining aubergine slices.

Cover with the remaining cheese mixture, sprinkle with the *kephalotyri* and breadcrumbs, and bake uncovered for 1 hour. If the top appears to be browning too quickly, loosely cover with a sheet of aluminium foil. (Do not press down, or you will remove the lovely crust when you take off the foil.)

Sprinkle with the reserved parsley and serve hot or warm.

To make individual casseroles Divide the aubergine slices, meat sauce, and cheese mixture between 8 or 10 individual baking dishes or small soufflé dishes, each about 7 cm/3 inches deep, layering the ingredients as above. Bake about 40 minutes.

To make *papoutsakia* Cut 5 large aubergines lengthways in half, sprinkle the cut sides with salt, and "sweat" for 30 minutes. Dry with paper towels. Fry in olive oil until the cut sides are golden brown and the skin is dark and wrinkled, drain between layers of paper towels, and carefully scoop out the flesh from each, leaving a 1 cm/½ inch shell. Fill the shells with the meat sauce and cover each with a layer of the cheese mixture. Sprinkle with the *kephalotyri* and breadcrumbs and bake 40-45 minutes.

Moussakas with Potatoes

Use only 2 large aubergines and substitute 450 g/1 lb small new potatoes, boiled in salted water for 10 minutes and cut in 6 mm/¼ inch slices, for the bottom layer of aubergine slices. Or omit the aubergines altogether, and substitute 1.4 kg/3 lb potatoes.

Moussakas with Courgettes

Substitute courgettes for the aubergines: trim 1.4 kg/3 lb courgettes, cut lengthways into 6 mm/¼ inch slices, and fry in olive oil until golden brown on both sides. Drain between layers of paper towels, and assemble as above.

Multi-coloured Moussakas

Use 450 g/1 lb new potatoes, boiled 10 minutes and sliced, as the bottom layer, and 450 g/1 lb courgettes and 1 large aubergine, sliced and fried, for the remaining layers. Proceed as directed above.

Smyrna Sausages
Soudzoukakia
Serves 6

These spicy sausages are the legacy of the Greeks who once lived in Smyrna (now Izmir, Turkey) and brought back to their home country a taste for Eastern flavourings. Here are two versions: In the first, the *soudzoukakia* are browned, then simmered for just a few minutes in a tomato sauce; in the second, they are marinated overnight in the tomato sauce before cooking. Either way they are a simple, tasty and economical dish.

1 medium onion, grated
2 tablespoons cumin seeds
2 tablespoons aged red wine vinegar
40 g/1½ oz fresh fine breadcrumbs
675 g/1½ lb lean lamb, finely minced twice
1 small bunch of flat leaf parsley, leaves finely chopped
1 clove garlic, finely chopped
1 egg, lightly beaten
Sea salt
1 tablespoon cracked black pepper, or to taste
3 tablespoons extra virgin olive oil
1 litre/1¾ pints Tomato Sauce made with cumin and parsley (page 321)

Combine the onion and 4 tablespoons water in a small saucepan, bring to a boil, and simmer until the water has evaporated, about 6 minutes. Take care not to let the onion burn. Meanwhile, in a small dry frying pan, gently heat the cumin seeds until aromatic, about 2 minutes. Pulverize them in a small mortar or spice grinder. Sprinkle the vinegar over the breadcrumbs and combine with the lamb, half the parsley, the garlic, egg, onion, cumin, and salt and pepper. Knead the mixture for a few minutes, cover tightly, and refrigerate for 1 hour.

Moisten your hands with cold water, divide the meat mixture into 18 portions, and shape them into 5 cm/2 inch-long sausages. Flatten them slightly between your palms.

Heat the olive oil in a large heavy frying pan and sauté the sausages until browned on both sides, about 12 minutes. (You can use 2 frying pans for greater speed.) Drain between layers of paper towels.

Bring the Tomato Sauce to a simmer in a shallow saucepan large enough to hold the sausages in a single layer. Add the sausages and simmer 3 minutes or until hot. Season to taste with salt and pepper.

Transfer to a warm serving platter and sprinkle with the rest of the parsley.

Grilled Kephtedes
Kephtedes sta Karvouna
Serves 6

Spicy beef and lamb patties are a traditional centrepiece for many outdoor parties and village gatherings. These grilled *kephtedes* are highly flavoured but simple food, usually served mounded on a platter with an array of colourful garnishes for an eye-catching presentation. They are good with aubergine dishes, *tsatsiki* (page 54), *khorta* (page 220), and fried potatoes.

350 g/12 oz lean beef, finely minced
350 g/12 oz lean lamb, finely minced
1 large onion, finely chopped
4 tablespoons finely chopped flat leaf parsley
2 tablespoons dried *rigani* (page 14), briefly pounded in a small mortar
1 teaspoon dried thyme, crumbled
75 g/3 oz fresh fine wholemeal breadcrumbs
1 tablespoon mustard seeds or 1/2 teaspoon powdered mustard
4 tablespoons dry red wine or 2 tablespoons aged red wine vinegar
Coarse-grain sea salt *and* cracked black pepper to taste
Extra virgin olive oil

For serving
2 small red or mild onions, quartered and thinly sliced
1 small bunch of flat leaf parsley, leaves coarsely chopped
3 ripe tomatoes, skinned and cut into small dice
1/2 medium cucumber, peeled and cut into small dice
Juice of 1/2 lemon
1 tablespoon sumak (see Note) or 1 teaspoon paprika *and* a large pinch of cayenne pepper
Watercress sprigs
Lemon wedges

Combine the beef, lamb, onion, parsley, *rigani*, thyme, and breadcrumbs in a large bowl. Heat the mustard seeds in a small dry frying pan over low heat until a few pop. Pulverize them in a mortar or spice grinder. Mix this powder with the wine and add to the meat, along with salt and pepper. Knead the mixture for a few minutes, tightly cover, and refrigerate for 1-4 hours.

Prepare the fire.

Moisten your hands with cold water and shape the meat mixture into 12 balls, flattening each one into a 2 cm/3/4 inch-thick patty.

Oil a grill rack and place it 10-12 cm/4-5 inches above the hot coals. Grill the *kephtedes*, basting frequently with olive oil, for about 8 minutes, until browned and crusty on both sides but still moist and pink in the centre.

Combine the onion, parsley, tomatoes, cucumber, lemon juice, sumak, and salt and pepper to taste and spread this mixture over a platter. Arrange the *kephtedes* on top, sprinkle with olive oil to taste, and surround with the watercress and lemon wedges.

Note Sumak, available from Greek and Middle Eastern shops, is the pulverized berry of a piquant herb. It has a coarse texture, pleasantly tangy acid flavour, and a deep auburn colour.

Marinated Smyrna Sausages
Soudzoukakia Marinata

1 onion, grated
115 ml/4 fl oz red wine
40 g/1¹/₂ oz fresh fine breadcrumbs
675 g/1¹/₂ lb lean lamb, finely minced twice
1¹/₂ teaspoons ground cinnamon, or to taste
¹/₄ teaspoon ground cloves
3 tablespoons finely chopped flat leaf parsley
1 egg, lightly beaten
Sea salt and cracked black pepper to taste
Olive oil, for frying
1 litre/1³/₄ pints Tomato Sauce made with cinnamon and parsley (page 321)
3 bay leaves

For serving
3 tablespoons finely chopped flat leaf parsley

Make the sausages and fry them as directed on page 159, substituting 4 tablespoons of the wine for the vinegar, the ground cinnamon and cloves for the pulverized cumin.

Bring the Tomato Sauce to a simmer and add the remaining wine and bay leaves.

Place the sausages in a non-reactive bowl and cover with the sauce. Cool, tightly cover, and refrigerate overnight.

To serve, heat the sausages in the sauce and serve warm or hot, sprinkled with the parsley.

Peppery Grilled Liver
Sikotakia Piperato tis Skhara
Serves 3 to 4

For this quick and easy popular delicacy tender lamb's liver is marinated in lemon juice, mustard, and olive oil, then dusted with crushed peppercorns and grilled. The secret is to grill just long enough to brown the outside but keep the inside moist and pink.

450 g/1 lb lamb's liver, cut into 6 mm/¹/₄ inch-thick slices
Juice of 2 lemons
¹/₂ teaspoon powdered mustard
6 tablespoons extra virgin olive oil
1¹/₂ tablespoons cracked black pepper

For serving
Watercress sprigs
1 tablespoon finely chopped Preserved Lemon (page 18) or finely grated lemon zest of 1 small lemon
4 tablespoons finely chopped flat leaf parsley
$1/_2$ teaspoon coarse-grain sea salt, or to taste
1 small red or mild onion, cut into thin rings
$1/_2$ teaspoon paprika
1 lemon, cut into wedges
2 ripe tomatoes, cut into wedges, or 8 tiny tomatoes

Trim off any membrane from the liver.

Whisk together the lemon juice, powdered mustard, and the olive oil in a non-reactive bowl. Add the liver, cover tightly, and set aside.

Prepare the fire.

Set a grill rack 7 cm/3 inches above the hot coals and lightly brush with olive oil. Remove the liver from the marinade, reserving the liquid, and sprinkle with the pepper. Grill until browned on both sides but still pink inside, about 2 minutes.

Meanwhile, chop the Preserved Lemon, parsley, and salt together to mix. Combine with the onion and paprika.

Arrange the liver in the centre of a warm platter and surround with the watercress and lemon and tomato wedges. Spoon over a few tablespoons of the marinade and scatter over the onion mixture. Serve immediately.

Note Grilled liver is also delicious prepared with the marinade for lamb (page 144) or pork (page 171).

Piquant Garlic Beef
Sofrito
Serves 6

In this classic recipe strong red wine vinegar, liberal amounts of perfumed mountain herbs, and a generous quantity of garlic turn modest beef stew into an outstanding dish. Richly flavoured *sofrito* is an island speciality from Corfu, and in tavernas there it is cooked in tightly sealed individual earthenware pots; at the table the lids are removed to release a wonderful fragrance and reveal meltingly tender beef in a thick, garlicky herb sauce. This special dish takes very little time to prepare. Serve with Aubergine Pilaf with Glazed Tomatoes (page 228), bowls of purple and green olives and *feta* cheese, and Island Greens Salad (page 218).

1 kg/$2^1/_4$ lb lean beef (top round or rump)
Plain flour, for dredging
$1/_2$ tablespoon cracked black pepper, or to taste
6 tablespoons extra virgin olive oil, or to taste

225 ml/8 fl oz aged red wine vinegar
8 bay leaves
3 tablespoons dried thyme, marjoram or rosemary, or a mixture
225 ml/8 fl oz Meat Stock (page 347) or water
Sea salt to taste
2–3 heads garlic to taste, cloves separated and peeled
4 tablespoons plain flour

For serving
Finely chopped flat leaf parsley
24 Elitses or Niçoise olives, drained

Heat the oven to 140C/275F/gas mark 1. Trim the meat of all fat and sinew and cut into 4 cm/1¹/₂ inch cubes. Dredge with flour, shaking off any excess, and sprinkle with the pepper.

Heat half the olive oil in a large heavy sauté pan and lightly brown half the meat over medium-low heat. Drain between layers of paper towels and transfer to a large heavy casserole. Repeat with the remaining meat.

Drain off any oil from the pan and add the vinegar. Bring to a boil, stirring in any residue from the bottom and sides of the pan with a wooden spoon. Simmer a few minutes to reduce slightly, and pour over the meat. Add the bay leaves, thyme, stock, salt, and the remaining olive oil and shake the casserole gently to mix. Add the garlic, pushing it down between the pieces of meat so its flavour will penetrate the dish.

Combine the flour and a few tablespoons water to make a thick paste. Spread it around the top rim of the casserole and the inner edge of the casserole lid. Place the lid in position, smooth the paste to make a good seal, and bake 3 hours.

Insert a blunt-ended knife between the lid and casserole to break the seal. Remove the lid and wipe the rim of the casserole clean. Season to taste with salt and pepper; the dish should be highly seasoned. Sprinkle with the parsley and olives, and serve immediately.

To serve in individual casseroles Divide the *sofrito* equally between 6 individual casseroles, seal them, and bake 2¹/₂ hours at 130C/250F/gas mark ¹/₂.

Aromatic Beef in Red Wine
Kapamas
Serves 6

This dish is said to be the invention of the nomadic tribes of antiquity who wandered all over Greece and the Balkans. That could explain the rich variety of seasonings used – the flavours of East and West are blended in a supremely aromatic and exotic concoction. After marinating for as long as eighteen hours in red wine, the beef is slowly cooked in a tightly sealed pot. Prepared and cooked a day ahead, *kapamas* becomes even more intensely flavoured. Serve with Garlic Potatoes with Juniper Berries (page 206), Potatoes in a Clay Pot (page 205), or a vegetable pilaf.

1.4 kg/3 lb lean beef (such as rump), in one piece

2 large onions, sliced

1 1/2 tablespoons ground allspice

2 large cloves garlic, each cut into 5 or 6 pieces

8 bay leaves

2 tablespoons dried *rigani* (page 14)

About 700 ml/1 1/4 pints dry red wine

2 rashers lean bacon, finely diced

115 ml/4 fl oz extra virgin olive oil

675 g/1 1/2 lb small boiling onions, peeled (page 132)

4 tablespoons plain flour *plus* flour for dredging

900 g/2 lb ripe tomatoes, skinned and diced, juices reserved

1 teaspoon honey

One 7 cm/3 inch cinnamon stick, broken in half

115 ml/4 fl oz Meat Stock or Light Meat Stock (page 347) or water

Sea salt *and* cracked black pepper to taste

1 dozen Thasos *or* Kalamata olives, rinsed, halved, and pitted

For serving

3 tablespoons finely chopped flat leaf parsley

2 tablespoons capers, rinsed

1 clove garlic, finely chopped

2 tablespoons finely grated lemon zest

Trim off any fat or sinew from the meat and cut into pieces about 7 cm/2 1/2 inches square and 2.5 cm/1 inch thick. Combine the meat, sliced onion, allspice, garlic, 4 of the bay leaves, 1 tablespoon of the *rigani,* and the red wine in a large non-reactive bowl. Cover and set aside in a cool place for 2-4 hours, or refrigerate for 12-18 hours.

Heat the oven to 140C/275F/gas mark 1. Place a large heavy sauté pan over low heat and fry the bacon in its own fat for 2-3 minutes. Transfer to a large heavy casserole. Add half the olive oil to the pan and sauté the boiling onions until lightly browned on all sides, about 10 minutes. Drain between layers of paper towels and set aside.

Remove the meat from the marinade, reserving the marinade, and pat dry with paper towels. Lightly dredge with flour, shaking off any excess. Add 3 tablespoons of the remaining olive oil to the pan and sauté half the meat over medium heat until lightly browned on both sides, about 10 minutes. Transfer to the casserole with a slotted spoon and repeat with the remaining meat.

Meanwhile, transfer the marinade to a saucepan. Bring to a boil, lower the heat, and simmer until reduced by one third. Once the meat is browned, strain the marinade through a sieve into the sauté pan, and discard the solids. Bring to a boil, stirring in all the residue from the bottom and sides with a wooden spoon.

Add the reduced marinade, tomatoes and their juices, honey, cinnamon, stock, salt and pepper, and the remaining 4 bay leaves and 1 tablespoon *rigani* to the casserole. Gently shake the casserole to mix everything together.

Make a thick paste with the 4 tablespoons flour and a few tablespoons water and spread it round the top rim of the casserole and the inner edge of its lid. Place the lid in position, smooth the paste to make a good seal, and bake 2 1/2 hours.

Insert a blunt-ended knife between the lid and casserole to break the seal, remove the lid and wipe the rim of the casserole clean. Add the onions. If there is more than about 350 ml/12 fl oz sauce, leave the casserole uncovered; if less, add a little water or stock and replace the lid. Bake 30 minutes longer.

Bring a small saucepan of water to a boil, add the olives, and remove the saucepan from the heat. Let stand for 5 minutes, then drain and rinse the olives, add to the casserole, gently shaking to mix, and bake about 5 minutes longer. Season with salt and pepper to taste. Meanwhile, chop the parsley, capers, garlic, and lemon zest together until well mixed.

Arrange the meat and onions on a warm platter and spoon over the sauce. Sprinkle with the parsley mixture and the remaining olive oil and serve hot.

Note If you plan to refrigerate the cooked dish overnight before serving, do not add the olives until re-heating.

Beef Stifado
Stifado Moschari
Serves 6 to 8

Beef *stifado* is one of the best examples of the wonderful braised dishes to be found in good tavernas throughout Greece. The secret to its fine flavour is long slow cooking, a generous quantity of spices, and a large quantity of onions – the same amount as meat. *Stifado* is traditionally made with wild rabbit (page 132) or hare (page 134), but a beef version is a popular city dish and an easy-to-make family favourite. Like most stews, beef *stifado* tastes even better when reheated, so it can be made ahead of time. Very good with Pilaf and Green Lentils (page 229) or crusty Country Bread (page 249).

1.2 kg/2½ lb lean beef, such as rump, or any cut suitable for braising
115 ml/4 fl oz extra virgin olive oil, or to taste
1.2 kg/2½ lb small boiling onions, about 2.5 cm/1 inch in diameter, peeled (page 132)
2 cloves garlic, finely chopped
6 large tomatoes, skinned, seeded, and diced
½ tablespoon honey
1 tablespoon tomato purée diluted with 4 tablespoons water
225 ml/8 fl oz dry red wine
One 5 cm/2 inch cinnamon stick
8 cloves
12 whole allspice
8 bay leaves
4 sprigs of dried thyme or *rigani* (page 14)
Zest of 1 orange, removed in large strips and tied together with kitchen string
Sea salt and cracked black pepper to taste

For serving
4 tablespoons finely chopped flat leaf parsley

Trim off any fat or sinew from the meat and cut into pieces about 4 cm/1¹/₂ inches square and 2 cm/¹/₂ inch thick.

Heat the oven to 150C/300F/gas mark 2. Heat half the olive oil in a heavy frying pan and lightly brown half the meat over low heat. Drain between layers of paper towels and transfer to a heavy casserole. Repeat with the remaining meat.

Add the onions to the pan and gently roll them around over low heat until a pale golden brown, about 10 minutes; transfer to the casserole. Add the garlic to the pan, heat until aromatic, then add the tomatoes and their juices, and the honey, and simmer gently for 2 minutes. Add the tomato purée, red wine, cinnamon stick, cloves, allspice, bay leaves, thyme sprigs, orange zest, and salt and pepper. Stir to mix and simmer 3 minutes. Transfer the tomato sauce to the casserole, add the remaining olive oil, and gently shake to mix everything together. Cover with a tight fitting lid and bake 2 hours, or until the meat is meltingly tender and the sauce is thick; check once or twice during baking and add water if necessary.

Discard the thyme sprigs and orange zest and check the seasonings. Sprinkle with parsley and serve hot.

Country Beef
Brizoles
Serves 6

Popular country food, these spicy steaks are ideal for large parties. Delicious, attractive, and colourful, this is such an easy dish you'll find yourself making it often. Bone-in steaks are essential for flavour and juiciness; try the variations with lamb or pork.

6 small beef steaks on-the-bone, about 225 g/8 oz each
Juice of 1 lemon
2 tablespoons ground coriander
¹/₄ teaspoon grated nutmeg or ground mace
1 tablespoon dried *rigani* (page 14)
¹/₂ tablespoon dried marjoram
1 teaspoon coarse-grain sea salt
1 tablespoon cracked black pepper
6 large ripe tomatoes, cut in half
1 teaspoon sugar
8 medium potatoes, peeled if desired, and cut lengthways in half or into quarters
6 large cloves garlic, each cut into 2 or 3 pieces
225 ml/8 fl oz extra virgin olive oil

For serving
4 tablespoons finely chopped flat leaf parsley

Trim off all fat from the meat and wipe it to remove any bone splinters. Place in a non-reactive bowl and pour over the lemon juice. Set aside.

Gently heat the coriander and nutmeg in a dry frying pan until aromatic, and transfer to a small mortar. Add the *rigani,* marjoram, salt and pepper, and pound until well mixed and slightly crushed. Rub the steaks all over with this mixture.

Heat the oven to 180C/350F/gas mark 4.

Lay the steaks in a single layer in a large baking dish, spaced well apart. Sprinkle the tomatoes with the sugar and place them between the steaks, cut sides up. Add the potatoes, arranging them so each piece is touching a steak. Press the garlic down between the meat and potatoes. Pour over any remaining marinating liquid, sprinkle with the olive oil, and add 115 ml/4 fl oz water to the dish. Bake uncovered, basting the beef and potatoes occasionally with the pan juices, for 1 hour or until the meat is very tender and the tomatoes are almost falling apart.

Season to taste with salt and pepper and sprinkle with the parsley. Serve hot.

Variations

Substitute 12 small lamb chops or 6 small shanks, trimmed of fat, for the beef, 3 tablespoons chopped fresh rosemary for the coriander, nutmeg, and marjoram, and vinegar for the lemon juice. Omit the tomatoes and leave the garlic cloves whole and unpeeled – your guests can spread the softened garlic on the cooked meat at the table.

Substitute pork chops, trimmed of fat, for the beef and 1 teaspoon ground cumin for the nutmeg. Cut 3 small aubergines in half, sauté them in 4 tablespoons olive oil, and add to the baking dish with the potatoes and tomatoes. Allow an additional 15 minutes baking time.

Spit-Roasted Suckling Pig
Gourounopoulo tis Souvla
Serves 8 to 12

The ancient Greeks worked hard to keep their gods happy and, when the occasion demanded it, a sacrifice was the best way to enlist divine help or give thanks for favours rendered – and the best sacrifice of all was a succulent pig! It's still a favourite celebration dish in Greece today, especially in late summer and early autumn. A true suckling pig weighs around 4.5-6.2 kg/10-14 lb and has a soft, pliant skin and mild gamy flavour. Greeks spit roast the meat without stuffing (a few bay leaves in the cavity are enough to lend a delicate fragrance) and baste it during cooking with a flavourful marinade so that the skin becomes crisp, brown, and sweetly scented. Serve in thick slices accompanied by Potatoes in a Clay Pot (page 205) and Beetroot Salad with Allspice (page 184) or an aubergine dish.

One 4.5-6.3 kg/10-14 lb suckling pig, prepared by the butcher
Wine vinegar, to rub over the pig
Coarse-grain sea salt
6 bay leaves
Juice of 3 lemons

¹/₂ tablespoon cracked black pepper
1 tablespoon honey
175–225 ml/6–8 fl oz extra virgin olive oil (to taste)
1 tablespoon dried thyme, crumbled
1 teaspoon dried summer savory (page 15), crumbled

For serving
Watercress sprigs
Elitses or Niçoise olives
Slices of aged *myzithra* cheese

Prepare the fire.

Scrub the pig's skin with a stiff brush and lightly wipe the pig inside and out with vinegar and then with salt. Place the bay leaves in the stomach cavity and sew up the cavity using a trussing needle.

Combine the lemon juice, pepper, ¹/₂ teaspoon salt, honey, and olive oil, and set this marinade aside. Tie the forelegs and hind legs of the pig together and secure it to the spit. Pierce the skin in a dozen places, baste liberally with the marinade, and place the spit 60 cm/2 feet above the hot coals. Roast, rotating the spit and basting the pig frequently, for 1¹/₄-2¹/₄ hours (depending on the size of the pig); catch the juices in a pan. Gradually bring the spit closer to the coals; after about an hour of roasting, add the thyme and savory to the marinade and continue basting. Check if the meat is cooked by inserting a sharp knife into the thickest part of the pig; the juices should run clear.

Carve into serving pieces and arrange on a warm platter. Pour off as much fat as possible from the pan juices, strain the remaining liquid, and pour over the pork. Surround with the watercress, olives, and cheese.

The Winemaker's Pork
Khirino Einopiou
Serves 4

In country districts the family pig is traditionally slaughtered on the day after the first autumn rain, and the Greek pork-eating season generally runs from September to late February. Legend has it that, because it is a source of formidable strength, pork is the food for warriors, and a neighbour of mine on Crete always serves this dish to the men who trample her grapes for wine-making – a job that calls for great perseverance and stamina. The flavours are indeed assertive – strong garlic, scented bay leaves, the bouquet of parsley and thyme, spicy coriander and mustard. Serve this pork and mushroom dish with potatoes and a green salad.

4 thick pork chops, 175–200 g/6–7 oz each after boning, trimmed of fat
2 cloves garlic, crushed
4 bay leaves, broken in half
6 sprigs of parsley

2 tablespoons coriander seeds or 1 tablespoon fennel seeds
1 tablespoon dried thyme, crumbled
About 700 ml/1¹/₄ pints dry red wine
1 tablespoon mustard seeds or ¹/₂ teaspoon powdered mustard
Coarse-grain sea salt
¹/₂ tablespoon cracked black pepper, or to taste
1 tablespoon aged red wine vinegar
5 tablespoons extra virgin olive oil
12 large white mushrooms, cut into quarters

For serving
24 Elitses or Niçoise olives, drained
Coarsely chopped flat leaf parsley or fresh coriander

Place the chops between 2 sheets of waxed paper. With a kitchen mallet or the side of a heavy knife, pound until an even 1 cm/¹/₂ inch thick. Combine the pork, garlic, bay leaves, parsley sprigs, half the coriander, the thyme and enough red wine to cover the pork in a non-reactive bowl. Cover and set aside.

Prepare the fire.

Heat the mustard seeds in a small dry frying pan until a few pop. Pound the mustard seeds and remaining coriander with salt and pepper in a small mortar until pulverized. Whisk the vinegar and olive oil together in a small bowl and whisk in the pulverized spices. Remove the pork from the marinade, dry with paper towels, and brush liberally with the spiced olive oil. Reduce the marinade to 175 ml/6 fl oz by rapid boiling in a saucepan over high heat, and strain.

Set a grill rack 10 cm/4 inches above the hot coals and brush with olive oil. Grill the pork until lightly browned on both sides, basting frequently with the oil and catching the juices in a pan. Raise the grill 5 cm/2 inches and grill 10-12 minutes longer. (For an attractive appearance, 'square' the chops: give them a 45° turn on each side halfway through the cooking time to give them 'grill marks'.) Meanwhile, brush the mushrooms liberally with the spiced oil and grill for 2-3 minutes, turning once.

Arrange the pork and mushrooms on a warm platter. Drain off the fat from the pan juices and add the juices to the marinade. Stir in the olives and the remaining spiced olive oil, and heat through. Pour over the pork and mushrooms, sprinkle with the parsley, and serve.

Mani Pork Souvlaki
Khirino Souvlakia Manis
Serves 6

During the period when Greece was part of the Ottoman Empire the Muslim occupation naturally discouraged the eating of pork. This did not, however, deter the rebellious inhabitants of the isolated and mountainous Mani region at the southern tip of the Peloponnese, who continued to raise pigs throughout the centuries of occupation and developed a long tradition of pork cookery. This is a simple and easy-to-prepare dish but, what it lacks in sophistication, it more than makes up for in flavour. The meat is marinated in a blend of coriander, juniper berries, and mustard, grilled with perfumed bay leaves, and garnished with fresh coriander. Serve with *pilafi* and Beetroot Island-Style (page 182) or *tsatsiki* (page 54).

1.2 kg/2¹/₂ lb boneless lean pork from the tenderloin or leg
1 tablespoon coriander seeds
6 juniper berries
3 tablespoons aged red wine vinegar
¹/₂ teaspoon powdered mustard
115 ml/4 fl oz extra virgin olive oil
18 bay leaves, each broken in half
1 tablespoon honey
Cracked black pepper and coarse-grain sea salt to taste

For serving
Coarsely chopped fresh coriander or watercress or purslane sprigs
Lemon wedges

Cut the meat into 2.5 cm/1 inch cubes and trim off any fat and sinew. Pound the coriander seeds and juniper berries in a small mortar until crushed and well mixed. Combine with the vinegar and mustard in a small bowl, and whisk in the olive oil. Combine the meat and marinade in a non-reactive bowl, mix together with your hands, and cover. Set aside 2-3 hours.

Prepare the fire.

Remove the meat from the marinade and thread alternatively with the bay leaves onto 6 skewers. Whisk the honey into the marinade and baste the meat liberally with this sauce, then sprinkle it with pepper.

Set a grill rack 10 cm/4 inches above the hot coals and lightly brush with olive oil. Grill the *souvlakia* until lightly browned on all sides, then raise the grill 5 cm/2 inches. Grill 10-15 minutes longer, basting frequently, or until the *souvlakia* are cooked.

Arrange on a warm platter, sprinkle with salt, pepper, and fresh coriander, and surround with the lemon wedges.

Traditional Pork and Bean Casserole
Khirino Khoriatiko
Serves 10-12

Robust flavours dominate this warming winter country dish; although similar to the comforting cassoulet of the Languedoc region of France, this casserole almost certainly predates it. The preparation is time-consuming, so it's best to assemble it one day for final cooking the next. It's ideal to serve at a supper party, so the quantities given here are large.

Pork and smoked ham are cooked with onions, garlic, red wine, and hillside herbs and tangy Eastern spices, then layered in a casserole with country sausages and dried butter beans that absorb all the rich flavours, and baked. Serve with olives, *feta* cheese, radishes, and country bread, accompanied by a red wine such as Nemea or Naousa.

675 g/1¹/₂ lb dried butter beans, soaked overnight in water to cover, cooked and drained; tinned beans are unsuitable for this recipe
1.4 kg/3 lb boneless lean pork shoulder
115 ml/4 fl oz extra virgin olive oil, or to taste
3 heaped tablespoons finely diced *pastourmas* ham (page 348) or pancetta or bacon
3 large onions, chopped
3 large cloves garlic, finely chopped
225 ml/8 fl oz red wine, *optional*
900 g/2 lb tomatoes, skinned and diced, juices reserved
1 teaspoon honey
4 tablespoons dried *rigani* (page 14)
1 tablespoon dried marjoram
1 tablespoon dried winter savory (page 15) or thyme
2 tablespoons ground coriander
5 cloves
4 juniper berries
1 small bunch of flat leaf parsley, leaves finely chopped
Sea salt to taste
1 tablespoon cracked black pepper, or to taste
225-350 ml/8-12 fl oz Meat Stock (page 347)
225 g/8 oz home-made (page 178) or commercial country sausages, grilled or sautéed
50 g/2 oz fresh wholemeal breadcrumbs
4 tablespoons grated *kasseri* or parmesan cheese
Juice of ¹/₂ lemon

Trim off any fat from the meat and cut into 2.5 cm/1 inch cubes. Heat 3 tablespoons of the olive oil in a heavy sauté pan and lightly brown half the meat over medium heat. Drain between layers of paper towels, and repeat with the remaining meat.

Drain off any fat from the pan, add the ham, and sauté 2-3 minutes. Add the onion and sauté, stirring occasionally, until light golden brown, about 15 minutes. Add the garlic, cook 1 minute longer, and add the red wine. Bring to a boil and boil a minute or two, then stir in the tomatoes with their juices, honey, *rigani,* marjoram, savory, coriander, cloves, juniper berries, parsley, salt, and pepper. Simmer until the liquid is reduced by half. Add 225 ml/8 fl oz of the stock and simmer 5 minutes longer.

Add the meat, cover, reduce the heat, and simmer 30 minutes longer; add stock or water if there appears to be less than 450 ml/16 fl oz of sauce. Season to taste with salt, pepper, and/or additional herbs; the sauce should be highly flavoured.

Heat the oven to 160C/325F/gas mark 3. Slice the sausage into 1 cm-/¹/₂ inch-thick slices and combine with the beans.

Sprinkle 2 tablespoons olive oil over the bottom of a heavy casserole and cover with one third of the sausages and beans. Cover with a layer of half the meat mixture, then half the remaining beans, then the remaining meat. Top with a layer of the remaining beans and sprinkle with the breadcrumbs and cheese. With the back of a wooden spoon, gently press down on the beans so some of the sauce rises to the surface.

Sprinkle with the lemon juice and the remaining olive oil, cover, and bake 45 minutes. Reduce the oven temperature to 150C/300F/gas mark 2 and bake 1-1¹/₂ hours longer, until a golden crust has formed. Remove the casserole lid and bake 10 minutes or until the crust is deep golden brown. Serve hot.

Pork Cretan-Style
Khirino Kritiko
Serves 6

An autumn and winter speciality on the island of Crete, this hearty dish makes the most of winter savory, a lovely mountain herb that has a particular affinity with pork. In rural communities, this popular Sunday dinner dish is still cooked in the traditional way – baked very slowly overnight in the village *fournos*. A crisp Purslane Salad (page 219) or Wild Greens Salad (page 221) provides a refreshing complement to the richness of the pork.

6 thick pork loin chops, on-the-bone (about 225 g/8 oz each) or boneless (175-200 g/6-7 oz each)

Juice of 3 lemons

2 medium aubergines

2 tablespoons coarse-grain sea salt, or to taste

2 tablespoons coriander seeds, lightly crushed

1 tablespoon cumin seeds

1¹/₂ tablespoons cracked black pepper, or to taste

2 tablespoons dried winter savory (page 15) or thyme

1 tablespoon dried *rigani* (page 14)

8 juniper berries

115-225 ml/4-8 fl oz extra virgin olive oil (to taste)

4 large potatoes, peeled and cut lengthways in half or into quarters

6 large tomatoes, skinned and cut in half

1 teaspoon sugar

6 large cloves garlic, feathery outer skins rubbed off

12 bay leaves

For serving

1 small bunch of flat leaf parsley, leaves finely chopped

Trim off any fat from the pork and wipe chops on-the-bone to remove any bone splinters. Combine the pork and lemon juice in a non-reactive bowl, cover, and set aside for 3 hours to marinate.

Slice off the stem ends of the aubergines. Cut lengthways in half and sprinkle the cut sides with 1 tablespoon of the salt. Set aside for 1 hour to "sweat".

Heat the oven to 160C/325F/gas mark 3. Heat the coriander and cumin seeds in a small dry frying pan over low heat until aromatic, about 1 minute. Combine the cumin, coriander, pepper, savory, *rigani*, juniper berries, and remaining salt in a mortar and pound until slightly pulverized. Remove the pork from the marinade, reserving any juices, and rub all over with this mixture. Arrange the pork chops in a large baking dish, spaced well apart. Set aside.

Heat 3 tablespoons of the olive oil in a large heavy frying pan. Thoroughly dry the aubergines with paper towels, fry until the cut sides are golden brown, about 6 minutes, and drain between layers of paper towels.

Add the potatoes to the baking dish, arranging them so that each one is touching a piece of meat. Sprinkle the tomatoes with the sugar and add to the dish, cut sides up. Add the aubergines, skin sides down, and place the garlic cloves between the pieces of meat.

Pour over the remaining olive oil and the reserved marinade and sprinkle with the bay leaves and any remaining herb mixture. Add 225 ml/8 fl oz water to the dish and bake boneless pork 30 minutes, pork on-the-bone 45 minutes, basting the meat several times with the pan juices; if the liquid evaporates, add a little more water. Reduce the oven temperature to 150C/300F/gas mark 2 and bake 15 minutes longer, or until the pork is cooked.

Spoon the pan juices over the pork and sprinkle with the parsley.

Variation

Substitute a 1.2 kg/2¹/₂ lb boneless pork loin roast for the pork chops. Marinate for 3 hours in the lemon juice, turning the pork occasionally. Rub all over with the herb and spice mixture, place in the centre of the baking dish, and pour over 115 ml/ 4 fl oz of the olive oil. Surround with the vegetables and garlic and sprinkle with bay leaves and remaining marinating liquid including any spice mixture. Bake 1 hour at 160C/325F/gas mark 3, basting frequently with the remaining olive oil. Bake 30 minutes longer at 150C/300F/gas mark 2, or until done; do not baste again.

Slice the pork, arrange in the centre of a warm platter, and surround with the vegetables. Spoon over the pan juices.

Pork Cutlets with Mustard Sauce
Khirino me Saltsa Moustarthas
Serves 4

Pork cutlets served with a tangy mustard sauce sharpened and spiced with lemon juice, garlic, and cumin are a popular autumn and winter lunch dish. Serve with Wild Greens Salad (page 221) and vegetable *pilafi*.

4 pork loin chops, about 175 g/6 oz each after boning, trimmed of all fat
Sea salt and freshly ground black pepper to taste
6 tablespoons extra virgin olive oil

3 tablespoons aged red wine vinegar *and* 2 tablespoons water or 5 tablespoons
Mavrodaphne wine or other heavy sweet wine
Juice of 1 small lemon
2 hard-boiled egg yolks, pressed through a sieve
1 1/2 tablespoons Dijon mustard
1/2 tablespoon honey
1/2 teaspoon ground cumin
1 large clove garlic, finely chopped
3 tablespoons finely chopped flat leaf parsley
1 tablespoon dried *rigani* (page 14), briefly pounded in a mortar

Sprinkle the pork chops with salt and pepper and place between 2 sheets of waxed paper. With a kitchen mallet or the back of a wooden spoon, pound until an even 1 cm/1/2 inch thick. Measure half the olive oil into a small bowl and set aside in a warm spot.

Heat the remaining olive oil in a heavy frying pan and sauté the cutlets over medium-low heat until lightly browned on both sides. Drain off any oil and add the vinegar and water. Cover, reduce the heat, and cook for 15 minutes, or until the cutlets are evenly pale all the way through.

Meanwhile, whisk together the lemon juice, egg yolks, mustard, honey, cumin, garlic, and salt and pepper and press through a fine sieve into a bowl. Add the warm olive oil, pan juices, parsley, and *rigani* and briefly whisk to mix. Arrange the pork on a warm platter and pour over the sauce.

Souvlaki Sausages
Sheftalia
Serves 4 as a main course, 12 as a *meze*

These delectable, highly seasoned sausages are popular street food all over Greece, and they are the perfect spicy snack at any time of the day. Meaty parcels of minced beef and pork mixed with onions, mint, parsley, and cumin are wrapped in caul fat and threaded onto skewers – in Greece double skewers, joined at one end, are sold for just this purpose. During grilling the fat melts to reveal the moist and tasty sausages inside. Perfect with *toursi* pickles, yogurt, or *tsatsiki,* and pitta, *sheftalia* can be served as a main course or a *meze*.

675 g/1 1/2 lb lean pork or 350 g/12 oz each of lean beef *and* lean pork,
finely minced twice
1 large onion, grated
2 tablespoons fresh mint leaves, finely chopped or 1 tablespoon dried mint, crumbled
1 small bunch of flat leaf parsley, leaves finely chopped
1 teaspoon ground cumin or 1/2 teaspoon ground allspice
2 tablespoons aged red wine vinegar
Coarse-grain sea salt to taste
1/2 tablespoon cracked black pepper, or to taste
Extra virgin olive oil, for grilling

225 g/8 oz pork caul fat (page 349)

For serving
1 small bunch of flat leaf parsley, leaves coarsely chopped
2 small red or mild onions, quartered and thinly sliced
2 lemons, cut into wedges
3 ripe tomatoes, cut into thin wedges

Combine the meat, onion, mint, parsley, cumin, 1 tablespoon of the vinegar, salt, and pepper in a large bowl. Knead for a few minutes, cover, and refrigerate for 1-2 hours.

Prepare the fire.

Add the remaining vinegar to a bowl of tepid water and soak the caul fat in it for 3 minutes. Separate the pieces, lay flat, and pat dry. With scissors or a sharp knife, cut into pieces approximately 10 x 7 cm/4 x 3 inches.

Divide the meat mixture into 12 portions. Moisten your hands with cold water and shape 1 portion into a 6 cm/2¹/₂ inch-long sausage. Lay it across a narrow end of a piece of caul fat, fold over the edge and sides, and roll up to make a firm parcel. Press down on the sausage firmly but gently to flatten it slightly; take care not to let the caul casing burst. Repeat with the remaining meat and caul fat.

Lightly brush 8 skewers with olive oil. Thread 3 sausages onto 1 skewer, running the skewer through a little off-centre; do not pack them closely together. Carefully insert a second skewer through the sausages, parallel to the first one, to keep the *sheftalia* balanced during grilling. Thread the remaining sausage the same way.

Set a grill rack 10-12 cm/4-5 inches above low coals and lightly brush with olive oil. Grill the sausages 10-15 minutes, turning them carefully so they brown evenly.

Using a fork, push the sausages off the skewers onto a warm platter. Sprinkle with some of the parsley and onion and surround with the lemon wedges. Serve the remaining parsley and onion and the tomatoes separately.

Spicy Sausages with Mustard Sauce
Loukhanika me Yefsi Pastourma
Makes 10 to 12 sausages

Highly spiced with cumin, cayenne pepper, and juniper berries and scented with rosemary and thyme, these sausages, which can be boiled or smoked, are exceptionally good. Although similar in flavour to the Greek delicacy *pastourmas* (spicy preserved veal or pork tenderloin), they are traditionally made with beef. The simple mustard sauce accompanying them is superb, and sets off the spicy sausages to perfection. Serve as a light lunch or supper dish with potatoes or *pilafi*. Or thinly slice the sausages and serve with olives and cheese as a *meze*.

40 g/1¹/₂ oz fresh wholemeal breadcrumbs (for boiled sausages only)

115 ml/4 fl oz (for boiled sausages) to 225 ml/8 fl oz (for smoked sausages) red wine or Meat Stock (page 347)

1¹/₂ tablespoons cumin seeds or 1 tablespoon ground coriander

6 juniper berries

1 teaspoon fresh rosemary

1 teaspoon dried savory (page 15) or thyme

¹/₂ teaspoon cayenne pepper, or to taste

900 g/2 lb lean beef or 450 g/1 lb each of lean beef *and* pork, finely minced twice, or 900 g/2 lb lean pork, very finely chopped

225 g/8 oz (for boiled sausages) to 450 g/1 lb (for smoked sausages) streaky bacon, finely diced or minced

1 clove garlic, crushed

1 tablespoon each of coarse-grain sea salt *and* cracked black pepper, or to taste

225 g/8 oz sausage casings or 1 prepared sheep's intestine (for a smoked sausage, page 349)

Extra virgin olive oil, for cooking the sausages

Mustard Sauce

2 tablespoons mustard seeds

1 tablespoon aged red wine vinegar

1 hard-boiled egg yolk, pressed through a sieve

1 teaspoon honey

2 tablespoons finely chopped flat leaf parsley

1 tablespoon yogurt, preferably home-made (page 8) or extra virgin olive oil

Sea salt *and* cracked black pepper to taste

Soak the breadcrumbs in the 115 ml/4 fl oz wine for 30 minutes.

Heat the cumin seeds in a small dry frying pan until aromatic. Pound the juniper berries, rosemary, savory, and cayenne pepper together in a small mortar until pulverized; or grind in a spice grinder. Combine the meat, streaky bacon, breadcrumbs (or 225 ml/8 fl oz wine), garlic, and salt and pepper in a large bowl. Sprinkle with the herb and spice mixture, knead for a few minutes, cover, and set aside for 1 hour.

With the sausage attachment on an electric mixer, or by hand, fill the casings and tie to make 10-12 cm/4-5 inch sausages. If they are to be boiled, pierce each sausage in several places.

To make one long sausage for smoking, tie a knot in one end of the intestine and carefully fill with the sausage mixture. Secure with a second knot and tie the two knotted ends together. Pierce in a dozen places. Cover with a clean tea towel, then with a board, and place weights (such as tinned fruit) on top. Leave to drain for at least 4 hours.

To boil the sausages Bring a large saucepan of water to a boil, add the sausages, reduce the heat, and simmer 1-1¹/₄ hours, or until cooked through. To check if the sausages are cooked, pierce one with a skewer; the meat should be an even colour all the way through.

To smoke the sausage(s) Follow the manufacturer's instructions for your particular type of smoker, using Mediterranean pine or lemon leaves or a mixture of both if possible. After smoking, hang the sausage(s) until needed.

To serve, lightly brush the boiled sausages with olive oil and bake for 30 minutes at

180C/350F/gas mark 4, turning them once. Or split the sausages lengthways, brush with olive oil, and grill until lightly browned on both sides. Smoked sausages need no cooking, but frying them in olive oil gives an even better flavour.

To make the mustard sauce Gently heat the mustard seeds in a dry heavy frying pan until they begin to pop, about 4 minutes. Pulverize them in a mortar or spice grinder and transfer the powder to a bowl. Add the vinegar, egg yolk, honey, parsley, yogurt, and salt and pepper, and mix until smooth with a wooden spoon.

The sauce can be served immediately or made ahead and refrigerated for up to 2 hours.

Note For a *meze* or to add to an omelette, slice boiled sausages into 1 cm/¹/₂ inch pieces and fry in a little olive oil.

Country Sausages
Loukhanika Khoriatika
Makes 12 to 14 sausages

Sausages are as much part of the Greek diet today as they were two thousand years ago. They have long added variety to family meals, provided an effective way of preserving meat, and given the cook a chance to create novel mixtures of herbs, spices, and meats. Traditionalists say that meat for sausages should be hand chopped (to preserve the moisture in the meat). Each different region has its own favoured ingredients and cooking methods, and speciality restaurants, called *kapnisteria,* cater for the popular taste in sausages and smoked meats. In this recipe the pork and beef mixture is strongly flavoured with herbs, spices, and orange zest, and pine nuts add a crunchy country texture. These are good thinly sliced as a *meze,* cooked in omelettes (page 77) or in vegetable dishes (page 180), or just grilled and served with crusty bread and salad.

1 teaspoon dried thyme
2 tablespoons fennel seeds or ¹/₂ teaspoon ground allspice
1 teaspoon ground coriander
1 bay leaf, ground
900 g/2 lb lean pork, finely diced or 450 g/1 lb lean pork, finely diced, *and*
450 g/1 lb lean beef, finely minced twice
225 g/8 oz streaky bacon
1 tablespoon cracked black pepper
1 tablespoon coarse-grain sea salt, or to taste
One 5 cm/2 inch strip of orange zest, blanched or dried (page 348), finely chopped
4 tablespoons lightly toasted pine nuts, coarsely ground
25 g/1 oz fresh wholemeal breadcrumbs, *optional*
1 clove garlic, crushed
3 tablespoons finely chopped flat leaf parsley
50-115 ml/2-4 fl oz red wine or Meat Stock (page 347), to moisten
225 g/8 oz sausage casings (page 349)
Extra virgin olive oil, for cooking the sausages

For serving
Lemon wedges
Coarsely chopped flat leaf parsley

Pound the thyme, fennel seeds, coriander, and bay leaf in a small mortar until well mixed and the fennel seeds are lightly pulverized.

Combine the meat, streaky bacon, pepper, salt, orange zest, pine nuts, breadcrumbs, garlic, parsley, and spice mixture in a large bowl. Knead for a few minutes and add enough wine to moisten. Cover and set aside for 30 minutes.

With the sausage attachment on an electric mixer or by hand, fill the casings and tie to make 10-12 cm/4-5 inch sausages. Pierce each sausage in several places.

To cook the sausages, heat 4 tablespoons olive oil in a heavy frying pan and fry the sausages over medium-low heat, turning them occasionally, until deep golden brown on all sides. Or brush the sausages with the olive oil and grill until browned on all sides.

To serve, surround with the lemon wedges and sprinkle with the parsley.

Vegetables and Salads

lakhanika ke salates

On taverna menus and at Greek family meals vegetables are often the main focus of attention. This relish for the variety and versatility of fresh vegetables, coupled with the national flair for creating exciting dishes with them, makes Greece a paradise for vegetable lovers.

At the height of the growing season Greek vegetable markets are ablaze with colour – mountains of shiny multi-hued aubergines, piles of courgettes, baskets of scarlet and green peppers, leafy bunches of purple beetroot, fronds of salad greens in infinite variety, mounds of tiny carrots, pyramids of huge red tomatoes, creamy sheaves of fresh celery and fennel, and banks of beans in red, pink, white, and purple. From this cornucopia the cook selects the best vegetables for a range of flavourful dishes: asparagus and new potatoes, or peas, carrots, and artichokes, to serve bathed in a delicate *avgolemono* sauce, or cucumbers, beetroot, or courgettes to turn into sweet and spicy salads. Perhaps carrots, onions, mushrooms, celery, or cauliflower are the best choice for succulent vegetable dishes à la grècque – juicy tomatoes, courgettes, and aubergines to stuff or to bake in aromatic casseroles.

Beans of all sorts appear on Greek family tables at least once a week. In summer bean dishes are made from the fresh varieties available in the market, in winter many of the same dishes are made from dried beans. These range from delicate purées and simple salads for *mezedes* to baked dishes that make substantial main courses.

The cooking method used has a great influence on the flavours of Greek vegetable cookery. Grills and griddles give the special smokey flavour essential to many aubergine dishes; *fournos* cooking produces a glorious texture in vegetables of all kinds, especially beans; and cooking in clay pots lends a unique earthy-sweet taste to potatoes and beetroot. The curious lemon astringency of vine leaves deserves special mention. Tender young leaves are stuffed with a rice mixture, while tougher leaves impart a subtle, enigmatic flavour to a wide range of grilled and baked dishes. Simply boiled or steamed vegetables are rare in Greece; most often they are served with traditional sauces such as the lemony *latholemono* and *avgolemono*, flavoured vinegar sauces, or intriguing concoctions based on pine nuts, walnuts, or almonds. Many of the recipes in this chapter make perfect first course or light lunches and suppers, as well as delicious side dishes.

Marinated Asparagus
Sparangia Latholemono
Serves 3 to 4

This superbly flavoured seasonal dish (see picture page 181) requires little work but it does demand top-quality ingredients: tender young asparagus with a fresh bright colour; a good fruity olive oil, and the juice of a plump fresh lemon. Choose asparagus of a similar thickness for even cooking. The dish can be prepared several hours ahead – the longer the asparagus rests in the marinade, the more mellow the flavour. Serve plenty of crusty bread for your guests to mop up the sauce.

900 g/2 lb asparagus
Coarse-grain sea salt
Juice of 1 large lemon
4 shallots, finely chopped
1 teaspoon dried *rigani* (page 14)
1 small bunch of flat leaf parsley, leaves coarsely chopped
1 teaspoon cracked black pepper
175 ml/6 fl oz extra virgin olive oil, or to taste

Break off the tough ends of the asparagus at the point where they snap easily and discard. Add 5 cm/2 inches of water and salt to taste to a shallow saucepan large enough to hold the asparagus in a double layer. Bring to a boil and add the asparagus. Simmer 3-5 minutes, or until barely tender, drain, and spread on paper towels to dry. (Or steam the asparagus as directed on page 187.)

Whisk together the lemon juice, shallots, *rigani,* parsley, pepper, salt to taste, and olive oil in a large shallow bowl. Add the asparagus and toss gently to coat. Cover and set aside at room temperature for up to 1 hour, or refrigerate for up to 4 hours, but remove from the refrigerator 15 minutes before serving.

To serve, carefully toss the asparagus with the marinade once more and transfer to a platter. Season to taste with salt and pepper and serve.

Note   Artichoke hearts, cauliflower florets, slender leeks, green beans, beetroot, and courgettes can all be prepared the same way.

Beetroot Island-Style
Panzaria Nisiotika
Serves 6 as a *meze,* 3 as a vegetable dish or for a light lunch

For this ancient dish island cooks choose small young beetroot, each purple-red globe nestling in glossy green leaves. Crisp leaves are a good indication of freshness but, even more important, they're packed with vitamins and minerals – so the Greeks make them an integral part of the dish. Clay-pot cooking gives the beetroot the best flavour but they can also be oven-baked or boiled. An appetizing light lunch or a good side dish for grilled or roasted pork or chicken, Beetroot Island-Style is also an attractive addition to a *meze* table with Fried Cheese (page 38), olives and Lamb's Liver with Lemon Juice and Rigani (page 35).

6 small beetroot (about 5 cm/2 inches in diameter) with their leaves
1 small red or mild onion, cut into thin rings
Strained juice of 1 large lemon
Coarse-grain sea salt and cracked black pepper to taste
1 teaspoon dried *rigani* (page 14)
75–115 ml/3–4 fl oz extra virgin olive oil, to taste

Trim the stalks and root ends from the beetroot. Reserve the green leaves and scrub the beetroot with a stiff brush under cold running water. Bake in a clay pot or baking dish (page 205), or boil 15 minutes in boiling (salted) water, or until just tender when pierced with the point of a knife. Drain, and when cool enough to handle, remove the skins with a small paring knife.

Place the onion in a glass or china bowl and sprinkle with half the lemon juice, salt and pepper, and *rigani*. Toss to mix, cover, and set aside.

Remove the tough stalks from the beetroot greens and discard any leaves that are not fresh and glossy; leave thin tender stalks intact but trim to 5 cm/2 inches. Thoroughly rinse, tear into pieces, and place in a saucepan. Add 4 tablespoons boiling water, cover, and cook 2-3 minutes over low heat, or until just tender; do not overcook. Drain in a colander set over a bowl, pressing the greens against the colander with the back of a wooden spoon. (Reserve the mineral-rich cooking liquid for soup stock.)

While the beetroot are still warm, cut lengthways into quarters (the traditional shape) or into 4 cm/1½ inch julienne (matchsticks). Combine with half the olive oil and half the remaining lemon juice and salt and pepper in a non-reactive bowl and toss to coat. Arrange the beetroot on one side of a platter and the greens on the other side. Sprinkle with the remaining olive oil and lemon juice and a generous amount of salt and pepper and scatter the onion over the beetroot. Serve warm or at room temperature.

Variations
Coarsely chop the cooked greens. Combine with the quartered beetroot and add the lemon juice, olive oil and salt and pepper; omit the onion and *rigani*.

To serve taverna-style, use only the beetroot; save the greens for Beetroot Greens Salad (page 222). Cut the cooked beetroot into julienne (matchsticks). Add the lemon juice, olive oil, salt and pepper, and 1 tablespoon crushed coriander seeds; omit the *rigani*. Immediately before serving, add 6 sprigs of fresh mint leaves torn into small pieces or 4 tablespoons coarsely chopped flat leaf parsley to the beetroot, gently toss together, and garnish with the onion.

Beetroot Salad with Allspice
Panzaria Kritika
Serves 4

Allspice features often in Cretan cookery, and this easy-to-make salad comes from a most unlikely source – a monastery on the island, where, on a quiet summer's day, I enjoyed a simple but delightful lunch. With typically Cretan hospitality the monks set before us large platters of this excellent salad, bowls of creamy fresh goat's cheese, and trays of grilled fish. You can prepare the dish up to 24 hours ahead; try it with egg dishes or grilled meats, or with cheese and fish.

6 small beetroot (about 5 cm/2 inches in diameter)
$^1/_2$ tablespoon ground allspice
Coarse-grain sea salt *and* cracked black pepper to taste
5 tablespoons extra virgin olive oil
Strained juice of 1 lemon

For serving
2 tablespoons fresh mint leaves or coarsely chopped fresh dill, *optional*
1 small red or mild onion, cut in half and thinly sliced
4 tablespoons coarsely chopped flat leaf parsley
12 Elitses or 8 Niçoise olives, drained

Heat the oven to 160C/325F/gas mark 3. Trim the stalks and root ends from the beetroot and scrub them under cold running water with a stiff brush. Line a heavy baking dish with aluminium foil (to prevent the beetroot from discolouring the dish), add the beetroot and 4 tablespoons water, and bake uncovered for 40 minutes or until just tender; add more water to the dish if necessary. (Or wrap each beetroot in aluminium foil and bake; allow an extra 30 minutes baking time.)

Peel the beetroot with a small paring knife and cut into 4 cm/1$^1/_2$ inch julienne (matchsticks). Place in a non-reactive bowl with the allspice, salt and pepper, olive oil, and half the lemon juice, gently toss together, cover, and set aside.

Just before serving, tear the mint leaves into small pieces. Combine the onion with the parsley, mint, remaining lemon juice, and salt.

Transfer the beetroot to a serving dish and sprinkle with the onion mixture, any marinade remaining from the beetroot and onion, and salt and pepper to taste. Scatter the olives over the beetroot and serve.

Artichokes City-Style
Aginares a la Polita
Serves 6

This fresh-tasting spring vegetable dish dates from the days of the Byzantine Empire, and the 'city' in question is thought to be Constantinople (now Istanbul), the glittering empire's capital. Artichokes, new potatoes, carrots, small onions, and broad beans cook slowly in a tightly closed casserole from which none of the delectable flavour can escape. The dish takes some time to prepare, but it can be made a day ahead for convenience.

2 lemons
12 small or 6 medium artichokes, preferably with 5 cm/2 inches of stem intact
1 tablespoon plain flour
Sea salt
6 small new potatoes, peeled if desired
6 small young carrots
12 boiling onions (about 2.5 cm/1 inch in diameter), peeled (page 132)
1.2 kg/2½ lb young broad beans, shelled
Freshly ground white pepper to taste
4 sprigs of fresh dill
115 ml/4 fl oz extra virgin olive oil, or to taste

For serving
Lemon wedges

Fill a large non-reactive saucepan with water and bring to a boil. Meanwhile, squeeze the juice from the lemons, set the juice aside, and add 2 of the lemon halves to a large bowl of iced water; whisk in the flour and 1 teaspoon salt. (Flour and salt help prevent the artichokes from discolouring.) Remove the outer leaves of the artichokes, leaving only the tender light green ones. With a sharp knife, slice off the top third of each artichoke, and scoop out the fuzzy choke with a small spoon. Peel the tough outer skin from the stems. Cut medium artichokes in half lengthways. Rinse, rub with a lemon half, and add to the bowl of iced water.

Cut potatoes larger than 2.5 cm/1 inch in diameter in half, and cut the carrots into 1 x 5-cm/½ x 2-inch sticks.

Drain the artichokes and add to the boiling water with the potatoes and onions. Boil 2 minutes, add the carrots, and boil 2 minutes longer, then add the broad beans and cook 1 minute longer. Drain, reserving 350 ml/12 fl oz of the cooking liquid.

Transfer the vegetables to a heavy saucepan large enough to accommodate them in a single layer, arranging the artichokes bottoms up. Add salt, pepper, most of the dill, and enough of the reserved cooking liquid to come halfway up the sides of the artichokes.

Whisk together the olive oil and two thirds of the reserved lemon juice and pour this *latholemono* sauce over the vegetables. Cut a piece of waxed paper to fit the saucepan, making a hole in the centre for the steam to escape. Gently press the paper down on top of the vegetables (to prevent the artichokes from discolouring) and cover the saucepan.

Set over medium heat and bring just to a simmer. Immediately reduce the heat to very low and simmer 25 minutes, or until the vegetables are just tender; there should always be about 225 ml/8 fl oz of liquid in the pan – add more of the reserved cooking liquid if necessary. Season the sauce to taste with the remaining lemon juice and olive oil, salt, and/or pepper. If there is more than 225 ml/8 fl oz sauce, pour into a small saucepan and reduce to 225 ml/8 fl oz by rapid boiling.

Place the artichokes bottoms up in the centre of a warm platter and surround with the other vegetables. Spoon over the sauce and garnish with the remaining dill. Serve hot, warm, or at room temperature, with bowls of lemon wedges.

Note   To make ahead, transfer the vegetables and sauce to a non-reactive bowl, let cool, cover, and refrigerate. Heat gently to warm or bring to room temperature before serving. Season the sauce to taste with salt, pepper, and/or lemon juice and serve.

Variations

Add 3 skinned, seeded, and diced ripe tomatoes and 1/2 teaspoon sugar to the saucepan with the drained vegetables. Do not add lemon juice to the cooking liquid, but sprinkle the vegetables with 2 tablespoons lemon juice to serve.

Serve with *avgolemono* sauce instead of *latholemono*. Add only 4 tablespoons olive oil and 2 tablespoons lemon juice to the vegetables. Just before the vegetables are cooked, whisk 2 egg yolks for 1 minute, whisk in the remaining lemon juice, and whisk 1 minute longer. When the vegetables are cooked, remove 225 ml/8 fl oz cooking liquid and cover the vegetables to keep warm. Gradually whisk the cooking liquid into the egg and lemon juice mixture, whisking 1 minute longer, and transfer to the top of a double boiler set over hot water. Cook over low heat, stirring constantly with a wooden spoon, until the sauce thickens enough to lightly coat the back of the spoon, about 1 minute. Arrange the vegetables on a warm platter, pour over the sauce, garnish with the dill, and serve at once.

Asparagus and New Potatoes Avgolemono
Sparangia me Patates ke Avgolemono
Serves 4

This is a spring dish of subtle delicacy and exquisite flavour. The gentle cooking method allows the potatoes to absorb a muted asparagus flavour; the vegetables are lightly coated with the classic *avgolemono* sauce. Serve as an elegant first course or lunch or as an accompaniment to grilled or roasted meats.

16 small new potatoes (about 675 g/1 1/2 lb), peeled if desired and cut in half or into quarters
675 g/1 1/2 lb asparagus
2 large eggs
Strained juice of 2 lemons
Sea salt and freshly ground white pepper to taste

minutes; take care not to break up the turnips when stirring. Add the grapes and currants and heat to warm through.

Combine the honey, ginger, rosemary, and vinegar, add to the pan, and simmer until the sauce is slightly syrupy, about 2 minutes. Serve immediately.

Sweet and Sour Courgettes
Kolokithaki Glykoxsino
Serves 6

The dominant flavour in this easy dish is cinnamon, but the sprinkling of lemon juice lends just the right hint of tartness to balance the sweetness of the sauce. Serve it with grilled chicken, pork, or swordfish.

900 g/2 lb courgettes, each preferably about 5 cm/2 inches long
Coarse-grain sea salt to taste
50 g/2 oz small dark seedless raisins
75 ml/3 fl oz aged red wine vinegar
5 tablespoons extra virgin olive oil
1 tablespoon ground cinnamon, or to taste
2 tablespoons aromatic honey diluted with 4 tablespoons hot water
1 teaspoon cracked black pepper, or to taste

For serving
1 small bunch of flat leaf parsley, leaves coarsely chopped
1 tablespoon dried *rigani* (page 14), briefly pounded in a mortar

Trim the courgettes and rub with a tea towel to remove any fuzz. If large, cut into pieces 5 cm/2 inches long and 2.5 cm/1 inch thick; if smaller than 5 cm/2 inches leave whole. Pat dry with paper towels and sprinkle lightly with salt. Combine the raisins and vinegar in a small non-reactive bowl.

Warm the olive oil in a heavy sauté pan large enough to hold the courgettes in a single layer and sauté the courgettes over low heat until just tender, about 8 minutes; stir occasionally with a wooden spoon so they cook evenly. Sprinkle the courgettes with cinnamon and add the raisins and vinegar, honey and water, and pepper. Gently shake the pan to mix, and cook until the sauce becomes slightly syrupy, about 3 minutes.

Transfer the courgettes to a serving dish, pour over the sauce, and sprinkle with the parsley, *rigani,* and salt and pepper to taste. Serve hot, warm, or cold.

Cucumber Salad with Honey Vinegar Sauce
Angouri Salata
Serves 4

Along with more dramatic treasures, archaeologists working on Minoan sites have also found cucumber seeds – remnants of sumptuous royal feasts or frugal family suppers long ago. This simple salad is based on a classic recipe and features ingredients that have been accessible to Greek cooks for centuries – good olive oil, aged red wine vinegar, and aromatic honey. Serve it with grilled meats or fish.

1 large cucumber, peeled
Coarse-grain sea salt
4 tablespoons aged red wine vinegar
2 tablespoons aromatic honey, such as Hymettus
$^1/_2$ teaspoon cracked black pepper, or to taste
2 tablespoons extra virgin olive oil
4 tablespoons fresh chervil, dill, or flat leaf parsley, coarsely chopped

For serving
12 Elitses or 6 Niçoise olives

Slice the cucumber paper-thin with a mandoline or knife, or cut into matchsticks. Place in a bowl, sprinkle with 1 tablespoon salt, and toss to mix. Cover and set aside for 1 hour.

Combine the vinegar, honey, pepper, and a pinch of salt in a non-reactive bowl. Whisk in the olive oil. Gently squeeze the cucumber slices, a handful at a time, between paper towels, to remove as much moisture as possible. Add the cucumber and chervil to the vinegar sauce and mix well.

Transfer to a shallow bowl or platter, scatter the olives over, and serve.

Carrots and Tiny Onions à la Grècque
Karotta ke Kremithi Mikri Khoriatiko
Serves 8 as a first course, 4 as a vegetable dish or as part of a buffet

Tiny delicately-sweet carrots are ideal for this spicy dish, but if they are not available buy the best fresh young carrots you can find. When you make this be sure to give the flavours time to mellow and mature. Serve as part of a buffet, as a first course, or as a side dish. Celery and cauliflower are also good prepared à la grècque (see the variations below).

350 g/12 oz slender young carrots, cut into 5 cm/2 inch lengths
4 tablespoons extra virgin olive oil
2 tablespoons dried coriander seeds, lightly crushed
450 g/1 lb small boiling onions, peeled (page 132)
450 ml/16 fl oz dry white wine
$^1/_2$ teaspoon ground mace
3 bay leaves
$^1/_2$ tablespoon aromatic honey, such as Hymettus
1 tablespoon cracked black pepper
Coarse-grain sea salt to taste

For serving
3 tablespoons coarsely chopped fresh coriander or finely chopped flat leaf parsley or 1$^1/_2$
tablespoons chopped fresh oregano or thyme
1 tablespoon finely grated lemon zest
Lemon wedges

Blanch the carrots in lightly salted boiling water for 1 minute, drain, rinse, and set aside.

Heat the olive oil in a large heavy saucepan over low heat. Add the coriander seeds and the vegetables in a single layer and stir with a wooden spoon to coat with the oil. Add the wine, mace, bay leaves, honey, pepper, and salt. Bring just to a boil, cover, reduce the heat, and simmer gently 20 minutes or until tender.

Transfer the vegetables to a non-reactive bowl and measure the liquid. If there is more than 350 ml/12 fl oz, return it to the saucepan and reduce by rapid boiling over high heat. Pour over the vegetables and set aside until cool. Cover the bowl and shake it gently to redistribute the vegetables in the marinade, and set aside in a cool spot for 1-2 hours before serving.

To serve, taste the marinade; if more salt is needed, combine it with the fresh coriander. Chop the coriander, lemon zest, and salt together just until mixed.

Transfer the vegetables to a shallow serving bowl and pour over most of the marinade (strain it first if you prefer). Sprinkle with the coriander mixture and serve with the lemon wedges.

Celery à la Grècque
Selino Khoriatiko

Substitute 1 head of celery for the carrots and onions and 1 tablespoon caraway seeds for the mace. Slice off the root end of the celery and rinse the sticks well. Remove the tough strings with a small sharp knife and cut the stalks on the diagonal into 5 cm/2 inch lengths. Blanch 2 minutes in lightly salted boiling water, drain, and dry on paper towels.

Cauliflower à la Grècque
Kounoupithi Khoriatiko

Substitute 1 medium head of cauliflower, broken into florets, for the celery and use parsley as the garnish. Trim as much stalk as possible from the florets and cut an "X" in the base of each with a small sharp knife. Blanch 1 minute in lightly salted boiling water and drain. Simmer in the marinade for only 6 minutes, or until barely soft.

Mushrooms à la Grècque
Manitaria Khoriatika
Serves 6 as a first course, 3 as a vegetable dish

There are many versions of this popular dish, but most are pale imitations of the original Greek creation, with little of the rich mix of spicy and earthy flavours that are its hallmark. The intensity of flavour can be adjusted according to taste – for a lightly spiced dish prepare only two hours ahead; for more mellow taste and texture leave overnight in the marinade; the dominant cinnamon tones can be similarly exploited or subdued.

450 g / 1 lb small white mushrooms
2-3 tablespoons extra virgin olive oil, to taste
One 7 cm / 3 inch cinnamon stick, broken in half
2 bay leaves
1 tablespoon coriander seeds, lightly crushed
350 ml / 12 fl oz dry white wine
Coarse-grain sea salt to taste
1 teaspoon cracked black pepper, or to taste

For serving
Chopped fresh thyme, oregano or coriander
Lemon wedges

Trim the mushroom stalks and brush or wipe the mushrooms.

Combine the olive oil, cinnamon stick, bay leaves, and coriander seeds in a heavy sauté pan large enough to hold the mushrooms in a single layer, and heat over low heat. Add the mushrooms, cover, and sweat 5 minutes, or until they have released most of their liquid and are slightly darkened and aromatic; don't let them become soft.

Bring the wine to a boil in a small non-reactive pan over high heat and reduce to 225 ml/8 fl oz by rapid boiling. Add to the mushrooms along with the salt and pepper. Bring to a boil, then transfer to a non-reactive bowl and set aside to cool. Cover and set aside for 2 hours in a cool place or refrigerate overnight.

To serve, transfer the mushrooms to a shallow bowl and pour (or strain) over the marinade.

Season to taste with salt and pepper. Sprinkle with the thyme and serve with lemon wedges.

Note Slender leeks, green beans, or artichoke hearts, all blanched 2 minutes, or quartered cooked beetroot, can be prepared the same way for multi-coloured variations.

Broad Beans in Vine Leaves
Fassoulakia sto Fourno
Serves 4 to 6

Young vine leaves appear in Crete's lively markets at the same time as broad beans, and this is the dish Cretan cooks make with the pick of the new spring crop. Since vine leaves and broad beans generally do not appear simultaneously in our own markets, brine-preserved vine leaves and green beans such as young limas make good substitutes. The leaves are not wrapped around the beans but, used to line the bottom of the baking dish and as a protective covering, they act as a flavouring agent. This dish is delicious with grilled or roasted meat or chicken.

900 g/2 lb very young broad beans in the pod or young lima beans or similar
About 30 fresh or brine-preserved vine leaves, rinsed
75-115 ml/3-4 fl oz extra virgin olive oil, to taste
Juice of 2 small lemons
Coarse-grain sea salt *and* freshly ground black pepper to taste

For serving
4 tablespoons finely chopped flat leaf parsley

Heat the oven to 160C/325F/gas mark 3. With a small paring knife, trim the ends of the beans. Remove a thin slice from each side of the broad beans, or remove the strings from limas or other beans (see Note). Blanch in lightly salted boiling water for 1 minute, remove with a slotted spoon, and set aside in a colander to drain. Add 6 or so vine leaves to the boiling water and blanch 5 seconds if fresh, 3 seconds if preserved; with a slotted spoon, transfer to paper towels to drain. Repeat with the remaining leaves.

Cover the bottom of a deep heavy baking dish, large enough to hold the beans in a double layer, with half the vine leaves, glossy sides down. Spread the beans over the leaves and add 4 tablespoons of the olive oil, half the lemon juice, and 225 ml/8 fl oz water. Sprinkle with salt and pepper and lay the remaining leaves on top, glossy sides up. Bake 50 minutes or until soft; test with a sharp knife, making sure to insert the point through a bean as well as the pod. Bake 15-30 minutes longer if necessary, and sprinkle with an additional 4-8 tablespoons water if the dish seems in danger of drying out.

Discard the top layer of leaves and transfer the beans to a warm serving dish. Sprinkle with the remaining lemon juice and olive oil and cooking liquid to taste. Season with salt and pepper and sprinkle with parsley. Serve hot, warm, or at room temperature.

Variations
Substitute 675 g/1½ lb white mushrooms or 900 g/2 lb waxy potatoes for the beans, or a

mixture of both. Trim the mushroom stalks to 1 cm/¹/₂ inch. Peel the potatoes if desired, cut into bite-size pieces, and cook 5 minutes in lightly salted boiling water. Bake mushrooms 25 minutes, potatoes or potatoes and mushrooms 40 minutes, or until tender.

Note Small young tender beans need only the ends trimmed off; larger beans have tough strings down the sides that should be removed. To do this quickly, hold a small paring knife firmly in one hand and trim the stem end of the bean from its outside curve nearly through to the inner side; the string will come away with the stem.

Stuffed Vine Leaves with Latholemono Sauce
Dolmades me Latholemono
Serves 8 as a first course, 4 as a main course

Dolmades – little rolls of savoury rice in vine leaves – are popular all over Greece and there are endless variations on the theme. Tiny versions, called *dolmadakia*, are served as a *meze*, while the larger *dolmades* can be first or main courses. Sometimes the filling is simply rice flavoured with allspice or cinnamon; sometimes it includes meat, pine nuts, currants, and fragrant herbs. *Dolmades* are not difficult to make but they do take time, so it's worth knowing that they freeze well (freeze before cooking).

75-115 ml/3-4 fl oz extra virgin olive oil, to taste
6 spring onions, trimmed, with best green parts left intact, and finely chopped
225 g/8 oz long-grain rice
1 teaspoon ground cinnamon
Sea salt
1 bay leaf
450 ml/16 fl oz Chicken Stock (page 344) or water
50 g/2 oz pine nuts
65 g/2¹/₂ oz currants or small dark seedless raisins
32 medium vine leaves or 40 smaller leaves, fresh or brine-preserved, *plus* extra leaves to make 1 layer in the baking dish
1 small bunch of fresh dill, coarsely chopped or 8 sprigs of fresh mint, leaves torn into small pieces
4 tablespoons finely chopped flat leaf parsley
Cracked black pepper to taste
Juice of 2 large lemons

For serving
Lemon wedges

Heat 2 tablespoons of the olive oil in a heavy saucepan and sauté the spring onions over low heat until soft, about 5 minutes. Add the cinnamon and rice and stir well with a wooden spoon.

Add salt to taste, the bay leaf, and stock. Raise the heat and boil uncovered until the liquid has disappeared and holes appear in the surface of the rice, about 8 minutes. Stir in the pine nuts and currants with a fork and cover the saucepan with 2 layers of paper towels and a tight-fitting lid. Set aside for 15 minutes in a warm spot such as the back of the stove.

Fill a large saucepan with water and bring to a boil. Trim off the stalks from the 32 medium or 40 smaller vine leaves and set aside.

Add the remaining leaves to the boiling water, 5 or 6 at a time, and blanch 3 seconds if preserved, 5 seconds if fresh. Remove with a slotted spoon, spread between layers of paper towels, and blot dry. Line a heavy shallow non-reactive and flameproof dish or sauté pan, large enough to hold the *dolmades* in a single tightly packed layer, with these leaves, glossy sides facing down. Blanch the reserved leaves, drain, and blot dry.

Remove the bay leaf from the rice and, with a fork, stir in most of the dill, the parsley, the juice of half a lemon, and salt and pepper to taste.

Place a vine leaf on a clean work surface, glossy side down and stalk end towards your wrist. Use 1 heaped teaspoon of filling each for first course *dolmas,* 1 tablespoon filling for main course *dolmas.* Place the filling in the centre of the leaf at its widest part, pull the stalk end over, and fold in both sides. Firmly roll up the package towards the point of the leaf. Repeat with the remaining leaves and rice; as you finish each *dolmas,* place it in the dish pressing tightly against the next one.

Pour over 2 tablespoons of the remaining olive oil and the juice of another half lemon and add enough water to barely reach the top of the *dolmades.* Cover with a plate slightly smaller than the dish and place a weight (such as a large tin of fruit) on top. Set the dish over medium-low heat and bring just to a boil, reduce the heat, and simmer small *dolmades* 25 minutes, larger ones 30 minutes. There should always be some liquid in the dish; if necessary add more water to barely reach the top of the *dolmades.*

Remove from the heat and, with the plate and weight still in place, set aside for 5 minutes if serving warm, or let cool.

Transfer the *dolmades* to a platter or individual plates and sprinkle with the remaining olive oil and lemon juice. Surround with the lemon wedges, or arrange them between the *dolmades,* and garnish with the remaining dill.

Note For a Cretan touch, substitute Green Grape Sauce (page 320) for half the water used to cook the *dolmades.* The sauce tenderizes the vine leaves to make lovely velvety *dolmades.*

Stuffed Vine Leaves with Avgolemono Sauce
Dolmades me Avgolemono
Serves 8 as a first course, 4 as a main course

These *dolmades* are more substantial than the previous version, filled with lamb and rice and flavoured with allspice and fresh fennel. They are especially good with a rich *avgolemono* sauce, but try them as well with the simpler *latholemono* sauce (page 347).

4 tablespoons extra virgin olive oil

1 large onion, finely chopped

225 g/8 oz lean lamb, finely minced

1 teaspoon ground allspice

Sea salt *and* freshly ground black pepper to taste

150 g/5 oz long-grain rice

275 ml/10 fl oz Light Meat Stock (page 347) or water

32 medium vine leaves or 40 smaller leaves, fresh or brine-preserved, *plus* extra leaves to make 1 layer in the baking dish

2 tablespoons finely chopped fresh fennel leaves *or* 2 tablespoons fresh mint leaves, torn into small pieces

1 small handful flat leaf parsley, leaves finely chopped

Juice of 2 large lemons

2 egg yolks

Heat half the olive oil in a heavy saucepan and sauté the onion over low heat until soft, about 8 minutes. Add the meat, raise the heat, and sauté until lightly browned, breaking up any lumps with a wooden spoon. Add the allspice, salt and pepper, and rice, and cook 1 minute, stirring. Add the stock and boil uncovered until the liquid has disappeared and holes appear in the surface of the rice, about 8 minutes. Cover the saucepan with 2 layers of paper towels and a tight-fitting lid and set aside for 20-25 minutes in a warm spot such as the back of the stove.

Prepare the vine leaves and line a dish as directed on page 196.

With a fork, stir the fennel, most of the parsley, half the lemon juice, and salt and pepper into the rice. Make the *dolmades* as directed on page 196. Pour the remaining olive oil and lemon juice over the *dolmades* and add enough water to barely cover them. Cover with a plate slightly smaller than the dish and place a weight on top. Set the dish over medium-low heat and bring to a boil, reduce the heat, and simmer small *dolmades* 25 minutes, larger ones 30 minutes. There should always be enough liquid to reach the top of the *dolmades;* add more water if necessary.

Pour off 275 ml/10 fl oz of the cooking liquid and strain it. Replace the plate and weight and set the dish aside in a warm spot.

Beat the egg yolks with a hand whisk or electric mixer until pale and frothy. Gradually add the remaining lemon juice and whisk 1 minute longer. Slowly add the strained cooking liquid, whisking constantly. Transfer to the top of a double boiler set over hot water and stir over low heat, using a figure-8 motion, until the sauce is thick enough to lightly coat the back of the spoon, about 6 minutes.

Arrange the *dolmades* on a warm platter or individual plates and pour over the sauce. Sprinkle with the remaining parsley and serve immediately.

Stuffed Vine Leaves and Courgette Flowers
Dolmades Kolokithokorfathes
Serves 8

A delight of late spring in Greece is a beautiful platter of stuffed vine leaves and stuffed courgette flowers, garnished with fresh fennel and wedges of lemon. Both are designed as tiny treats, small enough to be eaten in one mouthful, and stuffed with an aromatic flavoured rice. Stuffed courgette flowers may sound a trifle exotic but do try them – they're delicious and well worth the effort. Serve these as part of a buffet or a picnic.

115 ml/4 fl oz extra virgin olive oil
1 dozen spring onions, trimmed, with best green parts left intact, and finely chopped
4 tablespoons coarsely chopped fresh fennel leaves *or* 1 tablespoon ground fennel seed
225 g/8 oz long-grain rice
Sea salt to taste
450 ml/16 fl oz Chicken Stock (page 344) or water
24 small vine leaves (each one no more than 7 cm/3 inches across at its widest point), fresh or brine-preserved, *plus* extra leaves to make 1 layer in the baking dish
16 courgette flowers or additional vine leaves
1 small handful flat leaf parsley, leaves finely chopped
Strained juice of 2 large lemons
Freshly ground black pepper to taste

For serving
Sprigs of fresh fennel, *optional*
Lemon wedges

Heat 2 tablespoons of the olive oil in a heavy saucepan and sauté the spring onions over low heat until soft, about 5 minutes. Stir in the fennel and cook 1 minute. Add the rice, stirring with a wooden spoon to coat with the oil. Add salt to taste and the stock, raise the heat, and boil uncovered until the liquid has disappeared and holes appear in the surface of the rice, about 8 minutes. Cover the saucepan with 2 layers of paper towels and a tight-fitting lid and set aside for 20 minutes in a warm spot such as the back of the stove.

Prepare the vine leaves and line a dish as directed on page 196 (trim the 25 small leaves before blanching).

To prepare the courgette flowers, gently pull out the stamens, trim the stems, and rinse them by dipping in a bowl of cold water. Shake off the excess water and carefully wrap in a tea towel or use paper towels to pat dry.

With a fork, stir the parsley, the juice of half a lemon, salt, and pepper into the rice to make a highly-seasoned mixture with a distinct flavour of fennel.

Make the *dolmades* as directed on page 196. To fill a courgette flower, hold it in the palm of one hand and, with your thumb, gently push 1 heaped teaspoon of stuffing inside, taking care not to break the flower. Fold 1 petal over the stuffing, then fold in the other petals to make a secure little parcel. Arrange in the dish with the stuffed vine leaves.

Sprinkle all the *dolmades* with 2 tablespoons of the remaining olive oil and the juice of half a lemon and add water to barely reach the top of the *dolmades*. Place a plate slightly smaller than the dish on top of the *dolmades* and set a weight (such as a large tin of fruit) on the plate. Place the dish over medium-low heat and bring to a boil, reduce the heat to low, and simmer 25 minutes. There should always be liquid in the dish; add a little more water if necessary to barely reach the top of the *dolmades*. Remove from the heat and, with the plate and weight still in place, set aside to cool at room temperature.

To serve, arrange the *dolmades* on a platter and sprinkle with the remaining olive oil and lemon juice, and salt and pepper to taste. Garnish with the fennel sprigs and surround with the lemon wedges.

Note To store, let cool, transfer the *dolmades* to a non-reactive airtight container, and refrigerate for up to 2 days. Serve at room temperature.

Baked Aubergines with Tomatoes and Feta Cheese
Melitzanes me Feta
Serves 8

A slightly sweet, nutty flavour is the hallmark of this dish, and the secret lies in the quantity of olive oil used and in the preliminary cooking of the aubergines. An ideal buffet dish served hot or cold, especially with barbecued meats, this can easily be prepared for large numbers of people.

4 large aubergines (900 g–1.2 kg/2–2^1/$_2$ lb)
Sea salt
175–225 ml/6–8 fl oz extra virgin olive oil, to taste
350 g/12 oz *feta* cheese, cut into 8 slices
^{1}/$_2$ tablespoon cracked black pepper, or to taste
4 large ripe tomatoes, skinned, seeded, and diced, juices reserved
2 tablespoons tomato purée diluted with 4 tablespoons water
1 teaspoon honey
8 bay leaves

For serving
1 small bunch of flat leaf parsley, leaves coarsely chopped

Trim the ends from the aubergines and cut lengthways in half. Sprinkle with 2 tablespoons salt and set aside for 30 minutes to "sweat".

Heat the oven to 180C/350F/gas mark 4. Set a large heavy frying pan over medium heat and add 4 tablespoons of the olive oil. Thoroughly dry the aubergines with paper towels and fry half of them until the cut sides are dark golden brown and the skin is shrivelled and darkened, about

12 minutes. Drain between layers of paper towels. Heat 2 tablespoons of the remaining olive oil in the frying pan and fry the remaining aubergines. Drain.

Arrange the aubergines, cut sides up, in a heavy baking dish just large enough to hold them in a single layer. Sprinkle with the pepper and place a slice of *feta* on top of each one.

Combine the tomatoes and their juices, tomato purée, honey, and remaining olive oil and spoon over the *feta* and aubergines. Place a bay leaf on top of each and add just enough water to the dish to cover the bottom. Bake uncovered for 30-40 minutes, or until the aubergines are very soft. There should be about 450 ml/16 fl oz of sauce in the dish; add more water if necessary.

Serve directly from the baking dish, leaving the bay leaves in place as garnish. Sprinkle with the lemon juice, parsley, and salt and pepper to taste. Serve hot or warm.

Note   To grill aubergines, trim the aubergines, cut in half, and "sweat". Set a grill rack about 10 cm/4 inches above hot coals and brush both aubergines and grill with olive oil. Grill on both sides until dark golden brown and soft. Meanwhile, heat the oven and make the tomato sauce. Drain the aubergines on paper towels, arrange in the baking dish as directed, and bake.

Baked Summer Vegetables
Briami Mystras
Serves 6

Magnificent baked vegetable casseroles have been part of Greek life for centuries. The ingredients may vary from season to season, but they always have a rich, satisfying character and fresh flavour. Here the vegetables are slowly baked in an onion and tomato sauce until they have absorbed most of the spicy sauce; a cheesy breadcrumb topping adds a golden crusty finish. Serve with country bread, a green salad and slices of mild *feta* cheese. It's also a perfect accompaniment to grills.

2 medium aubergines (about 350 g/12 oz)
Sea salt
2 green bell peppers, roasted and skinned (page 343)
1 large onion, cut into quarters and thinly sliced
1 large clove garlic, finely chopped
6 large ripe tomatoes, skinned and diced, juices reserved
1 tablespoon honey
1 tablespoon ground cumin
3 tablespoons dried *rigani* (page 14)
5 tablespoons coarsely chopped flat leaf parsley
Freshly ground black pepper to taste
450 g/1 lb new potatoes
450 g/1 lb courgettes, cut into 6 mm/¼ inch slices
5 tablespoons hot water
40 g/1½ oz lightly toasted fresh breadcrumbs

50 g/2 oz grated *kasseri* or parmesan cheese

For serving
Juice of 1 large lemon

Trim the ends from the aubergines and cut into 4 cm/1¹/₂ inch cubes. Sprinkle with 1 tablespoon salt and set aside in a colander to "sweat" for 30 minutes. Slice the tops off the peppers, discard the cores and seeds, rinse off any remaining seeds, and cut lengthways into 6 mm/¹/₄ inch strips.

Heat 4 tablespoons of the olive oil in a large heavy sauté pan and cook the onion over medium-low heat until soft, about 8 minutes. Add the garlic, tomatoes and their juices, honey, cumin, *rigani,* half the parsley, salt, and pepper. Raise the heat, bring to a boil, and simmer 10 minutes, or until reduced by about one third, stirring occasionally with a wooden spoon.

Heat the oven to 190C/375F/gas mark 5. Place a second large heavy sauté pan over medium heat and add 4 tablespoons of the remaining olive oil. Thoroughly dry the aubergine with paper towels and fry until golden brown on all sides, about 10 minutes. Drain between layers of paper towels.

Peel the potatoes and cut into 6 mm/¹/₄ inch slices. Arrange them in the bottom of a deep heavy baking dish. Combine the aubergine, pepper, and courgettes and spread over the potatoes. Pour over the sauce, remaining olive oil, and the hot water, firmly shake the dish to distribute the sauce, cover, and bake 15 minutes. Reduce the oven temperature to 180C/350F/gas mark 4 and bake 20 minutes longer. Stir the vegetables, taking care not to break the potatoes, and bake uncovered 25 minutes longer or until the potatoes are just tender.

Taste the sauce and add salt and pepper if desired. Combine the breadcrumbs and cheese and sprinkle over the vegetables; with the back of a spoon gently press down on the vegetables so a little of the juices reaches the breadcrumbs. Bake, uncovered, 15 minutes longer or until golden brown.

Sprinkle with the lemon juice, pepper, and the remaining parsley. Serve hot, warm, or at room temperature.

Note To make individual casseroles, divide the ingredients between 6 small casseroles. Bake covered at 190C/375F/gas mark 5 for 15 minutes, uncovered at 180C/350F/gas mark 4 for about 25 minutes.

Sweet Sour Okra with Olive Oil
Bamies Psimenes
Serves 3 to 4

It is thought that this beautiful little vegetable was first brought to Greece from ancient Egypt, where it had arrived via the slave routes from central Africa. Today, its distinctive, slightly sour, flavour and exquisite shape, makes okra a popular vegetable in stews and an attractive side dish to grilled fish and meats. Choose okra with care – each pod should be small, firm, and a bright pale green. Greek cooks like okra to retain its colour, shape and juices in cooking so the pods are first sprinkled with wine vinegar or lemon juice and then left in the sun for a few hours, to shrivel slightly. Serve hot, with grills or eggs (page 74), or cold, as a *meze* or side dish.

450 g/1 lb small young okra, rinsed
3 tablespoons fresh lemon juice
4-6 tablespoons extra virgin olive oil to taste
1 tablespoon light honey or sugar
Coarse-grain sea salt *and* freshly ground black pepper to taste

For serving
Finely chopped flat leaf parsley

With a paring knife, trim off the okra stems; take care not to pierce the pods or they will disintegrate in cooking.

Spread the okra on a large china or glass plate and sprinkle with half the lemon juice. Set aside 2 hours, preferably in the sun.

Heat 3 tablespoons of the olive oil in a heavy sauté pan, large enough to hold the okra in a single layer. Add the okra and gently cook for 6 minutes or until the pods are very lightly browned; stir carefully once or twice. Drizzle over the honey, sprinkle with salt and pepper, and the remaining lemon juice, and add 175 ml/6 fl oz water to the pan. Cover and simmer 20 minutes or until the okra is tender; add a little more water to the pan if it is in danger of drying out, but do not disturb the okra.

Carefully transfer the okra and pan juices to a shallow serving dish and sprinkle with the parsley, salt and pepper to taste, and the remaining olive oil. Serve hot, warm, or cold.

Okra and Onions in Tomato Sauce
Bamies Ladera
Serves 4

The secret to the magnificent taste and texture of the stove-top stews (*ladera*) of the Greek taverna kitchen is slow cooking, seasonal flavour, and plenty of olive oil. Okra, a favourite ingredient in *ladera* dishes because of its sharp flavour and great affinity with olive oil, is perfect with chicken (page 125) or beef, or with a rich tomato sauce. The only real care needed in preparing this dish is in the preparation of the okra, to ensure it remains whole during the cooking and doesn't disintegrate into a glutinous mass. Serve warm, with country cheese (page 9), olives, and crusty bread, or cold, as a side dish to meat or fish grills.

550 g/1¼ lb fresh okra, rinsed and trimmed (see above)
2 tablespoons white wine vinegar

4–6 tablespoons extra virgin olive oil, to taste
225 g/8 oz tiny (pearl) onions, peeled (page 132) or 1 large mild onion, quartered and thinly sliced
1 clove garlic, finely chopped
$^{1}/_{2}$–1 teaspoon ground coriander, to taste (*optional*)
450 g/1 lb ripe tomatoes, skinned and diced, juices reserved
1 teaspoon honey or sugar
Coarse-grain sea salt *and* cracked black pepper to taste
Juice of $^{1}/_{2}$ small lemon

For serving
1 small bunch of flat leaf parsley, leaves coarsely chopped

Spread the okra on a glass or china plate and sprinkle with the vinegar. Set aside for 2 hours, preferably in the sun.

Warm 3 tablespoons of the olive oil in a large heavy frying pan and sauté the onions over low heat until soft, about 10 minutes. Add the garlic and coriander and heat until aromatic. Add the tomatoes and their juices, honey, salt, and pepper, and bring to a low boil. Reduce the heat and simmer, uncovered, for 10 minutes, or until the sauce is slightly thickened. Meanwhile, rinse the okra and pat dry with paper towels. Add to the pan with the remaining olive oil and gently simmer, uncovered, for 30 minutes or until the okra is tender but not disintegrating and most of the liquid has evaporated. Sprinkle with the lemon juice and most of the parsley and continue cooking for 10 minutes.

Leave in the pan to cool slightly. Transfer to a shallow serving dish, sprinkle with the remaining parsley, and salt and pepper to taste. Serve warm or cold.

Honey-Glazed Onions
Kremithia sto Fourno
Serves 4

Baked in a honey and wine mixture aromatized with pungent cloves, these onions emerge from the oven beautifully glazed in a light sauce. Meltingly soft and sweetly spicy, they are delicious with grilled or roasted meats and game.

675 g/1$^{1}/_{2}$ lb boiling onions (about 2.5 cm/1 inch in diameter), peeled (see Note)
2 tablespoons unsalted butter
2 tablespoons extra virgin olive oil
225 ml/8 fl oz Mavrodaphne or Madeira wine *and* 1 tablespoon honey, preferably Hymettus, or 225 ml/8 fl oz Chicken Stock (page 344) *and* 2 tablespoons honey, preferably Hymettus
4 cloves
Sea salt *and* freshly ground black pepper to taste

1 small bunch of flat leaf parsley, leaves coarsely chopped
1 tablespoon finely chopped Preserved Lemon (page 18) or 1 tablespoon finely grated lemon zest

Heat the oven to 160C/325F/gas mark 3. Arrange the onions in a heavy baking dish large enough to hold them in a single layer and dot with the butter and olive oil. Combine the wine and honey, 115 ml/4 fl oz water, cloves, salt and pepper in a small saucepan. Bring to a boil over medium-low heat and pour over the onions. Cover and bake 1 hour or until there is about 115 ml/4 fl oz of light syrupy sauce and the onions are very soft.

Chop the parsley, Preserved Lemon, a pinch of salt, and a generous amount of pepper together to mix. With a wooden spoon, gently roll the onions around in the sauce to glaze, and transfer to a warm platter, discarding the cloves. Pour over any remaining sauce and sprinkle with the parsley mixture. Serve hot or warm.

Note Peeling small onions is easier if they are blanched first: Slice the root end off each onion and remove the feathery outside layer of skin. Blanch the onions in boiling water for 5 minutes, drain, and peel.

Courgettes with Olive Oil and Herbs
Kolokithaki me Elaiolatho

Serves 4

When preparing this as a side dish for grilled or roasted meat or fish, I often bake a few extra courgettes – the next day they provide an instant *meze* or salad or make an unusual omelette filling for a quick and tasty lunch.

675 g/1¹/₂ lb small courgettes (5-7 cm/2-3 inches long)
4 tablespoons extra virgin olive oil, or to taste
Juice of 2 lemons
Sea salt *and* freshly ground black pepper to taste
4 tablespoons finely chopped flat leaf parsley
1 tablespoon dried *rigani* (page 14), briefly pounded in a mortar

Heat the oven to 180C/350F/gas mark 4.

Trim the courgettes and rub with a tea towel to remove any fuzz. Arrange in a heavy shallow baking dish large enough to hold them in a single layer. Pour over the olive oil and half the lemon juice and add 115 ml/4 fl oz water. Sprinkle with salt and pepper and bake uncovered for 10 minutes. Roll the courgettes around in the cooking liquid to coat, reduce the oven temperature to 150C/300F/gas mark 2, and bake 40 minutes longer, or until the courgettes are barely soft. Roll them around in the cooking liquid once or twice during baking, and add a few tablespoons water if needed – there should always be at least 4 tablespoons liquid in the dish.

Transfer the courgettes to a warm platter and sprinkle with a few tablespoons of the cooking liquid, the remaining lemon juice, the parsley, *rigani,* and olive oil, salt, and pepper to taste. Serve hot, warm, or cold.

Note To serve as a *meze* or salad, refrigerate the courgettes in the cooking liquid, covered, in a non-reactive container for up to 24 hours. Remove from the liquid and cut into 1 cm/^{1}/$_2$ inch slices. Sprinkle with lemon juice, olive oil, coarse-grain sea salt and cracked black pepper, a generous amount of finely chopped parsley, and *rigani.*

To use as a filling for an omelette, remove the courgettes from the cooking liquid, cut into thin slices, and drain on paper towels. Add to a barely set omelette, with a little finely chopped parsley, dried basil, freshly ground pepper, and a few tablespoons grated *feta* cheese.

Potatoes in a Clay Pot
Patates sto Fourno
Serves 4

The tradition of cooking in unglazed cooking pots dates from the Minoan period, the earliest Western civilization, but it thrives in modern Greece, and with good reason. Vegetables cooked this way need only to be scrubbed, no special care is needed in baking them, and they not only acquire a unique earthy flavour but also retain almost all their vitamins and minerals. Potatoes cooked in a clay pot develop a delightful slightly sweet flavour, making them especially good in salads or as a side dish for a delicately flavoured main course such as Baked Sole in Vine Leaves (page 104). This cooking method is also excellent for beetroot – during baking their natural crimson colour deepens to a rich dark purple and the texture turns velvety smooth.

675 g/1^1/$_2$ lb small new potatoes of a similar size

For serving
Coarse-grain sea salt *and* cracked black pepper to taste
Fresh lemon juice
1-2 tablespoons extra virgin olive oil or unsalted butter
Finely chopped flat leaf parsley, *optional*

Prepare the pot following the manufacturer's instructions or immerse it for 5 minutes in warm water. Pour out the water, add the potatoes, and cover with the lid.

Place in a cold oven and set the oven temperature to 160C/325F/gas mark 3. Bake 1^1/$_4$-1^3/$_4$ hours or until the potatoes are tender.

Transfer to a warm bowl and sprinkle with the salt and pepper, lemon juice, olive oil, and parsley.

Note You can bake the potatoes at a higher heat (220C/425F/gas mark 7) for a shorter time (50 minutes) or at a lower heat (120C/250F/gas mark ^{1}/$_2$) for a longer time (2 hours) if necessary, but always start with a cold oven. For easier cleaning, immerse the pot in hot water as soon as you remove the potatoes from it.

Beetroot in a Clay Pot
Panzaria sto Fourno

Prepare the pot as directed on page 205. Trim the stem and root ends from 6 small beetroot, about 5 cm/2 inches in diameter. Scrub with a stiff brush under cold running water, taking care not to break the skins. Add to the pot, cover, and place in a cold oven. Set the temperature to 160C/325F/gas mark 3 and bake 1½ hours or until the beetroot are tender.

When cool enough to handle, peel the beetroot and cut into quarters or slices. Sprinkle with sea salt and cracked pepper, the juice of 1 small lemon, extra virgin olive oil to taste, 1 tablespoon fresh oregano or dried *rigani,* and finely chopped flat leaf parsley. These are delicious with *pilafi, feta* cheese, or grilled swordfish.

Note If you are using the beetroot in a salad, season while they are still warm.

Garlic Potatoes with Juniper Berries
Patates Skorthou
Serves 4

This is a dish for those who like strong flavours – the taste of these tiny baked potatoes is anything but subtle. The finished dish has a bold expressive character and it's perfect with herbed roast chicken (page 122) or pork dishes. Real garlic lovers can press out the soft centres of the baked cloves and spread them on the potatoes or on toasted bread.

3 tablespoons extra virgin olive oil
2 tablespoons dried juniper berries, lightly crushed
8 large cloves garlic
675 g/1½ lb small new potatoes

For serving
Juice of 1 small lemon
Coarse-grain sea salt *and* cracked black pepper to taste
Finely chopped fresh oregano or dried *rigani* (page 14)
Triangles of toasted wholemeal bread, *optional*

Heat the oven to 180C/350F/gas mark 4.

Pour the olive oil into a heavy shallow baking dish large enough to hold the potatoes in a single layer. Sprinkle the juniper berries over the oil and place the dish in the oven for a few minutes to warm. Trim off the stem ends of the garlic cloves and rub off any feathery outer skin. Place the potatoes and garlic in the warm dish and roll them in the olive oil to lightly coat. Bake 10 minutes and roll the potatoes and garlic in the olive oil once more. Reduce the oven temperature to 150C/300F/gas mark 2 and bake uncovered for 50 minutes or until the potatoes are just tender.

Roll the potatoes in the olive oil to coat once more and transfer to a warm platter. Sprinkle with the lemon juice, salt and pepper, and oregano. Serve hot or warm, with toast, if desired.

Broad Bean Salad with Fennel and Black Olives
Fassoulakia Salata me Elies
Serves 3 to 4

Sweet young broad beans and fresh fennel usually appear in the markets at the same time and their very individual flavours complement each other well. This enticing salad is particularly good with sausages, egg dishes, or cold roast pork.

1.4 kg/3 lb broad beans in the pod
Juice of 1 large lemon, or to taste
75 ml/3 fl oz extra virgin olive oil, or to taste
Coarse-grain sea salt to taste
1 teaspoon cracked black pepper, or to taste
12 Amfissa or other mild black olives, cut in half and pitted
1 small red or mild onion, quartered and thinly sliced
5 tablespoons coarsely chopped fresh fennel or flat leaf parsley

Shell the beans and reserve 2 tender pods. Blanch the pods and beans in lightly salted boiling water for 5 minutes, drain, discard the pods, and rinse the beans. Remove the skins from the beans and place the beans in a non-reactive bowl. Add the lemon juice, olive oil, salt, and pepper, and gently stir to mix. Cover and set aside for 1-2 hours.

To serve, add most of the olives, onion, and fennel to the beans and season to taste with salt, pepper, lemon juice, and/or olive oil. Transfer to a platter, and garnish with the remaining olives, onion, and fennel.

Note Although it is not necessary to remove the skins of very young broad beans, Greek cooks prefer to remove the opaque skins to reveal the pretty shade of green within. Without their skins, broad beans also are easier to digest and have a subtly different flavour.

Variation
Substitute 675 g/1¹/₂ lb green beans, such as fine beans, for the broad beans. Trim both ends of the beans and, if necessary, with a small paring knife remove the strings along both sides. Cut into 4 cm/1¹/₂ inch pieces, blanch in lightly salted boiling water for 5 minutes or until barely tender, and rinse. Proceed as directed above.

Green Lentil Salad
Fakes Salata
Serves 8 to 10 as a *meze*, 4 as a salad

The ancient Greeks believed that the benign influence of green lentils could greatly improve a grouchy temper – I cannot verify this claim, but I have seen smiles of pleasure creep over the faces of my guests when they try this salad! Cumin, parsley, mint, and garlic enhance the rustic tones of the humble lentil and a *latholemono* dressing deepens all the flavours.

275 g/10 oz dried green lentils, picked over and rinsed
1 tablespoon cumin seeds, lightly pounded in a small mortar
1 small red or mild onion, cut into thin rings
Juice of 1 lemon
Coarse-grain sea salt *and* cracked black pepper to taste
1 small bunch of flat leaf parsley, leaves coarsely chopped
2 tablespoons fresh mint leaves or 1 teaspoon dried mint
1 large clove garlic, minced
4 tablespoons finely chopped Preserved Lemon (page 18)
4 tablespoons extra virgin olive oil
2 tablespoons Strained Yogurt (page 8)

For serving
Large pinch of sumak, cayenne pepper or paprika

Place the lentils in a large saucepan and add cold water to cover by 7 cm/3 inches. Bring to a boil, cover, reduce the heat, and simmer until soft but not disintegrating, about 30 minutes. Drain, gently shake the colander once or twice, and set aside to dry. Warm the cumin seeds in a small dry frying pan over low heat until aromatic, about 1 minute.

Combine the onion, half the lemon juice and cumin, and a large pinch of salt in a non-reactive bowl. Chop 1 tablespoon of the parsley and the mint leaves together just to mix; add to the onion. Set aside.

Chop the garlic, most of the Preserved Lemon, the remaining cumin, half the remaining parsley, and a pinch of salt together to mix. Combine with the lentils, remaining parsley and lemon juice, the olive oil, and salt and pepper to taste. Carefully stir to mix.

Transfer to a platter and sprinkle with the onion and its marinade. Spoon the yogurt over the centre and sprinkle with the remaining Preserved Lemon and parsley and the sumak. Serve at room temperature.

Note The lentils can be cooked and combined with their flavourings a day ahead, but do not marinate the onion until a few minutes before serving.

Black-Eyed Peas with Capers
Fassolia me Kapari
Serves 8 as a *meze*, 4 as a vegetable dish

A taverna favourite, this highly flavoured dish is eaten as a quick snack, a *meze*, or a side dish with grilled meats. The beans are mixed with a lovely sweet-sour sauce, piquant with plump capers, and a bed of rocket leaves supplies a refreshing complement. This dish can be prepared several hours ahead.

225 g/8 oz dried black-eyed peas, soaked for 6-8 hours in cold water to cover
1 tablespoon aromatic honey, such as Hymettus
3 tablespoons aged red wine vinegar, or to taste
Coarse-grain sea salt *and* cracked black pepper to taste
5 tablespoons extra virgin olive oil, or to taste
3 tablespoons capers, rinsed, and coarsely chopped if large
4 tablespoons finely chopped flat leaf parsley

For serving
1 small bunch of rocket leaves, torn into bite-size pieces *or* 1 small bunch of watercress, sprigs only
1 small red or mild onion, cut into thin rings
225 ml/8 fl oz Strained Yogurt (page 8)

Place the beans in a saucepan with cold water to cover. Bring to a boil, drain, and rinse out the saucepan. Return the beans to the pan, add cold water to cover by 7 cm/3 inches, and bring to a boil. Cover, reduce the heat, and simmer 20-30 minutes or until tender; take care not to overcook. Drain and set aside in a colander for a few minutes to dry.

Combine the honey, vinegar, and salt and pepper in a large bowl and gradually whisk in the olive oil. Add the beans, capers, and parsley, and mix with a spoon. Season with vinegar, olive oil, salt and/or pepper.

Line the edges of a platter or shallow bowl with the rocket leaves and place the beans in the centre. Scatter over the onion and serve the yogurt separately.

Summer Bean Salad
Kalokherini Salata Fassolion
Serves 12 as a *meze*, 6 to 8 as a salad or vegetable dish

In Greece dried beans and peas are not limited to winter dishes, but appear in various guises all year round – and there's a very good reason for this. At the height of the Greek summer the daytime temperatures are such that slaving over a hot stove is not an activity undertaken with enthusiasm. This is the time to take maximum advantage of the communal village oven. Food preparation can be done in the cool early morning and the main meal of the day taken to the *fournos* for baking; it's common practice to take to the oven not just a meat dish, but also a pot of beans to be baked alongside it. If the beans are not eaten that day they make a lovely cold salad for the next. In this recipe the country flavour of the beans is complemented by the sweet freshness of juicy ripe tomatoes, peppery watercress or purslane, and the perfume of bay leaves, thyme, and parsley. Serve this pretty dish as a *meze,* with crusty bread as a light lunch, or as a side dish for grilled meat, chicken, or liver.

275 g/10 oz dried cannellini or white haricot beans, soaked for 6-12 hours
in cold water to cover
1 onion, peeled and stuck with 2 cloves
1 small carrot, cut into 3 pieces
1 stick of celery, cut into 3 pieces
2 bay leaves
2 large sprigs of parsley
Juice of 1 large lemon
115 ml/4 fl oz extra virgin olive oil
Coarse-grain sea salt *and* cracked black pepper to taste
4 large ripe tomatoes, skinned and diced
Large pinch of sugar
1 large clove garlic, finely chopped
2 tablespoons fresh thyme, finely chopped or 1 tablespoon dried
thyme, crumbled
1 small bunch of watercress, leaves only, or 2 dozen small purslane sprigs

For serving
1 small red or mild onion, cut into thin rings
2 dozen Elitses or 1 dozen Niçoise olives, drained

Place the beans in a saucepan and add cold water to cover. Bring to a boil, drain, and rinse out the saucepan. Return the beans to the saucepan along with the onion, carrot, celery, bay leaves, parsley, and water to cover by 10 cm/4 inches. Bring to a boil, cover, reduce the heat, and simmer 50 minutes or until the beans are tender but not disintegrating. Drain and set aside in a colander for a few minutes to dry.

Combine the beans, half the lemon juice and olive oil, a large pinch of salt, and 1 teaspoon pepper in a large bowl. Stir to mix, taking care not to break up the beans. Cover and set aside for up to 1 hour.

Place the tomatoes in a sieve over a bowl and sprinkle with the sugar and a pinch of salt. Set aside.

Whisk together the remaining lemon juice, garlic, thyme, a large pinch of salt, and pepper to taste in a small non-reactive bowl. Add the remaining olive oil in a thin steady stream, whisking constantly. Add to the beans along with the watercress and tomatoes, and season to taste.

Transfer to a platter and sprinkle with the onion and olives. Serve at room temperature.

Note To bake, soak the beans for 6-12 hours in cold water to cover, drain, and place in a large saucepan with cold water to cover. Bring to a boil, drain, and transfer to a large deep casserole. Add the onion, carrot, celery, bay leaves, parsley, and water to cover by 10 cm/4 inches. Cover and bake 3-4 hours at 130C/250F/gas mark 1/2 or 2 hours at 180C/350F/gas mark 4 (the temperature can be varied to suit your oven schedule). Or, to reduce the baking time by 30 minutes, bring to a boil before placing the casserole in the oven.

Country Salad
Khoriatiki Salata
Serves 6 to 8

No Greek table is complete without a salad; unfortunately, the "Greek salads" served to tourists often fall very short of the real thing. *Khoriatiki salata* is authentic, and it changes with the seasons. In summer the main ingredients are tomatoes, cucumbers, salad greens, and bell peppers; in winter thinly shredded cabbage is dominant. To these are added crumbly *feta* cheese, local black olives, capers, perfumed *rigani,* and a well-flavoured olive oil. Present this salad on a good-sized platter and provide warm bread for your guests to dip into the flavourful juices.

1 large cucumber

4 large ripe tomatoes, skinned if desired

1/2 teaspoon sugar

Coarse-grain sea salt to taste

1 small green bell pepper, roasted and skinned (page 343), seeds wiped off, and cut lengthways into thin strips

1 large handful of salad greens, such as watercress or purslane sprigs or bite-size pieces of rocket leaves, endive or Cos lettuce

1 small red or mild onion, cut into thin rings

12-16 Kalamata olives, drained

8 *toursi* peppers, home-made (page 350) or bottled, drained, *optional*

225 g/8 oz *feta* cheese, drained and crumbled into large pieces

2 tablespoons small capers, drained

3 tablespoons dried *rigani* (page 14)

4 tablespoons finely chopped flat leaf parsley

115 ml/4 fl oz extra virgin olive oil, or to taste

Strained juice of 1 small lemon, *optional*

Cracked black pepper to taste

Trim and peel the cucumber. Cut in half lengthways, then into 1 cm/1/2 inch slices to make half moons. Core the tomatoes and cut into wedges. Sprinkle with the sugar and salt and set aside for 15 minutes. Spread the pepper strips on paper towels to dry.

Arrange the greens around the edge of a platter or shallow serving bowl. Make a circle of tomatoes on the inner part of this border of greens, and arrange a circle of the cucumbers inside it. Sprinkle over the bell pepper, onion, olives, and *toursi* peppers. Pile the cheese in the centre and sprinkle with the capers. Chop the *rigani* and parsley together to mix, and sprinkle

over the salad, along with the olive oil, lemon juice, and pepper.

Note For a winter salad substitute 1 small head of white or green cabbage (about 450 g/1 lb) for the tomatoes and cucumber. Core and rinse the cabbage, then slice very thinly or shred with a large-holed grater. Lightly mix together the cabbage and salad greens and arrange on a platter. Serve as described above.

Traditional Tomato Salad
Domata Salata Patroparadoti
Serves 4

Thick wedges of sweet juicy tomatoes, crumbly *feta* cheese, richly flavoured olives, fruity olive oil, and aromatic hillside herbs make a distinctively Greek combination. This salad, the centrepiece of every taverna table in summer, is the first dish I order each time I enter Greece – just to prove to myself that I'm really there.

6 large ripe tomatoes, skinned if desired

Coarse-grain sea salt *and* cracked black pepper to taste

$^1/_2$ teaspoon sugar

6 spring onions, trimmed, with the best green parts left intact, and thinly sliced

1 small bunch of flat leaf parsley, leaves coarsely chopped

12 Kalamata olives, drained

75 g/3 oz crumbled *feta* cheese

2 tablespoons dried *rigani* (page 14), briefly pounded in a small mortar, or 3 tablespoons fresh oregano leaves

6 tablespoons extra virgin olive oil, or to taste

$^1/_2$ tablespoon fresh lemon juice, *optional*

Core the tomatoes, cut into wedges, and arrange on a platter. Sprinkle with salt and pepper and the sugar, loosely cover, and set aside for 1 hour.

To serve, sprinkle the spring onions, parsley, olives, and *feta* over the tomatoes. Sprinkle the *rigani,* olive oil, and lemon juice over the salad, add olive oil and/or pepper to taste, and serve at once.

Tomato Salad with Rocket and Tiny Olives
Domatosalata me Rokka ke Elies
Serves 4

Rocket (*rokka*), said to be a native of the Greek islands, is mentioned frequently in myth and legend and still grows wild in the Greek countryside. Be sure to choose rocket that's crisp and bright green. With its slightly bitter, mustardy flavour rocket has a wonderful affinity with tomatoes, amply demonstrated by this summer salad. It's especially good with cheese dishes.

4–6 large ripe tomatoes, skinned if desired
Coarse-grain sea salt *and* cracked black pepper to taste
$^{1}/_{2}$ teaspoon sugar
1 small bunch of rocket, leaves trimmed and torn into large pieces
1 small red onion, cut into thin rings
24 Elitses or Niçoise olives, drained
$^{1}/_{2}$ tablespoon fresh lemon juice, *optional*
6 tablespoons extra virgin olive oil, or to taste

Core the tomatoes, cut into wedges, and sprinkle with salt and pepper and the sugar. Cover and set aside for 1 hour.

To serve, spread the rocket on a platter and arrange the tomatoes on top. Scatter over the onion and olives and sprinkle with the lemon juice, olive oil, and pepper. Serve immediately.

Orange Salad Cretan-Style
Salata Kritiki
Serves 6

Folklore has it that the Lasithi plateau on the island of Crete is the birthplace of watercress, and the Cretans certainly are very fond of its peppery bite. Watercress appears in a variety of classic recipes, including this vibrantly colourful traditional favourite.

4 small beetroot, cooked in a clay pot (page 206), peeled, and cut into julienne (large matchsticks)
Juice of 1 small lemon
6 tablespoons extra virgin olive oil, or to taste
Coarse-grain sea salt *and* cracked black pepper to taste
3 large navel oranges
1 large bunch of watercress, sprigs only

225 g/8 oz *feta* cheese, drained and cut into 1 cm/¹/₂ inch dice
12 Elitses or Niçoise olives, drained
2 tablespoons dried *rigani* (page 14), briefly pounded in a small mortar

Combine the beetroot, most of the lemon juice, 2 tablespoons of the olive oil, and salt and pepper in a non-reactive bowl. Cover and set aside.

Peel the oranges and remove any white pith with a sharp knife. Cut the oranges crosswise into 6 mm/¹/₄ inch slices. Remove the pithy centres with the point of a knife. Spread the slices on a plate, tightly cover, and refrigerate until chilled.

To serve, line the edges of a chilled serving platter with the watercress and lay the orange slices in a single overlapping layer on the inside edge of this border. Make a circle of the beetroot inside the oranges and drizzle their marinade over. Place the *feta* in the centre of the platter. Sprinkle the oranges with a little salt, and the beetroot and cheese with the *rigani* and olives. Sprinkle the remaining lemon juice and olive oil and pepper over the salad and serve at once.

Green Salads
Prasines Salatikes

Contrary to popular opinion, a green salad course did not originate with the French or the Italians but with the ancient Greeks. It was the custom to end a great feast with a simple salad, to refresh the palate after the excesses of a rich and heavy meal and, it was believed, to induce drowsiness (although we might suspect that the drowsiness had more to do with the copious quantities of wine consumed).

When Greeks order a green salad they expect to be served a traditional bowl of either Cos lettuce (*marouli*) or one of a variety of wild greens such as purslane, watercress, chicory, or young dandelions. With the exception of those composed of the delicately sweet Cos lettuce Greek salads have in common an earthy, slightly bitter, flavour that's much appreciated by the peoples of the eastern Mediterranean. This special flavour derives from the particular character of the soil of the region and cannot really be reproduced here. But in our markets we can occasionally find purslane, dandelion, and several varieties of chicory and, more frequently, rocket and watercress. Cos lettuce is usually available year-round: In the spring, when it is at its best, use the whole head of lettuce for these salads; in other seasons select just the tender sweet heart. The natural astringency of these greens finds perfect partners in the mellow richness of olive oil and the simple flavours of fresh lemon juice or red wine vinegar and sea salt.

Green Salad with Feta Cheese and Olives
Salatika me Feta
Serves 6 to 8

A refreshing and popular salad, perfect for a simple lunch or a side dish. When a variety of greens is available I like to make it with hearts of Cos lettuce, escarole lettuce, watercress, rocket, and tender young spinach leaves in about equal proportions. Be sure to use good-quality mild *feta* cheese or firm and crumbly goat's cheese.

2 small heads of Cos lettuce *or* 2 hearts of larger heads *or* 3 handfuls of a mixture of young spinach leaves, watercress sprigs, curly endive, young sorrel, escarole lettuce, rocket, and young dandelion leaves
Strained juice of 1 small lemon, or to taste
Coarse-grain sea salt *and* cracked black pepper to taste
5 tablespoons extra virgin olive oil, or to taste
1 small bunch of flat leaf parsley, leaves coarsely chopped
18 Kalamata olives *or* other Greek black or purple olives
225 g/8 oz mild *feta* cheese, cut into 1 cm/$^1/_2$ inch dice
6 spring onions, trimmed, the best green parts left intact, and thinly sliced, *or*
1 small red onion, quartered and thinly sliced
3 tablespoons dried *rigani* (page 14)

Prepare the greens (see recipe below).

Combine the lemon juice and salt and pepper in a non-reactive bowl. Whisk in the olive oil in a thin steady stream. Combine the greens, parsley, olives, *feta,* and spring onions in a serving bowl and pour over the dressing. Toss with a wooden spoon and fork, taking care to break up the cheese as little as possible. Sprinkle with the *rigani* and serve.

Easter Greens Salad with Latholemono Sauce
Salatika Paskhalina
Serves 4

A classic salad of mixed greens, spring onions, and Preserved Lemon, scented with fresh dill and parsley and tossed in an olive oil and lemon juice dressing. This is one of the salads on the traditional Easter table.

2 small heads of Cos lettuce *or* 2 handfuls of curly endive, escarole lettuce, young dandelion leaves, young spinach, young sorrel, rocket *and/or* watercress or purslane sprigs (page 220)
6 spring onions, trimmed, the best green parts left intact

Strained juice of ¹/₂ small lemon, or more to taste
1 small handful fresh dill, coarsely chopped *or* 1 teaspoon dill seeds (soaked for a few minutes in the lemon juice)
Coarse-grain sea salt *and* freshly ground black pepper to taste
4 tablespoons extra virgin olive oil, or to taste
1 small bunch of flat leaf parsley, leaves coarsely chopped
2 tablespoons finely chopped Preserved Lemon (page 18) *or* ¹/₂ tablespoon finely grated lemon zest, blanched in boiling water for 5 seconds and drained

Discard any stalks and imperfect leaves from the greens, rinse well, and tear into large bite-size pieces. Spin dry in a salad spinner or shake off any excess water and loosely wrap in a clean tea towel. Refrigerate for up to 12 hours.

To serve, cut the spring onions lengthways into quarters, then into 2.5 cm/1 inch lengths. Combine the lemon juice (and dill seeds) and salt and pepper in a non-reactive bowl and gradually whisk in the olive oil. Combine the greens, spring onions, fresh dill, parsley, and Preserved Lemon in a serving bowl, and pour the *latholemono* sauce over. Toss with a wooden spoon and fork and add lemon juice, salt, and/or pepper to taste. Serve immediately.

Note Greek cooks take pride in slicing Cos lettuce as thinly as possible. This does indeed produce a sophisticated salad but also results in the loss of much vitamin C contained in the leaves. I prefer to tear the green leaves, minimizing the loss of this delicate vitamin.

Island Greens Salad
Salatika Nisiotika
Serves 6 to 8

Batavia lettuce is now sometimes available in our shops, and its flavour is very similar to that of the wild greens popular throughout Greece and the islands. Escarole lettuce is from the same botanical family and its tender, mildly astringent inner leaves are a delicious addition to a green salad. If you cannot find these bitter greens add a finely sliced Belgian endive or a few beautiful deep crimson radicchio leaves to give your salad an intriguing bite and lift it out of the ordinary. Choose Belgian endives with tightly closed heads, and buy the freshest escarole greens you can find – the flavour changes to an unpleasant bitterness once they're past their peak. For this popular island salad choose several contrasting types of salad greens. Fresh lemon juice is the perfect dressing – as a general rule, the more bitter the greens, the more lemon juice you'll need.

3 handfuls of watercress, escarole lettuce, young spinach leaves, curly endive, young dandelion, young sorrel, radicchio, purslane, Cos lettuce *and/or* rocket
2 slices wholemeal bread, crusts removed and cut into 1 cm/¹/₂ inch dice
Coarse-grain sea salt *and* freshly ground black pepper to taste
4 tablespoons extra virgin olive oil, or to taste
1 large clove garlic, cut into 2 or 3 pieces

2 tablespoons finely chopped Preserved Lemon (page 18) *plus* 2 tablespoons of its oil
(see Note)

Juice of $^1/_2$ small lemon, or to taste

1 small bunch of flat leaf parsley, leaves coarsely chopped

24 Elitses or Niçoise olives, drained

1 small red onion, quartered and thinly sliced

3 tablespoons fresh herbs such as marjoram, basil or oregano or 2 tablespoons dried *rigani*
(page 14)

Prepare the greens (page 218).

Sprinkle the bread dice with salt and a generous amount of pepper. Warm half the olive oil in a large heavy frying pan and sauté the garlic over low heat until it becomes aromatic, 2-3 minutes. Remove with a slotted spoon and discard. Raise the heat to medium and fry the bread dice until golden brown on all sides. Drain between layers of paper towels.

Combine the Preserved Lemon and its oil, lemon juice, and pepper to taste, in a non-reactive bowl, and gradually whisk in the remaining olive oil.

Combine the greens, parsley, olives, onion, herbs, and crôutons in a serving bowl. Pour over the dressing and toss with a wooden spoon and fork. Add salt and pepper, olive oil, and/or lemon juice to taste and serve at once.

Note You can substitute the juice of 1 whole lemon plus 2 tablespoons extra virgin olive oil for the Preserved Lemon, oil, and juice of $^1/_2$ a lemon if necessary.

Purslane Salad
Salatika Glistritha
Serves 4

If you have a garden, purslane is very easy to grow and it can be made into a wonderfully refreshing salad, either on its own or with other salad greens for variety in taste and texture. Or try adding other vegetables to the greens, such as beetroot, potatoes, young broad beans, tomatoes, or chickpeas and other dried beans.

2 large handfuls of purslane, sprigs only or 1 small handful of purslane, sprigs only *and* 2
handfuls of rocket, escarole lettuce, Cos lettuce *and/or* young spinach leaves

2 spring onions, trimmed, the best green parts left intact, and thinly sliced, *optional*

Coarse-grain sea salt *and* cracked black pepper to taste

Strained juice of 1 lemon, or to taste

5 tablespoons extra virgin olive oil, or to taste

Thoroughly rinse the purslane and remove the small fleshy leaves in clusters (the stalks are easily broken with your thumbnail). Prepare the greens (page 218).

Combine the greens and spring onions in a salad bowl and sprinkle with salt and pepper, lemon juice, and olive oil. Toss with a wooden spoon and fork and add salt, pepper, and/or lemon juice to taste. Serve immediately.

Purslane and Young Beetroot
Salatika Glistritha ke Panzaria
Serves 4

Sweet young beetroot and crunchy peppery purslane make an appealing combination. With its pretty crimson-green contrast, this is an attractive side dish for grilled meat, chicken, or fish and egg dishes. Other Mediterranean greens such as rocket, watercress, young dandelion leaves, or escarole lettuce can be substituted for the purslane.

3 medium young beetroot, baked in a clay pot (page 206) or boiled, and peeled
Generous pinch of ground cloves
Coarse-grain sea salt *and* cracked black pepper to taste
Strained juice of 1 large lemon
6 tablespoons extra virgin olive oil, or to taste
2 handfuls of purslane
2 spring onions, white parts only, thinly sliced

Cut the beetroot into julienne (large matchsticks). Place in a non-reactive bowl, sprinkle with the cloves, salt and pepper, and half the lemon juice and olive oil. Gently toss together, taking care not to break the beetroot. Cover and set aside for 1 hour or refrigerate for up to 4 hours.

Thoroughly rinse the purslane and remove the small fleshy leaves in clusters.

Combine the beetroot, purslane, and remaining lemon juice and olive oil in a salad bowl. Add salt and pepper to taste, sprinkle with the spring onions, and serve immediately.

Wild Greens
Agria Khorta

To Greeks *khorta* means green vegetables or wild greens, sometimes even including grass; to compound the confusion wild greens are occasionally called wild herbs, and all these may be called *salatika*! For the sake of clarity, here the term refers only to wild leaf greens such as mustard, dandelions, and chicory, and green leafy vegetables (such as beetroot and turnip greens and radish tops).

Young tender leaves may be used in green salads but the most popular method of preparing *khorta* is to boil the greens and serve as a vegetable, warm or at room temperature, dressed with olive oil and vinegar. Crusty bread, yogurt, country cheeses, and olives are traditional accompaniments. *Khorta* is also a favourite filling for pies and a delicious addition to casseroles.

After the first autumn rains wild greens grow in abundance on the hillsides and in the fields and the sight of village women picking their favourites for the family meal is common; during the season Greek markets also stock many different varieties of *khorta*. Among them is tender *vlita,* known here as amaranth greens and sometimes available in speciality shops and markets. Some Chinese markets offer purple or water spinach, which has a similar sweet/sour flavour and makes a delicious substitute for spinach in Cretan pies (page 58). Purslane, dandelion greens, radish tops, turnip and beetroot greens, ruby chard and sprouting broccoli are all occasionally available.

Wild greens continue to grow in Greece throughout the winter and short spring. Wild chicory (*radiki*), in particular, is at its best in March and April, just before its clear blue flowers appear, and a bowl of this bitter green has pride of place as an accompaniment to the Paschal lamb on the traditional Easter table. Come the early summer, however, the dry season and a shortage of water means the absence of the traditional and healthy *khorta* dishes from Greek tables until the autumn.

Wild Greens Salad
Khorta Salatika
Serves 4

The combination of bitter greens, mustard, vinegar, olive oil, and sea salt creates a delicious explosion of flavours in this salad. Choose only fresh young tender leaves and tear them into pieces, rather than chopping, to preserve as much vitamin C as possible. Cast-iron pots produce an unpleasant flavour in *khorta* and also reduce the valuable vitamin content, so always cook them in a stainless steel or enamel-lined saucepan; wild greens do not shrink in cooking as much as cultivated greens.

550 g/1 ¹/₄ lb wild greens such as turnip greens, radish tops, amaranth greens, water
spinach, ruby chard or mustard greens (charlock)
¹/₂ teaspoon Dijon mustard
2–3 tablespoons aged red wine vinegar (to taste) or juice of 1 small lemon
5 tablespoons extra virgin olive oil, or to taste
Coarse-grain sea salt *and* cracked black pepper to taste

Rinse the greens in several changes of cold water. Remove any tough stalks from the turnip greens and radish tops and tear the leaves into bite-size pieces. Break off the tender sprigs of leaves from the amaranth greens, water spinach, or mustard greens and discard any tougher stalks.

Steam the greens, or place in a saucepan, add 4 tablespoons boiling water, and cook, stirring once or twice with a fork: Amaranth greens and young ruby chard take only 1-2 minutes, turnip greens and radish tops take 3-4 minutes, and water spinach and mustard around 5 minutes – take care not to overcook. Drain well in a colander, pressing the greens against the sides with a wooden spoon.

To serve, combine the Dijon mustard and vinegar and whisk in the olive oil. Pour over the greens and sprinkle with a generous amount of salt and pepper. Serve warm or at room temperature.

Beetroot Greens Salad
Salatika Panzaria

Serves 3

Village cooks would not dream of throwing away the crisp green leaves of young beetroot. Instead they cook them (reserving the vitamin-rich cooking liquid for soup) and turn them into this nutrient-packed salad.

Fresh green leaves from 6 young beetroot
4 tablespoons boiling water
Juice of 1 small lemon or 2 tablespoons aged red wine vinegar
4 tablespoons extra virgin olive oil, or to taste
1 teaspoon dried *rigani* (page 14), briefly pounded in a small mortar
¹/₂ teaspoon coarse-grain sea salt, or to taste
Cracked black pepper to taste

Remove the thicker stalks from the beetroot greens but leave tender thin stalks intact. Rinse well, and tear into bite-size pieces.

Place in a stainless steel or enamel-lined saucepan, add the boiling water, cover, and boil until barely tender, about 2 minutes. Drain in a colander, pressing the greens against the sides with a wooden spoon to extract as much moisture as possible.

Transfer to a platter and gently separate the leaves with a fork. Sprinkle with the lemon juice, olive oil, *rigani,* salt, and pepper. Serve warm or at room temperature.

Dandelion Greens Salad
Radiki Salatika

Serves 4

Most Greek markets boast several varieties of dandelion greens and those snapped up the most quickly are always the wild ones. Our own garden dandelions are often tough and not usually suitable for cooking, but some speciality shops sell cultivated dandelion greens in season and they make a delicious *khorta.*

450 g/1 lb young dandelion leaves
115 ml/4 fl oz boiling water
1 small clove garlic, finely chopped
Juice of 1 small lemon, or to taste
4 tablespoons extra virgin olive oil
Coarse-grain sea salt *and* cracked black pepper to taste

Discard the coarse dandelion stalks, thoroughly rinse the leaves, and tear the leaves into 5-7 cm/2-3 inch pieces.

Place in a stainless steel or enamel-lined saucepan, and add the boiling water. Cover, and boil 1-2 minutes. Drain well in a colander, pressing the greens against the sides with a wooden spoon.

Transfer to a platter and gently separate the leaves with a fork. Whisk together the garlic, lemon juice, and olive oil and pour over the greens. Sprinkle generously with salt and pepper and serve warm or at room temperature.

Note If you use wild dandelion leaves, blanch them in boiling water for 1 minute to remove bitterness and drain before boiling a second time.

Pilafs and Pastas

pilafi ke macaronia

Savoury rice dishes are known in Greece as *pilafi*. The rice is always cooked according to a basic method; to it are added meat, vegetables, or fish and one of a range of aromatic sauces to create any number of variations.

For any pilaf dish good-quality long-grain rice, such as Carolina or Patna, is essential. This is first cooked in olive oil or butter and then all the stock or water is added at once. The rice is removed from the heat and left in a warm spot while the grains absorb the liquid. For a successful pilaf, therefore, both rice and stock must be carefully measured; the amount of stock should be exactly double the quantity of rice.

In a properly made pilaf the rice grains are dry, firm, and separate and have a pleasantly mild and nutty flavour. The simple instructions for the *pilafi* included should produce perfect results every time. *Pilafi* is the ideal accompaniment to casseroles and stews and vegetable pilaf the perfect one-dish meal.

There are two types of Greek *macaronia,* or pasta. One made with unbleached plain (soft wheat) flour, is used to make thin flat strips like noodles or tagliatelle or shapes like ravioli, and cooked while fresh. The second type is made from durum (hard wheat) flour and is dried and stored. Because of its high gluten content and an ability to retain its shape during cooking, this type is ideal for baked dishes such as *youvetsi* (spiced meat and *macaronia*) and *pastitsio* (page 238). Many of these *macaronia* are simple to make at home and their delicate flavour and ability to absorb aromatics makes them a perfect foil for sauces.

One unusual *macaronia* still made in villages, though difficult to duplicate here, deserves special mention. *Trahanas* is made from stiff dough of hard-wheat flour, eggs and yogurt or soured milk. The dough is rolled out, spread out to dry in the sun for a day or two, then forced through a special sieve to make an oatmeal-textured pasta. *Trahanas* is sometimes served as a pasta course but more often appears in a soup flavoured with lemon juice, wine, egg yolks, or tomatoes.

Greek grocery shops sometimes sell fine-ground *farina* (semolina), a durum (hard-wheat) flour particularly suited to *macaronia*. *Macaronia* made with *farina* is a deliciously

authentic country flavour and is ideal for use in oven-baked dishes such as Stuffed Macaronia in Country Broth (page 242). However making *macaronia* with *farina* is not easy, and a machine is necessary to work the dough to the right texture. Greek grocery shops are also the place to find the long thin rolling pin needed to stretch the dough out and the special rolling pin covered with indented squares for cutting macaronia squares for Macedonian Pie (page 240).

As wheat was cultivated in Greece well before classical times, it's highly probable that *macaronia* has been produced there since antiquity – and there is indeed archaeological evidence to point in that direction. That being so, the simple and flavoursome recipes included here, popular all over Greece and the islands in regional variations, are based on a rich and ancient culinary tradition.

rice dishes
Pilafi

Perfect Pilaf
Pilafi
Serves 4

This simple bay-scented pilaf is excellent with casseroles and grilled dishes. A good fruity olive oil and a well-flavoured stock produce the best results and a last minute sprinkling of parsley and paprika adds a touch of colour. (If necessary, it can be reheated over a heat diffuser mat or in a double boiler.)

2 tablespoons extra virgin olive oil
350 g/12 oz long-grain rice, such as Carolina or Patna
3 bay leaves
1 tablespoon sea salt, or to taste
700 ml/1¼ pints hot Chicken or Light Meat Stock (pages 344 and 347) or water

For serving
Juice of ½ lemon
Finely chopped flat leaf parsley
Pinch of paprika
Cracked black pepper to taste

Heat the olive oil in a heavy saucepan and stir the rice over low heat until the grains whiten, about 2 minutes. Add the bay leaves, salt, and stock, raise the heat to medium, and boil uncovered, without stirring, until the liquid has disappeared and holes appear in the surface of the rice, about 10 minutes. Remove from the heat, cover with a clean tea towel and a tight-fitting lid, and set aside for 30-40 minutes in a warm spot such as the back of the stove. The grains will become firm, dry, and separated.

Transfer the rice to a warm platter or bowl and lightly separate the grains with a fork. Discard the bay leaves and sprinkle the pilaf with the lemon juice, parsley, paprika, and pepper. Serve hot or warm.

Pilaf with Currants and Pine Nuts
Pilafi me Stafili Korinthiako
Serves 4

The strong clove, fresh ginger root, and orange zest flavourings reveal the Eastern influences behind this spicy pilaf. Currants and pine nuts are traditional additions sometimes cooked with the rice, sometimes added at the last minute. Adding them after the rice has absorbed all the liquid seems the best way to preserve their textures and distinctive flavours. Always served cold, this is especially good with game.

4 tablespoons extra virgin olive oil, or to taste
350 g/12 oz long-grain rice, such as Carolina or Patna
4 cloves
2.5 cm/1 inch piece of fresh ginger root, peeled
1 bouquet garni (2 bay leaves, 3 sprigs of parsley *and* 1 sprig of thyme, tied together)
5 cm/2 inch strip of orange zest
700 ml/1¼ pints hot Chicken Stock (page 344) or water
1 teaspoon sea salt, or to taste
115 g/4 oz currants, soaked in 2 tablespoons Mavrodaphne wine or warm water for 1 hour
50 g/2 oz lightly toasted pine nuts *or* coarsely chopped walnuts

For serving
Juice of 1 small lemon
½ small red onion, thinly sliced
2 tablespoons finely chopped flat leaf parsley or coarsely chopped fresh coriander
1 tablespoon finely chopped Preserved Lemon (page 18), *optional*
Cracked black pepper to taste

Heat half the olive oil in a heavy saucepan, add the rice, and stir over low heat until the grains whiten, about 2 minutes. Add the cloves, fresh ginger root, bouquet garni, orange zest, stock, and salt. Raise the heat to medium and boil uncovered, without stirring, until the liquid has disappeared and holes appear in the surface of the rice, about 10 minutes. Stir in the currants and pine nuts with a fork and remove from the heat. Cover with a clean tea towel and a tight-fitting lid and set aside 30-40 minutes in a warm spot such as the back of the stove.

Discard the ginger root, bouquet garni, and orange zest, and turn the pilaf out onto a platter. Lightly separate the grains with a fork and set aside to cool.

To serve, sprinkle with the lemon juice, onion, parsley, Preserved Lemon, salt, pepper, and remaining olive oil.

Aubergine Pilaf
with Glazed Tomatoes
Pilafi me Melitzanes ke Domates

Serves 4

Serve this flavourful pilaf, garnished with thin strips of smoky grilled peppers and caramelized tomatoes, as a side dish for grilled meats or chicken, *souvlakia,* or sausages. For vegetable lovers it makes a satisfying lunch or supper.

2 medium aubergines
Coarse-grain sea salt
4 tablespoons extra virgin olive oil
1 $^1\!/_2$ tablespoons unsalted butter
25 g/1 oz *fides* (vermicelli), broken into small pieces
1 small onion, finely chopped
275 g/10 oz long-grain rice, such as Carolina or Patna
4 cloves
2 bay leaves
575 ml/1 pint hot Chicken or Light Meat Stock (pages 344 and 347) or water
50 g/2 oz lightly toasted almonds or walnuts, coarsely chopped
50 g/2 oz currants or small dark seedless raisins
12 large cherry tomatoes or tiny tomatoes (about 2.5 cm/1 inch in diameter)
$^1\!/_2$ teaspoon sugar, or to taste
Cracked black pepper to taste
2 medium green or yellow bell peppers

For serving
Juice of $^1\!/_2$ lemon
4 tablespoons coarsely chopped flat leaf parsley
Strained Yogurt (page 8)

Trim the ends from the aubergines and cut into 2 cm/³/₄ inch dice. Sprinkle with ¹/₂ tablespoon salt and set aside for 30 minutes to "sweat".

Dry the aubergines with paper towels. Heat 3 tablespoons of the olive oil in a large heavy frying pan and lightly brown the aubergines on all sides over medium heat. Drain between layers of paper towels and set aside.

Melt the butter in a heavy saucepan and cook the vermicelli over low heat until the butter turns a deep golden brown, about 6 minutes; take care not to burn the butter. Add the onion and cook 5 minutes. Stir in the rice, cloves and bay leaves and cook, stirring, until the grains whiten, about 2 minutes. Add the stock and salt to taste, raise the heat to medium, and boil uncovered, without stirring, until the liquid has disappeared, and holes appear in the surface of the rice, about 10 minutes. Stir in the aubergines, almonds, and currants with a fork. Remove from the heat, cover with a clean tea towel and tight-fitting lid, and set aside for 30-40 minutes in a warm spot such as the back of the stove.

Fifteen minutes before you are ready to serve, heat the grill. With a sharp knife, slash open the top of each tomato and sprinkle the insides with a pinch of salt, the sugar, and a generous amount of pepper. Arrange the peppers on a grill pan and grill 5 cm/2 inches from the heat, turning, until the skin is shrivelled and darkened. Remove from the pan and arrange the tomatoes on the pan. Brush with the remaining olive oil and grill until the tops are darkened and slightly caramelized. While the tomatoes are cooking, remove the cores and seeds from the peppers. Rub off the skin and any remaining seeds with your fingers, dry with paper towels, and cut into thin strips. Turn the pilaf out onto a warm platter. Arrange the peppers on top, surround with the tomatoes, and sprinkle with the lemon juice and parsley. Serve hot or warm, with bowls of yogurt.

Pilaf with Green Lentils
Pilafi me Fakes
Serves 4

Those who are fond of the flavour of good olive oil will appreciate this dish. Coriander, allspice, and bay leaves perfume the lentils and rice, and when they are cooked, a sweet-and-sour honey, vinegar, and olive oil sauce is poured over them. The result is a highly seasoned pilaf with an unusual combination of flavours. Broad Beans and Sweet Carrot Pilaf (page 230) is the spring version of this winter dish.

115 g/4 oz green lentils, picked over, rinsed, and soaked for 2 hours in cold water to cover
5 tablespoons extra virgin olive oil
1 medium onion, cut into quarters and thinly sliced
1 1/2 tablespoons dried coriander seeds, crushed or 1 tablespoon ground coriander
1/2 teaspoon ground allspice
3 bay leaves
350 g/12 oz carrots, halved or quartered lengthways and cut into 2.5 cm/
1 inch lengths
175 g/6 oz long-grain rice, such as Carolina or Patna
450 ml/16 fl oz hot Chicken or Light Meat Stock (pages 344 and 347) or water
1 teaspoon sea salt, or to taste
1 tablespoon aromatic honey, such as Hymettus

1 tablespoon aged red wine vinegar
3 tablespoons finely chopped flat leaf parsley
1 tablespoon dried *rigani* (page 14), crumbled
$^1/_2$ teaspoon cracked black pepper, or to taste

For serving
Strained Yogurt (page 8)

Drain the lentils and place in a saucepan with water to cover. Bring to a boil, drain, rinse, and set aside.

Heat 2 tablespoons of the olive oil in a heavy saucepan and sauté the onion over low heat until soft, about 6 minutes. Stir in the coriander, allspice, and bay leaves, add the carrots, and cook, stirring occasionally, 5 minutes longer. Stir in the rice and cook, stirring, until the grains whiten, about 2 minutes. Add the lentils, stock, and salt to taste. Raise the heat to medium and boil uncovered, without stirring, until the liquid has disappeared and holes appear in the surface of the rice, about 10 minutes. Remove from the heat, cover with a clean tea towel and tight-fitting lid, and set aside for 30 minutes in a warm spot such as the back of the stove.

Combine the honey and vinegar in a small saucepan, stir in the remaining olive oil, and heat to warm. Stir in the parsley, *rigani,* pepper, and salt to taste. Turn the pilaf out onto a warm platter and pour over the honey sauce. Serve hot with bowls of yogurt.

Broad Beans and Sweet Carrot Pilaf
Pilafi me Fava ke Karotta
Serves 4

When the first broad beans and tender young carrots appear in the market this popular spring dish is served in homes throughout Greece. The carrots cook to a sweet velvety texture with the rice, the crunchy beans are added at the last minute. Served warm or cold, with a bowl of yogurt and a green salad or wild greens dish, this is a satisfying meal on its own. It's also a perfect complement to grilled lamb.

3 tablespoons extra virgin olive oil
2 shallots, finely chopped
450 g/1 lb young carrots, halved or quartered lengthways and cut
into 2.5 cm/1 inch lengths
175 g/6 oz long-grain rice, such as Carolina or Patna
1 teaspoon sea salt, or to taste
1 teaspoon honey
2 bay leaves
175 ml/6 fl oz hot Chicken Stock (page 344) or water

175 ml/6 fl oz hot water
675 g/1¹/₂ lb broad beans in the pod, shelled
Juice of 1 lemon
Cracked black pepper to taste

For serving
Small sprigs of fresh dill or young mint, torn into small pieces just before using

Heat 2 tablespoons of the olive oil in a heavy saucepan and sauté the shallots over low heat until soft, about 5 minutes. Add the carrots and cook 2-3 minutes, stirring with a wooden spoon. Add the rice and cook, stirring, until the grains whiten, about 2 minutes. Add 3/4 teaspoon of the salt, the honey, bay leaves, stock, and water. Raise the heat to medium and boil uncovered, without stirring, until the liquid has disappeared, and holes appear in the surface of the rice, about 10 minutes. Remove from the heat, cover with a clean tea towel and tight-fitting lid, and set aside for 30-40 minutes in a warm spot such as the back of the stove.

Peel the skins from the broad beans (see **Note,** page 207). Heat the remaining olive oil in a small saucepan, add the beans, cover, and cook 4 minutes over low heat to soften. Add half the lemon juice, the remaining salt, and pepper.

Stir the beans and cooking juices into the pilaf with a fork and turn out onto a warm platter. Sprinkle with the remaining lemon juice and the dill.

Spinach Pilaf
Spanakorizo
Serves 4

In traditional kitchens this classic country dish is made in a heavy, round-bottomed pan so that the pilaf can be turned out to make an attractive mound. Serve *spanakorizo* as a simple lunch or supper dish, with olives and slices of *feta* cheese, or as an accompaniment to grilled meats.

2 medium leeks
5 tablespoons extra virgin olive oil, or to taste
1 clove garlic, finely chopped (*optional*)
Large pinch of ground cumin
900 g/2 lb tender fresh spinach, rinsed twice and stalks discarded
6 sprigs of fresh dill, chopped (*optional*)
Coarse-grain sea salt *and* freshly ground black pepper to taste
175 g/6 oz long-grain rice, such as Carolina or Patna
350 ml/12 fl oz Chicken Stock (page 344) or water

For serving
Juice of ¹/₂ lemon

Slice off the roots and green tops of the leeks. Cut a slit lengthways halfway through each leek, keeping the original shape intact. Hold upright under running water and gently pull the layers apart, one at a time, to wash out any grit or dirt. Shake off any excess water and blot dry with paper towels.

Heat 3 tablespoons of the olive oil in a large heavy saucepan or casserole. Thinly slice the leeks, add to the pan, and sauté over low heat, stirring occasionally, until soft, about 10 minutes. Add the garlic and cumin, stir to mix, and continue cooking until aromatic.

Slice the spinach into 2 cm/¹/₂ inch ribbons and add to the pan with the dill, 1 teaspoon salt (or to taste) and pepper. Stir with a wooden spoon and cook until the spinach has reduced in bulk by half, about 1 minute. Add the rice, stir once, then add the stock. Raise the heat to medium and boil uncovered, without stirring, until the liquid has disappeared, and holes appear in the surface of the rice, about 10 minutes. Remove from the heat, cover with a clean tea towel and tight-fitting lid, and set aside for 30-40 minutes in a warm spot such as the back of the stove.

To serve, hold the serving dish over the top of the pan and, using both hands, invert the pan to turn out the pilaf onto the dish. Whisk together the lemon juice and remaining olive oil and pour over the pilaf. Sprinkle with salt and pepper to taste and serve hot, warm, or at room temperature.

Variations

Substitute 675 g/1¹/₂ lb young beetroot greens or ruby chard for the spinach and omit the dill.

Substitute 350 g/12 oz young rocket leaves, torn into pieces, or small clusters of watercress or purslane, or turnip greens or mustard greens, torn into small pieces, for the spinach, and omit the dill. Add the greens to the pan *after* the rice has absorbed the liquid; fork the greens into the rice. Cover the pan and set aside in a warm spot as described. For serving, substitute ¹/₂ tablespoon (or to taste) aged red wine vinegar for the lemon juice and be generous with the salt and pepper.

Saffron Rice with Mussels
Mythia me Risi
Serves 4

On the last day of one of the cooking courses I ran on the island of Crete a large basket was delivered to one of my students. Inside was a marine treasure trove – sea urchins, baby squid, mussels, shrimp, cuttlefish, razor clams, and sea anemones. Using this generous gift, we made a lovely saffron pilaf. Here is a simpler version of that delightful dish – try it also with baby squid, cuttlefish, shrimp, or a combination of seafood.

1 teaspoon saffron threads
32–40 mussels
3 tablespoons extra virgin olive oil
3 shallots, finely chopped
275 g/10 oz long-grain rice, such as Carolina or Patna
2 bay leaves

450 ml/16 fl oz hot water
65 g/2½ oz lightly toasted pine nuts
50 g/2 oz currants or small dark seedless raisins
4 tablespoons chopped flat leaf parsley
Sea salt and cracked black pepper to taste
Juice of ½ lemon

For serving
Lemon wedges

Heat the saffron in a small dry frying pan until aromatic, about 1 minute. Set aside.

Discard any open mussels and those with broken shells. With a stiff brush, thoroughly scrub the mussels under cold running water and pull off their "beards". Place in a large saucepan, cover, and set over medium-high heat. Holding the lid firmly in place, shake the saucepan once or twice. After a minute or two all the mussels should have opened; discard any that do not open. Pour the mussel broth into a small bowl, crumble in the saffron, and set aside. Remove all but 8 mussels from their shells, reserving the juices, and set aside.

Heat half of the olive oil in a heavy saucepan and sauté half the shallots over medium-low heat until pale golden, about 5 minutes. Stir in the rice, and cook, until the grains whiten, about 2 minutes. Strain the saffron broth and add to the rice with the bay leaves and hot water. Raise the heat to medium and boil uncovered, without stirring, until all the liquid has disappeared and holes appear in the surface of the rice, about 10 minutes. Stir in the pine nuts and currants with a fork. Remove from the heat, cover with a clean tea towel and tight-fitting lid, and set aside for 30 minutes in a warm spot such as the back of the stove.

Five minutes before you are ready to serve, heat the remaining olive oil in a small frying pan and sauté the remaining shallots over low heat until soft, about 3 minutes. Add the parsley, salt and pepper, and half the lemon juice and heat to warm. Add the shelled mussels, cover, and heat 1 minute over very low heat.

Stir the mussel and parsley mixture into the pilaf with a fork, turn out onto a warm platter, and sprinkle with the remaining lemon juice and reserved mussel juices. Surround with the lemon wedges and the mussels in their shells and serve at once.

Spiced Prawn Pilaf
Pilafi Aromatiko me Garithes
Serves 4

Although this island pilaf is simple to make, it looks splendidly exotic and colourful, with its coriander- and turmeric-flavoured rice, sweet tomato and prawn sauce, and garnish of yogurt, parsley, and piquant capers. Although saffron is popular for colouring and flavouring *pilafi,* the Greeks use it only in dishes made with a very light stock, which preserves its delicate fragrance and colour. As this pilaf is cooked in a heavier stock, the preferred aromatic is the less subtle (less expensive) turmeric.

675 g/1¹/₂ lb medium prawns in the shell
4 tablespoons extra virgin olive oil
1 large onion, chopped
1 stick of celery, chopped
3 bay leaves
2 shallots, finely chopped
1 teaspoon ground coriander
¹/₂ teaspoon turmeric
275 g/10 oz long-grain rice, such as Carolina or Patna
¹/₂ teaspoon sea salt, or to taste
3 ripe medium tomatoes, skinned, seeded, and diced
Pinch of sugar
¹/₂ teaspoon cracked black pepper, or to taste
1 teaspoon dried *rigani* (page 14), crumbled

For serving
5 tablespoons Strained Yogurt (page 8)
2 tablespoons finely chopped flat leaf parsley
1 tablespoon capers, rinsed and coarsely chopped

Rinse the prawns, and shell all but 4 reserving the shell. De-vein all the prawns, cover, and refrigerate.

Heat 1¹/₂ tablespoons of the olive oil in a heavy saucepan, and sauté the onion and celery over low heat until golden, about 15 minutes. Add the prawn shells (or 2 shelled prawns), 1 of the bay leaves broken into 2 pieces, and 450 ml/16 fl oz water. Bring to a boil over medium heat, cover, reduce the heat, and simmer 40 minutes. Strain the stock through a fine sieve into a bowl, pressing the solids against the sides of the sieve with the back of a wooden spoon. Add water if necessary to make 600 ml/1 pint and set aside.

Heat 1 tablespoon of the remaining olive oil in a heavy saucepan and sauté the shallots over low heat until pale golden, about 6 minutes. Stir in the coriander, turmeric, rice, and remaining 2 bay leaves. Cook, stirring, until the rice whitens, about 2 minutes. Add the prawn stock and salt, raise the heat to medium, and boil uncovered, without stirring, until the liquid has disappeared, and holes appear in the surface of the rice, about 10 minutes. Remove from the heat, cover with a clean tea towel and tight-fitting lid, and set aside for 30 minutes in a warm spot such as the back of the stove.

Heat the remaining olive oil in a heavy sauté pan. Lightly toss the prawns in their shells 2 minutes over medium-low heat and add the shelled prawns. Cook, stirring occasionally, until pink and opaque all the way through, 3-5 minutes. Remove with a slotted spoon and keep warm. Add the tomatoes, sugar, and pepper to the pan. Cook 1 minute, add the *rigani*, and return the shelled prawns to the pan. Lower the heat, simmer 1 minute longer, and season to taste. Warm the yogurt in a small saucepan over low heat.

Turn the pilaf out onto a warm platter, pour over the tomato and prawn sauce, and spoon the yogurt on top. Sprinkle with the parsley and capers and garnish with the prawns in the shell. Serve at once.

Pasta
Macaronia
Serves 4 (Makes about 450 g/1 lb dough)

Although you can use a pasta machine to do some of the work in making *macaronia,* I usually prefer to roll out the dough by hand.

Macaronia cut in 6 mm/¹/₄ inch-wide strips (what the Italians call tagliatelle) are easy to produce without a machine. For a soft and pliant dough all the ingredients should be at room temperature and the dough should be well kneaded.

275 g/10 oz unbleached plain flour or semolina (*farina* page 344)
3 large eggs

Mound 250 g/9 oz of the flour on a large clean work surface and make a deep hollow in the centre. Break the eggs into the hollow and lightly beat them with a fork. Little by little draw in the flour with your fingers and mix it with the eggs. Continue until you have incorporated all the flour; add some or all of the remaining flour if the dough feels sticky. Knead the dough for at least 5 minutes, until the dough leaves the work surface clean, adding a little more flour if necessary. Tightly wrap the dough in cling film and set aside for 10-30 minutes; do not refrigerate.

Lightly dust a rolling pin and a clean work surface with flour. Divide the dough into 6 portions and roll out each as thin as possible without tearing. Use the rolling pin to push, rather than press, the dough into a large rectangular shape. Trim the sides of each sheet and loosely roll it up into a cylinder. With a sharp knife, cut each cylinder crosswise into strips of desired width. Separate the strips, and spread them on clean tea towels or a pasta drying rack to dry slightly, about 15 minutes, before cooking. They are ready to cook when they are no longer sticky but are not so dry that they would crack if folded.

Macaronia with Olive, Anchovy, and Sweet Tomato Sauce
Macaronia me Elies ke Saltsa Domatas
Serves 4

Strong flavours and bold colour contrasts make this simple dish exceptionally attractive and appetizing. The cooked *macaronia* is coated with an anchovy-garlic paste, and then a sweet tomato sauce is poured over it. Interestingly enough, although basil is seen growing in pots all over Greece, this is one of the few basil-flavoured Greek dishes I know.

3 whole salted anchovies (page 343), filleted, or 6 salted anchovy fillets
115 ml/4 fl oz extra virgin olive oil, or more to taste
2 cloves garlic, thinly sliced

12 Nafplion or other Greek green olives, blanched in boiling water for
3 seconds, patted dry, pitted, and coarsely chopped
6 large ripe tomatoes, skinned
1 teaspoon honey
$^1/_2$ teaspoon cracked black pepper, or to taste
Sea salt to taste
2 tablespoons fresh basil or 1 tablespoon chopped fresh thyme or oregano
1 recipe *macaronia* (page 235), cut into 6 mm/$^1/_4$ inch strips and dried for 15 minutes

Soak the anchovy fillets in cold water for 5 minutes. Rinse, pat dry, and cut into small pieces. Place in a small bowl with 2 tablespoons of the olive oil and set aside.

Fill a large saucepan with lightly salted water and bring to a boil. Meanwhile, heat 2 tablespoons of the remaining olive oil in a small heavy frying pan and sauté the garlic over a low heat until aromatic; do not let it colour. Transfer the garlic and oil to a wooden mortar or bowl, add the anchovies and their oil, and pound together until mixed but not smooth. Return the mixture to the frying pan, add the olives, and heat to warm.

Cut the tomatoes in half, squeeze out the seeds, and slice into thin wedges. Heat 1 tablespoon of the remaining olive oil in a second small frying pan over medium heat and add the tomatoes, honey, salt, and pepper. Cook just until the tomatoes begin to lose their shape, about 1 minute. Tear the basil leaves into small pieces and stir into the tomatoes. Add the *macaronia* to the boiling water and cook until they rise to the surface, about 3 minutes; drain immediately.

Combine the *macaronia* and olive sauce in a warm shallow bowl. Pour over the tomatoes, sprinkle with the remaining olive oil, and serve at once.

Macaronia with Chicken and Wild Greens
Macaronia me Kotopoulo ke Khorta
Serves 4

This popular dish is simple and quick to prepare but it does require top-quality ingredients. Be sure to use a well-flavoured olive oil, plump olives, and the freshest young beetroot or dandelion greens you can find.

225 g/8 oz thin 2.5 cm/1 inch-long strips of cooked chicken
2 tablespoons aged red wine vinegar or 1 tablespoon balsamic vinegar
Freshly ground black pepper to taste
4 tablespoons extra virgin olive oil
1 clove garlic, cut into 2 or 3 pieces
1 large handful tender young beetroot greens or dandelion greens, tough stalks removed and
leaves torn into small pieces

4 tablespoons boiling water
50 g/2 oz lightly toasted pine nuts
24 Elitses or 12 Niçoise olives, drained, pitted, and coarsely chopped
1 recipe *macaronia* (page 235), cut into 6 mm/¼ inch strips and dried for 15 minutes
Sea salt to taste

For serving
Grated aged myzithra, *halloumi,* or *kasseri* cheese

Combine the chicken, vinegar, pepper, and 1 tablespoon of the olive oil in a bowl, toss to mix and set aside.

Heat most of the remaining olive oil in a large heavy frying pan and sauté the garlic over low heat until pale golden; don't let it burn. Discard the garlic and set aside the pan.

Fill a large saucepan with lightly salted water and bring to a boil. Meanwhile, place the greens in a heavy saucepan, add the boiling water, cover, and gently boil 1 minute. Drain well, spread between layers of paper towels, and blot dry.

Return the frying pan to low heat and add the chicken, pine nuts, and olives. Cook 3 minutes, stirring occasionally with a fork. Add the greens and heat through. Add the *macaronia* to the boiling water and cook only until they rise to the surface, about 3 minutes; drain.

Combine the chicken mixture and *macaronia* in a warm earthenware bowl and toss to mix. Sprinkle with the remaining olive oil and salt and pepper to taste. Serve at once, with bowls of cheese.

Macaronia and Spicy Meat in a Pie
Pastitsio
Serves 8

This traditional dish, composed of layers of *macaronia,* in a sweet and spicy meat sauce, and a creamy cheese sauce, makes no pretensions to elegance but its heady aroma, beautiful bubbling and golden-crusted appearance, and utterly delicious taste are pleasure enough. It needs only the simplest of accompaniments – a salad of wild greens (page 221) is ideal.

5 tablespoons extra virgin olive oil
2 large onions, finely chopped
675 g/1½ lb lean beef or lamb or a mixture of both, minced
115 ml/4 fl oz red wine or 2 tablespoons aged red wine vinegar
6 large ripe tomatoes, skinned, seeded, and diced, juices reserved
1½-2 tablespoons ground cinnamon
Large pinch of cayenne pepper
1 tablespoon dried marjoram, crumbled

1 small handful flat leaf parsley, leaves finely chopped
Sea salt *and* cracked black pepper to taste

White Sauce
50 g/2 oz unsalted butter
4 tablespoons plain flour
850 ml/1¹/₂ pints warm milk
¹/₂ teaspoon grated nutmeg
3 eggs, separated
2 egg yolks
675 g/1¹/₂ lb macaroni or penne
115 g/4 oz small-curd cottage cheese, drained
75 g/3 oz grated *feta* cheese
2 tablespoons unsalted butter, melted
75 g/3 oz fresh fine breadcrumbs, dried 5 minutes in a low oven
25 g/1 oz grated *kasseri* or parmesan cheese
8 Elitses or Niçoise olives, drained, pitted, and each cut in half

Warm half of the olive oil in a heavy frying pan and sauté the onion over medium-low heat until pale golden, about 5 minutes. Add the meat, raise the heat, and cook, stirring and breaking up any lumps with a spoon, until lightly browned, about 6 minutes. Add the red wine and boil until reduced by half. Add the tomatoes and their juices, 1 tablespoon of the cinnamon, and the cayenne pepper, and cook until the liquid is reduced by half. Add the marjoram, half the parsley, a pinch of salt, and a generous amount of pepper. Simmer 5 minutes longer and add cinnamon, salt and pepper to taste; the sauce should be highly flavoured.

Fill a large saucepan with lightly salted water and bring to a boil. Meanwhile, melt the butter in a heavy saucepan and stir in the flour with a wooden spoon to make a roux. Cook, stirring, over low heat until the roux is smooth and light and gold in colour. Stir in the milk 115 ml/4 fl oz at a time, adding more only when the sauce is smooth. Cook, stirring, until the sauce comes to a low boil. Remove from the heat, stir in the nutmeg and 5 egg yolks, and set aside.

Arrange a rack in the centre of the oven and heat the oven 180C/350F/gas mark 4.

Cook the macaroni in the boiling water until barely soft, about 10 minutes. Drain and rinse briefly under cold running water. Shake the colander once or twice and set aside to dry.

Stir the cottage cheese, most of the *feta* cheese, and a little pepper into the white sauce. Whisk the egg whites until they hold soft peaks and fold half of them into the white sauce. Combine the remaining egg whites and *feta* cheese, the parsley, 225 ml/8 fl oz of the white sauce, a pinch of cinnamon, and the macaroni in a large bowl.

Brush a baking dish with half the melted butter and 1 tablespoon of the remaining olive oil, and sprinkle with half the breadcrumbs. Spread one third of the macaroni mixture over the bottom of the dish and cover with half the meat filling. Spread a thin layer of macaroni over the meat, cover with the remaining filling and then the remaining macaroni. Cover with the white sauce, lightly smooth the top with a spatula, and sprinkle with the remaining breadcrumbs and the *kasseri* cheese. Set 2 olive halves, cut sides down, in the centre of each of which will be 8 serving portions and sprinkle with the remaining olive oil and melted butter.

Bake 40 minutes, or until a deep golden brown. Let rest for 10 minutes before cutting into serving portions.

Macedonian Pie
Laganes
Serves 10

I once spent a week in a Macedonian village where the inhabitants seemed to exist solely on this glorious dish. *Laganes* (from which the Italian word *lasagna* derives) is an extravagant pie of thin *macaronia* squares, layered with three sauces, spicy sausages, and wild greens, and topped with *kasseri* cheese and breadcrumbs. Freshly baked, with each component in perfect balance, this dish is a triumphant success.

350 g/12 oz unbleached plain flour or semolina (*farina*, page 344) or a mixture of both
4 large eggs

Meat Sauce
2 tablespoons extra virgin olive oil
1 large onion, finely chopped
450 g/1 lb lean beef, finely minced
4 tablespoons finely chopped flat leaf parsley
1 tablespoon dried *rigani* (page 14), crumbled
1 teaspoon ground allspice
115 ml/4 fl oz dry white wine
5 cm/2 inch strip of orange zest
3 bay leaves
Sea salt *and* cracked black pepper to taste

Sausage Filling
Two 10-13 cm/4-5 inch sausages (pages 175, 176 or 178), casings discarded, cut
into small dice or 175 g/6 oz finely diced lean prosciutto ham
1 tablespoon extra virgin olive oil
Fresh leaves from 6 young beetroot, cooked, drained, and chopped
(page 222) or 225 g/8 oz fresh spinach, chopped

White Sauce
700 ml/1¼ pints milk
3 tablespoons unsalted butter
3 tablespoons unbleached plain flour
½ teaspoon grated nutmeg
3 egg yolks
225 g/4 oz grated *graviera* or gruyère cheese

2 tablespoons unsalted butter, melted
3 tablespoons extra virgin olive oil
115 g/4 oz fresh fine breadcrumbs, briefly dried in a low oven
115 g/4 oz small-curd cottage cheese, drained
75 g/3 oz grated *feta* cheese

700 ml/1¼ pints Tomato Sauce (page 321), made with cinnamon and parsley
2 tablespoons grated *kasseri* or parmesan cheese

Make a dough with the 350 g/12 oz flour and 4 eggs, as directed on page 235. Wrap the dough in cling film and set aside.

To make the meat sauce, heat the olive oil in a heavy frying pan and sauté the onion over medium-low heat until pale golden, about 8 minutes. Add the meat, raise the heat, stirring with a wooden spoon to break up any lumps, and cook, until lightly browned, about 5 minutes. Add the parsley, *rigani,* allspice, wine, orange zest, bay leaves, and salt and pepper, and simmer until most of the liquid has evaporated. Set aside.

To make the sausage filling, heat the olive oil in a second frying pan and lightly brown the diced sausage. Drain on paper towels, combine with the beetroot greens and set aside.

Divide the dough into 6 portions. Dust a rolling pin and a clean work surface with flour. Roll out each portion as thin as possible into a 15 cm/6 inch-wide strip. Trim the edges and cut in half lengthways, then into 7 cm/3 inch squares. Lightly dust with flour and spread on clean tea towels for a few minutes to dry. Fill a large saucepan with lightly salted water and bring to a boil.

Meanwhile, to make the white sauce, heat the milk just to a simmer and remove from the heat. Melt the butter in a heavy saucepan and stir in the flour with a wooden spoon. Cook, stirring, over low heat until smooth and light gold in colour. Briskly stir in the milk 115 ml/4 fl oz at a time, adding more only when the sauce is smooth. Cook, stirring, until the sauce comes to a low boil. Remove from the heat, stir in the nutmeg, egg yolks, and *graviera* cheese, and set aside.

Add the *macaronia* squares to the boiling water, 4 or 5 at a time, and cook until they rise to the surface, about 4 minutes. Drain on paper towels.

Arrange a rack in the centre of the oven and heat the oven to 190C/375F/gas mark 5. Brush a large heavy baking dish, at least 6 cm/2½ inches deep, with half the melted butter and 2 tablespoons of the olive oil and sprinkle with half the breadcrumbs. Cover the bottom of the dish with a single layer of *macaronia*. Remove the orange zest and bay leaves from the meat sauce and spoon half the meat sauce over the *macaronia*. Combine the cottage cheese, *feta* cheese, and ½ teaspoon pepper, and spoon half of this mixture over the meat. Spoon over 115 ml/4 fl oz white sauce and cover with a third of the remaining *macaronia*. Spread the sausage filling over the *macaronia,* cover with half the tomato sauce, and then with half the remaining *macaronia*. Spoon over the remaining meat sauce and cottage cheese mixture, and then 115 ml/4 fl oz of the white sauce. Cover with the remaining *macaronia,* tomato sauce, and, finally, the white sauce. Sprinkle with the remaining breadcrumbs, the *kasseri,* and remaining olive oil and melted butter.

Bake 30 minutes, or until golden brown and aromatic. Let rest 10 minutes before cutting into serving portions.

Stuffed Macaronia in Country Broth
Macaronia Yemista

Serves 4

These stuffed *macaronia* are traditionally served at celebrations, and I first sampled them at a country wedding on the island of Crete. Squares of *macaronia* are stuffed with a spicy meat or chicken mixture, baked until golden brown, and served in large shallow bowls with broth to moisten and plump the *macaronia,* and a sprinkling of olive oil. Bowls of cheese, warm yogurt, or tomato sauce and a salad of wild greens (page 221) are traditional accompaniments.

75 ml/3 fl oz extra virgin olive oil, or more to taste
1 large onion, finely chopped
350 g/12 oz lean beef or lamb, finely minced twice
1.1 litres/2 pints Light Meat or Chicken Stock (pages 347 and 344) or Meat Stock (page 347)
1 teaspoon ground cinnamon, or to taste
Sea salt *and* freshly ground black pepper to taste
1 tablespoon dried *rigani* (page 14), crumbled
4 tablespoons finely chopped flat leaf parsley
275 g/10 oz unbleached plain flour or semolina (*farina*, page 344) or a mixture of both
3 large eggs

For serving
Grated aged *myzithra*, or *kasseri*, or parmesan cheese, or 700 ml/1¼ pints Strained Yogurt
(page 8), or Tomato Sauce (pages 321 and 322), made with *rigani* or parsley, warmed

Heat 2 tablespoons of the olive oil in a heavy frying pan and sauté the onion over medium-low heat until golden, about 12 minutes, stirring frequently. Add the meat and cook, stirring to break up any lumps, until lightly browned and any meat juices have evaporated. Spread on paper towels to drain, drain off the fat from the pan, and wipe it out. Return the meat and onion mixture to the pan, add 115 ml/4 fl oz of the stock, the cinnamon, salt and pepper, *rigani,* and parsley. Simmer 5 minutes over low heat and set aside.

Make a dough with the flour and 3 eggs as directed on page 235.

Divide into 6 portions and let rest for 10 minutes. Dust a rolling pin and clean work surface with flour and stretch and roll out each as thin as possible without tearing. Trim the edges and cut into 5 cm/2 inch strips, then 5 cm/2 inch squares. You should have 40 squares.

Heat the oven to 190C/375F/gas mark 5. Place 1 teaspoon of filling in the centre of each square and, with lightly dampened forefinger and thumb, gently pull 2 opposite corners of each square up and together. Repeat with the other 2 corners so they all meet in the centre to make a neat packet.

Brush a heavy baking dish, at least 5 cm/2 inches deep and large enough to hold all the *macaronia* in a single layer, with olive oil. Arrange the *macaronia* in it and brush them with olive oil. Bake 10 minutes, then reduce the oven temperature to 180C/350F/gas mark 4 and bake 10-15 minutes longer, or until light golden brown. Season the remaining stock to taste and pour into the dish. Bake 15-20 minutes longer, or until the *macaronia* are tender; taste one to test.

Divide the *macaronia* and stock between individual shallow bowls, sprinkle with the remaining olive oil, and serve with bowls of the cheese, yogurt, or Tomato Sauce.

Variations
Cooked chicken cut into tiny dice can be substituted for the meat, or substitute the filling for Baked Cheese and Spinach Pies (page 57).Use 115 ml/4 fl oz white wine and 1 litre/1³/₄ pints home-made Chicken Stock instead of Light Meat Stock.

Stuffed Macaronia with Tomato Sauce
Macaronia Yemista me Saltsa Domatas
Serves 4

This is the Greek version of ravioli – *macaronia* stuffed with a nutmeg-spiced chicken and cheese mixture.

275 g/10 oz unbleached plain flour
4 large eggs
2 litres/3¹/₂ pints Chicken Stock (page 344) or water
225 g/8 oz finely diced cooked chicken
2 tablespoons finely chopped flat leaf parsley
2 egg yolks
2 tablespoons minced shallots
¹/₄ teaspoon grated nutmeg
50 g/2 oz feta or *kasseri* cheese
75 g/3 oz small-curd cottage cheese, drained
Sea salt *and* cracked black pepper to taste

For serving
225 ml/8 fl oz Scorched Tomato Sauce (page 323)
115 ml/4 fl oz Rich Chicken Stock (page 344)
Extra virgin olive oil, to taste
Grated aged *myzithra* or *feta* cheese

Make a dough with the flour and 3 of the eggs, as directed on page 235. Divide into 6 portions and let rest for 10 minutes. Lightly dust a rolling pin and clean work surface with flour and roll out the dough as thin as possible without tearing. Trim the edges, cut into strips 6 cm/2¹/₂ inches wide, then into 6 cm/2¹/₂-inch squares; you should have at least 24. Spread them out to dry for a few minutes. Bring the chicken stock to a low boil.

Meanwhile, combine the chicken, parsley, egg yolks, shallots, nutmeg, *feta,* cottage cheese and salt and pepper. Beat the remaining egg with a little water. Place 1 tablespoon of the filling in the centre of each *macaronia* square, lightly brush the edges of each square with the beaten egg, and fold over to form a triangle. Trim into half-moons with a pastry wheel, firmly pressing the edges together to seal.

Add half the *macaronia* to the stock and cook until they rise to the surface, about 6 minutes. Drain, keep warm, and cook the remaining *macaronia.*

To serve, combine the Scorched Tomato Sauce and Rich Chicken Stock in a saucepan, season to taste, and heat to warm; do not boil. Transfer the *macaronia* to a warm earthenware bowl and pour over the tomato sauce and olive oil. Gently toss together and serve at once, with bowls of the cheese.

Variations
Substitute a cheese (page 56), cheese and spinach (page 57), wild greens (page 58), or meat (page 62) filling for the chicken filling; you will need only half the quantity of filling those recipes make.

Kritharaki with Brown Butter and Cheese
Kritharaki me Voutiro ke Tyri
Serves 4 to 6

Archaeological evidence suggests that *kritharaki* may have been an early "convenience food", sold in the marketplaces of ancient Greece. The tiniest grains of *kritharaki* are no larger than pearl rice, the largest are the size of cantaloupe seeds; you can find it in Greek or Middle Eastern shops – it is also called *manestra* or *orza.* Goats' butter is the traditional flavouring but brown butter and lemon juice make a fine substitute. Be generous with the cheese and fresh herbs.

350 g/12 oz medium-size *kritharaki*
850 ml/1¹/₂ pints home-made Light Meat or Chicken Stock (pages 347 and 344),
Meat Stock (page 347) or water
75 g/3 oz unsalted butter
Juice of 1 large lemon, or to taste
115 g/4 oz finely grated aged *myzithra* or *kasseri* cheese
1 small handful fresh herbs, leaves only, snipped or finely chopped
1 small handful flat leaf parsley, leaves coarsely chopped
6 spring onions, best green parts only, finely sliced
Coarse-grain sea salt *and* cracked black pepper to taste

Bring the stock to a boil in a large saucepan. Add the *kritharaki* and simmer until barely tender, about 10 minutes. Drain, and briefly refresh under cold running water. Rinse out the saucepan.

Meanwhile, heat the butter in a small heavy saucepan over a very low heat until deep golden brown, about 10 minutes. (Keep the heat very low or the solids in the butter will burn.) Strain through 2 layers of muslin into a bowl and add most of the lemon juice.

Return the *kritharaki* to the rinsed-out saucepan. Add the butter mixture, the cheese, herbs, parsley, spring onion, salt and pepper, and remaining lemon juice. Stir just to mix, heat to warm, and transfer to a warm serving bowl. Serve at once.

Note Your choice of herbs to flavour *kritharaki* depends on what is available and the dish it is to be served with. The quantity of herbs you use depends on their strength. Fresh oregano, chervil, thyme, borage, or coriander are all good choices. Herbs with a mild flavour, such as chervil, are simply snipped into small pieces, but stronger herbs, such as oregano, must be finely chopped.

Breads

psomia

Bread is a fundamental part of Greek life – it appears in some form at every meal and special festive breads are of great significance in religious festivals and family celebrations. Greek bakeries, piled high with breads of every conceivable size and shape, have a special magic. In rural communities bread is still baked in the *fournos* and the village baker supplies a range of breads, from the basic everyday loaf to wonderful crusty wholemeal, barley, or stone-ground breads, as well as one or two savoury or fruit breads.

Savoury breads are seasonal and vary from region to region and baker to baker. The one essential common ingredient is a good fruity olive oil, which results in a wonderfully supple dough with an appealing aroma and the characteristic flavour and texture of all Greek breads. Flavoured with cheese, olives, fennel, or herbs these savoury breads invariably appear as round loaves but you may prefer to make the dough into rolls. And if you have savoury bread left over, just sprinkle slices of the bread with olive oil and crisp them in a low oven; dipped into red wine and accompanied by fresh cheese and olives, they are a delectable, traditional, and quickly made snack.

Sweet breads, such as Currant Bread (page 262), are enjoyable all year round and *paximathi*, a sweet anise-flavoured hard bread, is a universal treat with coffee. The flavourings used in sweet breads hint at their ancient origins – *mastic* (page 14), *petimezi* (page 306), cinnamon, allspice, vanilla, and nutmeg are all traditional.

Both sweet and savoury breads play a central role in Greek religious life, as part of Orthodox ritual and as celebration food. The women of each church congregation make a dense-textured bread for the celebration of the Eucharist, and a special bread flavoured with mastic is made for Saints' days. These church breads are known as *artos*, the ancient Greek word for bread. A flat sesame seed bread called *lagana* is baked to mark the first day of Lent; later, this important fast is broken by the sharing of the rich Easter Bread (page 259). At Christmas and New Year, more festive sweet breads (pages 260 and 261) appear – ornately decorated or shaped and gleaming with sugary glaze. And throughout the year, for any celebration – an engagement, a wedding, the birth of a child – there is the all-purpose festive bread called *tsoureki* (page 258).

Many of these breads are not difficult to make at home, although they do take a little extra time. Most can be frozen very successfully, so you can make extra loaves or rolls to serve with Greek meals later, and they also keep extremely well.

notes on
successful bread making

Making bread is wonderfully satisfying and not at all difficult if you follow some simple guidelines. These tips should help you succeed in making a variety of delicious breads, both savoury and sweet.

Equipment you will need

• Large mixing bowl
• Dough scraper
• Scales and measuring spoons; heavy baking trays
• Oven thermometer; clean tea towels; clingfilm; an uncluttered, clean work area
• Draught-free warm spot
• Loaf pans are useful but not essential

Ingredients

Flour: These recipes use wholemeal flour, pastry flour, wholewheat flour, and unbleached plain flour. Other flours, such as stone-ground, can be substituted; you will usually need to use less of them and to knead the dough for a longer time. Flour measurements are approximate; the important thing is to add enough flour to make the dough the required texture. I use organic flour whenever possible.

Salt: Salt serves two primary functions in bread making: It helps retain moisture in the dough and acts as a flavour enhancer. Use only sea salt – the taste of the chemical additives in other salts is intensified in bread. Salt must be dissolved before it is incorporated into the dough; fine-grain sea salt dissolves the most quickly.

Olive oil: The "secret" ingredient in Mediterranean breads, it makes a pliant, easy-to-handle dough. Pungent extra virgin olive oil gives the most authentic taste, but use less-expensive refined olive oil, if you prefer.

Yeast: For convenience, these recipes use active dry yeast. However, do use fresh yeast if you can find it since it gives a better flavour; one small cake is equivalent to one tablespoon active dry yeast. Dissolve in liquid heated to 30-32C/85-90F instead of 43C/110F.

Techniques

Temperature: Temperature is an important factor during all stages of bread making. Yeast is a living organism; it weakens and dies if over-heated, refuses to work if too cold. It is activated only at specific temperatures, and once activated, will die if left too long (usually more than about twelve minutes) without a "host" (the flour). Mixing bowls should be lukewarm. Kneading warms the dough so that it will rise. The oven must be hot enough for a quick rise, but not too hot or the dough may collapse. After 10 minutes or so the temperature is usually reduced so that the loaf cooks through. Oven temperatures must be exact – use an oven thermometer.

Kneading dough: Use a lightly floured board or work surface for kneading dough, and press into the dough with your knuckles each time you fold it over. Kneading enables the dough to rise. A few minutes practice is all you need to become competent, and it is a very satisfying culinary skill but, if you prefer, you can use the dough hook attachment on an electric mixer.

Rising: To rise properly, bread dough needs warmth and contact with the yeast micro-organisms that exist in the air. High humidity can cause bread to rise faster so be prepared to reduce the rising time if the atmosphere is humid. Cold will slow down the rising process: if you have to leave the dough for more than 2 or 3 hours, refrigerate it to prevent it over-rising and breaking. If it should over-rise and collapse, knead again and bake immediately.

Flavour: In addition to the type of flour used and any added flavourings, the taste of bread is also affected by:
Yeast – too much adversely flavours the dough
Salt – without it the bread, whether savoury or sweet, will be flat-tasting
Water – any unpleasant flavours in treated water are intensified in bread; use bottled water for best results
Rising – the longer the rise, the greater the flavour – cover the dough or bowl with clingfilm to minimize contact with the air and slow down the rising

Making a good crust: A simple way to create a good bread crust is to spray the dough with a plant mister once or twice during baking. Slashing the top of the dough with a clean razor blade or very sharp knife gives the bread an attractive appearance; this can be done either before the second rise, in which case the crust will separate quite dramatically during baking, or just before baking. Wet doughs (such as that for spinach bread) cannot be slashed, nor can over-risen dough. Greek bakers usually slash only round loaves; a traditional design is two or three parallel lines cut diagonally across the centre.

Country Bread
Khoriatiko Psomi
Makes 2 loaves

This is the flavourful bread that appears daily on village tables. It's easy to make, has an excellent crumb, and a good strong flavour enhanced with honey and olive oil.

2 tablespoons active dry yeast
225 ml/8 fl oz tepid (43C/110F) water
2 tablespoons honey
2 teaspoons fine-grain sea salt

1 egg, lightly beaten
175 ml/6 fl oz milk, heated to tepid (43C/110F)
2 tablespoons olive oil
2 tablespoons unsalted butter, melted
500-550 g/18-20 oz wholemeal flour or 275 g/10 oz wholemeal flour and 200-250 g/ 7-9
oz graham flour (available in health food shops)

Sprinkle the yeast over 4 tablespoons of the tepid water and set aside in a warm spot for 10 minutes, or until foamy.

Combine the honey, salt, egg, milk, remaining water, 1 tablespoon of the olive oil, and half the butter in a bowl. Sift 275 g/10 oz of the flour into a large mixing bowl, make a well in the centre, and stir in the yeast and honey mixtures. Knead for 10 minutes, gradually adding enough of the remaining flour to make a firm, smooth, and elastic dough. Tightly cover the bowl and set aside in a warm draught-free spot for 1¹/₂ hours, or until doubled in bulk.

Lightly oil a heavy baking tray. Knead the dough 1 minute. Form into 2 round loaves and place well apart on the baking tray. Cover with a clean tea towel and set aside for 1 hour in a warm spot to rise.

Heat the oven to 190C/375F/gas mark 5.

Brush the loaves with the remaining olive oil and butter and bake 40 minutes, or until lightly browned and, when tapped on the bottom, sound hollow. Cool on a rack.

Shepherd's Bread
Artos Voskou
Makes 2 round loaves or 10 rolls

This strongly flavoured, densely-textured bread is sometimes made into a large round loaf, often with a hole in the centre, sometimes into long or round rolls. Greeks have been baking tasty country bread like this for centuries; originally made with oat bran and barley meal it's now more commonly made with oat and wheat brans and stone-ground flour. This bread is delicious served with grilled meats, salads, and sheep's or goat's cheeses or just dipped in olive oil or red wine. Try making it with fresh sheep's milk (available in health food shops) instead of water, as the ancient Greeks did.

2 tablespoons honey
3 teaspoons sea salt
5 tablespoons olive oil
115 g/4 oz wheat bran
100 g/3¹/₂ oz oat bran
450 ml/16 fl oz lukewarm water or sheep's or goat's milk
350-400 g/12-14 oz wholemeal flour

Combine the honey, salt, 3 tablespoons of the olive oil, the wheat bran, oat bran, and water in a large jar. Tightly cover and set aside for 18-22 hours in a warm draught-free spot to ferment.

After about 12 hours the mixture should begin to give off an aroma rather like that of fresh beer; let ferment longer. Don't worry if it takes a few hours longer to give off the characteristic aroma.

Sift 150 g/5 oz of the flour, mix it into the fermenting bran mixture with a wooden spoon, replace the lid, and set aside for 4 hours longer in the same warm spot. The dough will have developed a sponge-like texture.

Sift 200 g/7 oz of the remaining flour into a large mixing bowl, make a well in the centre, and pour in the bran mixture. Knead thoroughly for at least 5 minutes, adding additional flour if necessary to make a firm dough – it will never feel as smooth or as elastic as dough made with yeast.

Lightly brush a heavy baking tray with some of the olive oil. Form the dough into 2 round loaves or 10 round or long rolls and arrange on the tray, spaced well apart. Cover with cling film and set aside for 2-3 hours in a warm draught-free place to rise. The dough will increase in bulk by only about one third.

Heat the oven to 180C/350F/gas mark 4.

Brush the loaves or rolls with the remaining olive oil and bake 15 minutes, then reduce the oven temperature to 160C/325F/gas mark 3. Bake loaves 50 minutes longer, rolls 30 minutes longer, or until they sound hollow when lightly tapped on the bottom. Cool on a rack.

Store Cupboard Bread
Paximathi me Salata
Serves 4 to 6

Bread quickly becomes stale in hot climates, and this bread is a country solution to the problem. Baked until it becomes hard and dry, it can be stored almost indefinitely. Then, when it is needed, it is soaked in wine, olive oil, or water and almost magically regains its dense and delicious texture. A village neighbour spreads chopped sweet tomatoes over the bread and sprinkles them with pungent herbs, making a simple and delicious summer lunch. Serve with Purslane Salad (page 2219) and bowls of olives and cheese.

The Greeks also double-bake rolls and thick slices of bread, but the method works only with coarse or densely textured bread; softer, loose-textured loaves just become soggy if revived in the same way.

1 round loaf Shepherd's Bread (page 250), cut in half horizontally
115 ml/4 fl oz water
Juice of 1 lemon
6 large ripe tomatoes, skinned, seeded if desired, and diced
1/2 teaspoon sugar
1 teaspoon coarse-grain sea salt, or to taste
1-2 teaspoons cracked black pepper to taste
175-225 ml/6-8 fl oz extra virgin olive oil to taste
1 small red or mild onion, cut into thin rings

4 tablespoons finely chopped flat leaf parsley
2 tablespoons dried *rigani* (page 14) or 1 tablespoon dried thyme, crumbled

Heat the oven to 110C/225F/gas mark ¹/₂.

Place the bread, cut sides up, on a heavy baking tray, and bake 30 minutes or until hard, turning once. Cool on a rack.

Place the bread on a plate and sprinkle the water and lemon juice evenly over it. Set aside for 30 minutes, or until the liquids are absorbed. Sprinkle the tomatoes with the sugar, salt, and pepper, and set aside.

Pour 115 ml/4 fl oz of the olive oil over the bread, set aside for a few minutes, then spoon over the tomatoes. Scatter the onion over the tomatoes and sprinkle with the parsley, *rigani*, and remaining olive oil. Serve at once.

Pitta Bread
Pita
Makes 6 medium pitta breads

The perfect bread to accompany *souvlakia* and other grilled meats, *pita* is soft-textured and mildly sweet. It's also straightforward to prepare and well worth making since the flavour of home-made *pita* is far superior to that of the bland commercial product. It keeps well for a few days and can be frozen. There are a surprising number of ways to make it, but the following is the one I find works the best.

1 teaspoon light honey
175-225 ml/6-8 fl oz tepid (43C/110F) water
1 tablespoon active dry yeast
1 teaspoon fine-grain sea salt
3 tablespoons olive oil
150 g/5 oz wholemeal flour
115 g/4 oz unbleached plain flour

Combine the honey and 4 tablespoons of the tepid water in a bowl and sprinkle the yeast over. Set aside for 10 minutes in a warm spot. Dissolve the salt in the remaining tepid water and add 1¹/₂ tablespoons of the olive oil.

Sift the wholemeal flour and 50 g/2 oz of the plain flour into a large bowl, make a well in the centre, and pour in the yeast and salt mixtures. Mix with your hands, adding up to 4 tablespoons additional water or up to 50 g/2 oz additional plain flour if necessary to make a moist but firm dough. Transfer to a lightly floured surface and knead 10 to 15 minutes, until smooth and elastic. Transfer to a lightly oiled bowl, and brush with olive oil. (The oil keeps the dough moist while rising.) Cover the bowl with a slightly damp tea towel and set aside in a warm draught-free spot for 2 hours, or until at least doubled in bulk.

Arrange 1 rack close to the bottom of the oven, 1 to the top, and heat the oven to 220C/

425F/gas mark 7.

Knead the dough 2 minutes and divide into 6 portions. Set aside for 10 minutes in a warm spot to rest, then flatten each portion with your palm. Lightly flour a work surface and roll the dough into 6 mm/¹/₄ inch-thick rounds or ovals. Brush a heavy baking tray with the remaining olive oil and slide the pitta rounds onto it, spacing them at least 10 cm/4 inches apart. (Don't brush the pittas or they will not rise properly.)

Place the baking tray on the lower oven rack and bake 3 minutes. Quickly transfer to the top rack and bake 3 or 4 minutes longer, or until the pittas are puffy but not even lightly browned. They should still be soft. (If your oven is small and you need to use 2 baking sheets or more, place the second sheet in the oven when you move the first to the top rack.)

Stack between warm and very slightly damp clean tea towels and set aside in a draught-free spot until cool. Seal in plastic bags to store.

Olive Bread
Eliopsomo
Makes 1 large round loaf or 2 small ones

This aromatic bread changes its character with the seasons. In spring it's gently perfumed with fresh rosemary or fennel; in winter dried thyme or mint gives it a more pungent but less subtle flavour. Olive bread has a long-standing tradition in Greek life and is believed to have appeared on Minoan tables three thousand years before the birth of Christ. This is a modern version of an ancient recipe, made with added yeast, but it retains all the rustic simplicity and taste of the original. Cut it into thin slices and serve with *mezedes,* sausages, or omelettes.

1 teaspoon honey
225 ml/8 fl oz tepid (43C/110F) water
1¹/₂ tablespoons active dry yeast
115 ml/4 fl oz extra virgin olive oil
1 teaspoon fine-grain sea salt
350–400 g/12–14 oz wholemeal flour
12 plump Greek or other oil-cured olives, pitted
1 large onion, finely chopped
1 tablespoon fresh rosemary or fennel leaves, finely chopped or
1 tablespoon dried thyme or mint, crumbled

Dissolve the honey in the water in a small bowl and sprinkle the yeast over. Set aside in a warm place until foamy, about 10 minutes. Whisk in 3 tablespoons of the olive oil and the salt.

Sift 200 g/7 oz of the flour into a large mixing bowl, make a well in the centre, and add the yeast mixture. Knead 10 minutes, adding enough of the remaining flour to make a firm but elastic dough. Set aside in a warm draught-free place for 2 hours, or until at least doubled in bulk.

Heat 3 tablespoons of the remaining olive oil in a heavy frying pan and sauté the onion over low heat until pale golden, about 10 minutes. Set aside.

Blanch the olives in boiling water for 1 second; drain and dry with paper towels. Cut 5 of the olives into small pieces and finely chop the rest. Add the olives and rosemary to the onions and stir to mix. Add to the dough and knead 1 minute.

Brush a heavy baking tray with olive oil. Form the dough into 1 or 2 slightly flattened round loaves on the tray, spaced well apart. Cover with a clean tea towel and set aside for 1 hour in a warm draught-free spot.

Heat the oven to 190C/375F/gas mark 5.

Bake the bread 10 minutes, reduce the oven temperature to 180C/350F/gas mark 4, brush with the remaining olive oil and bake 25-35 minutes longer, or until the bread is deep golden brown and sounds hollow when tapped on the bottom.

Note Also try plump fleshy Amfissa olives instead of the more pungent oil-cured ones.

Cheese Mint Bread
Tyropsomo Thiosmou
Makes 3 small loaves

The characteristic, rather musty, flavour of *halloumi* cheese is particularly suited to bread made with olive oil. If it is unavailable, *feta* cheese makes a perfectly good substitute, but it should be drained well before using. This densely textured bread, fragrant with mint, is traditionally made in small loaves, ideal for picnics or to serve with salads.

75-150 ml/3-5 fl oz tepid (43C/110F) water
1 tablespoon active dry yeast
5 tablespoons extra virgin olive oil
1 teaspoon fine-grain sea salt
300 g/11 oz wholemeal flour
2 tablespoons dried mint, finely crumbled
Scant 225 g/8 oz *halloumi* or *feta* cheese, cut or crumbled into small pieces
1 tablespoon fresh lemon juice

Pour 75 ml/3 fl oz of the water into a small bowl and sprinkle the yeast over. Set aside in a warm place until foamy, about 10 minutes. Whisk in 4 tablespoons of the olive oil and the salt.

Sift the flour into a large mixing bowl, make a well in the centre, and pour in the yeast mixture. Knead 10 minutes, adding some, or all, of the additional water if necessary to make a firm elastic dough. Transfer to a lightly oiled bowl, and brush the dough with olive oil. Tightly cover the bowl with cling film and set aside for 2¹/₂ hours in a warm draught-free spot. It will not quite double in bulk, but the long resting time produces a well-flavoured bread.

Knead in the mint. Divide the dough into 3 portions. Form each into a ball, then flatten on a board to a thickness of 2 cm/3/4 inch. Place one third of the cheese in the centre of each and bring up the edges of the dough to barely enclose the cheese, but do not seal. Transfer to a lightly oiled heavy baking tray, cover with a clean tea towel, and set aside for 1 hour in a warm draught-free spot.

Heat the oven to 180C/350F/gas mark 4.

Combine the remaining olive oil and the lemon juice and lightly brush the loaves with this mixture. Bake 10 minutes, reduce the oven temperature to 160C/325F/gas mark 3, and bake 40 minutes longer or until golden brown.

Rigani Cheese Bread
Tryopsomo Riganato
Makes 1 large round loaf

I first tasted this delicious bread at a picnic high in the Pindus mountains – an appropriate setting for a bread heavily scented with mountain herbs. The great round loaf, with its glistening olive oil glaze and rich cheese flavour, was the delicious centrepiece of the outdoor feast; around it were spread olives, *kephtedakia* (page 32), Smoked Fish Salad (page 31), and *mezedes* of aubergine and other vegetables.

1 tablespoon active dry yeast
225 ml/8 fl oz tepid (43C/110F) water
3 tablespoons olive oil
$^1/_2$ teaspoon fine-grain sea salt
300–400 g/11–14 oz wholemeal flour
2 tablespoons dried *rigani* (page 14), crumbled
$^1/_2$ tablespoon dried mint, finely crumbled
350 g/12 oz *feta* cheese, well drained and finely crumbled
1 egg yolk beaten with 2 tablespoons warm water

Sprinkle the yeast over the water and set aside in a warm place until foamy, about 10 minutes. Whisk in 2 tablespoons of the olive oil and the salt.

Sift 300 g/11 oz of the flour into a large mixing bowl, make a well in the centre, and pour in the yeast mixture. Knead 10 minutes, adding the remaining flour if necessary to make a firm, elastic dough. Transfer to a lightly oiled bowl, tightly cover with cling film, and set aside for 2 hours in a warm draught-free spot.

Knead in the *rigani*, mint, and *feta* until evenly distributed throughout the dough. Lightly oil a heavy baking tray and place the dough in the centre. Form into a round loaf and flatten to a thickness of 5 cm/2 inches. Cover with a clean tea towel and set aside for 1 hour in a warm draught-free spot. The dough will rise only slightly.

Heat the oven to 180C/350F/gas mark 4.

With a sharp thin blade, slash the top of the loaf diagonally in 2 or 3 parallel lines, brush with the remaining olive oil, and bake 25 minutes. Brush with the beaten egg yolk and bake 15 minutes longer, or until the bread is deep golden brown and sounds hollow when tapped on the bottom.

Fennel Bread
Marathopsomo
Makes 1 large or 2 smaller loaves

Fennel bread changes its character during the year, according to the type of fennel used to flavour it. The finest-flavoured loaves appear on Greek tables in early spring when succulent young fennel is at its best. Later in the season finely chopped larger fennel sprigs are used, and, for the rest of the year, the bread is made with pulverized fennel seeds. This exquisite bread is the perfect complement to a light meal of Beetroot Island-Style (page 182), olives, and *myzithra* cheese (page 11). Its distinctive flavour is also superb with grilled fish, chicken, or pork.

1 tablespoon active dry yeast
225 ml/8 fl oz tepid (43C/110F) water
5 tablespoons extra virgin olive oil
1 teaspoon fine-grain sea salt, or to taste
300-400 g/11-14 oz wholemeal flour
1 large handful of fennel sprigs or 3 tablespoons fennel seeds
2 medium onions, finely chopped
Juice of 1 large lemon
115 g/4 oz *feta* cheese, well-drained and finely crumbled
1 teaspoon coarse-grain sea salt, or to taste
6 Elitses or Niçoise olives, blanched in boiling water for 5 seconds, drained,
pitted, and halved

Sprinkle the yeast over the water and set aside in a warm place until foamy, about 10 minutes. Whisk in 2 tablespoons of the olive oil and 1/2 teaspoon of the fine-grain sea salt.

Sift 300 g/11 oz of the flour into a large bowl, make a well in the centre, and pour in the yeast mixture. Knead 10 minutes, adding the remaining flour if necessary to make a firm elastic dough. Transfer to a lightly oiled bowl, brush the dough with olive oil, tightly cover with cling film, and set aside for 2 hours in a warm draught-free spot. The dough will not quite double in bulk.

Blanch fresh fennel in boiling water for 5 seconds, pat dry with paper towels, and chop finely. (Or pound fennel seed and the remaining fine-grain salt in a mortar, or grind in a coffee grinder until almost pulverized, just before the seeds become a powder.) Combine the fresh fennel and remaining fine-grain salt (or the pounded fennel), onion, most of the lemon juice, and 2 tablespoons olive oil, and knead into the dough along with the cheese.

Lightly oil a baking tray. Form the dough into 1 or 2 round loaves and flatten to 5 cm/ 2 inches. With a clean thin blade, slash 2 parallel lines diagonally across the top of the loaf(ves), and set aside for 1 hour in a warm draught-free spot. The slashes will open as the dough rises.

Heat the oven to 180C/350F/gas mark 4.

Sprinkle the coarse-grain salt inside the slashes and gently press the olives into the tops of the loaf(ves), cut sides down. Brush with the remaining olive oil and lemon juice and bake smaller loaves 35 minutes, 1 large loaf 50 minutes, or until browned and the bread sounds hollow when tapped on the bottom.

Spinach Bread
Spanakopsomo
Makes 1 large round loaf or 2 smaller ones

Traditionally this bread is made with wild greens. Spinach gives a smoother, lighter bread (and is easier to find), but you may like to try the ancient *khorta* version too. This flattish, chewy bread with its distinctive flavour is perfect with salads, egg dishes, and cheese and olives.

1 teaspoon honey
2 teaspoons fine-grain sea salt
175 ml/6 fl oz tepid (43C/110F) water
1 tablespoon active dry yeast
5 tablespoons olive oil
400 g/14 oz wholemeal or spelt flour (available in health food shops)
900 g/2 lb fresh spinach
2 large mild onions, finely chopped
1 large clove garlic, finely chopped
1 1/2 tablespoons cumin seeds or 1 tablespoon ground cumin
Juice of 1 lemon

Combine the water, honey, and 1 teaspoon of the salt in a medium bowl and sprinkle the yeast over. Set aside in a warm place until foamy, about 10 minutes. Whisk in 2 tablespoons of the olive oil, then sift in 75 g/3 oz flour and stir to mix. Set aside in a warm draught-free spot for 1 hour, or until sponge-like in texture.

Meanwhile, rinse the spinach in several changes of cold water, remove the tough stalks and leaves, and cut tender leaves into 6 mm/1/4 inch strips. Set aside. Heat 2 1/2 tablespoons of the olive oil in a large heavy frying pan and sauté the onion over a low heat until pale golden, about 15 minutes. Heat the cumin in a small dry frying pan until aromatic, and pulverize it in a mortar or grinder. Add the cumin, garlic, and remaining salt to the onion. Stir in the spinach and cook 5 minutes, stirring frequently, until soft. Sprinkle with the lemon juice and drain in a colander set over a bowl. Set aside, reserving the cooking liquid.

Sift 225 g/8 oz of the remaining flour into a large bowl, make a well in the centre, and pour in the yeast sponge. Knead 10 minutes, adding enough of the reserved cooking liquid to make a firm but elastic dough. Transfer to a lightly oiled bowl, tightly cover with cling film, and set aside for 2 hours in a warm draught-free place.

Add the *feta* to the dough and knead 1 minute. Add the spinach mixture, sprinkle with the remaining flour, and quickly mix together – the dough will be quite moist and loose; do not knead it again.

Brush a baking tray with olive oil and place the dough on it. Form into 1 large round loaf or 2 smaller ones spaced well apart. Cover with a clean tea towel and set aside for 1 hour in a warm draught-free spot.

Heat the oven to 190C/375F/gas mark 5.

Bake the bread 20 minutes, reduce the oven temperature to 180C/350F/gas mark 4, brush with the remaining olive oil, and bake 20-30 minutes longer, until golden brown.

Festive Bread
Tsoureki
Makes 2 braided loaves or 3 long loaves

During any major religious festival, this shiny glazed celebration bread is attractively displayed in every Greek cake shop and coffee house window, and laden baskets of the loaves hang from the ceiling of every bakery.

However, many Greeks still prefer to make their own *tsoureki,* and every family has a favourite flavouring – orange, lemon, mastic, vanilla, allspice, or cloves and bay are the most popular. The traditional shape is a braided or round loaf, but forming the dough into long loaves makes it easier to store and cut. It makes delicious toast, and it keeps for well up to one week.

175 g/6 oz light brown sugar
115 ml/4 fl oz tepid (43C/110F) water
2 tablespoons active dry yeast
300 g/11 oz unbleached plain flour
275-300 g/10-11 oz unbleached pastry flour
115 ml/4 fl oz *plus* 2 tablespoons milk, heated to tepid (43C/110F)
2 tablespoons olive oil
5 eggs
Juice of ¹/₂ orange
2 tablespoons finely grated orange zest, briefly dried in a low oven and pulverized in a mortar with ¹/₂ teaspoon sugar, or 1 ¹/₂ tablespoons orange extract
¹/₂ teaspoon vanilla extract
1 teaspoon ground allspice *or* 1 teaspoon mastic granules (page 14), pulverized in a mortar with ¹/₂ teaspoon sugar
1 teaspoon fine-grain sea salt, or to taste
50 g/2 oz unsalted butter, melted
1 egg yolk
1 tablespoon honey
4 tablespoons sesame seeds *or* blanched slivered almonds

Dissolve 1 teaspoon of the brown sugar in the water and sprinkle the yeast over. Set aside in a warm place until foamy, about 10 minutes.

Sift 200 g/7 oz of the plain flour into a large bowl, make a well in the centre, and pour in the yeast mixture. Knead and gradually add the 115 ml/4 fl oz milk, remaining plain flour, and 175 g/6 oz of the pastry flour, or enough to make a light, smooth, and elastic dough. Turn onto a lightly floured surface and knead 10 minutes. Transfer to a lightly oiled bowl, and brush with olive oil. Cover with a warm damp tea towel and set aside in a warm draught-free place for 1 hour, or until at least doubled in bulk.

Beat the eggs in a large bowl until light and frothy and beat in the remaining brown sugar, the orange juice, orange zest, vanilla, allspice, and salt. Add to the dough with 3 tablespoons of the melted butter and knead in enough of the remaining pastry flour to make a soft dough. Transfer to a lightly floured surface and knead 3 minutes.

Divide the dough into 6 portions. With the palms of your hands, roll each into a 23 cm/9 inch rope, slightly fatter in the middle and with pointed ends. Brush a large heavy baking tray with the remaining melted butter. Lay 3 ropes on it side by side, loosely braid, and tuck the pointed ends underneath so the loaf ends are rounded. Repeat with the remaining 3 ropes, spacing the 2 braided loaves well apart. To make long loaves, either form the dough into loaves on the baking tray or place in buttered loaf tins. Loosely cover with cling film and set aside in a warm draught-free place for 2 hours, or until doubled in bulk.

Heat the oven to 200C/400F/gas mark 6.

Whisk together the egg yolk, honey, and the 2 tablespoons milk and brush the loaves with this mixture. Sprinkle with sesame seeds and bake 10 minutes. Reduce the oven temperature to 180C/350F/gas mark 4 and bake 20 minutes longer, or until a beautiful honey brown. Transfer to racks to cool.

Easter Bread
Lambropsomo
Makes 2 braided or large round loaves

The almond-topped bread that breaks the Lenten fast has pride of place on the Easter Sunday table. Rich in eggs and butter (foods forbidden during Lent), these shiny loaves display all the baker's artistry with their splendid decorations of spring flowers, leaves, or berries shaped in dough. Many of these Easter breads are so beautifully crafted that they are used as wall decorations throughout the year. Red eggs, signifying both rebirth and the blood of Christ, are an important part of the decoration – they delight the children but, unlike our traditional Easter eggs, are never eaten.

6 white eggs, at room temperature
2 teaspoons red food colouring
A few drops of blue food colouring
1 tablespoon olive oil
1 recipe Festive Bread dough (page 258), made without allspice or mastic
75 g/3 oz blanched slivered almonds

Half fill a stainless steel saucepan with water, bring to a boil, and add the food colourings. Gently boil the eggs 20 minutes; add a little more colouring if necessary to produce deep crimson eggs.

Let the eggs cool in the water, remove them, and set aside to dry. Dip a paper towel in the olive oil, and rub each egg all over with it.

Form the dough into 2 braided (see recipe above) or round loaves on buttered baking trays; if making round loaves reserve a little of the dough for decoration. Roll the reserved dough into thin ropes with the palms of your hands and break off small pieces to make into spring symbols, such as flowers, leaves, or berries. Decorate the tops of the round loaves with these shapes. Set the loaves aside for 2 hours in a warm draught-free spot to rise.

Heat the oven to 200C/400F/gas mark 6.

Place the eggs either around the centres of the round loaves or between the decorations, or arrange the eggs between the braids. Brush with the egg and honey glaze, sprinkle with the almonds, and bake 10 minutes. Reduce the oven temperature to 180C/350F/gas mark 4 and bake 20 minutes longer, or until golden brown, and transfer to racks to cool.

Discard the eggs once the bread is cut.

Christmas Bread
Christopsomo
Makes 2 shaped or round loaves

This enticingly festive bread is the focal point of a strong religious tradition. After midnight mass on Christmas Eve, each family gathers together to share the loaf, in great anticipation of who will find the lucky coin baked inside. The head of the household first breaks off a piece and sets it aside "for Christ"; then pieces are given to guests sharing the celebration. The next two pieces are for himself and the female head of the household, and finally the remainder is shared between the others at the table, men first, then women and, lastly, the children. Whoever finds the coin will be blessed with good luck; if it is found in the piece reserved for Christ, the money is given to the church or to charity. For a traditional Christmas table the bread is baked in the shape of any "blessing" the family would like to give thanks for, such as livestock or produce of the fields, and many city-dwelling cooks still shape their Christmas breads into these ancient symbols of good fortune.

1 recipe Saint Basil's Bread (page 261), substituting:
3 cloves, 2 bay leaves *and* one 5 cm/2 inch cinnamon stick for the aniseed;
2 tablespoons lemon zest *or* lemon extract for the orange zest, *optional; and* 75 g/3 oz blanched slivered almonds for the sesame seeds
2 egg whites
75 g/3 oz caster sugar
Pinch of salt
12 small walnut halves
50 g/2 oz candied fruit, cut into tiny dice

Form the dough into 2 loaves on a buttered baking tray and let it rise a second time (page 261).

Heat the oven to 190C/375F/gas mark 5.

Whisk the egg whites until thick but not stiff, then whisk in the sugar and salt. Brush the loaves generously with this glaze. Arrange the walnut halves on top, gently pushing them onto the dough, then sprinkle over the candied fruit. Lightly brush with the remaining glaze and bake 40-50 minutes, or until deep chestnut brown. Cool on a rack.

Saint Basil's Bread
Vasilopitta
Makes 1 large round loaf, 2 long loaves, or 18 rolls

Named for a founding father of the Orthodox church, this is the traditional New Year's bread and, like Christmas Bread, has a lucky coin baked inside. At the last chime of midnight on New Year's Eve the head of the family breaks the bread and divides it between those gathered for the celebration. Appropriately, for a bread made in honour of a Byzantine saint, the Eastern spice *mahlepi* is a favourite flavouring, but aniseed is also popular and whole aniseed gives the bread an interesting texture and a pungent festive aroma. This delectable loaf is a year-round favourite in non-traditional households. The traditional shape is a very large round loaf with a smaller loaf on top, but it's easier to store if you make it into two long loaves or rolls. It keeps well and can also be frozen.

2 tablespoons whole aniseed or 1 tablespoon *mahlepi* seeds (available in Greek or Middle Eastern shops), lightly crushed

2 tablespoons active dry yeast

225 ml/8 fl oz *plus* 2 tablespoons milk, heated to tepid (43C/110F)

300 g/11 oz unbleached plain flour *and* 300-400 g/11-14 oz wholemeal or spelt flour *or* 600-700 g/22-25 oz unbleached plain flour

7 eggs

225 g/8 oz honey

1 teaspoon fine-grain sea salt, or to taste

150 g/5 oz caster sugar

175 g/6 oz unsalted butter, melted

5 tablespoons light olive oil

2 tablespoons finely grated orange zest, briefly dried in a low oven and pulverized in a mortar with 1 teaspoon sugar, or 2 tablespoons orange extract

115 g/4 oz sesame seeds

Combine the aniseed and 115 ml/4 fl oz water in a small saucepan, bring to a boil, and simmer 1 minute. Set aside to cool. Strain and set aside the liquid (or set aside both seeds and liquid).

Pour 225 ml/8 fl oz milk into a medium bowl, sprinkle the yeast over, and set aside for 10 minutes in a warm spot, or until foamy. Stir 115 g/4 oz of the plain flour into the yeast with a wooden spoon, tightly cover, and set aside in a warm draught-free spot for 1 hour, or until it has become sponge-like in texture.

With a wire whisk or electric mixer, beat 6 of the eggs, the honey, salt, and all but 2 teaspoons of the sugar in a large bowl until light and frothy. Sift the remaining plain flour and 200 g/7 oz of the wholemeal flour into another large bowl, make a well in the centre, and pour in the yeast sponge, aniseed liquid (and seeds if desired), about 115 g/4 oz of the butter, 4 tablespoons of the olive oil, the orange zest, and the egg mixture. Knead 5 minutes, transfer to a lightly floured surface, and knead 10 minutes longer, adding enough of the remaining flour to make a soft smooth dough.

Transfer to a lightly oiled bowl and brush the dough with the remaining olive oil. Tightly cover and set aside in a warm draught-free spot for 2 hours, or until at least doubled in bulk.

Transfer to a lightly floured surface and knead 5 minutes. Divide into 2 portions, one twice as large as the other. Liberally butter a baking tray with the remaining butter and place the larger portion on the tray. Form it into a round loaf about 5 cm/2 inches thick, and flatten the top slightly with your palm. Form the smaller portion into a round loaf about 2.5 cm/1 inch thick, flattening it on the bottom, and centre it on top of the larger one. (To make long loaves, either form into loaves on the baking tray or place in buttered loaf pans. To make rolls, divide the dough into 18 portions and form into round or long rolls on a buttered baking tray, spaced at least 7 cm/3 inches apart.) With a wooden skewer or equivalent, write the year on top for New Year's bread or make a simple design. Loosely cover with cling film and set aside for 30 minutes in a warm draught-free spot.

Heat the oven to 190C/375F/gas mark 5.

Beat the remaining egg with the reserved 2 teaspoons sugar and the 2 tablespoons milk and liberally brush the dough with this glaze. Sprinkle over the sesame seeds and bake 40-50 minutes, or until deep chestnut brown. Cool on a rack.

Currant Bread
Stafithopsomo
Makes 2 medium loaves or 12 rolls

With a more refreshing and lighter flavour than the familiar sweet raisin bread, this currant loaf is easy to make and has an attractive country character. It can be shaped into loaves or rolls and it makes perfect breakfast bread with yogurt, honey, and fresh fruit. Or try it toasted, with jam or preserves.

150 g/5 oz *plus* 1 tablespoon honey
2 tablespoons unsalted butter, melted
1 1/2 teaspoons fine-grain sea salt, or to taste
300 ml/1/2 pint milk, heated to tepid (43C/110F)
2 tablespoons active dry yeast
400 g/14 oz wholemeal flour
150 g/5 oz unbleached plain flour
1/2 teaspoon ground cloves
2 eggs, lightly beaten
1 tablespoon light olive oil
225 g/8 oz currants

With a whisk, combine the 150 g/5 oz honey, half the butter, the salt, and 225 ml/8 fl oz of the milk in a small bowl. Sprinkle the yeast over and set aside in a warm place until foamy, about 10 minutes.

Sift both flours and the ground cloves into a large mixing bowl; remove and set aside 150g/ 5 oz. Make a well in the centre of the remaining flour, and stir in the yeast mixture and the eggs. Turn out onto a floured work surface and knead 4-5 minutes, or until the dough is light, smooth, and elastic. Transfer to a lightly oiled bowl, brush the dough with the remaining olive oil, tightly cover with cling film, and set aside in a warm draught-free place for 30 minutes, or until increased in bulk by one third.

Sprinkle the currants and half the reserved flour mixture over the dough, and knead 5 minutes, adding some or all of the remaining flour, if necessary, to make a firm elastic dough. Cover the bowl and set aside in a warm draught-free place for 2 hours, or until doubled in bulk.

To make loaves Divide the dough into 2 portions. Lightly brush two 23 x 13 cm/9 x 5 inch loaf tins with the remaining melted butter. Place 1 piece of dough in the centre of each, or roll each piece into a 23 x 30 cm/9 x 12 inch rectangle. Starting with a shorter side, roll up each rectangle to make a 23 cm/9 inch loaf.

To make rolls Divide the dough into 12 portions and shape into rolls. Brush a heavy baking tray with the remaining melted butter and set the rolls on it, spaced well apart.

Cover the loaves or rolls with a clean tea towel and set aside for 1 hour in a warm draught-free place, to rise.

Heat the oven to 190C/375F/gas mark 5.

Whisk together the 1 tablespoon honey and the remaining milk and lightly brush the top of the dough to glaze. Bake loaves 1 hour, rolls 25 minutes, or until they sound hollow when tapped on the bottom. Transfer to a rack to cool.

Pies, Pastries, Cakes, and Biscuits

glykes, pittes, tartes, ke biscotakia

Greeks have a great fondness for syrup-drenched pastries, pies, and cakes, but they rarely end a meal with them. Fresh fruit is the usual dessert and the Greek sweet tooth is satisfied between meals, most often at a pastry shop. Every village has at least one of these *zacharoplastia*, and in large cities the visitor is tempted at every turn by ornate examples of sculptured sweetness.

The skill of the *zacharoplastis* ("sugar sculptor") elevates cake and pastry making to fine art and the range of these sugary concoctions is breathtaking. Gloriously honeyed pastries such as *baklava*, syrup-laden *kataifi* (page 268), and creamy Filo Custard Pie (page 267) are displayed alongside regional specialities such as the wonderful lemon pie from the island of Kos.

To mark historic occasions the pastry maker bakes special celebration cakes; for festivals he bakes traditional sweet breads (pages 258 to 263), tiny sweet pies (page 270), and a variety of fragrant honey cakes (page 280), just as Greek bakers have done since ancient times.

Many of these traditional pastries and cakes are known as *glyka tou tapsiou*, meaning "sweets from the baking tin". After baking they are drenched in honey or syrup perfumed with orange flower water or rosewater or an aromatic spice. These, and the other pastries included here, are ambrosial. Serve them as snacks or dessert and, in the Greek fashion, provide Greek coffee (page 336) and tall glasses of ice-cold water – perfect complements to the richness of these sweets.

Filo
Phyllo
Makes 450 g/1 lb pastry

The golden pies in the windows of Greek pastry shops owe their crisp beauty to *phyllo* pastry. Paper-thin sheets of *phyllo* are difficult to make at home, but excellent *phyllo* is available ready-made, fresh or frozen. It is generally sold in 450 g/1 lb packets, each containing between 16 and 26 sheets of pastry, measuring 30 x 45 cm/12 x 18 inches. Frozen *phyllo* must be allowed to thaw slowly in the refrigerator or it will become soggy. Unopened commercial *phyllo* can be refrigerated for up to five days but, once opened, it should be used within twenty-four hours.

Working with *phyllo* is straightforward if you bear in mind that, since it contains little oil, it must be kept moist or it will dry out and become impossible to manipulate. So cover it first with cling film, then with a slightly damp tea towel (if the pastry touches the towel it will disintegrate). You can also protect the *phyllo* by working quickly but carefully.

If you would like to make your own *phyllo* you will need a large smooth tabletop or marble slab, a long thin rolling pin – and patience. *Phyllo* pastry must be stretched as thin as possible. In some small Greek villages, making *phyllo* is a group effort, requiring four people: One stands at each corner of the rolled-out dough and each helps to pull and stretch out the pastry until it is paper-thin.

300 g/11 oz plain flour
1 teaspoon fine-grain sea salt
175-225 ml/6-8 fl oz cold water
2 tablespoons olive oil

Sift 250 g/9 oz of the flour and the salt into a large mixing bowl and gradually add enough of the water to make a firm but moist dough. Transfer to a floured work surface and knead 15 minutes, or until smooth and elastic. Sprinkle with half the olive oil and continue kneading, then sprinkle with the remaining olive oil and knead until it has all been incorporated. Tightly wrap in cling film and refrigerate 1 hour to firm.

Lightly flour a tabletop or marble slab. Break off an egg-sized piece of dough and roll it out, rolling first in one direction, then turning the pastry and rolling again. Lightly flour the board as necessary. As the sheet becomes larger and thinner, use the rolling pin to help turn the pastry, or a broom handle if the rolling pin is too short. When the pastry is paper-thin, trim the edges, cut into rectangles about 30 x 45 cm/12 x 18 inches, and stack between lightly floured tea towels. Set aside to dry for 10 minutes before using or storing. Repeat with the remaining dough.

To freeze, stack half the *phyllo* on waxed paper, cover with another sheet of waxed paper, and roll up loosely. Repeat with the remaining *phyllo,* wrap each roll in cling film, and store in sealed freezer bags for up to 3 months.

Filo Custard Pie
Galaktoboureko
Serves 12 to 15

This magnificent syrupy pie is best eaten very fresh. The light custard filling is scented with vanilla and lemon; the syrup, poured hot over the baked pie, is sharpened with lemon and orange – or, often, perfumed with cloves and rosewater (page 349). Be sure to use unsalted butter, which is essential to the subtle and fragrant flavour.

1.1 litres/2 pints milk
5 large eggs, separated
225 g/8 oz vanilla sugar (page 16) or 200 g/7 oz caster sugar *and*
1 teaspoon vanilla extract
175 g/6 oz semolina (*farina*, page 344)
1 tablespoon unsalted butter

450 g/1 lb packet filo pastry (page 266)
225 g/8 oz clarified butter (page 12) or unsalted butter, melted

Syrup
300 g/11 oz honey
225 g/8 oz caster sugar
Zest of 1 orange, removed in thin strips
Juice of 1 small lemon
3 tablespoons orange flower water, or to taste

For serving
Sifted icing sugar
Ground cinnamon

Heat the milk to just below a boil. Remove from the heat and set aside. With an electric mixer or whisk, beat the egg yolks and sugar (and vanilla) in a large bowl until pale and creamy. Beat in the semolina and gradually beat in the hot milk. Rinse out the saucepan and return the custard mixture to low heat. Cook, stirring constantly in a figure-8 motion with a wooden spoon, until the custard is firm enough to come away from the sides of the pan, about 6 minutes. Transfer to a bowl. Secure the butter on the tip of a knife and rub it over the surface of the custard; the butter will immediately melt to make a thin oily layer, preventing a skin from forming. Lightly press waxed paper on top and set aside to cool.

Arrange a rack in the centre of the oven and heat the oven to 190C/375F/gas mark 5.

Remove the packet of filo pastry from the refrigerator and set aside unopened.

With a wire whisk, beat the custard until smooth. Whisk the egg whites in a copper or other mixing bowl until they hold stiff peaks. Stir one third of the whites into the custard to lighten it, then quickly fold in the remainder.

Divide the filo into 2 portions. Rewrap 1 and refrigerate. Lightly brush a 23 x 32 cm/9 x 13 inch cake tin, at least 6 cm/2¹/₂ inches deep, with melted butter. Line with 1 pastry sheet, carefully pushing it up the sides with your knuckle (fingernails tear filo). Lightly brush with butter and lay another sheet on top. Repeat with the remaining un-refrigerated filo, but do not brush the last sheet. Pour the custard into the tin, taking care not to disturb the filo lining the sides. Lightly smooth with a spatula and gently fold over any filo extending beyond the edges of the tin.

Remove the second portion of the filo from the refrigerator. Lay 1 sheet on top of the custard letting it hang over the sides of the tin and lightly brush with butter. Repeat with the remaining filo, but do not butter the last sheet. Ease the fingers of one hand down between the edge of the pie and sides of the tin. Gently pull the bottom edges of the pie slightly towards the centre and lightly tuck the top sheets in around the bottom of the pie. Liberally butter the top sheet. With a thin sharp knife, score the top 2 sheets into 7 cm/3 inch squares or into diamonds with 5 cm/2 inch-long sides.

Reduce the oven temperature to 180C/350F/gas mark 4. Bake for 40 minutes, or until the pastry is a deep golden brown and the custard is set: Gently shake the pie – it should sway only slightly; loosely cover with aluminium foil if it seems to be browning too quickly.

Meanwhile, combine the honey, sugar, orange zest, and 450 ml/16 fl oz of water in a syrup pan or heavy saucepan. Bring slowly to a boil and simmer 10 minutes, or until the syrup lightly coats the back of a metal spoon. Set aside.

As soon as you remove the pie from the oven, immediately cut down through the score marks to the bottom of the tin. Add the lemon juice and orange flower water to the syrup, strain, reserving the zest, and pour over the hot pie. Cover the tin with a clean tea towel, making sure the towel does not touch the top of the pastry, and set aside; the trapped steam softens the top layers of filo. Refrigerate if serving time is more than 2 hours away.

To serve, cut through the score marks once more to loosen the pieces. Liberally sprinkle with the icing sugar, lightly sprinkle with the cinnamon, and scatter the reserved orange zest over. Spoon over any syrup remaining in the tin, or serve the syrup separately if you prefer.

Kataifi Nut Rolls with Caramel Syrup
Kataifi Bourekakia
Makes approximately 24 pastries

Aromatic nut-filled pastries made from very thin strands of vermicelli-like pastry, *kataifi* are sumptuous honey-sweet treats. The pastry, also called *kataifi,* is available frozen in Greek and Middle Eastern shops, and the preparation, although it sounds complicated, is really not difficult. For best results make these a day ahead and pour on the hot syrup as soon as you remove the cake tin from the oven: The *kataifi* will be sticky-sweet underneath but will remain crisp and golden on top. My favourite filling is made with pistachio nuts but almonds or walnuts are also good. For a dish of unashamed extravagance serve with Rich Cream (page 310).

275 g/10 oz finely chopped unsalted skinned (page 303) pistachio nuts, walnuts or blanched almonds

1 egg white

450 g/1 lb honey
1 teaspoon ground cinnamon, or more to taste
275 g/10 oz clarified butter (page 12) or unsalted butter, melted
450 g/1 lb packet *kataifi*
200 g/7 oz sugar
Strained juice of ¹/₂ lemon

Heat the oven to 180C/350F/gas mark 4.

Whisk the egg white in a small bowl until it holds stiff peaks. Stir in the nuts, 4 tablespoons of the honey, the cinnamon, egg white, and 2 tablespoons of the butter and set aside.

Loosen the strands of *kataifi:* Place the *kataifi* in the centre of a clean work surface, pull off a small amount, and gently squeeze it in one hand. With your other hand pull apart the strands, but avoid tearing them. Repeat with all the pastry, but work fast (don't spend more than 1 minute doing this – *kataifi* dries out very quickly).

Lay a small handful in the palm of one hand and form into a rectangular shape. Place 1 tablespoon filling in the centre, fold over the edges, and roll up towards your fingertips to make a parcel. As you finish each pastry, arrange it in 25 cm/10 inch round or 23 x 32 cm/9 x 13 inch cake tin in tight concentric circles (round tin) or lines (rectangular tin). Spoon the remaining butter evenly over the pastries and bake 40 minutes, or until crisp and deep golden brown.

Meanwhile, melt the sugar in a syrup pan or small heavy saucepan and cook over a low heat until a deep gold (light caramel). While the sugar cooks, combine the remaining honey with 275 ml/10 fl oz water in a heavy saucepan, slowly bring to a boil, and simmer 6 minutes, or until it lightly coats the back of a metal spoon. Wrap your hand in a tea towel and carefully spoon the honey syrup into the caramel – don't pour: Caramel can spit and burn. Stir in the lemon juice.

As soon as you remove the pastries from the oven, pour the hot syrup over them. Cover the tin with a clean tea towel, making sure it does not touch the pastries, and set aside to cool. Serve the pastries directly from the cake tin or piled high on a platter.

Kataifi Custard Pie in Rosewater Syrup
Kataifi me Krema
Serves 16 to 20

This easy-to-make pie is composed of layers of crisp golden *kataifi* and smooth rich custard. The *kataifi* are saturated with an exotic perfumed syrup of honey, cloves, lemon juice, and rosewater and the result is mouth-watering. Serve with Rich Cream (page 310) and Greek Coffee (page 336).

50 g/2 oz rice flour
225 g/8 oz caster sugar
700 ml/1¹/₄ pints milk
5 egg yolks

1 teaspoon vanilla extract
450 g/1 lb packet *kataifi* (page 269)
275 g/10 oz clarified butter (page 12) or unsalted butter, melted and strained through
muslin
450 g/1 lb aromatic honey (page 17)
6 cloves
Strained juice of 1 small lemon
3 tablespoons rosewater, or to taste

For serving
Kaymaki rolls (page 310), *optional*

Combine the rice flour with 50 g/2 oz of the caster sugar and enough of the milk to make a smooth paste. Warm the remaining milk over low heat and whisk it into the paste. Rinse out the saucepan, return the milk mixture to the pan, and slowly bring to a boil, stirring constantly with a wooden spoon. Reduce the heat to very low and simmer, stirring, 3 minutes or until smooth and thick. Beat together the egg yolks and vanilla, and briskly whisk into the milk mixture. Cook, stirring, 1 minute longer; don't let the custard boil. Set aside to cool.

Heat the oven to 180C/350F/gas mark 4. Loosen the strands of *kataifi* as directed on page 269 and place in a large bowl. Brush two 23 cm/9 inch or 25 cm/10 inch cake tins, one at least 7 cm/3 inches deep, with melted butter and add the remaining butter to the *kataifi*. With your fingers, quickly coat the strands with butter, divide between the tins, and spread evenly. Bake 30-40 minutes, or until crisp and a deep golden brown. Set aside to cool in the tins.

While the *kataifi* is baking, combine the honey, cloves, remaining sugar, and 350 ml/12 fl oz water in a heavy saucepan. Bring to a boil, then gently boil 10 minutes, or until the syrup coats the back of a metal spoon. Set aside to cool slightly.

Discard the cloves and stir the lemon juice and rosewater into the syrup. Pour two thirds of the warm syrup over the cooled *kataifi* in the deeper tin. Set aside for 5 minutes, or until the syrup is absorbed by the pastry.

Cover the syrup-drenched *kataifi* with the custard and place the second *kataifi* layer on top. Gently press down on it and spoon over the remaining syrup. Cover the tin with a clean tea towel and set aside for at least 1 hour. Cut into slices and serve.

Tiny Sweet Filo Pies
Bourekakia
Makes approximately 24 pastries

Traditionally shaped into triangles, squares, rectangles, cigars, or coils, these crisp golden glazed pastries are stuffed with a range of delectable fillings. Pistachio nuts, almonds, or walnuts are favourites, combined with honey and cinnamon, custard, or fresh cheese. For a spectacular display on a buffet table make them in a variety of shapes and with a choice of fillings. For this recipe, you can either make one of the two fillings given below or one of the fillings detailed on pages 273, 274, and 275.

Nut filling
150 g/5 oz finely chopped walnuts
150 g/5 oz finely chopped blanched almonds
150 g/5 oz aromatic honey (page 17)
1 teaspoon finely grated lemon zest
1 teaspoon ground cinnamon
1 egg, lightly beaten

Custard filling
600 ml/1 pint milk
4 large eggs, separated
115 g/4 oz vanilla sugar (page 16) or 115 g/4 oz caster sugar *and* 1/2 teaspoon
vanilla extract
75 g/3 oz semolina (*farina*, page 344)
1 tablespoon unsalted butter

275 g/10 oz clarified butter (page 12) or unsalted butter, melted
450 g/1 lb packet filo pastry (page 266)

Syrup
275 g/10 oz aromatic honey (page 17)
115 g/4 oz caster sugar
Zest of 1 lemon, removed in thin strips
Juice of 1/2 lemon
2 tablespoons rosewater or orange flower water, *optional*

For serving
Sifted icing sugar
75 g/3 oz finely chopped unsalted pistachio nuts, walnuts or blanched almonds

To make the nut filling, combine the ingredients in a large bowl.

To make the custard filling, heat the milk to just below a boil. Remove from the heat and set aside. With an electric mixer or whisk, beat the egg yolks and sugar (and vanilla) in a large bowl until pale and creamy. Beat in the semolina and gradually beat in the hot milk. Rinse out the saucepan and return the custard mixture to low heat. Cook, stirring constantly in a figure-8 motion with a wooden spoon, until firm enough to come away from the sides of the saucepan, about 5 minutes. Transfer to a bowl. Secure the butter on the tip of a knife and rub it over the surface of the custard. Lightly press waxed paper on the top of the custard and set aside to cool.

Heat the oven to 180C/350F/gas mark 4. Brush two baking trays with some of the melted butter.

Divide the filo into 2 portions. Rewrap 1 and refrigerate. Fold half the remaining sheets in half, loosely cover with cling film and then a slightly damp tea towel, and set aside. Lay the remaining sheets, stacked on top of each other, on the table, with the shorter side facing you.

To make triangles Cut the filo sheets lengthways into 4 strips and stack the strips on top of each other. Lightly brush the top strip with melted butter and carefully remove from the pile, then lightly butter a second strip and place it on top of the first. Place 1 tablespoon nut filling or 2 tablespoons custard filling on the bottom end of the buttered strips. Take the bottom right corner of both strips between finger and thumb and fold over to the left side to make a triangle. Gently pull up the bottom left corner and fold up to make a second triangle. Continue folding until you reach the top. Place seam side down on the baking tray. Repeat with the remaining filo and filling.

To make rolls Cut the filo sheets lengthways into 3 strips and stack on top of each other. Lightly brush the top strip with melted butter and carefully remove from the pile, then lightly butter a second strip and place it on the first. Spread $1^1/_2$ tablespoons nut filling or 3 tablespoons custard filling along the bottom of the strip, leaving a 2 cm/$3/_4$ inch border along the lower edge and the sides. Fold the lower edges of the strips over the filling and roll over twice, then bring both sides over the filling, lightly brush with butter, and roll up the strip. Place seam down on the baking tray.

Cigars are small, thin rolls; rectangles and squares are made similarly but folded up, not rolled. If you prefer, all can be made with 1 filo strip instead of 2.

To make coils Cut the filo sheets lengthways into 3 strips and stack on top of each other. Lightly brush the top strip with melted butter and carefully remove from the pile. Spread 1 tablespoon nut filling or 2 tablespoons custard filling along the bottom, leaving a 2 cm/$3/_4$ inch border along the lower edge and the sides. Fold the lower edge over the filling and fold over both sides. Firmly roll up, and lightly brush with butter. Place a finger on one end of the cylinder and, with the other hand, wrap it around to make a tight coil. Tuck the outside end in and under, and set seam side down on the baking tray.

Brush the pastries with the remaining melted butter and bake 20-25 minutes, or until crisp and golden.

While the pies are baking, combine the honey, sugar, lemon zest, and 225 ml/8 fl oz water in a syrup pan or a small heavy saucepan. Bring to a boil and simmer 10 minutes, or until the syrup lightly coats the back of a metal spoon. Set aside to cool slightly, then add the lemon juice and rosewater.

Dip the hot pastries in the warm syrup a few at a time and pile on a platter. Sprinkle with the icing sugar and nuts, and serve warm or cold. Serve any remaining syrup in a bowl.

Nut Pastries in Fragrant Honey Syrup
Floyeres
Makes approximately 24 pastries

With regional variations these crisp nut pastries are made throughout Greece and the islands. Sometimes they are baked, sometimes fried, and they may be shaped into half-moons, small circles, or squares. The filling given here is heady with cinnamon and cloves; these can also be made with the filling for Sweet Cheese Pastries (page 274) or any of those suggested for Tiny Sweet Filo Pies (page 270), and honey can be substituted for the syrup.

Pastry
225 g/8 oz unbleached plain flour
Pinch of salt
2 tablespoons icing sugar
25 g/1 oz unsalted butter, melted
2 tablespoons olive oil
2 egg yolks, lightly beaten
1 tablespoon finely grated orange zest, briefly dried in a low oven and pulverized in a
mortar with 1 teaspoon sugar, or 1 teaspoon orange extract
Juice of 1 small orange

Filling
2 egg whites
250 g/9 oz unsalted skinned (see page 303) pistachio nuts, walnuts or blanched almonds,
chopped
$1/_2$ teaspoon ground cloves
1 teaspoon ground cinnamon
115 g/4 oz aromatic honey, such as Hymettus
150 g/5 oz unsalted butter, melted
2 egg yolks, lightly beaten with 2 tablespoons water

Syrup
275 g/10 oz aromatic honey, such as Hymettus
One 7 cm/3 inch cinnamon stick, broken in half
4 cloves
Zest of 1 lemon, removed in thin strips
3 tablespoons orange flower water, or to taste

For serving
50 g/2 oz unsalted skinned pistachio nuts, walnuts or blanched almonds, chopped
Sifted icing sugar

To make the pastry, sift the flour, salt, and sugar into a large bowl. Add the butter, olive oil, egg yolks, orange zest, and orange juice, and knead well for 5 minutes. Add cold water if necessary to make a smooth dough. Tightly cover with cling film and refrigerate for 1 hour.

To make the filling, beat the egg whites until they just hold soft peaks. Combine the nuts, cloves, cinnamon, honey, and egg whites, and set aside.

Heat the oven to 180C/350F/gas mark 4. Lightly brush 2 baking trays with melted butter.

Divide the dough in half, rewrap 1 portion, and refrigerate it. Lightly flour a clean work surface. Roll out the dough as thin as possible and cut into 7 cm/3 inch circles with a biscuit cutter or inverted glass or into 5 cm/2 inch squares with a knife. Place 1 tablespoon filling in the centre of half the circles or all the squares. Dip your forefinger in water and lightly dampen the pastry edges. Place a second circle on top of the first, or pull the corners of each square almost into the centre to make a smaller square with a little filling exposed, and lightly press the edges together. Seal each circle by pressing the edge with the prongs of a fork or pastry wheel, or pinch the edge at 1 cm/$1/_2$ inch intervals to make a decorative border. Set the pastries 2.5 cm/1 inch apart on the baking trays, and repeat with the remaining dough and filling.

Brush with the remaining butter and bake 15 minutes, or until the pastry is set. Brush with the beaten egg yolks and bake 10 minutes longer, or until a deep golden brown. Transfer to a rack to cool.

Combine the honey, 350 ml/12 fl oz water, cinnamon stick, cloves, and lemon zest in a syrup pan or a heavy saucepan. Bring to a boil and simmer 5 minutes. Add the orange flower water and keep the syrup hot over low heat. Dip the warm pastries in the syrup a few at a time and pile high on a warm platter. Sprinkle with the nuts and icing sugar, and serve warm.

Sweet Cheese Pastries
Skaltsounakia
Makes approximately 24 pastries

A speciality of the island of Crete, *skaltsounakia* are made with a lemon-scented pastry and filled with a sweetened mixture of *myzithra* and *feta* cheeses. Serve with bowls of warm Hymettus honey or syrup fragrant with orange flower water (page 17 or 19).

Pastry
225 g/8 oz unbleached plain flour
Pinch of salt
1 tablespoon finely grated lemon zest, briefly dried in a low oven and pulverized in a mortar with 1 teaspoon sugar
115 g/4 oz unsalted butter, cold, cut into small pieces
2 egg whites
1 teaspoon vanilla extract
1-3 tablespoons cold milk or water

Filling
350 g/12 oz fresh myzithra cheese (page 11) or drained small-curd cottage cheese, pressed through a fine sieve
25 g/1 oz grated *feta* cheese
2 egg yolks, lightly beaten
150 g/5 oz aromatic honey, such as Hymettus
1 teaspoon vanilla extract
2 tablespoons brandy, *optional*
1 teaspoon ground cinnamon, or to taste
50 g/2 oz unsalted butter, melted
2 egg yolks, lightly beaten

For serving
Ground cinnamon or orange flower water
Sifted icing sugar

To make the pastry, sieve the flour into a large bowl. Stir in the salt and lemon zest, add the butter, and lightly rub the mixture together with your fingers until it resembles coarse bread crumbs. Whisk the egg whites until they just hold soft peaks. Add the whites and vanilla to the flour and knead well, adding milk or water if necessary to make a smooth and elastic dough. Tightly cover with cling film and refrigerate for 1 hour.

To make the filling, lightly mash the *myzithra* in a bowl. Add all the remaining filling ingredients and mash lightly with a fork until well mixed but not smooth. Set aside.

Heat the oven to 180C/350F/gas mark 4. Lightly brush 2 baking trays with melted butter.

Divide the dough in half, rewrap 1 portion, and refrigerate it. Lightly flour a clean work surface. Roll out the dough as thin as possible and cut into 10 cm/4 inch circles with a biscuit cutter or inverted glass or into 10 cm/4 inch squares with a knife. Place 1 heaped tablespoon filling in the centre of each. Dip your forefinger in water and lightly dampen the pastry edges. Fold over circles to make half-moons and seal by gently pressing the edges together with a pastry wheel or the prongs of a fork; or pull the corners of each square almost into the centre to make a smaller square with a little filling exposed, and lightly press the edges together. Set the pastries 2.5 cm/1 inch apart on the baking trays, and repeat with the remaining dough and filling.

Brush with the remaining butter and bake 15 minutes, or until the pastry is set. Brush with the beaten egg yolks and bake 10 minutes longer, or until golden brown. Cool on a rack.

Sprinkle with the cinnamon (or orange flower water) and sugar, and serve warm or at room temperature, with bowls of honey or a syrup of your choice.

Kos Lemon Pie
Lemonopitta tou Ko
Serves 10 to 12

A strong refreshing lemon flavour is the hallmark of this easy-to-make island speciality. For best results use whole blanched almonds and grind them yourself. And use a light touch when making the dough; the essence of this pie is its melt-in-the-mouth pastry and the perfect blend of the fresh natural ingredients. Serve this attractive midsummer dessert surrounded by lemon leaves if available.

Pastry
115 g/4 oz unbleached plain flour
4 tablespoons icing sugar
1/2 tablespoon finely grated lemon zest
Pinch of salt
115 g/4 oz unsalted butter, cold, cut into small pieces
2 egg yolks
1 teaspoon vanilla extract

Filling
115 g/4 oz unsalted butter, at room temperature

115 g/4 oz honey
5 egg yolks
225 g/8 oz finely ground blanched almonds
Strained juice of 2 lemons
4 tablespoons smooth Rich Cream (without crust, page 310) or double cream
115 g/4 oz caster sugar
Zest of 2 lemons, removed in thin strips
Juice of 1 lemon

For serving
Sifted icing sugar

To make the pastry, sift the flour and icing sugar into a large cold bowl, stir in the lemon zest and salt, and add the butter. Quickly and lightly rub the mixture together with your fingers until it resembles coarse breadcrumbs. Beat the egg yolks and vanilla together and stir into the flour mixture. Pull the dough together into a ball with your fingers, adding cold water only if necessary to make a soft dough. Tightly cover with cling film and refrigerate for 30 minutes.

Set a rack in the centre of the oven and heat the oven to 190C/375F/gas mark 5.

Lightly flour a work surface and roll out the pastry to fit a 23 cm/9 inch or 25 cm/10 inch tart tin with a removable bottom. To transfer the pastry, wrap it around the rolling pin, lift above the tin, and unroll over the rim. With your thumb or knuckle, gently press the pastry into the tart tin, then roll the rolling pin over the rim to trim the edges. Line with aluminium foil and bake 6-8 minutes or until just set. Set aside, and lower the oven temperature to 160C/325F/gas mark 3.

To make the filling, beat the butter and honey with an electric mixer or by hand until pale and creamy. Beat in the egg yolks one at a time. Then stir in the almonds, the juice of 2 lemons, and the cream. Pour into the pastry shell and lightly smooth the top with a spatula. Bake 30-40 minutes, or until golden brown and set.

Meanwhile, combine the sugar, lemon zest, and 125 ml/4 fl oz water in a syrup pan or small heavy saucepan. Slowly bring to a boil, then simmer 6 minutes or until the syrup lightly coats the back of a metal spoon. Set aside to cool slightly.

Add the lemon juice to the barely warm syrup and strain, reserving the zest. Pour the syrup over the warm pie, remove from the tin, and liberally sprinkle with icing sugar and the reserved zest. Serve immediately.

Note To make the pastry in the food processor, chill the processor container and metal blade in the refrigerator for 1 hour. Working very quickly, process the flour, sugar, lemon zest, and butter until the mixture resembles coarse breadcrumbs. Add the egg yolks and vanilla and pulse just to mix. (It is unlikely that you will need to add water.) Wrap and refrigerate.

Sticky Yogurt Cake
Yiaourtopitta Glykisma
Serves 14 to 18

When the occasion calls for a really sticky cake, with lashings of syrupy sweetness, this is the treat to make. It's one of the best examples of the Greek tradition of *glyka tou tapsiou*, meaning "sweets from the baking pan". In a traditional version there would be even more of the sticky lemon syrup. Increase the amount of syrup if you like, but it's quite sweet as it is. This cake can be made in advance and in fact tastes even better if the flavours are allowed to mellow for a day. Serve, cut into slices, with Greek Coffee (page 336).

550 g/1¼ lb aromatic honey, such as Hymettus or orange blossom

Zest of 1 lemon, removed in thin strips

175 g/6 oz caster sugar

75 g/3 oz unsalted butter, melted

4 eggs, separated

225-250 g/8-9 oz unbleached plain flour

2 teaspoons baking powder

450 ml/16 fl oz Strained Yogurt (page 8), beaten until smooth

Juice of ½ lemon

Combine the honey, lemon zest, 2 tablespoons of the sugar, and 450 ml/16 fl oz water in a syrup pan or heavy saucepan. Bring to a boil and simmer 10 minutes, or until the syrup lightly coats the back of a metal spoon. Set aside to cool.

Meanwhile, remove the zest from the cooled syrup and stir in the lemon juice.

Set a rack in the centre of the oven and heat the oven to 190C/375F/gas mark 5. Brush a round 23 cm/9 inch cake tin at least 6 cm/2½ inches deep with 1 tablespoon of the melted butter and place on a baking tray.

With an electric mixer, beat the egg yolks and remaining sugar together until pale and thick. Sift in 175 g/6 oz of the flour and the baking powder and stir to mix. Stir in the remaining butter and the yogurt. Sift in enough of the remaining flour to make a dough stiff enough to come away from the sides of the bowl. (The consistency of the yogurt affects the quantity of flour needed.)

Whisk the egg whites until they hold stiff peaks and stir one third of the whites into the flour mixture. Fold in the remaining whites and pour into the cake tin. Bake 35 minutes, or until golden brown and a cake tester is clean when removed.

As soon as you remove the cake from the oven, spoon the syrup over the top, letting it run down the sides. Cover the tin with a clean tea towel and set aside until cool.

Note For a traditional version of this cake, increase the quantity of syrup by half: Use 900 g/2 lb honey, zest of 1½ lemons, 115 g/4 oz sugar, 450 ml/16 fl oz water, and the juice of 1 small lemon.

Almond Cake in Honey Syrup
Revani
Serves 15 to 20

This cake has a pleasant almond and yogurt flavour and the syrupy coating can be orange- or lemon-scented, according to your taste. It will keep for up to one week in an airtight container, but it is likely to magically disappear long before that. Serve it cut into squares or diamond shapes, with *kaymaki* rolls (page 310) and Greek Coffee (page 336).

450 g/1 lb aromatic honey (page 17)
350 g/12 oz caster sugar
Zest of 1 large navel orange or 2 lemons, removed in thin strips
1 1/2 tablespoons unsalted butter, melted
6 eggs separated
225 g/8 oz fine-grain semolina (*farina*, page 344)
75 g/3 oz blanched almonds, coarsely ground
225 ml/8 fl oz Strained Yogurt (page 8), beaten until smooth
75 g/3 oz chopped blanched almonds
Strained juice of 1 large navel orange *or* 2 lemons
2 tablespoons orange flower water, or to taste

Combine the honey, 115 g/4 oz of the sugar, the zest, and 350 ml/12 fl oz water in a syrup pan or heavy saucepan. Bring to a boil, and simmer 10 minutes or until the syrup lightly coats the back of a metal spoon. Let cool.

Heat the oven to 180C/350F/gas mark 4. Brush a 23 cm/9 inch square cake tin, at least 6 cm/2 1/2 inches deep, with the melted butter.

With an electric mixer or by hand, beat the remaining sugar and the egg yolks together until pale and thick, about 5 minutes. Stir in the semolina, ground almonds, and yogurt. Whisk the egg whites until they form stiff peaks and stir one third into the semolina mixture. Fold in the remaining whites, pour into the cake tin, and sprinkle with the chopped almonds. Bake 40-45 minutes, or until golden brown.

Meanwhile, stir the orange juice and orange flower water into the cooled syrup.

As soon as you remove the cake from the oven, spoon the syrup and zest over the top, letting it run down the sides. Cover the tin with a clean tea towel and set aside for at least 2 hours before serving.

Honey Puffs
Loukoumades
Makes about 36 pastries

Tucked away in the back streets of many Greek towns are tiny cafés that serve only these light fluffy puffs of yeast batter bathed in a velvety honey and cinnamon syrup. The pastries are made to order and served with a glass of iced water to cleanse the palate after the sweetness.

Make the batter at least two hours ahead. It should be of a pouring consistency but only just. As a *loukoumades* cook once explained to me, the batter is right "when the dough needs a little help to leave the hand or the spoon." Then fry the pastries when your guests are ready to eat – and not a minute before.

2 teaspoons active dry yeast
3 tablespoons *plus* 1 teaspoon caster sugar
175-275 ml/6-10 fl oz tepid (43C/110F) water
225 g/8 oz unbleached plain flour
Pinch of salt
2 tablespoons olive oil
Peanut or corn oil, for deep-fat frying
550 g/1¼ lb aromatic honey, such as Hymettus
2 tablespoons fresh lemon juice
2 tablespoons rosewater, or to taste, *optional*

For serving
1½ tablespoons ground cinnamon

Dissolve the yeast and 1 teaspoon of the sugar in 4 tablespoons of the tepid water and set aside until foamy, about 10 minutes.

Sift the flour and the salt into a large bowl and add the yeast mixture, olive oil, and 115 ml/4 fl oz of the tepid water. Beat with a wooden spoon or an electric mixer to make a soft dough, adding more warm water if necessary to make it just firm enough to need scooping off a spoon. Tightly cover and set aside in a warm draught-free spot for 2-3 hours to rise. The dough is ready when the surface bubbles and blisters; if the batter seems thin, beat in a little more sifted flour. Knead 2 minutes and set aside.

Heat the oil to 190C/375F (or until a little batter dropped in sizzles immediately) in a large saucepan or deep-fat fryer. Dip a spoon in the hot oil, then scoop up about 1 tablespoon of dough, and use a second spoon to push it off into the oil. Don't hold the spoons too high above the oil or you will be splashed. Fry 5 or 6 *loukoumades* at a time until deep golden brown on all sides, about 3 minutes. Remove with a slotted spoon and drain on paper towels.

Combine the honey and 225 ml/8 fl oz water in a heavy saucepan, bring to a boil, and simmer 3 minutes. Stir in the lemon juice and rosewater. Remove from the heat. Dip the *loukoumades* in the syrup a few at a time and heap on a warm platter or individual plates (5-6 per person). Mix the cinnamon with the remaining sugar and sprinkle over the pastries. Drizzle over a few threads of syrup and serve immediately.

Honey Cakes
Melomacarona (Finikia)
Makes 24 small cakes

These light and crumbly cakes, Phoenician in origin, are offered to visitors at Christmas and New Year's gatherings. The dough is shaped into small flat ovals and marked with a criss-cross design; after baking, each cake is dipped into a sweet syrup and sprinkled with nuts, cinnamon, and sugar for an attractive finishing touch. *Melomacarona* can be kept for up to one week in an airtight container.

115 g/4 oz unsalted butter, melted
115–175 ml/4–6 fl oz olive oil
175 g/6 oz fine-grain semolina (*farina*, page 344)
5 tablespoons caster sugar
2 tablespoons brandy, *optional*
1 tablespoon finely grated orange zest, briefly dried in a low oven and pulverized in a mortar with 1 teaspoon sugar, or $^1/_2$ tablespoon orange extract
550 g/1$^1/_4$ lb aromatic honey, such as Hymettus
115–175 g/4–6 oz unbleached plain flour
1 teaspoon baking powder
$^1/_4$ teaspoon grated nutmeg
$^1/_2$ teaspoon ground cloves
Strained juice of $^1/_2$ lemon
Strained juice of 1 small orange or 2 tablespoons orange flower water

For serving
150 g/5 oz finely chopped walnuts or blanched almonds
1 teaspoon ground cinnamon

Combine 6 tablespoons of the butter and 115 ml/4 fl oz of the olive oil in a large bowl. Gradually stir in the semolina, 2 tablespoons of the sugar, the brandy, orange zest, and 175 g/6 oz of the honey. Sift together the flour, baking powder, nutmeg, and cloves, and stir into the semolina mixture. Turn out onto a lightly floured surface and knead 10 minutes, or until soft and pliant. If it seems stiff, add a little more oil; if thin, more flour.

Heat the oven to 180C/350F/gas mark 4. Brush 2 baking trays with the remaining melted butter.

Form the dough into egg-sized ovals and set them 5 cm/2 inches apart on the baking trays. With the back of a fork, lightly press down twice on top of each oval to make a criss-cross design, slightly flattening them at the same time. Bake 20 minutes, or until lightly browned. Transfer to a rack to cool.

While the cakes are cooling, bring the remaining honey and 350 ml/12 fl oz water to boil in a saucepan and simmer 4 minutes. Remove from the heat and add the lemon and orange juices. With a spoon, place the barely warm cakes in the hot syrup a few at a time. Leave them in the syrup 1 minute, and transfer to paper cake cases or a serving platter.

Combine the nuts, cinnamon, and remaining sugar, and sprinkle over the cakes.

Shortcakes
Kourabiethes
Makes about 36 shortcakes

No festive table in Greece would be complete without a large platter piled high with these snowy white, sugar-dusted shortcakes. Scented with cloves and rosewater, these buttery treats are perfect with fruit desserts and spoon sweets. Their flavour improves with age – store them at room temperature in an airtight container with icing sugar sprinkled over each layer, and dust with fresh sugar before serving. A variation of these can be made with blanched almonds (see below).

450 g/1 lb unsalted butter, at room temperature
115 g/4 oz caster sugar
1 teaspoon vanilla extract
2 egg yolks
2 tablespoons brandy, *optional*
350–400 g/12–14 oz unbleached plain flour
1 teaspoon baking powder
25 g/1 oz unsalted butter, melted
12–36 cloves, as desired

For serving
3 tablespoons rosewater
225 g/8 oz icing sugar

With an electric mixer or by hand, beat the room-temperature butter in a large bowl until light and fluffy. Beat in the sugar, vanilla, egg yolks, and brandy. Sift in 225 g/8 oz of the flour and the baking powder and beat to mix. Gradually stir in enough of the remaining flour to make a soft dough. (Traditional cooks use their fingers to do this; it is easier to judge the right moment to stop.) Tightly cover and refrigerate for 1 hour.

Heat the oven to 160C/325F/gas mark 3. Lightly brush 2 baking trays with the melted butter and dust them with flour.

Break off pieces of dough the size of very small eggs and shape into balls, ovals, pears, S-shapes, or crescents. Set 5 cm/2 inches apart on the baking trays.

Press 1 clove into each of 12 of the shortcakes or into every one if you prefer. Bake 15 minutes, or until firm and very pale gold. Transfer to racks to cool.

Sprinkle the shortcakes with the rosewater. Spread half the icing sugar on a plate and arrange the shortcakes side by side on the sugar. Liberally dust with the remaining sugar.

Variations
Substitute 150 g/5 oz finely ground lightly toasted blanched almonds for 115 g/4 oz of the flour.

In a small mortar, pulverize 1 teaspoon mastic granules (page 14) with 1 tablespoon sugar, and add with the eggs. Omit the brandy and the cloves.

Hazelnut Biscuits
Foundoukia Biscotakia
Makes 30 to 36 biscuits

The perfect accompaniment to fruit desserts and cream desserts, these sweet and spicy mouthfuls are easy to make – and they are irresistible!

25 g/1 oz unsalted butter, melted
2 tablespoons unbleached plain flour
225 g/8 oz unsalted butter, at room temperature
50 g/2 oz caster sugar
150 g/5 oz aromatic honey, such as Hymettus or orange blossom
3 eggs
425 g/15 oz hazelnuts or walnuts, finely ground
$1/2$ teaspoon ground cloves
1 teaspoon ground cinnamon

For serving
175 g/6 oz icing sugar

Heat the oven to 160C/325F/gas mark 3. Lightly brush 2 baking trays with the melted butter and dust with flour.

Beat the room-temperature butter and the sugar in a bowl of an electric mixer or a large mixing bowl until pale and creamy, about 5 minutes. Beat in the honey, then beat in the eggs 1 at a time. Stir in 275 g/10 oz of the hazelnuts, the cloves, and the cinnamon. Add some or all of the remaining hazelnuts to make a mixture just stiff enough to hold its shape.

Place heaped tablespoons of the mixture 5 cm/2 inches apart on the baking trays, and use your fingers to pull each gently up into a cone shape. Bake 20-25 minutes or until firm but not hard. Transfer to racks to cool.

Liberally dust with the icing sugar and pile high on a platter.

Fruit Desserts, Puddings and Creams, and Sweetmeats

frouta, krema, ke glykisma

For most Greeks, after a meal, juicy refreshing fruit is the dessert of choice. Fruits of all kinds appear on Greek tables in various seasons – although it's said that modern Greeks have nowhere near the choice of fruits that were available to their classical ancestors: For example, it is believed that there were over one hundred varieties of pear in ancient Greece.

The fruits most commonly associated with Greece are the grape and the fig. Legend has it that Hercules ate vast quantities of figs and that, on one campaign, Alexander the Great's army survived for a time on only figs, so it's not surprising that even modern Greeks believe figs to be a source of strength and stamina! The wild figs of the Greek countryside are usually small and often seedless but filled with the most heavenly sweet nectar. In the early 1900's Greek immigrants took cuttings of Smyrna figs, a particularly luscious variety, to California, where they now produce magnificently plump and juicy Calimyrna figs, a lovely green-amber fruit perfect for drying. More widely available in Britain is the deep rich purple Turkish fig. Either of the figs is perfect for the desserts, jams, and spoon sweets included here. Grapes, in contrast, are a relative newcomer to Greek dessert tables. Until recent years, they were grown only for wine making or drying.

Also based on fruits (although young vegetables and nuts can be used) are spoon sweets, *glyka tou koutaliou*, a very Greek speciality. Preserving ripe fruits and nuts in honey was a technique much favoured by both the Minoans and the ancient Greeks. These honey-coated delicacies are a fundamental part of the Greek expression of friendship and welcome, and

every guest entering a Greek house is offered a lace-covered tray holding small silver bowls of spoon sweets along with a glass of iced water, a small cup of thick strong coffee, and a small glass of liqueur. The rims of the bowls are indented to hold long-handled spoons with which the visitor scoops up the mellifluous treat. In this ritual the sweet offering is a traditional symbol of hospitality: It is extremely impolite to refuse it.

Spoon sweets are probably best described as a cross between a jam and a preserve. Almost any fruit can be used to make them, but those made with tiny whole fruits are the most treasured of all. Spoon sweets made from sour cherries and fragrant citrus blossoms are especially delectable. All of these sweets are excellent with ice cream, pancakes, and, surprising as it may sound, with pungent goat's or sheep's cheeses.

Puddings, creams, and sweetmeats are rarely eaten straight after a meal in Greece but instead at various times throughout the day or night – whenever the need for something sweet overwhelms! In summer the whole family may go out to the pastry shop or café late in the evening to enjoy ice creams, sweetmeats, velvety smooth rice puddings, creams made from pistachios or almonds, and elaborate honeyed pastries. Many of these sweet treats have been enjoyed by generations of Greeks since antiquity – the chewy honey-sesame sweetmeats called *pasteli,* for example, were presented to victorious athletes at the classical Olympic games. And many other creams, puddings, sweetmeats, and spoon sweets are based on ancient flavours and fragrances. With their unusual tastes, textures, and aromas they are unmistakably Greek.

Platter of Fresh Fruits
Freska Frouta
Serves 4

Magnificent platters of prepared fresh fruit must have been one of the earliest Greek desserts. Use only fruit in perfect condition and keep the arrangement simple but colourful. Since most fruits discolour very quickly, prepare them just a few minutes before serving. Allow half a dozen pieces of fruit per person.

Choose from any of the following:

$1/2$ small sweet melon such as honeydew or Persian
$1/4$ small watermelon
1 crisp sweet apple, cored and cut into 8 wedges
1 ripe pear, cored and cut into quarters
225 g/8 oz large sweet grapes, cut into 4 clusters
1 large prickly pear, peeled (page 298), and cut into quarters
8 strawberries, with their stems if possible
16 cherries, with their stems if possible
4 ripe figs, halved
2 peaches or nectarines, peeled, pitted, and cut into quarters

For serving
Green leaves such as those of the fig, strawberry, lemon or apple, rinsed and patted dry
350 g/12 oz myzithra cheese, cut into 8 slices
Hymettus or other aromatic honey

Remove the seeds from the honeydew melon, cut it into 4 slices, and cut off the rind. Cut the watermelon flesh into 4 or 8 chunks.

Line a serving plate with the leaves and arrange the fruit attractively on the leaves. Serve with a plate of the sliced cheese and small bowls of the honey.

Note   Mulberries, apricots, plums, and quince are other traditional Greek fruits. For breakfast, serve with Strained Yogurt (page 8), honey, and Currant Bread (page 262).

Fruits in Sweet Wine and Honey
Frouta Glykisma
Serves 6

At summer tables today it is still traditional to dip fresh fruit into a glass of sweet wine before eating it, but the fruit can also be poached in wine. For this versatile, not-too-sweet dish you can use a variety of fruits, including peaches, nectarines, plums, apricots, cherries, figs, pears, apples, and quinces or melons. The fruit should be ripe but it does not have to be perfect to produce a special dessert. Here the flavouring for the poaching syrup is vanilla, coriander, and lemon but you can also try cinnamon, cloves, or orange (see below). For a particularly delicate flavour add the pits of fruits such as apricots to the poaching liquid. Serve poached fruit on its own or with biscuits, Rich Cream (page 310), and chilled Samos wine.

450 ml/16 fl oz sweet Samos wine or 225 ml/8 fl oz Mavrodaphne wine
150 g/5 oz aromatic honey, such as Hymettus
One 5 cm/2 inch piece of vanilla bean or 1 teaspoon vanilla extract
24 coriander seeds
Zest of ¹/₂ small lemon, removed in thin strips
6 portions of any of the fruits mentioned above

Combine the wine, honey, vanilla, coriander seeds, and lemon zest, and enough water to cover the fruit in a large saucepan, slowly bring to a boil, and simmer 5 minutes.

Meanwhile, remove the stems from the fruit (or trim those of figs), and remove any pits carefully so the fruit does not lose its shape. Use a pitter for cherries and a small paring knife for plums and apricots. Cut melon into bite-sized pieces. Peel apples, pears, and quinces and cut into slices. If you are poaching apricots, crack a few pits with a nutcracker, remove the kernels, and add to the poaching liquid.

Add the fruit to the poaching liquid in small batches, slightly raise the heat, and return to a gentle simmer. Poach until barely tender: figs, grapes, or melons 1-2 minutes, apricots or gooseberries about 4 minutes, plums or cherries about 6 minutes, and apple, pear, or quince slices about 8 minutes. Transfer to paper towels to drain and place in a serving bowl.

Raise the heat and boil the poaching liquid until it is slightly syrupy and lightly coats the back of a metal spoon. Let cool slightly, strain, and pour over the fruit. Set aside for up to 2 hours, or cover and refrigerate for up to 24 hours. Serve at room temperature.

Note Strawberries, other soft berries, and citrus fruit segments need no poaching; just macerate them in a little honey or sugar before pouring the warm syrup over them.

Peaches in Sweet Wine and Honey
Glykisma me Rodakina

Choose 6 small or 3 large ripe peaches with no bruise marks or soft spots, and handle them carefully; do not peel until after poaching so the fruit retains flavour and colour. Substitute 3 cloves and one 7 cm/3 inch cinnamon stick for the vanilla and coriander. Cut larger peaches in half and discard the pits; to pit a small peach, hold it firmly, insert the point of a paring knife into its stem end, carefully loosen the pit, and then push it out from the other end. Poach small peaches or peach halves 5 minutes, larger whole peaches 8 minutes.

Note Nectarines can be substituted for the peaches.

Fragrant Apricot Ice Cream
Verikoka Pagota Aromatika
Serves 6

Apricots, said to originate in China, are thought to have been brought to Greece by the Phoenicians. In those days they were probably made into creams or sweetmeats, but modern Greeks are more likely to use this ancient flavour in ice creams. Make this rich ice cream in early summer when apricots are ripe and sweet. Serve it prettily garnished with toasted almonds and small colourful flowers, and accompanied by glasses of sweet Samos liqueur.

900 g/2 lb fresh apricots
1 teaspoon vanilla extract
150 g/5 oz aromatic honey (such as Hymettus), or to taste
3 eggs, separated
75 ml/3 fl oz Rich Cream (without crust, page 310) or 175 ml/6 fl oz double cream
2 tablespoons Samos liqueur or apricot ratafia, *optional*

For serving
Toasted slivered almonds
A few citrus blossoms or borage flowers or other fragrant, decorative
(non-poisonous) flowers

Fill a large saucepan with water and bring to a boil. Drop the apricots into the boiling water, remove the saucepan from the heat, count to 3, then carefully remove the apricots with a slotted spoon. Peel with a small paring knife, cut each in half, and discard the pits. If they are not quite ripe, bring about 115 ml/4 fl oz water to boil in a heavy saucepan, add the apricots, and simmer 5 minutes. Drain and reserve the cooking liquid. Process the apricots until smooth in a food processor fitted with the plastic blade. Add the vanilla and most of the honey. Add the remaining honey to taste, and add some of the reserved cooking liquid if necessary to produce a mixture the consistency of double cream.

Place 225 ml/8 fl oz of this purée in a non-reactive bowl, tightly cover, and refrigerate. Whisk the egg yolks until thick and pale and gradually add the remaining purée, whisking constantly. Transfer to a small heavy saucepan or the top of a double boiler set over hot water. Heat over low heat, stirring constantly, until thick enough to lightly coat the back of the spoon, about 5 minutes. Immediately transfer to a bowl. Let cool.

Stir the Rich Cream until smooth (or whisk double cream until slightly thickened), and lightly whisk in the cooled custard. Transfer to an ice cream machine and freeze according to the manufacturer's instructions. When the mixture is almost frozen, whisk the egg whites until they hold soft peaks, fold into the custard, and freeze until firm.

Add the liqueur to the reserved purée. Stir in honey to taste if desired and add some of the reserved juice or water if necessary to give a pouring consistency.

To serve, spoon the sauce onto chilled plates, place small scoops of ice cream in the centre of the sauce, and sprinkle with the toasted almonds and blossoms. Serve immediately.

Note You can also freeze this ice cream in the freezer. Pour the cooled custard into metal pans and freeze, stirring occasionally, until almost firm. Whisk the egg whites until they hold firm peaks and fold them into the custard until thoroughly combined. Freeze until firm.

Honey Ice Cream with Fresh Fig Compôte
Pagoto me Sika ke Khimo Rothion
Serves 6

In early autumn tall glasses of honeyed ice cream topped with a syrupy compôte of figs and pomegranate juice are served in pastry shops throughout Greece. It's an elegant and refreshing dessert, rich with the deep, luscious flavours of the two best fruits of the season. Serve it with Shortcakes (page 281) or Hazelnut Biscuits (page 282).

2 large ripe pomegranates
1 tablespoon fresh lemon juice

150 g/5 oz honey, preferably Hymettus
450 g/1 lb fresh figs, peeled, and each cut into 4 or 6 wedges
225 ml/8 fl oz milk
One 5 cm/2 inch piece of vanilla bean, split or 1 teaspoon vanilla extract
4 egg yolks
1 tablespoon caster sugar
175 ml/6 fl oz Rich Cream (*kaymaki*, without crust, page 310) or
225 ml/8 fl oz double cream

Scoop out the flesh and seeds from the pomegranates and place in a food processor bowl fitted with the plastic blade. Blend at low speed just until the flesh is separated from the seeds, about 15 seconds. (A gentle touch is essential or the juice will be tannin-flavoured, a result of working the membranes too vigorously.) Strain the juice through 2 layers of muslin into a non-reactive bowl. Stir in the lemon juice and 2 tablespoons of the honey, then add the figs. Tightly cover and refrigerate for 2-3 hours, shaking the bowl occasionally, to redistribute the figs in the sauce.

Place the milk and vanilla bean in a heavy saucepan and heat over low heat until very hot, but not boiling. Remove from the heat. With a hand whisk or electric mixer, whisk the egg yolks and sugar until pale and frothy, about 2 minutes. Gradually add the hot milk, whisking constantly, until it lightly coats the back of a spoon. Transfer to a bowl and set aside to cool.

Remove the vanilla bean from the custard and discard. Add the remaining honey to taste. Whisk the *kaymaki* until smooth (whisk the double cream until thick), and stir into the custard. Transfer to an ice cream machine and freeze according to the manufacturer's instructions, or pour into metal pans and freeze until firm, stirring occasionally.

To serve, place 2 or 3 small scoops of ice cream in tall parfait glasses and spoon over the fig and pomegranate compôte.

Fresh Fig Custard
Freska Sika Afrothi
Serves 6

This fluffy custard is perfect for figs that are too battered to serve on their own. You can use any variety of fig, although deep purple figs will give the custard the most spectacular colour. Adding the optional egg white will produce a custard somewhat like a soufflé although it will not rise very high. You can make this in a large soufflé dish or individual dishes, and it can be served hot or at room temperature.

175 g/6 oz caster sugar
450 g/1 lb figs, preferably purple, peeled, and each cut into 4 or 6 wedges
115 g/4 oz unsalted butter
3 tablespoons plain flour
175 ml/6 fl oz milk

One 5 cm/2 inch piece of vanilla bean or 1 teaspoon vanilla extract
4 large eggs separated
1 egg white, *optional*

For serving
Sifted icing sugar

Heat the oven to 220C/425F/gas mark 7. Combine 115 g/4 oz of the sugar and 4 tablespoons water in a syrup pan or a heavy saucepan and bring to a boil over low heat. Raise the heat and boil rapidly for 3-4 minutes, or until the syrup lightly coats the back of a metal spoon. Add the figs, gently shake the saucepan to coat the figs, and reduce the heat to very low. Simmer 6-8 minutes, or until the figs darken a little. Set aside.

Melt half the butter in a heavy saucepan over low heat. Stir in the flour with a wooden spoon and cook, stirring, 2 minutes longer, or until the roux turns a medium gold. Meanwhile combine the milk, 1 tablespoon of the remaining sugar, and the vanilla in another saucepan and heat to just under a boil. Whisk the milk into the roux and cook, whisking constantly, until the custard reaches a low boil. Reduce the heat, simmer a few minutes longer, and remove from the heat.

Brush a 1.1 litre/2 pint soufflé dish with the remaining butter and sprinkle with the remaining sugar. Invert over the sink and tap sharply to remove excess sugar.

Remove the vanilla bean from the custard and stir in the egg yolks one at a time. Stir in the figs and their syrup just to combine. With a hand whisk or an electric mixer, whisk the egg whites until they hold stiff peaks. Stir one third of the whites into the fig custard, then lightly fold in the remaining whites and transfer to the soufflé dish. Reduce the oven temperature to 190C/375F/gas mark 5 and bake 30 minutes. Gently shake the dish – it should wobble only slightly. Bake another 5-10 minutes if necessary.

Dust the custard with the icing sugar and serve immediately. Or let cool, dust with the sugar, and serve warm or at room temperature.

To make individual custards Butter small (225 ml/8 fl oz) soufflé or other oven-proof dishes, sprinkle with sugar, and divide the custard equally between them. Bake 20-25 minutes at 180C/350F/gas mark 4.

Variation

Double the quantity of vanilla and add 75 g/3 oz *myzithra* cheese (page 11) or 4 tablespoons Rich Cream (page 310) to the custard after the egg yolks. Bake at 180C/350F/gas mark 4 and increase the baking time by 5-10 minutes; if the custard browns too quickly, loosely cover with aluminium foil. This custard is especially good warm.

Sweet-Baked Figs
Sika sto Fourno
Serves 4

Firm but not under-ripe figs are the kind to choose for this dish. They are baked whole in a honeyed orange juice syrup until they are soft, sweet, and shiny. Arranged on a white serving platter, sprinkled with syrup and fragrant orange flower water, they make an elegant and delicious dessert. Also try baking figs in Mavrodaphne or Samos wine instead of orange juice. Fresh *myzithra* (page 11) is the traditional accompaniment.

12-16 small fresh figs or 8 large figs
4-5 tablespoons honey, preferably Hymettus or caster sugar (to taste)
$1/_2$ teaspoon vanilla extract
Strained juice of 1 large navel orange or 115 ml/4 fl oz Mavrodaphne or
sweet Samos wine

For serving
2 tablespoons orange flower water, *optional*

Heat the oven to 160C/325F/gas mark 3. Rinse the figs and trim the stems. Arrange in a single layer, stem ends up, in a heavy baking dish.

Combine the honey, vanilla, and orange juice in a small saucepan and gently heat until the honey has dissolved. Pour over the figs, and add enough water to cover the bottom of the dish. Bake, uncovered, fifteen minutes and baste the figs with the juices in the dish. Bake small figs 40 minutes longer, large figs 1 hour longer, basting occasionally; add a few tablespoons water if necessary so there is always some liquid in the dish.

Transfer the figs to a platter, spoon over the syrup, sprinkle with the orange flower water, and serve.

Anoula's Dried Figs
Sika Xsera
Serves 6

This recipe comes from my neighbour on Crete, Anoula. Each year she dries hundreds of figs, first laying them out in the sun for three days on a bamboo frame covered with dried grass, then completely drying them in a low oven. The most attractive figs from this abundance are packed into wooden boxes to be given as gifts; others are threaded on long grass strings and hung from storage room rafters, to serve later as a *meze;* and still others are kept for spicy sweet desserts like this one.

18 plump dried figs, preferably organic Greek
6 bay leaves

One 5 cm/2 inch cinnamon stick
One 2.5 cm/1 inch piece of lemon zest
700 ml/1¼ pints Mavrodaphne wine or strong freshly brewed tea, strained
115-225 g/4-8 oz sugar
18 lightly toasted blanched almonds

For serving
2 tablespoons fresh lemon juice or orange flower water

Rinse the figs, trim the stems, and combine the figs, bay leaves, cinnamon stick, lemon zest, and wine in a non-reactive bowl. Cover and set aside overnight.

Transfer to a heavy saucepan and slowly bring to a boil. Simmer 10 minutes, then transfer the figs with a slotted spoon to paper towels to drain. Measure the cooking liquid, return it to the saucepan, and add half as much sugar as measured liquid. Raise the heat and boil 10 minutes, or until the syrup lightly coats the back of a metal spoon. Strain and set aside.

With a small knife, make an incision in each fig just below the stem. Insert an almond into each fig, leaving the tip exposed. Place the figs in a bowl and pour over the syrup. Let cool, tightly cover, and set aside for 2-6 hours.

To serve, arrange the figs on a platter with the almonds upwards, pour over any remaining syrup, and sprinkle with the lemon juice.

Dried Apricots with Sweet Samos Wine
Verikoka Xsera me Krasi Samiotiko

Substitute sun-dried apricots for the figs and sweet Samos wine for the Mavrodaphne. Omit the bay leaves and cinnamon. Simmer only 2 minutes.

Minoan Dates and Prunes
Mourmathes Xsera ke Damaskina
Serves 6

Dried prunes were exported to Egypt by the Minoans; dates imported from Egypt by the same route. This ancient dish remains a favourite of Cretan islanders. An attractive dessert, it is easy to prepare. When choosing the fruit, select large California prunes and dates if possible (avoid sticky shiny dates, which are too sweet for this recipe).

12 large prunes, soaked in 450 ml/16 fl oz Mavrodaphne wine or strong freshly
brewed tea for 4–12 hours
75–115 g/3–4 oz sugar
12 large dates, preferably Medjool
225 ml/8 fl oz Rich Cream (without crust, page 310) or 175 g/6 oz mascarpone cheese
12 toasted blanched almonds, coarsely chopped

Transfer the prunes and their liquid to a heavy saucepan and slowly bring to a boil. Simmer 2 minutes, then, using a slotted spoon, transfer the prunes to paper towels to drain. Measure the cooking liquid, return it to the saucepan, and add half as much sugar as the measured liquid. Raise the heat and boil 10 minutes, until the syrup lightly coats the back of a metal spoon. Set aside.

Make a lengthways incision in each fruit and carefully remove the pits. For a neat appearance, tuck in the sides of the prune incisions with the point of a small knife. Arrange the prunes and dates on a platter.

Beat the Rich Cream until firm enough to hold its shape and divide in half. Using one half, place a spoonful of cream in each date. Whisk 3 tablespoons of the remaining syrup into the remaining cream and whisk until stiff. Fill each prune with a spoonful of this mixture.

Sprinkle the almonds over the prunes, and sprinkle with some or all of the remaining syrup if desired. (Dates need no added sweetness.) Serve immediately.

Morello Cherry Spoon Sweet
Vissino
Makes 1.3–1.6 litres/2¼–2¾ pints

Morello cherries are much loved by Greeks and have been popular since classical times. The delicious summer fruit is eaten both fresh from the tree, juicy and sharp, or as a preserve, mellowed by sugar and brandy. Dried cherries are eaten with strong country cheese as a simple *meze*, cherry juice is fermented into liqueur, and plump and luscious cherries are made into this delicious spoon sweet. Morello cherries are occasionally available in our markets; sweet cherries are not a perfect substitute, but they too can be made into a satisfactory spoon sweet (recipe follows). The perfect accompaniment for both versions is *myzithra* cheese (page 11).

900 g/2 lb Morello (sour) cherries
1 kg/2¼ lb sugar
1 teaspoon vanilla extract
2 tablespoons fresh lemon juice

Thoroughly wash and sterilize six 275 ml/½ pint jars and set aside in a warm spot.

Working over a bowl to catch any juices, remove the pits from the cherries with a cherry-pitter or small paring knife. Reserve the juice. Crack 12 of the pits and remove the kernels. Wrap these in a small square of muslin, tying up the edges to make a bag. Set aside.

Combine the sugar, any reserved juices, and 4 tablespoons water in a large heavy saucepan and melt the sugar over very low heat. Raise the heat to medium-low and boil 1 minute, stirring vigorously. Add the cherries and bag of kernels and boil 12 minutes. Remove any froth with a slotted spoon, taking care not to stir into the syrup. With the slotted spoon, transfer the cherries to paper towels to drain, leaving as much syrup as possible in the pan. Discard the bag of kernels. Add the vanilla to the syrup, raise the heat, and boil rapidly until the syrup reaches 114-116C/235-240F on a sugar thermometer (or a little syrup dropped into a glass of cold water immediately forms a soft ball). Add the lemon juice, and set aside to cool slightly.

Divide the cherries between the sterilized jars and add enough syrup to cover. (Use any remaining syrup for drinks or to pour over ice cream.) Let cool, tightly cover, and store at room temperature for up to 6 months.

Sweet Cherry Spoon Sweet
Kerasi

Use 1.2 kg/2¹/₂ lb small ripe but firm sweet cherries, 900 g/2 lb sugar, 2 teaspoons vanilla extract, and the juice of 1 small lemon. Boil the cherries in the syrup for 10-15 minutes or until they are plump and a little translucent. Drain and proceed as directed above.

Fresh Fig and Honeydew Spoon Sweet
Sika ke Peponi Glyko
Makes 1.3-1.7 litres/2¹/₄-3 pints

Perfectly ripe melons and figs need no adornment and are deliciously refreshing to eat just as they are. But bruised or less-than-perfect fruits can be made into this ancient spoon sweet, an ideal way to enjoy all their juicy flavour.

One 900 g/2 lb honeydew or other sweet melon
450 g/1 lb fresh figs, trimmed, peeled, and cut into 6-8 wedges
Strained juice of 2 large lemons
675-900 g/1¹/₂-2 lb sugar

Thoroughly wash and sterilize six 275 ml/¹/₂ pint jars. Cut the melon in half, remove the seeds, and dice the flesh. Place the figs, melon, and lemon juice in a large heavy saucepan and simmer 20-30 minutes, or until the fruit is soft. Transfer to a non-reactive sieve set over a bowl and press the fruit through with a wooden spoon.

Measure the purée, return it to the rinsed-out pan, and add exactly the same quantity of sugar. Slowly bring to a boil to dissolve the sugar, then raise the heat. Boil rapidly, stirring occasionally to prevent sticking or burning, until the syrup reaches 114-116C/235-240F on a sugar thermometer (or a little syrup dropped into a glass of cold water immediately forms a soft ball), about 20 minutes. The mixture will be thick and a deep reddish brown. Let it cool slightly.

Fill the jars, let cool completely, and cover tightly. Store at room temperature for up to 4 months.

Lemon Blossom Spoon Sweet
Glyko Lemonanthos
Makes approximately 700 ml/1¹/₄ pints

The perfumed blossoms of rose, orange, grapefruit, jasmine, and honeysuckle can all be made into delectable spoon sweets, but the most exquisitely fragrant of them all is made from lemon blossom. For this recipe you need the flower petals only, so enlist a friend's help to gather them. One of you holds a bag under a blossom-laden branch while the other gently shakes the flowers so that the petals fall into the bag. (Be sure to leave some blossom on the tree so that, in a few months' time, you can gather a harvest of perfumed juicy lemons!)

175 g/6 oz lemon petals
450 g/1 lb sugar
Juice of 1 lemon

Thoroughly wash and sterilize three 275 ml/¹/₂ pint jars.

Combine the petals with the sugar and set aside, uncovered, for 4-6 hours. With your fingers, toss the petals occasionally, gently rubbing them together so they bruise lightly. Your kitchen will smell wonderful!

Slowly bring 115 ml/4 fl oz water and half the lemon juice to a boil in a large heavy non-reactive saucepan. Add the petals and sugar, reduce the heat to very low, and cook until the sugar has dissolved. Raise the heat, gently boil 20 minutes, and set aside to cool.

Strain through a sieve, preferably plastic, set over a bowl and discard the solids. Return the syrup to the rinsed-out pan, add the remaining lemon juice, and boil until the syrup reaches 114C/235F on a sugar thermometer (or a little syrup dropped onto a cold plate retains its shape). Let cool slightly.

Fill the jars, let cool completely, and cover tightly. Store at room temperature for up to 3 months.

Prickly Pear Spoon Sweet
Glyko Frangosika
Makes approximately 1.4 litres/2½ pints

The large prickly pear bush (also known as cactus pear) is a common sight all around the eastern Mediterranean. Its sweet ruby-red fruits, occasionally available here in the autumn, taste wonderful chilled, with a little lemon juice sprinkled over them. Or choose tender prickly pears to make this colourful spoon sweet, especially good with *myzithra* (page 11) or pungent *kephalotyri* cheese (page 10).

8 medium to large prickly pears (about 1.4 kg/3 lb)
350-450 g/12 oz-1 lb sugar
Strained juice of 1 small lemon

Thoroughly wash and sterilize five 275 ml/½ pint jars and set aside in a warm spot.

Without touching it – or your hand will be covered with tiny hair-like spines – secure 1 prickly pear with a fork and slice off each end with a sharp knife. Make 4 or 5 lengthways incisions through the skin, and lift it off. Without letting the exposed fruit touch the work surface (to avoid the spines), transfer it to a clean cutting board and cut into small pieces. Repeat with the remaining fruit.

Place the fruit, including the seeds, in a large heavy saucepan and simmer until tender, about 10 minutes. Transfer to a sieve, preferably plastic, set over a bowl, and press the fruit through it. Discard the seeds. Measure the purée, return it to the rinsed-out pan, and add the lemon juice and 175 g/6 oz sugar for every 225 ml/8 fl oz purée. Slowly bring to a boil over medium-low heat. Raise the heat and rapidly boil, stirring occasionally to prevent sticking or burning, until the purée reaches 114-116C/235-240F on a sugar thermometer (or a little purée dropped onto a cold plate retains its shape). Let cool slightly.

Fill the jars, let cool completely, and cover tightly. Store at room temperature for up to 3 months.

Vanilla Rice Pudding
Risogalo me Vanillia
Serves 6

The enticing moist and creamy rice puddings of Greece, never thick or overly sweet, bear no resemblance to any versions remembered from childhood. Greeks enjoy them as a snack as well as a satisfying end to a meal and this vanilla-flavoured pudding is one of the most popular. Other traditional flavourings are mastic (page 14), lemon (page 18), and orange (page 19).

175 g/6 oz pudding or short-grain rice
700 ml/1¼ pints milk
75 g/3 oz *plus* 1 tablespoon caster sugar or vanilla sugar (page 16), or more to taste

1 cm/¹/₂ inch strip of orange zest
Pinch of salt
1 tablespoon unsalted butter
1 egg
¹/₂ teaspoon vanilla extract, or to taste
1 tablespoon fresh lemon juice, or more to taste
75 ml/3 fl oz Rich Cream (without crust, page 310) or 115 ml/4 fl oz double cream

For serving
Ground cinnamon
Sifted icing sugar

Place the rice in boiling water and leave for 5 seconds; drain, and rinse. Bring the milk almost to a boil in a heavy saucepan, and stir in the rice, the 75 g/3 oz sugar, the orange zest, salt, and butter. Reduce the heat to very low and simmer uncovered, stirring occasionally to prevent sticking, for 1 hour, or until thick and creamy. Remove from the heat and set aside.

Whisk together the egg, vanilla, lemon juice, and remaining 1 tablespoon sugar until pale and thick, about 2 minutes. Remove the orange zest from the rice mixture and stir half the rice into the egg mixture. Return this to the saucepan and stir to combine. Gently cook over low heat, stirring well, for 2 minutes. Stir in the Rich Cream and add more sugar or lemon juice if desired. (If using double cream, beat until slightly thickened, then stir into rice mixture.) Divide between individual dishes and chill.

To serve, liberally dust with the cinnamon and icing sugar.

Aromatic Rice Pudding
Risogalo Aromatiko
Serves 6

Mastic, the resin of the mastic tree, was greatly valued by the ancient gourmets as a flavouring for puddings, spoon sweets, and bread.

There is no substitute for the strong, rather mysterious taste and perfume of mastic – look for small packets of the granules in Greek and Middle Eastern shops. It is particularly good combined with other flavours of antiquity such as those of Sweet-Baked Figs (page 292), Glazed Sweet Chestnuts (page 305), or the spoon sweets (pages 295-298). Serve small quantities of this delectable pudding, since the flavours are strong and too much can be overpowering.

115 g/4 oz pudding or short-grain rice
850 ml/1¹/₂ pints milk
Pinch of salt
1 tablespoon unsalted butter
50 g/2 oz vanilla sugar (page 16) or 50 g/2 oz caster sugar *and* ¹/₂ teaspoon vanilla extract, or more sugar to taste

1 tablespoon mastic granules
1 tablespoon fresh lemon juice

For serving
Sifted icing sugar
Finely chopped toasted almonds

Place the rice in boiling water and leave for 5 seconds; drain, and rinse. Bring the milk almost to a boil in a heavy saucepan, and add the rice, salt, butter, all but 1 tablespoon of the sugar, and the vanilla. Reduce the heat to very low and simmer uncovered, stirring occasionally to prevent sticking, for 1 hour, or until soft and creamy. Remove from the heat before all the liquid evaporates; the mixture thickens on cooling. Set aside.

Pound the mastic in a mortar with the remaining sugar to a fine powder (or grind in a clean coffee grinder). Stir this powder, the lemon juice, and more sugar if desired into the warm rice. Divide between individual dishes, let cool, cover, and chill.

To serve, dust with the icing sugar and sprinkle with the almonds.

Lemon Rice Pudding
Risogalo me Lemoni
Serves 6

These refreshing, meltingly creamy puddings can be served on their own, or with Lemon Blossom Spoon Sweet (page 297). With their golden brown topping of caramelized sugar, they look extremely pretty.

175 g/6 oz pudding or short-grain rice
Finely grated zest of 1 lemon
700 ml/1¼ pints milk
115 g/4 oz caster sugar, or to taste
Pinch of salt
1 tablespoon unsalted butter
3 eggs, separated
½ teaspoon vanilla extract
Strained juice of 1 lemon, or to taste
75 ml/3 fl oz double cream

For serving
Sifted icing sugar

Place the rice with the lemon zest in boiling water and leave for 5 seconds; drain, and rinse. Bring the milk nearly to a boil in a heavy saucepan and stir in the rice and lemon zest, half the sugar, the salt, and the butter. Reduce the heat to very low and simmer uncovered, stirring occasionally

to prevent sticking, for 1 hour, or until thick and creamy. Set aside.

Set a rack in the centre of the oven and heat the oven to 180C/350F/gas mark 4. Whisk together the egg yolks, vanilla, most of the remaining sugar, and most of the lemon juice until pale and creamy; lightly beat the cream until slightly thickened. Add this mixture to the rice, and add sugar and the remaining lemon juice to taste. Whisk the egg whites in a large copper or mixing bowl until they hold stiff peaks. Stir one third of the whites into the rice, and lightly fold in the remainder. Divide between 6 dishes and smooth the tops.

Place in a shallow baking dish and add water to come 2.5 cm/1 inch up the sides of the dishes. Bake 25 minutes, or until barely set.

Meanwhile, heat the grill. Place the puddings on the grill pan and sprinkle with the remaining 2 tablespoons sugar. Grill 7-10 cm/3-4 inches from the heat source until caramelized and golden brown, about 2 minutes.

Serve warm, at room temperature, or chilled, lightly dusted with the icing sugar.

Orange Rice Pudding
Risogalo me Portokali

Substitute the juice of 2 sweet oranges and the finely grated zest of 1 sweet orange for the lemon juice and lemon zest.

Remove the zest of the second orange with a stripper or zester. Combine an additional 115 g/4 oz sugar and 115 ml/4 fl oz water and boil to a light syrup, about 8 minutes. Add the orange zest and simmer 5 minutes longer. Remove the zest with a slotted spoon, drain on paper towels, and coarsely chop. Reserve the syrup.

To serve, sprinkle the puddings with chopped orange zest, some of the syrup, and orange flower water if desired. Dust with icing sugar and a pinch of cinnamon.

Almond Creams
Krema Amigdalou
Serves 6

The perfect dinner party dessert after a rich main course, these light creams have a delicate sweet almond flavour enhanced with a subtle hint of mace. Garnished with a scattering of honeyed almonds and fresh or crystallized flowers, they have an elegant appearance and an unusual exotic taste. The almond cream must be prepared at least 6 hours before serving to allow the flavours to develop.

3 tablespoons cornflour
2 tablespoons ground rice (available in health food shops)

450 ml/16 fl oz milk
4 tablespoons aromatic honey, such as Hymettus
1 egg yolk
200 g/7 oz freshly ground blanched almonds
¹/₄ teaspoon ground mace

For serving
Sifted icing sugar
50 g/2 oz honeyed blanched almonds (see Note), lightly crushed *or* toasted blanched almonds, finely chopped
Fresh or crystallized violets or rose petals, *optional*

Combine the cornflour and ground rice with 4 tablespoons of the milk and stir until smooth. Warm the remaining milk in a large saucepan and whisk it into the cornflour mixture. Return it to the rinsed-out saucepan and slowly bring to a boil, stirring. Simmer 1 minute, stirring, then transfer to a non-reactive bowl. Stir in the honey, egg yolk, almonds, and mace. Let cool, cover, and refrigerate for at least 6 hours, or overnight.

Set a sieve, preferably plastic, over a bowl and press the almond cream through with a wooden spoon. Divide between individual bowls, lightly dust with the icing sugar, and sprinkle with the almonds. Serve cold, garnished with the flowers.

Note To make honeyed almonds, heat the oven to 150C/300F/gas mark 2. Toast 24 whole blanched almonds, turning once so they brown evenly, until pale golden brown, about 10 minutes. Combine with enough honey to coat (about 3-4 tablespoons) and spread on a lightly buttered baking tray. Bake 8 minutes, or until the honey coating hardens. Cool on the baking tray, and store in an airtight jar between layers of waxed paper.

Pistachio Creams
Krema Fistikiou
Serves 6

The aromatic flavour of pistachio nuts in this beautiful pale green cream is enhanced with fragrant honey and vanilla. For an elegant and sophisticated dessert, serve with a bowl of perfectly ripe pears.

175 g/6 oz unsalted pistachio nuts
2 tablespoons cornflour
2 tablespoons semolina (*farina*, page 344)
450 ml/16 fl oz milk
4-8 tablespoons aromatic honey, such as Hymettus (to taste)
One 5 cm/2 inch piece of vanilla bean or 1 teaspoon vanilla extract
2 egg yolks

For serving
Sifted icing sugar

Wrap the pistachio nuts in a tea towel, rub briskly, and remove the loosened skins with your forefinger and thumb. Coarsely chop about 6 nuts and set aside for garnish. Finely chop the remaining nuts and set aside.

Combine the cornflour and semolina with 4 tablespoons of the milk and stir until smooth. Warm the remaining milk in a large saucepan and whisk it into the cornflour mixture. Return it to the rinsed-out saucepan and slowly bring to a boil, stirring well. Add the honey and vanilla and simmer 2 minutes, stirring. Transfer to a non-reactive bowl, and stir in the egg yolks and finely chopped nuts. Let cool, cover, and refrigerate for at least 6 hours or overnight.

Set a sieve, preferably plastic, over a bowl and press the pistachio cream through with a wooden spoon. Discard the vanilla bean. Divide between individual bowls, lightly dust with the icing sugar, and sprinkle with the reserved nuts. Serve cold.

Sweet Chestnuts and Lemon Cheese
Kastana Glykisma me Kaymaki
Serves 8

The chestnut season is always anticipated with relish in Greece and, for a few weeks in the autumn, small braziers appear at every street corner and the debris of roasted chestnuts cover the pavements. Syrupy chestnut desserts are popular, especially this treat, based on thick and mellow *kaymaki* cream, perfumed with lemon, vanilla, and cloves. You can use double cream instead of *kaymaki* with no great loss of character to the dish, but make the lemon cheese at least four hours in advance for the richest flavour and texture.

Lemon cheese
450 ml/16 fl oz Rich Cream (without crust, page 310) or double cream
Finely grated zest of 1 lemon
Strained juice of 1 lemon
115 g/4 oz caster sugar
3 egg whites
675 g/1½ lb chestnuts, shelled and skinned (page 305)
50 g/2 oz vanilla sugar (page 16) or 50 g/2 oz caster sugar and ½ teaspoon vanilla extract
225 ml/8 fl oz milk
3 cloves

For serving
75 g/3 oz unsalted pistachio nuts, shelled, skinned (pages 303–304), and coarsely chopped

To make the lemon cheese, line a sieve, preferably plastic, with a single layer of damp muslin large enough to hang over the sides and set over a bowl.

Whisk together the Rich Cream, lemon zest, lemon juice, and sugar in a bowl until the mixture is just stiff enough to hold its shape. Take care – it will curdle if overworked. Whisk the egg whites until they hold stiff peaks and fold quickly and lightly into the cream. Transfer to the sieve, pull the corners of the muslin up and together, and tie with string to make a bag. Hang the bag over the bowl or the sink, away from heat or direct sunlight, and let drain 4 hours, occasionally giving the bag a firm squeeze to remove as much moisture as possible. Set aside, or refrigerate in the muslin bag for up to 4 hours.

Prepare the chestnuts no more than 2 hours before serving. Combine the chestnuts, sugar, vanilla, milk, and cloves in a heavy saucepan and simmer until all the milk is absorbed, about 15 minutes. Discard the cloves. Fit a moulis-légumes with the medium disc and pass the chestnuts through into a bowl.

Lightly spoon one third of the chestnut mixture into a glass serving bowl. Don't flatten the top – that would spoil its airy texture. Gently smooth half the cheese over the top, then carefully add half of the remaining chestnut mixture. Add another layer of cheese, reserving a little for decoration, and finish with a layer of the remaining chestnut mixture. Garnish with the reserved cheese and the pistachio nuts. Serve immediately, or refrigerate for up to 6 hours.

Glazed Sweet Chestnuts
Zakharota Kastana Glykisma
Serves 4

During the long slow baking of this sweet and spicy dish the fruity aromatic Mavrodaphne wine permeates the chestnuts and glazes them with a deep red syrup. Easy to make, this dessert is ideal for dinner parties since it can be made a day ahead. It is equally delicious warm or cold and is traditionally accompanied by fresh *myzithra* cheese (page 11), Rich Cream (page 310), or Lemon Cheese (page 304).

16 fresh plump chestnuts (see Note)
4 tablespoons honey or caster sugar
$^1/_4$ teaspoon ground allspice
350 ml/12 fl oz Mavrodaphne wine

Heat the oven to 150C/300F/gas mark 2. Fill a medium saucepan with water and bring to a boil.

Using a small knife with a strong blade (or a special chestnut knife), make an incision around the middle of each chestnut shell, beginning and ending on the flat side; take care not to cut into the chestnut. Add to the boiling water, and boil 10 minutes; then turn off the heat. Remove 2 or 3 chestnuts at a time and, as soon as they are cool enough to handle, carefully peel off the shells and inner skins, leaving the chestnuts whole. Work quickly – warm chestnuts are much easier to peel. Arrange in a single layer in a heavy baking dish just large enough to hold them.

Combine the honey, allspice, and wine, and pour over the chestnuts. Bake uncovered 1$^1/_2$ hours, gently turning the chestnuts in the syrup about every 20 minutes. Handle the chestnuts with care;

they break easily. At the end of the baking time there should be about 6 tablespoons syrup: add a little more wine or water if necessary, or bake 15-30 minutes longer to reduce the syrup.

Cool in the dish, then gently roll the chestnuts in the syrup. Transfer to a shallow serving dish or individual dishes and pour over any remaining syrup. Serve at room temperature or cold.

Note To use tinned chestnuts, rinse, drain, and dry with paper towels. Bring the wine, honey, and allspice to a boil in a large saucepan, add the chestnuts, and gently simmer 5 minutes. With a slotted spoon, transfer the chestnuts to paper towels to drain. Rapidly boil the cooking liquid until it is syrupy and coats the back of a metal spoon, about 8 minutes. Transfer the chestnuts to a serving dish and pour the syrup over. Let cool and serve.

Moustalevria Sweetmeats
Moustalevria Glykisma
Makes approximately 18 pieces

This jelly-like sweet, made from grape must and flour, was probably one of the very first sweetmeats. It was a popular sweet in ancient Greece and down through the centuries Greeks have had a special fondness for its unusual flavour. In the villages *moustalevria* is still made in the traditional way: The grapes are trodden by women (men tread the grapes for wine) and the must is first clarified with wood ash from the *fournos,* then boiled until it forms a light syrup called *petimezi.* This is then thickened with flour, semolina, or cornflour to make the sweetmeat. The exact moment for removing the sweetmeat from the heat is judged in dramatic fashion by slipping a piece of flaming charcoal into the mixture – if the flame stays alive it is ready. For this recipe, you need to prepare the grape juice a day or two before making *petimezi,* a true must is grape juice that is just beginning to ferment. However, *petimezi* can be prepared ahead and stored for up to three months. Use it to flavour fruit salads, biscuits, breads, cakes, and Moustalevria Pudding (page 307) as well as these sweetmeats.

2.3 kg/5 lb large sweet grapes
2 tablespoons wood ash (available from shops specializing in equipment for home-made wine)
6 tablespoons honey
6-8 level tablespoons sifted plain flour
A few drops of olive oil
Ground cinnamon
About 50 g/2 oz lightly toasted sesame seeds

Fill a large saucepan with water and bring to a boil. Stem the grapes and add them all at once to the boiling water. Count to 5 and drain.

Peel the grapes with your finger nails or a small paring knife and, with a wooden spoon, press them through a sieve, preferably plastic, set over a bowl. Strain the juice through muslin into a saucepan and discard the pulp. There should be about 1.6 litres/2¾ pints juice.

Cut out a 15 cm/6 inch square of a double layer of muslin, place the wood ash in it, and tie up the edges to make a bag. Add to the juice, bring to a boil, and simmer 10 minutes. Discard the bag of ash and pour the juice into a non-reactive bowl. Cover and set aside for 1-2 days.

Line a sieve with 2 layers of muslin and set over a saucepan. Strain the must into the saucepan, add the honey, and boil until it reaches 110-112C/225-230F on a sugar thermometer, the light thread stage. To test, dip the tip of a pair of scissors into the syrup. Remove them and open them – if the syrup (*petimezi*) forms a thread between the blades, it is ready. Set aside to cool. Measure the *petimezi*, and place 2 level tablespoons flour for each 225 ml/8 fl oz *petimezi* in a bowl. Add enough *petimezi* to make a thin paste, and bring the remaining *petimezi* to a boil in a large saucepan. Whisk the boiling *petimezi* into the paste, and return it to the rinsed-out saucepan. Simmer over low heat, stirring frequently with a wooden spoon, until it reaches the soft ball stage on a sugar thermometer (114-116C/235-240F), or test by dropping a small amount of the *moustalevria* onto a cold plate: It should keep its shape. Lightly wipe a baking tray with the olive oil and carefully pour on the *moustalevria* to make a 1 cm/^{1}/$_2$ inch layer. Set aside to cool.

Sprinkle the cinnamon on a plate and sesame seeds on another. Cut the *moustalevria* into 2.5 cm/1 inch squares and gently roll them first in the cinnamon, then in the sesame seeds. Store in an airtight container between layers of waxed paper for up to 1 month.

Moustalevria Pudding
Moustalevria
Serves 4

A variation of the mixture used for making *moustalevria* sweetmeats makes an unusual pudding. Here raisin juice is used for a quicker and easier version of *moustalevria*. Do not be tempted to use grape juice – it is not a successful substitute and produces an unpleasant flavour in this pudding.

350 g/12 oz small dark seedless raisins soaked in 115 ml/4 fl oz Mavrodaphne wine and
115 ml/4 fl oz hot water for 2 hours or 350 ml/12 fl oz *petimezi* (see above)
75 g/3 oz semolina (*farina*, page 344)
1 tablespoon honey

For serving
50 g/2 oz finely chopped walnuts or blanched almonds or lightly toasted sesame seeds
Ground cinnamon

Fit a moulis-légumes with the fine blade and pass the raisins and their liquid through into a bowl. (Or process in a blender or food processor.) Set a sieve over a bowl and press the mixture through with a wooden spoon. Add water if necessary to make 350 ml/12 fl oz liquid.

Combine the semolina, honey, and 4 tablespoons of the raisin juice to make a paste, then stir in the remaining juice. Transfer to a heavy saucepan and slowly bring to a boil. Simmer over very low heat until the mixture comes away from the sides of the saucepan, about 4 minutes, stirring constantly with a wooden spoon; take care not to let it burn.

Divide between small bowls and cool. Cover tightly and refrigerate until chilled, or up to 2 days. To serve, sprinkle with the nuts and cinnamon.

Honey Sesame Sweetmeats
Pasteli
Makes 16 pieces

In summer the cry of the *pasteli* vendor is a familiar sound in every Greek village and town and he has no lack of customers for this traditional sweet, rich, and nourishing sweetmeat. It is also very good crushed and sprinkled over ice cream.

200 g/7 oz sesame seeds
450 g/1 lb aromatic honey, such as Hymettus or orange blossom
2 tablespoons fresh lemon juice
1$^1/_2$ tablespoons unsalted butter, melted
1 tablespoon orange flower water, *optional*

Heat the oven to 180C/350F/gas mark 4. Line a 20 x 10 cm/8 x 4 inch loaf tin with waxed paper. Spread the sesame seeds on a baking tray and bake 5 minutes to toast lightly. Set aside.

Combine the honey and 4 tablespoons water in a small saucepan and slowly bring to a boil. Add the lemon juice and sesame seeds and gently boil until the mixture reaches the soft ball stage (114-116C/235-240F) on a sugar thermometer, or a small amount forms a slightly misshapen ball when dropped into a glass of cold water.

Brush the prepared tin with the melted butter and pour in the honey and sesame seed mixture. Sprinkle with the orange flower water and set aside to cool.

Turn out, peel off the paper, and, with a sharp knife, cut into pieces about 2 x 5 cm/$^3/_4$ x 2 inches. Store up to 1 month between layers of waxed paper in an airtight container.

Rich Cream
Kaymaki
Makes 225-275 ml/8-10 fl oz (plus the crust)

Thick rich eastern Mediterranean *kaymaki* (literally, "frothy cream") is unique, but two more readily available products have a similar flavour and texture. Clotted (Devon) cream, and imported Italian mascarpone cheese both make good substitutes, or you can make your own. Make this when you plan to be in the kitchen for a couple of hours – for an even, smooth texture and a thick crust you need to stir the hot cream at regular intervals. Be sure to use meticulously clean utensils and keep the cooking heat very low (or use a heat diffuser mat). *Kaymaki* should be made at least 18 hours before you need it; it can be stored for up to a week.

1 litre/1³/₄ pints double cream

Slowly bring the cream almost to a boil in a heavy saucepan, stirring occasionally with a wooden spoon. Reduce the heat to as low as possible, or place the saucepan on a heat diffuser mat. Lift a ladleful of cream about 30 cm/12 inches above the saucepan, and pour it back in a thin steady stream; repeat 2 or 3 times. Repeat this procedure every 10 minutes or so over the next 1¹/₂ hours, and stir the cream occasionally to make sure it does not stick.

Leave the cream undisturbed over the lowest heat for 30 minutes longer; it will have reduced by at least two thirds. Remove the saucepan from the heat and let it cool.

Loosely cover with a clean tea towel and set aside for 2 hours.

Remove the tea towel, tightly cover, and refrigerate for at least 12 hours, or overnight.

Cut the crust on top of the cream into 2.5 cm/1 inch-wide strips. Gently fold one end of a strip over the handle of a wooden spoon and roll it up (cut in half if the roll becomes too thick or unwieldy), and slide off onto a plate. Repeat with the remaining strips. The remaining *kaymaki* will have the texture of thick airless cream. It can be refrigerated in a tightly covered container for up to 1 week; refrigerate the rolls for up to 3 days.

Note Serve *kaymaki* rolls on their own or with desserts such as Kataifi Nut Rolls with Caramel Syrup (page 268) or Almond Cake (page 278). *Kaymaki* cream can be added to ice cream (page 289) or rice pudding (page 299) for an especially good flavour. Or whisk it together with a little sweet wine or lemon juice for a perfect accompaniment to fresh or poached fruit or sweet pastries.

Sauces

saltses

The philosopher Plato believed that, although anyone can grill food, only a skilled chef could flavour a sauce. It may be impudent to disagree with the great man but if that were true most of us would immediately abandon any attempt at sauce making.

Greek sauces are generally not awesomely complex – the ubiquitous *latholemono* (lemon juice and olive oil) and *lathoxsitho* (wine vinegar and olive oil) do not even require recipes since they are simple mixtures of oil and an acid, blended and seasoned to taste. The sauces in this chapter are those the visitor to Greece is likely to encounter most often. They range from two contrasting mayonnaises and the famous *avgolemono* and *skordalia* to creamy sauces based on walnuts, almonds, or pine nuts, a piquant anchovy sauce, and several very different tomato sauces. Throughout the book, of course, there are many more unusual sauce recipes detailed in individual recipes.

Many of the sauces have ancient origins and would traditionally be made with a wooden mortar and pestle. For modern cooks food processors and blenders now make speedy work of many of them and produce excellent results with fine flavours and textures.

A good sauce harmonises all the flavours of a dish and brings out the essential character of the individual ingredients. These versatile sauces will add verve and vivacity to your Greek meals.

Avgolemono Sauce
Avgolemono
Serves 4

Avgolemono seems to add the perfect finishing touch to practically any dish, except those containing tomatoes or garlic. Its delicate flavour is ideally suited to fish dishes, turns a simple chicken dish into one of elegant subtlety, marries well with lamb or pork, enhances pungent vine leaves, and lifts plain vegetables into the luxury class.

Avgolemono is simply a mixture of eggs, lemon juice, and broth. For a rich deep-yellow sauce, suited to vegetables and roast meats, yolks alone are used. For casseroles and soups Greeks prefer a lighter sauce, made with whole eggs.

The key to successful *avgolemono* is to use gentle heat, as high temperatures will cause the sauce to curdle, and to make it just before serving; this is not a sauce you can keep warm or reheat. The amount of lemon juice is adjusted to taste or to complement different dishes. *Dolmades,* for example, need little lemon juice because of the astringency of the vine leaves, while a mellow-flavoured chicken dish benefits from a larger amount.

3 large egg yolks
5-6 tablespoons strained fresh lemon juice, to taste
225 ml/8 fl oz strained hot broth (from the dish to be sauced)

Whisk the yolks, using a hand whisk or electric mixer, for 2 minutes, or until pale and frothy. Slowly add the lemon juice and whisk 1 minute longer. Add one third of the broth in a thin steady stream, whisking steadily, then quickly whisk in the remainder. Transfer to a small heavy saucepan or the top of a double boiler set over very hot water. Gently heat, stirring constantly in a figure-8 motion, until just thick enough to lightly coat the back of a wooden spoon, about 4 minutes. Do not stop stirring the sauce or let it boil or it will curdle. When it is ready, immediately remove from the heat (and saucepan) and serve.

Whole Egg Avgolemono for Soups and Casseroles
Serves 4 to 6

Avgolemono made with both egg whites and yolks is a beautiful pale lemony colour. However, egg whites cook faster than yolks so there is a risk of the sauce looking stringy. To avoid this Greek cooks whisk the egg whites until stiff before adding the yolks and lemon juice.

2 large eggs, separated
115 ml/4 fl oz strained fresh lemon juice, or to taste
115 ml/4 fl oz hot soup or broth (from dish to be sauced)

Whisk the egg whites with a hand whisk or electric beater until they hold stiff peaks. Add the yolks, whisk 1 minute longer, then add the lemon juice. Continue whisking until very pale and frothy. Pouring from a height of about 30 cm/12 inches, slowly add the soup or broth to the egg and lemon juice mixture, whisking constantly. (By the time the liquid reaches the egg mixture it will no longer be hot enough to curdle the sauce.) Off the heat, add the *avgolemono* to the soup or casserole and stir or shake gently to blend the flavours. Set aside in a warm place for a few minutes; do not return to the heat. Serve immediately.

Garlic Almond Sauce
Skordalia
Serves 6 to 8

This thick and creamy blend of garlic, almonds, and olive oil has been a favourite since the days of the ancient Greeks. However, since almonds are now expensive, modern versions often substitute breadcrumbs or potatoes for some or all of the ground almonds. For a truly excellent sauce use fresh sweet garlic and take a few minutes to blanch and grind fresh whole almonds. Serve *skordalia* with vegetable dishes such as fried courgettes and aubergines or baked beetroot or with grilled or baked fish or chicken.

115 g/4 oz ground almonds or 75 g/3 oz ground almonds *and* 25 g/1 oz fresh
breadcrumbs (made from white or wholemeal bread, crusts removed)
4-6 large cloves garlic, crushed
Sea salt to taste
$^1/_2$ teaspoon freshly ground white pepper, or to taste
4 tablespoons aged red wine vinegar or the juice of 1 large lemon
175-225 ml/6-8 fl oz extra virgin olive oil or 115 ml/4 fl oz extra virgin olive oil *and* 5-8
tablespoons broth (from the dish to be sauced)

For serving
12 Elitses or Niçoise olives

Place the almonds (and breadcrumbs), garlic, salt, and pepper in a food processor or blender container. With the machine running, slowly add half the vinegar and 175 ml/6 fl oz olive oil. Add some or all of the remaining vinegar and olive oil if necessary: The sauce should be creamy, with a slightly piquant flavour, and thick enough to hold its shape. Slightly more liquid is needed if you use breadcrumbs. Serve immediately, or refrigerate for up to 24 hours in a tightly covered jar.

To make the traditional way Pound the almonds, garlic, salt, and pepper in a large wooden mortar until well mixed and fairly smooth. Add the breadcrumbs, if using, and pound to mix. Gradually add the vinegar and olive oil, pounding constantly, until you have a thick sauce. It will not be as smooth as a food processor version but will have a superior flavour produced by the continual working together of the ingredients.

Note You can remove the powerful garlic aroma from a wooden bowl by wiping with lemon juice or bicarbonate of soda.

Potato Skordalia
Skordalia me Patates
Serves 6 to 8

This sauce should be made only in a mortar or bowl, as food processors ruin the texture of cooked potatoes. Use firm good-quality boiling potatoes and, for a sauce with a glorious deep yellow colour and rich flavour, add an egg yolk.

450 g/1 lb boiling potatoes or 225 g/8 oz boiling potatoes *and* 50 g/2 oz breadcrumbs
(made from white bread, crusts removed)
4-6 large cloves fresh garlic, crushed
1 egg yolk, *optional*
Sea salt to taste
$^1/_2$ teaspoon freshly ground white pepper, or more to taste
4 tablespoons aged red wine vinegar, or more to taste
175-225 ml/6-8 fl oz extra virgin olive oil

Fill a large saucepan with slightly salted water and bring to a boil. Cut the potatoes into halves or quarters, add to the boiling water, and cook 15 minutes, or until just tender. Drain, and peel when cool enough to handle. Push the potatoes through a potato ricer or moulis-légumes into a large mortar or bowl; add the breadcrumbs, if using, the garlic, egg yolk, salt, and pepper. With a pestle or wooden spoon, pound until fairly smooth and well mixed. Gradually add the vinegar and then the olive oil, pounding constantly, until the sauce is thick. Add more vinegar, if liked. Serve immediately, or refrigerate in an airtight container for up to 3 hours.

Piquant Almond Sauce
Amigdalosaltsa Pikantiki
Serves 2 to 3

Fresh young almonds are a favourite *meze* wherever raki is enjoyed – as I discovered when I lived in a Cretan village house surrounded by magnificent almond trees. Sitting under their beautiful flowering branches in my first spring there I contemplated the lovely dishes I would make when the almonds were ready in the autumn – not realizing that my trees and their almonds were considered public property by the villagers! Along with everyone else I enjoyed "my" almonds in the village café where tables were piled high with them. The Greek love of almonds dates back to ancient times, as does this pungent sauce. Served with baked, poached, or steamed fish or chicken it elevates simply prepared food to the realms of elegance.

50 g/2 oz freshly ground almonds
2 tablespoons aged red wine vinegar, or more to taste
1 1/2 tablespoons dried *rigani* (page 14)
2 tablespoons finely chopped flat leaf parsley
1/4 teaspoon powdered mustard
1 teaspoon aromatic honey, such as Hymettus
Sea salt *and* freshly ground black pepper to taste
4 tablespoons extra virgin olive oil
50-115 ml/2-4 fl oz Light Meat, Chicken or Fish Stock (pages 347, 344, and 345)

Place the almonds, vinegar, *rigani*, parsley, mustard, honey, and salt and pepper in a food processor or blender container. With the machine running, add the olive oil and then 4 tablespoons stock in a thin steady stream to make a thick sauce. For a thinner sauce, add up to 4 tablespoons additional stock. Add vinegar to taste, but its flavour should not be overpowering. Serve at room temperature or heat over low heat until warm.

Almond, Yogurt, and Coriander Sauce
Amigdalosaltsa me Yiaourti
Serves 3 to 4

This popular sauce, which can also be served as a *salata,* is delicious with grilled meats, *souvlakia,* aubergines, *pilafi,* fried fish, or vegetables.

50 g/2 oz freshly ground almonds
1/2 teaspoon ground coriander
1 clove garlic, finely chopped
1 teaspoon aromatic honey, such as Hymettus
Juice of 1 small lemon
Sea salt *and* freshly ground black pepper to taste
115-225 ml/4-8 fl oz Strained Yogurt (page 8)
4 tablespoons coarsely chopped flat leaf parsley
4 tablespoons coarsely chopped fresh coriander

Place the almonds, ground coriander, garlic, honey, half the lemon juice, and salt and pepper in a food processor or blender container. With the machine running, add yogurt a tablespoon at a time until the sauce has the desired consistency. Add the parsley and fresh coriander and pulse or blend just to mix. Add salt, pepper, and/or lemon juice to taste and serve immediately.

Walnut Sauce
Karythosaltsa
Serves 6

Fresh walnuts are one of the incomparable delights of late summer and early autumn on the Greek islands and this is the sauce the islanders make with them. With its velvet texture and fine flavour it is the traditional accompaniment to fried mussels, grilled or fried fish, grilled or fried aubergines, and courgettes or chicken. New-crop walnuts with golden or pale brown inner skins are best for this sauce but if these are hard to find, use the freshest walnuts available. This sauce freezes exceptionally well – freeze it in small amounts and you'll have delicious instant sauce for a variety of grilled and fried dishes. It can also be used to thicken and enhance the pan juices of baked chicken or fish dishes.

225 g/8 oz walnut pieces
25 g/1 oz fresh breadcrumbs (made from wholemeal bread, crusts removed), soaked for
5 minutes in 4 tablespoons broth (from the dish to be sauced) or milk (see Note)
2 tablespoons extra virgin olive oil (see Note)
1 large clove garlic, finely chopped
Sea salt *and* freshly ground white pepper to taste
2–4 tablespoons fresh lemon juice *or* white wine vinegar (to taste)

Optional flavourings
$^{1}/_{2}$ teaspoon grated nutmeg *or* 1 teaspoon ground allspice (for chicken)
1 teaspoon finely grated horseradish *and* 1 small handful flat leaf parsley, leaves
coarsely chopped (for mussels, fish, or vegetables)
1 tablespoon finely chopped fresh thyme (for vegetables)

Walnuts with light-brown inner skins must be peeled: Blanch them in boiling water for 5 seconds and drain. Wrap in a tea towel, rub briskly to remove the skins, and set aside to dry.

Pulverize the walnuts and breadcrumbs in a food processor container, then add the olive oil in a thin steady stream, processing until smooth. Add the garlic, salt, and pepper, half the lemon juice, and the chosen flavouring(s) and process until mixed. Add salt and pepper and/or the remaining lemon juice to taste. Add more broth if necessary to produce a thick but pouring sauce, or add more breadcrumbs to thicken the sauce. Serve warm or cold.

To make the traditional way Pound the walnuts in a large wooden mortar with a pestle until the oil is released, 10-15 minutes. Add the breadcrumbs and pound to mix. Slowly add the olive oil, pounding constantly. Add the garlic, salt, and pepper, lemon juice, and chosen flavouring and pound until creamy, fairly smooth, and of a pouring consistency (it will not be as smooth as a machine-made sauce).

Note The amount of oil in walnuts varies, so the texture of the sauce may be different each time you make it. Be prepared to add varying amounts of broth, and/or olive oil.

Pine Nut Sauce
Koukounaria Saltsa
Serves 4

Along much of Greece's dramatic rocky coastline the magnificent umbrella-shaped Mediterranean pine dominates the landscape. Every three years the glossy brown cones mature and ripen, and inside each is the edible kernel known to us as the pine nut. This extended ripening period and the fact that these pine trees thrive only along coastlines mean that pine nuts have always been relatively scarce and, therefore, expensive. But the delicate creamy blend of nuts, lemon juice, olive oil, and fresh chives in this traditional sauce more than justifies the extravagance. Serve with grilled or baked chicken or fish.

175 g/6 oz pine nuts
1 small clove garlic, finely chopped, *optional*
Sea salt to taste
1/4 teaspoon freshly ground white pepper, or to taste
2 tablespoons fresh lemon juice or 1 tablespoon aged red wine vinegar, or more to taste
3 tablespoons extra virgin olive oil, or more to taste
4-6 tablespoons broth (from the dish to be sauced) or additional extra virgin olive oil
4 tablespoons chopped fresh chives

Place the pine nuts, breadcrumbs, if using, garlic, salt, and pepper in a food processor or blender container. With the machine running, gradually add the lemon juice, olive oil, and 4 tablespoons broth and process until the sauce resembles thick cream. Add broth or olive oil if a thinner consistency is desired, and add salt or a few drops of lemon juice to taste; take care not to overpower the delicate flavour of the pine nuts. Add the chives and pulse just to mix. Serve immediately.

To make the traditional way Place the pine nuts, garlic, salt, and pepper in a wooden mortar and pound with a pestle until smooth and well mixed, about 10 minutes. Add the breadcrumbs, if using, and pound to mix. Gradually add the olive oil and broth, pounding constantly. The sauce will not be as smooth as a food processor version, but the flavour will be more distinctive. Stir in the chives just before serving.

Note Pine Nut Sauce can be refrigerated in an airtight container for up to 24 hours or frozen for up to 1 month, but do not add the chives until just before serving.

Mayonnaise
Mayonaiza
Serves 3 to 4

The flavour of mayonnaise is determined by the olive oil used. A light olive oil will produce the lightest mayonnaise, Kalamata or other extra virgin olive oils the fruity, traditional Greek version. Greek cooks sometimes add a few spoonfuls of yogurt to mayonnaise to lighten both colour and flavour. Serve this mayonnaise with cold poached or baked fish, shellfish, chicken, and salads.

2 large egg yolks, at room temperature

Large pinch of powdered mustard

115 ml/4 fl oz extra virgin olive oil

1–2 tablespoons fresh lemon juice to taste

Sea salt *and* freshly ground white pepper to taste

1–2 tablespoons Strained Yogurt (page 8), *optional*

Place the egg yolks and mustard in a large non-reactive bowl and whisk together 1 minute with a small whisk or 2 forks (held slightly apart, in the same hand). Add 4 tablespoons of the olive oil drop by drop, whisking constantly and pausing once or twice to add a few drops of lemon juice. Slowly add the remaining olive oil in a thin stream, whisking constantly. Add salt and pepper, whisk in the yogurt to taste, and serve.

Note To store, add 1 tablespoon boiling water to the finished mayonnaise. Cover tightly and refrigerate no longer than 4 hours.

To rescue curdled mayonnaise, place 1 room-temperature egg yolk in a clean bowl and slowly add the curdled mayonnaise, whisking constantly.

Garlic and Watercress Mayonnaise
Skortho ke Karthamon Mayonaiza
Serves 4

This piquant mayonnaise adds a delightful dash of the unexpected to *kephtedes* or everyday grilled chicken, and it can be quickly made in the food processor.

1 bunch of fresh watercress, green leaves only

1 teaspoon finely grated fresh horseradish

Large pinch of powdered mustard

1 tablespoon capers, rinsed and patted dry

2–4 large cloves garlic, finely chopped, to taste

Sea salt to taste

2 egg yolks, at room temperature

115 ml/4 fl oz extra virgin olive oil

Strained juice of $^1/_2$ lemon, or more to taste

Blanch the watercress in boiling water for 5 seconds, drain, spread between layers of paper towels, and blot dry.

Place the horseradish, mustard, capers, garlic, salt, egg yolks, and watercress in a food processor or blender container and, with the machine running, add 4 tablespoons of the olive oil drop by drop. Gradually add the remaining olive oil and the lemon juice. Add more lemon juice and/or salt to taste and serve immediately.

To make the traditional way Boil 2 eggs for 4 minutes, peel, and remove the yolks with a small spoon. They should be soft but not runny. Chop together the blanched watercress, horseradish, mustard, and capers. Pound the garlic and a large pinch of salt to a purée in a large mortar or bowl. Add the egg yolks and watercress mixture and pound until well mixed. Add half the olive oil drop by drop, still pounding, then add the remaining olive oil and the lemon juice in a steady stream. The sauce should be thick and well mixed, but it will not be as smooth as a food processor version.

Green Grape Sauce
Agouritha
Makes approximately 175 ml/6 fl oz

This unusual sauce is made from the juice of under-ripe grapes (known here as *verjuice*). Made in traditional homes on Crete, it is used to flavour pork and game dishes and Stuffed Aubergines (page 85). The small hard pickling grapes found in Indian and Chinese produce shops in early summer are exactly right for this sauce; if it proves impossible to find suitable grapes, *agouritha* can also be made with gooseberries, rhubarb, crab apples, or lemons or limes (see below). With its clear sharp tang, this is a particularly effective flavouring for baked fish and chicken dishes and a perfect marinade for lamb. It can be frozen; since only a little sauce is required to flavour the dish, freeze it in an ice cube tray and store the cubes in a bag, ready to use.

450 g/1 lb small hard white grapes (on the stem)

Blanch the grapes in boiling water for 5 seconds and remove with a slotted spoon. Drain between layers of paper towels and blot completely dry, then carefully separate the grapes from the stem.

Set a plastic sieve over a non-reactive bowl and push the grapes through with a wooden spoon. Don't be tempted to use a food processor because the metal blade reacts harshly with the sour juice, giving an unpleasant metallic flavour to the sauce. Even the plastic blade of a food processor will "overwork" the grape skins and spoil the delicate flavour. When you have extracted as much of the juice and pulp from the grapes as possible, rinse the sieve, line it with a layer of muslin, and place over another clean non-reactive bowl. Press the purée through a second time; the result will be a lovely smooth sauce.

Refrigerate for up to 1 week in a covered jar or freeze for up to 2 months.

Substitutes

Substitute 225 g/8 oz firm sour gooseberries for grapes; avoid large pink ones – they are usually sweet and watery. Snip off both ends with small scissors, and simmer 10 minutes in 4 tablespoons water. Large gooseberries may need a little longer to soften.

Substitute 225 g/8 oz rhubarb, trimmed and the "strings" removed. Cut into 1 cm/1/2 inch slices and simmer 10 minutes in 4 tablespoons water. Use pink rhubarb only when the green colour of classic *agouritha* is not an integral part of the dish.

Substitute 450 g/1 lb crab apples, peeled, cored, and cut into quarters. Simmer in a few tablespoons water until soft, about 30 minutes.

If you can find neither under-ripe grapes nor a substitute, use the juice of 2 limes and 1 lemon (about 150 ml/5 fl oz). However, this mixture does not have quite the same depth of flavour, nor does it have the property that turns the sauce slightly sweet when cooked, as do grapes, gooseberries, rhubarb, and crab apples, but it works well in such dishes as Stuffed Aubergines with Green Grape Sauce (page 85).

Tomato Sauce
Saltsa Domatas
Makes approximately 1 litre/13/4 pints

The secret of the deliciously sweet tomato sauces of Greece is vine-ripened tomatoes (although when they are unavailable Greek cooks cheat a little by adding a spoonful of honey). You can vary this basic sauce depending on the herbs and spices used. Make large quantities whenever there is a good supply of top-quality tomatoes, and store for use later.

4 tablespoons extra virgin olive oil
1 large onion, chopped
2.3 kg/5 lb ripe tomatoes, skinned and diced, juices reserved
4 tablespoons dry red wine or hot water
1 tablespoon tomato purée
1 tablespoon honey
Sea salt *and* freshly ground black pepper to taste

Any one of the following groups of flavourings
1 teaspoon ground cinnamon or one 7 cm/3 inch cinnamon stick *and* 4 tablespoons chopped flat leaf parsley or fresh mint or 2 tablespoons dried *rigani* (page 14)
or

12 sprigs of parsley *and* 4 bay leaves
or
4 tablespoons chopped fresh basil, parsley or marjoram *and* 4 cloves *and* 1 large
clove garlic, finely chopped
or
1 teaspoon ground cumin *and* 12 sprigs of parsley

Warm the olive oil in a large non-reactive frying pan and sauté the onion over low heat until soft, about 10 minutes. Combine the red wine, tomato purée, and honey, and add to the frying pan. Stir in the tomatoes, salt and pepper, and the flavourings. Raise the heat and boil uncovered, stirring occasionally, 30-40 minutes, or until thick enough to stay separated for a few seconds when a wooden spoon is drawn across the bottom of the pan.

Set a sieve over a bowl. Remove the bay leaves or cinnamon stick, if using, and press the sauce through the sieve with the back of a wooden spoon. Add more salt and pepper to taste (if it is to be stored, season before using). Serve warm or cold.

Note To store, fill small sterilized jars with the sauce. Invert a metal spoon 2.5 cm/1 inch above a jar and pour a thin stream of olive oil onto the spoon. It will reach the surface of the sauce at an angle, ensuring that it is not disturbed. Use only enough olive oil to make a thin layer for an airtight seal. Repeat with the remaining jars and cover tightly and refrigerate for up to 3 months. Use the sealing olive oil for cooking or stir into the sauce when serving.

Light Tomato Sauce
Saltsa Domatas Elafria
Makes 225 to 350 ml/8 to 12 fl oz

Make this elegant sauce when tomatoes are at their summer sweetest. Aromatized with cinnamon and pungent herbs it has a subtle fresh taste and a smooth thin consistency. It must be made as close as possible to serving time since the flavour begins to acidify in just a few hours. This sauce is excellent with *macaronia* or *pilafi*, grilled fish or aubergines, and simple summer vegetable dishes.

5 tablespoons extra virgin olive oil, or to taste
1 small onion, finely chopped
1 clove garlic, finely chopped, *optional*
4 large ripe tomatoes, skinned and diced
$^1/_2$ teaspoon honey
One 7 cm/3 inch cinnamon stick, broken in half
Sea salt *and* freshly ground black pepper to taste

Optional flavourings
2 tablespoons fresh mint, parsley, marjoram, basil or oregano
or

1 tablespoon dried rigani (page 14)

or

1 teaspoon dried thyme

or

1 tablespoon Mavrodaphne or Madeira wine, or to taste

Warm half the olive oil in a heavy frying pan and sauté the onion over low heat until barely soft, about 6 minutes. Chop the fresh herbs, if using, and add the garlic, tomatoes, honey, cinnamon stick, salt and pepper, and half the flavouring herb to the onions. Raise the heat and boil 3 minutes. Discard the cinnamon stick. Pour off any liquid in the pan and set aside.

Set a sieve, preferably plastic, over a bowl and press the sauce through with a wooden spoon. Stir in the wine, if using, and the remaining olive oil. The sauce should be the consistency of thin cream; if too thick, add some or all of the reserved cooking liquid. Season with salt and pepper and stir in the remaining flavouring herb. Serve warm or cold.

Scorched Tomato Sauce
Saltsa Domatas Kapsalismeni
Serves 3 to 4

When whole tomatoes are grilled until their skins blacken and blister, their flavour becomes wonderfully sweet and mellow – the perfect base for a full-flavoured sauce. In tavernas, where the grill is in constant use, this sauce is made in vast quantities. It's simple to make and a wonderful complement to grilled or barbecued fish, chicken, or lamb, and vegetable *pilafi*.

4 large ripe tomatoes

1–2 teaspoons aromatic honey, such as Hymettus

1 large clove garlic, minced

1 tablespoon dried marjoram or 1¹/₂ tablespoons dried *rigani* (page 14), crumbled

1 teaspoon ground paprika

Coarse-grain sea salt *and* cracked black pepper to taste

1 small bunch of flat leaf parsley, leaves coarsely chopped

4 tablespoons extra virgin olive oil

Heat the grill.

Set the tomatoes on a grill pan close to the heat until blackened and blistered on top, about 5 minutes. Remove from the heat and, when cool enough to handle, skin, discard the seeds, and place the pulp in a sieve set over a bowl. Set aside to drain for a few minutes, and reserve the juice.

Transfer the pulp to a food processor or blender container and add the honey, garlic, marjoram, paprika, salt and pepper, and half the parsley. Pulse to mix, and add the olive oil in a thin steady stream, pulsing until well mixed and fairly smooth. Stir in the remaining parsley and enough of the reserved juice to make the desired consistency, and season to taste with salt and pepper. Serve at room temperature or heat gently to warm.

To make the traditional way Prepare the tomatoes as directed above.

Chop half the parsley, the garlic, the marjoram, paprika, and salt and pepper together to mix. Place in a large wooden mortar, pound 1 minute, then add the tomato pulp and honey and pound to blend. Continue pounding as you add olive oil. Stir in enough of the reserved juice to make the desired consistency, and stir in the remaining parsley. Season to taste.

Peloponnese Honey Sauce
Saltsa Peloponissou
Serves 3

This piquant sauce is perfect for grilled white-fleshed fish, especially bass or halibut, or for grilled pork, *souvlakia*, or sausages. It's simple to make but the flavours are complex and tantalizing. Make the sauce with a wooden mortar and pestle or in a china or glass bowl using a wooden spoon – metal bowls or utensils will interact with the flavour of the egg yolk and subtly alter the taste of the finished sauce. Serve warm or cold.

2 soft-boiled eggs (boiled 4 minutes)

2 tablespoons aromatic honey, such as Hymettus

Sea salt to taste

1 teaspoon cracked black pepper

4 tablespoons aged red wine vinegar or 2 tablespoons balsamic vinegar diluted with 2 tablespoons warm water

1 tablespoon small capers, rinsed

2 tablespoons finely chopped flat leaf parsley

Slice the top third off each egg and spoon out the creamy yolk into a wooden mortar or non-reactive bowl. Add the honey, salt and pepper, and pound until smooth. Add the vinegar a few drops at a time, pounding constantly.

Transfer to a sieve, preferably plastic, set over a bowl and press the mixture through with the pounder. Stir in the capers and parsley and salt and pepper to taste. Serve immediately, or gently heat until warm. Do not let the sauce become too hot or the egg yolks will curdle.

Anchovy Sauce
Saltsa Antsouyias
Serves 3 to 4

In a few Greek markets, such as Athinas in central Athens, it's still possible to buy whole anchovies preserved in brine, sometimes sold straight from the huge wooden barrels in which they were packed. Tinned anchovies do not have the same special flavour but unless you can track down brine-preserved anchovies in a Greek or Middle Eastern shop, they are the kind to use for this creamy sauce. Make the sauce as close to serving time as possible. It's especially good with grilled tuna or swordfish.

1 large shallot, chopped or 2 spring onions, white parts only, chopped
1 large clove garlic, cut into 2 or 3 pieces
6–8 salted anchovy fillets, rinsed (to taste)
Finely grated zest of $1/2$ lemon
1 tablespoon capers, rinsed
Juice of 1 small lemon, or to taste
5 tablespoons extra virgin olive oil, or to taste
2 tablespoons finely chopped flat leaf parsley
$1/2$ teaspoon cracked black pepper, or to taste

Place the shallot, garlic, anchovies, lemon zest, capers, and lemon juice in a food processor or blender container. With the machine running, add the olive oil in a thin steady stream. Add the parsley and pepper and pulse just to mix. The sauce will have the consistency of fairly thick cream. For a thinner sauce add more lemon juice, which will give a more piquant flavour, or olive oil, which will mellow the flavour. Serve at room temperature.

To make the traditional way Finely chop the shallot, garlic, anchovies, and capers together. Place in a wooden mortar and pound with the pestle until well mixed and fairly smooth, about 10 minutes. Slowly add the lemon juice and about 115 ml/4 fl oz olive oil, pounding constantly, until thick. Stir in the parsley and pepper.

Appendices

pickles

toursia

Although *toursia* means "pickles", the term is generally now applied only to vegetables such as artichokes, cauliflower, cucumber, and peppers that have been traditionally prepared and flavoured and stored in wine vinegar, sometimes spiced. Other vegetables and fruits of all kinds, are also pickled in great quantities: lemons are salted and stored in olive oil (page 18), capers are packed in brine (page 16), and tomatoes sun-dried and stored in olive oil. *Toursia* are served as *mezedakia* with ouzo or raki (page 338), or with other *mezedes,* such as preserved meats, cheeses, radishes, wild artichokes, and young broad beans. They are rarely served with a main course.

Vegetables used for pickling must be fresh, unblemished, and very clean. Use an enamel-lined, stainless steel, or other non-reactive saucepan and sterilized wide-necked jars with tight-fitting lids.

spiced pickled peppers
piperies mikres toursi
Yields approximately 2.75 litres/5 pints

For pickling the Greeks use long, slender, waxy yellow or pale green peppers. They can be very mild, almost sweet, or quite tangy. If your peppers are tangy, omit the honey and cinnamon in the spiced vinegar, and add dried red chilli peppers to the jar. These are delicious with tomato or beetroot salads, or with *feta* cheese.

36 slender peppers, 5-7 cm/2-3 inches long, stems trimmed to 6 mm/¹/₄ inch
3 tablespoons coarse-grain sea salt
6 dried red chilli peppers, *optional*
1.1 litres/2 pints Spiced Vinegar (page 328)
Olive oil, for sealing the jars

Place the peppers in a glass or china bowl, sprinkle with the salt, and add water to barely cover. Cover and set aside for 6 hours, occasionally stirring the peppers.

Rinse the peppers and spread on paper towels to dry. Loosely pack into 1.1 litre/2 pint jars, add 1 or 2 red chilli peppers to each jar, cover with the Spiced Vinegar, and seal with a thin layer of olive oil. Tightly cover and store at room temperature for at least 3 weeks, or up to 3 months, before using. Refrigerate after opening.

Pickled Tiny Stuffed Aubergines
Melitzanakia Yemista Toursi
Makes approximately 2.75 litres/5 pints

For this pretty, delicate pickle choose slender baby aubergines about 5 cm/2 inches long. To keep the filling in place, you use the stronger "strings" removed from the celery stalks (for Filling 1) or the parsley or wild celery stalks (for Filling 2). Store for up to eight weeks at room temperature, and refrigerate and use within one week once the jar is opened.

900 g/2 lb small aubergines

Filling 1
2 large cloves garlic, finely chopped
2 large sticks of celery, tough strings removed and reserved, cut into 7-10 cm/3-4 inch pieces
2 tablespoons finely chopped celery leaves (see wild celery page 351)

1 red bell pepper, roasted, seeded, and skinned (page 343), rinsed, and
cut into thin strips
3 tablespoons finely chopped flat leaf parsley
1 tablespoon olive oil

Filling 2
3 large cloves garlic, finely chopped
2 young carrots, peeled if desired, and grated
2 tablespoons finely chopped flat leaf parsley
1 tablespoon finely chopped fresh mint
1 tablespoon olive oil
Pine nuts, small blanched almonds *or* walnut pieces (1 for each aubergine)
Slender flat leaf parsley *or* wild celery stalks (page 351), each with a few leaves
attached (1 stalk for each aubergine)
5 red chilli peppers, *optional*
700 ml/1¼ pints white wine vinegar combined with 450 ml/16 fl oz water *and* 2
tablespoons coarse-grain sea salt *or* 1.1 litres/2 pints Spiced Vinegar (see Note)
Olive oil, for sealing jars

Slice off the ends of the aubergines and carefully make a short lengthways incision in each aubergine. Blanch in boiling salted water for 2 minutes, remove with a slotted spoon, and dry between layers of paper towels.

Blanch the celery pieces for 5 minutes, remove with the slotted spoon, and drain on paper towels; finely chop. Blanch the celery strings or the parsley stalks for 6 seconds, and drain. Cut 6 of the pepper strips into 1 cm/½ inch pieces and set aside; finely chop the rest.

Combine the garlic, celery, celery leaves, chopped bell pepper, parsley, and olive oil (for Filling 1), or combine the garlic, carrots, parsley, mint, and olive oil (for Filling 2). Loosely stuff the aubergines with the filling. Arrange the bell pepper strips along the aubergine incisions or place a pine nut in each aubergine. Firmly wrap a celery string around each aubergine (Filling 1) or wrap with a parsley stalk, starting with the leafy end over the filling but leaving the pine nut slightly exposed (Filling 2). Place the aubergines upright in 600 ml/1 pint jars, packing quite tightly. Push 1 red chilli pepper down between the aubergines in each jar, cover with the vinegar, and seal with a thin layer of olive oil. Tightly cover the jars and set aside for 2 weeks before using.

Note To make Spiced Vinegar, combine 700 ml/1¼ pints white wine vinegar, 450 ml/16 fl oz water, 2 tablespoons coarse-grain sea salt, 1 dozen allspice berries, 6 cloves, 1 teaspoon black peppercorns, one 5 cm/2 inch cinnamon stick, and 1 tablespoon honey in a large saucepan and bring to a boil. Simmer 5 minutes, strain, and let cool.

Pickled Cucumbers
Angourakia Toursi
Yields approximately 3 litres/5¼ pints

Leave tiny (2.5-5 cm/1-2 inch long) cucumbers whole, and cut larger ones lengthways into quarters or into thick slices. Store at room temperature for at least two weeks or up to four months before using, and refrigerate after opening. Use these as a garnish for Pork in Aspic (page 36) or Fried Cheese (page 38), or serve with other small appetizers.

900 g/2 lb pickling cucumbers, stems trimmed
2 large cloves garlic, cut into large slivers, optional
12 black peppercorns
6 sprigs of fresh dill or 1 tablespoon dill seeds
12 small fresh vine leaves, tough stems trimmed, blanched in boiling water for 5 seconds, optional
450 ml/16 fl oz white wine vinegar
3 tablespoons coarse-grain sea salt
½ teaspoon honey
Olive oil, for sealing the jars

Blanch the cucumbers in boiling water for 1 minute and dry between layers of paper towels. Fill three 1.1 litre/2 pint jars with the cucumbers and divide the garlic, peppercorns, dill, and vine leaves between them. Combine the vinegar, salt, honey, and 225 ml/8 fl oz water and pour over the cucumbers. Cover with a thin layer of olive oil and tightly cover the jars.

jams and preserves
glyka

From the wide choice of fruits available to them, Greeks make a variety of delicious jams and preserves. Three of my particular favourites are those made from figs, quinces and loquats. They are not difficult to make, calling for time, patience, and careful observation rather than professional skill, but the following tips may be helpful.

Jam sets thanks to the work of the enzyme pectin (present in large quantities in fruits such as apple and quince, in smaller amounts in other fruits – it's especially low in strawberries). But to work effectively pectin needs the help of both acid, in the fruit or in added lemon juice, and sugar, so it's important to judge the proportion of sugar to fruit carefully and to add the sugar at the right moment, usually when the fruit is already cooked or softened. At that point some of the fruit's own sugar will have started to work with the pectin. Once the sugar has been added, careful observation is crucial. If you do not boil the mixture sufficiently you will end up with a crystallized jam, while over-boiling will give you a runny syrup instead.

Another common problem is the formation of mould on top of the stored jam. To guard against this it's a good idea to add some form of alcohol to the jam mixture – whisky, cognac, Armagnac, or, in true Greek fashion, raki, all serve the purpose. The same result is achieved by pouring melted wax over the surface of the jam, but the alcoholic option is easy and adds flavour as well.

Fresh Fig Jam
Sika Glyka
Makes 1.75-2.3 kg/4-5 lb jam

For this richly flavoured jam you can use any variety of fig but the fruit must be ripe. If you have unsprayed figs the skin can be left on the fruit (almost all shop-bought figs are sprayed) – they give the jam a beautiful deep colour, especially if you use deep purple figs. Otherwise the figs must be peeled. The tart apples in this recipe serve a dual purpose: Rich in pectin, they help the jam to set, and they are also an economic way of increasing the amount of jam you can produce from a reasonable quantity of the more expensive figs.

900 g/2 lb fresh ripe figs, rinsed or peeled, and stems trimmed
450 g/1 lb tart apples, such as Granny Smiths
1 teaspoon fennel seeds
Finely grated zest of 1 lemon
Strained juice of 3 large lemons
900 g/ 2 lb sugar

Thoroughly wash and sterilize five 450 g/1 lb jam jars.

Cut each fig in 6 or 8 pieces. Peel, core, and thinly slice the apples. Place the fennel seeds on a small square of muslin and tie up the edges to make a bag.

Place the figs, apples, bag of fennel seeds, lemon zest, and lemon juice, in a large heavy saucepan, cover, and bring slowly to a boil. Simmer 30 minutes or until the figs are tender, stirring occasionally to ensure that the fruit does not stick. Discard the bag of fennel seeds, add the sugar, stir well with a wooden spoon, and raise the heat. Boil 5 minutes, or until the setting point (105-106C/220-222F) is reached: To test, either use a sugar thermometer or drop a small quantity of jam onto a chilled plate – if it appears to be covered by a light skin, it is ready. If not boil a few minutes longer and test once more; remove the saucepan from the heat each time you test and, to prevent the figs from burning, stir vigorously with a wooden spoon.

Pour into the jars and cover the surface of the jam with circles of waxed paper or with melted wax. Tightly cover the jars and store at room temperature.

Quince Jam
Glyka Kidoni
Makes approximately 1.4-1.75 kg/3-4 lb jam

Throughout Greek myth and legend the quince is associated with love, marriage, and fertility, and it was actually a golden quince that Paris awarded to the goddess of love, Aphrodite, when he made the ill-fated judgement that sparked off the Trojan war. For Greeks the quince is still the love-fruit and its blossoms or fruit are an integral part of the Greek marriage ceremony.

In season Cretan markets display green-gold ripening quinces in abundance; in Britain, unfortunately, they are not so easy to find. If you spot quinces in your local shop, do not hesitate to buy them. They are versatile fruits to cook with: The ancient Greeks made them into a sweetmeat, but they can also be poached (page 287) or baked like apples and, when cooked, take on a beautiful deep red colour. They are lovely baked with a little sweet white wine, sugar, and a few cloves or a vanilla bean (rinse and core the quinces, and bake in a low oven until tender). Half a quince, finely chopped, is also a wonderfully aromatic addition to apple and pear pies and tarts. Or use their delicately perfumed flavour in this delicious jam. Be sure to choose firm under-ripe quinces; ripe yellow ones are pulpy, and not suitable for jam.

900 g/2 lb under-ripe quinces
2 small lemons
900 g/2 lb sugar
2 teaspoons vanilla extract

Thoroughly wash and sterilize four 450 g/1 lb jam jars.

Fill a large bowl with iced water. Quarter 1 lemon, squeeze the juice into the bowl, and add the quarters. Squeeze the juice from the remaining lemon and set aside. Wipe the quinces to remove the fuzzy down on their skins. Peel, quarter, and core, and tie the peelings and cores up in a piece of muslin to make a bag. Thinly slice or julienne the quinces, dropping them into the iced water. When all are prepared, drain the quinces, pat dry with paper towels, and place in a large heavy saucepan. Add 700 ml/1¼ pints water and the muslin bag. Slowly bring to a boil, and simmer 15 minutes. Remove the muslin bag, squeeze it over the pan to extract as much juice as possible, and discard.

Add the sugar, reserved lemon juice, and the vanilla to the quinces and simmer until the sugar is dissolved. Raise the heat and rapidly boil until the setting point is reached (as directed on page 330).

Fill the jars, cover the surface of the jam with circles of waxed paper or with melted wax, and tightly cover the jars. Store at room temperature for up to 6 months.

Loquat Preserve
Glyka Mespilonta
Makes 450-900 g/1-2 lb preserve

The refreshing, delicately flavoured loquat is native to China but throughout southern Greece and Crete loquat trees, laden with clusters of small orange-gold fruits, are a common sight. The loquat conveniently ripens in late spring, at the end of the orange season and before summer fruits appear in the markets. This lovely jam is absolutely delicious with biscuits, pancakes, or almond cakes and it is especially good with Rich Cream (page 310).

675 g/1¹/₂ lb large unblemished loquats
Strained juice of 1 lemon
One 5 cm/2 inch strip of lemon zest
225-350 g/8-12 oz sugar

Thoroughly wash and sterilize four 225 g/8 oz jam jars. Rinse the loquats and trim out their flower ends with a small paring knife. Cut into pieces and discard the pits. Work quickly – the fruit discolours easily.

Place the loquats in a heavy saucepan with the lemon juice, zest, and 4 tablespoons water, cover, and bring slowly to a boil. Reduce the heat and simmer 30-40 minutes, or until the loquats turn deep auburn. (This slow cooking is essential to release the loquats' sugar and to make a well-flavoured preserve.)

Fit a moulis-légumes with the fine blade and set it over a non-reactive bowl. Discard the lemon zest and pass the loquats through the moulis-légumes. Measure the pulp, return it to the rinsed-out saucepan, and add exactly the same amount of sugar. Slowly bring to a boil and simmer for 15-20 minutes, or until the setting point (105-106C/220-222F) is reached (test as directed on page 330).

Fill the jars, cover the surface of the jam with circles of waxed paper or with melted wax, and tightly cover the jars. Store at room temperature for up to 4 months.

beverages
pota

Greeks are connoisseurs of water and many will tell you without hesitation that cold water, pure and crystalline, is the only truly refreshing drink. As one English writer describes it, "*The glass of water appears everywhere; it is an adjunct to every kind of sweetmeat and even to alcohol. It has a kind of biblical significance. When a Greek drinks water he* tastes *it and, pressing it against the palate, savours it.*" This fondness for water does not stop them, however, from delighting in a range of deliciously flavoured non-alcoholic drinks. Some of the best are made with the syrup of spoon sweets or with the spoon sweet itself. Other popular traditional drinks are made with almonds, citrus fruits, and pomegranates.

Morello Cherry Syrup
Vissinatha

A popular and thirst-quenching drink is made from the syrup remaining from Morello Cherry Spoon Sweet (page 295). Fill a tall glass with ice, add syrup to taste, and fill with cold water.

The syrup of any spoon sweet can be used in the same way – lemon blossom syrup (page 297) is especially good.

Submarines
Ypovrikhia

This is the colloquial name for a traditional way to serve spoon sweets. A long-handled spoon is used to scoop up the sweet and then is immersed in a tall glass of ice-cold water. The fondant-like spoon sweet remains attached to the spoon, hence the drink's name. Favourite versions are those made from vanilla, Morello cherries (page 295), or mastic (page 14). Sipping *ypovrikhia* under a shady tree is an exceedingly pleasant way to while away the afternoon.

Almond Drink
Soumada
Makes about 850 ml/1½ pints syrup

This refreshing drink, especially delicious on a hot summer's day, is the traditional beverage to serve at weddings. The classic way to make the syrup is to pound the almonds and sugar in a mortar, but a food processor will produce a similar flavour using far less time and energy. Process only a small quantity at a time or the almonds will not be properly pulverized. The syrup keeps indefinitely in airtight bottles.

200 g/7 oz blanched almonds
675 g/1½ lb sugar
1 litre/1¾ pints water
A few drops of bitter almond essence or almond extract, *optional*

With a nut grinder or a food processor, finely chop the almonds – but do not pulverize. Transfer 2 tablespoons of the chopped almonds to a mortar, or remove all but 2 tablespoons from the processor bowl and set aside. Add 1 tablespoon each of sugar and water to the smaller amount of almonds, and pulverize to a paste. Remove and set aside, and repeat with the remaining almonds, adding sugar and water to each 2 tablespoons of chopped almonds.

Combine the remaining sugar and water in a heavy saucepan, bring to a boil, and gently boil 10 minutes. Stir in the almond paste with a wooden spoon and boil 10 minutes longer, stirring frequently to prevent sticking; do not leave unattended – the syrup easily boils over. Set aside to cool. Strain into a bowl through 2 layers of muslin, and squeeze the muslin to extract all liquid. Add almond essence if desired – the almond flavour should be unmistakable, but not overpowering. Store at room temperature in airtight bottles.

To serve, pour syrup to taste over crushed ice in a tall glass and add cold water.

Lemonade
Lemonada
Makes about 700 ml/1¼ pints syrup

This is a simple and unusual way to make any citrus drink. The light syrup keeps in the refrigerator for up to two weeks.

550 g/1¼ lb sugar
700 ml/1¼ pints water
Zest of 1 lemon
1 clove
One 5 cm/2 inch cinnamon stick

For serving
Freshly squeezed lemon juice, to taste
Slices of lemon dipped in sugar

Combine the sugar, water, lemon zest, clove, and cinnamon stick in a heavy saucepan and bring to a boil. Gently boil 10 minutes and set aside to cool.

Strain into clean bottles or jars and refrigerate.

To serve, pour lemon juice and syrup to taste over ice in a tall glass, and add cold water. Balance a slice of lemon dipped in sugar on the rim of the glass.

Pomegranate Refresher
Granita
Serves 4

The flavour of this sweet and pretty drink is best when the pomegranates are juiced within an hour or two of serving.

4 large ripe pomegranates
Juice of $1/2$ small lemon
5 tablespoons sugar, or to taste

For serving
A few drops orange flower water or rosewater, *optional*

Use a lemon squeezer or juice extractor, or a food processor fitted with the plastic blade, to juice the pomegranates (page 289).

Strain the juice through 2 layers of muslin into a non-reactive pitcher. Stir in the lemon juice and sugar with a wooden spoon and stir until the sugar has completely dissolved. Chill.

Serve over crushed ice, and sprinkle with orange flower water or rosewater if desired.

coffee
kafes

Old ways die hard in Greece and, although tradition is now changing slowly, the best coffee is still to be found in the *kafenion* (café) – until very recently, an exclusively male domain. Women generally drink coffee at home or in the *zacharoplasteion* (pastry shop). Coffee is rarely served in tavernas or traditional restaurants.

Greeks make coffee the way it is made throughout the Middle East – in a long-handled small brass pot (*briki*) with a broad lip, tapering towards the top. It is almost always served already sweetened, in tiny straight-sided cups. When you order your coffee you are asked how you would like it made, as sugar is added to the coffee grounds at the same time as the water. Some Greeks assert that there are at least 50 ways to make and flavour coffee but, in general, you are likely to be offered only *sketo* ("unsweetened"), *metrio* ("with some sugar"), and *glyko* ("sweet").

Greek coffee is made with thoroughly pulverized, well-roasted coffee beans. Brazilian is the coffee bean of choice although it is the length of time the beans are roasted that really defines Greek coffee's special character. Since the coffee grounds are poured into the cup it's essential that they are powder-fine.

To make Greek coffee at home you will need a *briki*. They are available in a range of sizes, from 1-cup to generous 8-cup versions. Both *brikia* and traditional cups can be bought from Greek and Middle Eastern shops; if you prefer to use larger espresso cups, increase the quantity of coffee and sugar by one half. Serve the coffee steaming hot.

Greek Coffee
Kafes
Serves 4

Greek coffee is always served with tall glasses of iced water.

4 coffee cups water
4 teaspoons powder-fine ground coffee, or heaped to taste
4 teaspoons sugar, or heaped to taste

Bring the water to a boil in a 4- to 6-cup *briki*. Remove from the heat and sprinkle the coffee and sugar over the water. Bring to a boil again, and remove from the heat. Stir until the froth has disappeared, and return to a high heat. Remove from the heat, stir until the froth disappears, and bring to a boil one more time. (This process is necessary to infuse the coffee and make a thick froth; the alternative is a thin liquid.)

Divide the froth between the cups (it's said to bring good luck) and carefully pour in the coffee to the brim. The froth will rise to the surface. Serve at once.

Herb Teas
Tsai Votana

In Greek villages tea means *faskomilo,* an infusion of the three-lobed sage (*salvia triloba*), a more aromatic member of the same botanical family as garden sage (*salvia officinalis*). Village folklore attributes great powers to sage tea, as a blood purifier or euphoric or to help relieve chest colds and upset stomachs. The sage is infused in boiling water for three to five minutes, according to taste, and the sweetener is honey.

Many other ancient herb teas are still enjoyed by Greeks today. Like sage tea these are not only refreshing and reviving drinks, but also have medicinal properties. Chamomile (*kamomili*) is the favourite, especially as a relaxing night-time tea or to ease head colds. Mint (*thiosmos*) is taken for a fever, thyme (*thimari*) when bronchitis threatens, and Cretan dittany (*dictamos*) when health or spirits are low. Most of these teas can be bought in Greek grocery shops. Or, if you feel adventurous, take your symptoms to a herbalist in a Greek market, and try the recommended concoction!

alcoholic drinks
pota einopnevmatoda

In Greece grapes are used to make a variety of alcoholic drinks in addition to wine. Once the grapes have been harvested and pressed, their remnants are distilled to produce two distinctive popular and highly potent liquors.

Aniseed-flavoured ouzo is the traditional accompaniment to *mezedes* throughout most of Greece. In the old-style cafés it is served straight, in a small glass, with a tall glass of cold water. Serving ouzo over ice is a modern innovation. The ouzo sold in Greece is usually much stronger than exported varieties.

Raki has a markedly different flavour, often somewhat similar to that of tequila. Only small quantities are bottled commercially but it is readily available in areas where it is produced (or in households with relatives in those areas). Until recently, it was made at home, or communally in the village, but today its manufacture requires a license. On the islands of Crete and Santorini and in other ancient wine-producing areas raki (known as *tsigouthia* or *tsipoura*) is the favourite liquor to drink with *mezedes*. Good raki is delicious; bad raki best avoided.

Other alcoholic drinks produced in Greece include brandy (frequently, slightly sweetened); *mastiha,* a mastic-flavoured liquor; a refreshing lager-style beer; and a number of flavoured liqueurs.

The Wines of Greece

Dionysus, the Greek god of wine, was the son of Zeus and the Theban princess Semele. The story runs that he passed on to the Greeks the secrets of wine making he had learned from the satyr Silenus. That much is myth: What is fact is that as their empire expanded the Greeks introduced both the vine and wine making to the rest of Western Europe.

Wine, along with bread and olives, has been part of Greek culture since the very earliest times and the poets of antiquity, Greek and Roman, praised the delights and variety of Greek wines. There is still an enormously rich variety of wines in Greece, and modern Greece has inherited grape varieties yielding wines that are often quite different in aroma and flavour from the well-known international varieties.

The Greek relationship with wine, as you might expect between old friends, is easy and natural. Greeks enjoy wine without fuss or unnecessary ceremony, without heated discussions of vintages or close scrutiny of labels. In general, Greek society still follows the precepts of the physician Hippocrates, who advised that wine was beneficial if taken at the right time and in the right quantity.

For Greeks the right time to drink wine is with food, whether a full meal, *mezedes*, or a snack. Greek wine is the natural accompaniment to Greek food: A taverna meal and a glass of local wine, taken outside in the warm pine-scented air, perhaps with a view of the sea or the vine-covered hillsides, may not be the "hautest" of cuisines but it is a moment of inspired magic.

More importantly, the experience of Greek wine and food together brings us exciting new harmonies of flavour. Particularly stimulating to non-Greeks are the unexpected aromas of wines produced from grapes indigenous to Greece but unknown outside the country (see *Reading the Wine Label*, page 341).

The last fifteen years have seen a tremendous renaissance in Greek wine making, with fresh, fruity wines now being made by all sections of the wine producing industry – the major exporting giants such as Boutari, Kourtakis, and Tsantalis, the smaller boutique wineries, and some of the cooperative ventures. Exciting use is being made of a number of high quality native Greek varieties as well as the noble ones of Cabernet Sauvignon, Chardonnay, and others. Stainless steel vats, temperature control, and new oak, allied to a better understanding of the grapes themselves on the part of an enthusiastic younger generation of winemakers, have resulted in many exciting wines, often offering a new flavour dimension, which are regularly winning prizes world wide. And it should not be forgotten that for many years Greece has been justly famous for great dessert wines such as Muscat of Samos, Lemnos and Patras, and Mavrodaphne of Patras.

The wine most associated with Greece is, of course, retsina. The Greek taste for retsina dates back three thousand years; it is the pine-laced wine of the ancients. This very individual wine is not to everyone's taste but a chilled glass of retsina or *kokkineli* (the rosé version), with its surprising stringency, is just right with *mezedes*.

Retsina is not a true table wine but an aromatized wine. Its origins are very old and arise from the Greek habit of storing wine in airtight jars sealed with a mixture of clay and resin, the flavour of which seeped into the wine. Because of the exclusion of air, these wines kept far longer than was usual, but the ancients assumed that this was due to the resin instead, and began to add this to their wines.

In some quarters retsina is not taken very seriously, a pity since the finest retsina from Attica and Evia, made from the *savatiano* grape, has a delicate aroma and a distinctive, pleasant, and very refreshing flavour. In these areas, retsina is the true traditional accompaniment to the Easter feast of Paschal Lamb and *kokoretsia* (page 145), and it marries well with dishes accompanied by a garlic sauce.

However, if you are entertaining friends at a Greek meal you may prefer a choice of wines. Since the annual wine production of many Greek vineyards is small, their wines are rarely exported and sampling them is a treat to be enjoyed during a visit to the country. (For more information on Greek vineyards and their wines, I recommend you to *The Greek Wine Guide*, by Nico Manessis, published by Olive Press, 1999.) Below you will find a consumer guide to some of the Greek wines that can occasionally be found here, and some helpful hints on reading a Greek wine label.

Once you start to sample Greek wines, you will begin to appreciate that they have a very special colour, aroma, and flavour and that they enhance the dishes in this book as no other wines can.

consumer's guide to greek wines and spirits

From a period of relative obscurity Greek wines are now appearing on the wine lists of good restaurants and on the shelves of some of our more intrepid vintners.

The Producers

The following list is alphabetical and by no means complete. It is based on producers whose wines are usually available on the export markets, rather than only in Greece, where many other fine wines can be found.

Antonopoulos: Red and white wines, including Adoli Ghis, Mantinia, Cabernet Nea Dris and Chardonnay

Averoff: Red Katogi

J. Boutari: Large range of wines, including white Santorini, red Naoussa, and retsina

N. Cosmetatos: White wines under the brand name of Gentilini

Emery: Red, white, rosé, and sparkling wines

Gaia: Red and white Notios, and white Thalassitis

Ktima Gerovassiliou: Red and white wines

Ktima Hatzimichali: Red and white wines, including ones from Chardonnay, Cabernet Sauvignon, and Merlot grapes

Kourtakis S.A: Wide range, including red and white Vins de Crete, Nemea and Patras, under the brand name of Kouros, retsina, and Mavrodaphne of Patras

Chateau Lazaridi: Red, white, and rosé wines under the chateau name

Ktima Kosta Lazaridi: Red, white, and rosé wines under the brand name of Amethystos, and Chateau Julia

Markovitis: Red Naoussa and Chateau Pegasos

Chateau Matsa: White wines under chateau name and Laoutari

Ktima Mercouri: Red wines under the ktima (domaine) name and white Foloe

Oenoforos: White Asprolithi, rosé Esperitis, and red Cabernet

Ktima Papaioannou: Red Nemea, white and rosé wines

Parparoussis: White wine and red Nemea

Samos Coop: Every level of sweetness in muscat wines, notably the sweet Nectar

Semeli S.A: White and rosé wines, and red Nemea and Chateau Semeli

Skouras Winery: Cambello red, white and rosé, a red Nemea, and red and white Megas Oenos

Ktima Spyropoulou: White wines, including Mantinia

Strofilia: White, rosé, and red wines under the Strofilia name

Tsantalis: Wide range of red, white, and rosé wines, including red Nemea, Naoussa, and Rapsani. Also muscat wines and Mavrodaphne of Patras

Tselepos: White Mantinia, and red Ktima Tselepou

Spirits

Ouzo: The traditional spirit flavoured with aniseed. Producers include Tsantalis and Babatzim

Distillates: Rarely available outside Greece at present. Producers include Averoff, Babatzim, Ktima Kosta Lazaridi, and Paparoussis

Reading the Wine Label

Apart from the language itself, there are two possible areas of confusion for the Greek wine buyer – Greek Legislative Wine Categories, and indigenous grape varieties.

Legislative Categories:

Appellation Greece follows EU viticultural policies. There are 27 appellations in Greece today. O.P.A.P. is equivalent to the French A.O.C., and O.P.E. is equivalent to V.D.Q.S.

Many of the new top quality wines do not qualify for O.P.A.P. or O.P.E. since they are made either outside a quality wine region or because different grape varieties than those permitted under quality wine legislation have been used.

These wines are found labelled either as Vins de Pays or as Table Wine.

A few of the more common indigenous grape varieties:

White grapes:

Assyrtico Grown on Santorini and other Aegean islands; many styles of wine produced from bone-dry, to sherry-like Visanto.

Lagorthi Once rare, this grape is making a come-back owing to its steely, lightly aromatic qualities.

Malagousia Rediscovered in the 1960s, this is now producing rich wines, and is increasingly used in high quality blends for its aromatic characteristics.

Moschofilero Produces some of the best Peloponnese white wines, with a delicate aromatic quality. At its best, very fine.

Muscat Grown on Samos and Cephalonia, and around Patras; yields wines from very dry to sweet, and sun-dried dessert wines.

Robola Popular on the Ionian islands; thought to have been introduced by the Venetians in the thirteenth century.

Roditis Grown extensively on the mainland; produces a wide spectrum of styles and quality.

Savatiano The predominant grape of Attica and Evia and the principal variety for retsina; also produces a range of branded table wines and vin de pays.

Vilana Unique to Crete; light, aromatic and fresh when well-handled.

Red grapes:

Aghiorghitiko 'St. George'. One of the best red varietals, unique to Nemea, Peloponnese.

Liatiko A speciality of Crete and believed to be an ancient varietal; ripens very early and is often mixed with other grape varieties.

Limnio Originally from Lemnos but now grown in Khalkidiki and Drama, it is believed to be a very ancient varietal. It has a unique flavour, and marries well with oak.

Mandelaria An island grape, now grown mainly on the Cyclades, Rhodes and Crete. It gives immense colour to the wine.

Mavrodaphne Grows around Patras; the Greek name means 'black laurel', and it makes a port-like dessert wine. It is increasingly used in blends.

Xynomavro The best red varietal of northern Greece; produces full-bodied wines such as Naoussa and Goumenissa. Quality can vary, vintages important.

Glossary

Anchovies No Greek market would be complete without its large wooden barrels of anchovies, which owe their unique flavour to the traditional preservation methods used. The small whole anchovies (just the heads are removed) are immersed in a heavy brine, lightly dried in the sun until the brine crystallizes into salt, and then packed into barrels. A good anchovy packer uses the same brine several times and it's in this recycling that the secret of the Greek anchovies lies. Anchovies packed in re-used brine have the strong traditional flavour familiar to the ancient Greeks, and these are the ones most sought after by today's connoisseurs. They can occasionally be found in Greek shops here; only the two fillets are used – lift each one from the backbone with the tip of a small knife. Imported tinned or bottled anchovy fillets packed in olive oil are the best substitute.

Avgolemono Probably the best-known Greek flavour, this blend of lemon juice and eggs can become a delicious sauce for fish, chicken, or vegetables or a fine delicate soup based on a good Chicken Stock (page 344).

Bell Peppers The distinctive flavour bell peppers impart to Greek dishes is thanks to a method of roasting (scorching) them over an open flame or hot embers. In Greece large fleshy bell peppers are always stuffed; Greek cooks choose slender, mildly flavoured varieties for roasting. These are difficult to find here but you can obtain a similar flavour by "scorching" bell peppers. Using tongs, hold the pepper over an open flame or hot embers (or use a grill), turning it until it is blistered and blackened on all sides. Cool in a paper bag or in a bowl covered with cling film to make removing the skin easier. Remove the core and seeds and rub off the skin and any remaining seeds with your fingers. Do not rinse – water affects flavour and storage life. To store, cut roasted peppers into strips, place in clean jars, cover with olive oil, and seal with a lid. Store for up to 2 months. Once the peppers are used, the storage oil can be used for flavourful grilling or cooking or on salads.

Cephalopods (squid, cuttlefish, and octopus) The name *cephalopod* derives from the Greek for "head and legs" – these sea creatures consist of just a head, tentacles, and a body bag or sac. Apart from the larger cuttlefish, which has a single bone in its sac, cephalopods have no bones. What they do have, however, is an ink sac that nature has provided for their protection.

Under threat of attack from a predator the cephalopod squirts out ink and, under cover of the ensuing darkness, it slips away to safety. This ink not only protects the cephalopod but is useful to the cook too. It has a slight salty flavour, lends a unique colour and sheen to sauces, and acts as a thickener. Some fish purveyors will clean cephalopods for you (even tiny ones retain grains of sand in their body bags) but avoid ones that are already cleaned since these may not be fresh. See also Octopus and Squid.

Chicken Stock Although Greek chickens are often scrawny, they are invariably free-range and have a superb flavour.

To make approximately 1.7 litres/3 pints of excellent stock: Cut up a chicken into 6 or 8 pieces, discard excess fat, trim the giblets, discarding the liver, and rinse the chicken and giblets. Place the chicken pieces and giblets in a large saucepan or stockpot along with 1 carrot (unpeeled), cut into large pieces; 1 stick of celery, cut into large pieces; 1 medium onion, peeled and quartered; 3 bay leaves; 3 sprigs of parsley; 12 peppercorns; pinch cayenne pepper; 2 cloves; ¹/₂ teaspoon saffron threads, gently heated in a small frying pan until fragrant; and 2.3 litres/4 pints water (or enough to cover). Bring slowly to a boil, skim off any froth, cover, reduce the heat, and simmer 1¹/₄ hours. Strain the stock and make fat-free (see Meat Stock) and, if desired, reduce for easier storage by rapid boiling.

To make Rich Chicken Stock: Boil the stock until reduced by one third. Use the chicken meat in pies, salads, or sandwiches.

See also Meat Stock, Lamb Stock, Fish Stock, and Vegetable Stock.

Croûtons Crunchy, olive oil-rich croûtons give Greek soups and salads a very special character.

To make croûtons: Remove the crusts from densely textured white or wholemeal bread, and cut the bread into 6 mm/¹/₄ inch cubes. Add a 3 mm/¹/₈ inch layer of extra virgin olive oil to a heavy frying pan and heat over moderate heat. Fry the bread cubes until golden brown on all sides. Drain on paper towels.

The secret of successful croûtons is to use fruity olive oil and not to allow it to reach smoking temperature. In Greece it is common to see packets of croûtons of very hard dark bread, made by the baker when he bakes Store Cupboard Bread (page 251).

Dolmas (Dolmades) These are small parcels of vine-leaf wrapped rice and herbs; sometimes meat and/or vegetables are added (pages 194 and 196). Tiny *dolmades*, suitable for *meze,* are called *dolmadakia.* In winter *dolmades* are made with cabbage leaves (page 92); in spring with courgette blossoms (page 198).

Farina (**Semolina**) Available in Greek shops and health food shops. Fine-ground *farina* has the texture of coarse flour and is used to make *macaronia* (pages 235, 238, and 242). Medium- or coarse-grain *farina* is used in puddings (pages 303 and 307) and coarse-grain *farina* is used in custards (pages 267, 270, 278, and 280).

Fava This "Old World" bean is the one most frequently used in Greek cooking. Very young favas (broad beans) are shelled and eaten raw as *meze,* or cooked in the pod. Fresh favas are made into *salata* (page 40), oven-baked with lamb (page 151) or chicken, eaten cold as a salad (pages 53 and 207) or warm as a vegetable dish (page 193). They are dried for the winter and made into one of the most popular Greek *mezedes* (page 52). *Fava* is also the name given to a *salata* made from fresh or dried fava beans (page 41) or split peas.

Filo These very thin pastry sheets (the word means "leaves") are the basic ingredient for sublimely syrupy sweet pastries and aromatic savoury pies. For information on making home-made filo pastry and on using home-made or commercial filo, see page 266 and specific recipes.

Fish When buying fish your best guide is your nose – fresh fish smells good. It's also good to inspect the head – this is the first part of the fish to go bad. (In Greece all fish except anchovies and sardines are sold with their heads intact; headless fish are assumed to have been frozen). Check the eyes too – they should be dark, clear, and except for deepwater fish such as the grouper, protruding. Gills should be red and the flesh spring back when prodded. If you are in a any doubt, pick the fish up by its tail; if the body bends, do not buy it.

Cleaning and Scaling Fish Cleaning a fish means to gut it, leaving head and skin intact. To gut a fresh fish, which should be done as soon as possible, slit open the belly with a sharp knife and pull out everything in the cavity; run your finger and thumb along the inside of the fish to check. Trim the fins with scissors and pull out the gills; if necessary, loosen them with a small paring knife. With a scaling knife or the back of a table knife, remove the scales by scraping from the tail to the head, and thoroughly rinse the fish. If you plan to grill a large fish do not scale it – the scales will protect it from the fierce grilling heat; just gut and thoroughly rinse the fish.

Filleting Fish Agres of Rhodes, in the second century A.D., is said to have been the first person to think of filleting fish. Fish filleted just before cooking has the best flavour, so always fillet fish yourself. It is easy to remove fish fillets with a filleting knife, which has a long, thin, supple blade. First, to remove the skin, ease the point of the knife under the skin at the tail and firmly pull the skin towards the head. Then, run the point of the knife around the side of the fish and lift off the fillet.

Scoring Fish When grilling large fish you need to make sure they cook in the centre but do not burn on the outside. To ensure that they cook through, make two or three deep parallel diagonal incisions on each side of the fish with a sharp knife.

Fish Stock Bony fish make the best-flavoured stock, and including fish heads in the stock will produce a smooth velvety texture. In Greece favourite fish to use as a base for stock are the John Dory (page 346) and the scorpion fish (*scorpena*).

To make approximately 850 ml/1¹/₂ pints stock: Place 675 g/1¹/₂ lb cleaned, gutted, and scaled fish (see Cleaning and Scaling Fish, above) or fish pieces in a large saucepan and add 1 sliced onion; 1 carrot (unpeeled), cut into large pieces; 2 bay leaves; 4 sprigs of parsley or 4 tablespoons parsley stalks; 1 stick of celery, cut into large pieces, or a small handful of wild celery leaves (page 351); a large pinch of saffron threads, heated in a frying pan over low heat until fragrant, optional; 1 tablespoon olive oil; 6 peppercorns; and water to cover. Bring slowly to a boil, reduce the heat, and simmer 1 hour. Strain through a large sieve lined with 2 layers of muslin, let cool, and refrigerate for up to 2 days.

Any flakes of fish can be seasoned and coated in a *rigani*/parsley-flavoured *latholemono* sauce and served with olives and cheese, as a *meze*. Or lightly mix them with some mayonnaise (page 319) or add to a *pilafi* (page 226).

Fournos The traditional clay oven that was once part of every Greek house (see page 23). Today when Greeks speak of the *fournos* they usually mean the local bakery. The baker will cook his customers' food in his oven once the day's bread is baked, saving time and money (the upkeep of a *fournos* is very expensive now). Casseroles, breads, pies, and vegetables baked in a *fournos* have a unique taste.

Game When dealing with game it is helpful to understand the principal of hanging, the process by which game is tenderized. Wild birds and animals, because of the action of internal bacteria, do not putrefy but rather dry after death. Domestic animals and birds, by contrast, are invaded by external bacteria that quickly cause decomposition, the effects of which are harmful to us. Therefore, it is essential that you know the origin of any bird or animal you wish to hang. Game that has been quickly and cleanly killed, that has only a few shot holes, can be hung; if the flesh is torn or the game has come into contact with our environment it should be prepared for the table right away. To hang game choose a cool place inaccessible to flies (a cellar is ideal). The length of hanging time will depend on the weather, age of the game, and, above all, personal taste. The right moment is usually when a tail feather can be plucked. To enjoy game safely avoid any you have not seen in its fur or feathers and cook only that which you have seen hung. For those who dislike the idea of dealing with hanging game, marinating is the answer. Game immersed in acids, such as wine or vinegar, undergo a process similar to hanging, and the meat is tenderized and flavour improved. See also Hare, Kid, Partridge, Pigeon/Squab.

Hare A hare is larger than a rabbit, usually weighing around 3.2-3.6 kg/7-8 lb (2.3 kg/5 lb after skinning). To cut a hare into serving pieces, cut off the front and back legs. Cut the body in half down the backbone. Cut each half into 4 or 5 pieces, similar in size to the legs. Hare meat can be tough, so it should be marinated for 1-2 days before cooking (page 133).

John Dory (*Christopsaro*) John Dory, with its firm white flesh and sweetly delicious flavour, is popular for use in filleted fish dishes (page 102). However, since most of the fish is head and belly, it is the perfect choice for soups and dishes requiring a rich stock. Its Greek name, meaning, "Christ's fish", derives from the two black spots behind the enormous head, said by some Greek fishermen to be the finger prints of St. Christopher, who plucked it from the water while he was carrying Christ on his back.

Kephtedes Aromatic round, oblong, or square croquettes of meat, chicken, fish, or vegetables, unchanged in form and flavour since antiquity. *Kephtedes* vary in size from very small (*kephtedakia*), for a *meze*, to large enough for a main course. They can be grilled, fried, or poached and are served with a variety of sauces (pages 32, 33, and 160).

Khorta Wild greens that grow in Greek meadows and on hillsides during the autumn, winter, and spring. These greens are rich in vitamins and minerals and have in common a slightly bitter flavour that makes them delicious with *latholemono* (see below) or *lathoxsithi* (an olive oil and vinegar sauce). Served cold, as a cooked greens salad, *khorta* becomes *khorta salatika* (page 221).

Kid In Greece kid often replaces the Paschal Lamb (page 142) for the Easter Sunday feast. Spit-roasted kid makes an unusual centrepiece for an outdoor party. Whole kid can be bought during spring from speciality butchers or by mail order; leg of kid is often available until early summer. It can be prepared with the marinade on page 147. Usually older and larger than lamb when slaughtered, kid needs a longer roasting time, so the fire heat must be steadier and constant. Build the fires with coals spread out over a large area and levelled. When the fire is ready, arrange the spit about 60 cm/2 feet above the glowing coals but slightly to one side. Roast a 10-11 kg/22-24 lb kid 3-3½ hours, slowly bringing the turning split closer to the embers, until the kid is only 12-15 cm/5-6 inches away from the heat. Baste frequently, catching the juices in a pan. Near the end of the cooking time be especially careful that the less fleshy sections of meat do not burn – push most of the embers under the rump, leaving only a shallow layer under the shoulders and rib cage.

Klephtiko   This term refers to dishes baked in paper, an ancient and practical cooking method (page 155) that seals in all the delicious juices of the meat or fish. Modern cooks have discovered that vegetables taste delectable when cooked this way too.

Lamb Stock   Light and distinctively flavoured lamb stock is a delicious ingredient of *souvlakia* (page 350) and casseroles.

To make approximately 1.4 litres/2¹/₂ pints stock: Place 900 g/2 lb cracked lamb bones and any scraps of lamb meat in a large heavy saucepan with 12 black peppercorns; 1 carrot (unpeeled), cut into large pieces; 1 sliced onion; 1 stick of celery cut into large pieces; and water to cover. Bring to a boil, cover, reduce the heat, and simmer 3 hours. Strain and make fat-free (see **Meat Stock** below). Use within 2 days or freeze.

Latholemono   A light blend of fruity extra virgin olive oil and perfumed lemon juice, this is a fresh-tasting and traditional sauce for salads and sautéed or grilled meat and fish. Made with red wine vinegar instead of lemon juice *latholemono* becomes *lathoxsithi,* a sauce made in the kitchens of antiquity.

Lobster   For home cooks, the easiest method of killing a live lobster is to plunge it head-first into a large pot of rapidly boiling water. Add 1 tablespoon salt and 4 tablespoons vinegar for each 1.1 litres/2 pints of water. Once the water returns to the boil after the lobsters have been added, reduce the heat slightly and cook 6 (450- 675 g/1-1¹/₂ lb lobsters) to 10 (larger ones) minutes longer. Drain, and blot dry with a cloth.

Macaronia   Greek pasta; home-made pastas are also known as *zimarika* (literally, "dough"). A wide variety of *macaronia* is available here in Greek and Middle Eastern shops; one popular type of small pasta is called *kritharaki* (page 244).

Meat Stock   Greeks have great faith in the sustaining powers of good meat stock; it is excellent on its own as a stock or as a basis for heartier soups, sauces and casseroles. Most butchers will give you bones (veal bones produce a lovely gelatinous stock).

To make approximately 2.3 litres/4 pints Light Meat Stock: Add 3 tablespoons olive oil to a heavy baking dish or roasting pan. Arrange 1.7 kg/4 lb beef, veal, or lamb bones (including shin, knuckle, and marrow bones, sawn through by the butcher and thoroughly rinsed) in it in a single layer, and add 1 large onion, sliced in half, cut sides down. Bake 1 hour at 190C/375F/gas mark 5 or until well browned. Transfer to a large stockpot or saucepan, add 2.3 litres/4 pints water, bring to a boil, and remove any froth from the surface with a slotted spoon. Add 1 tablespoon black peppercorns; 2 bay leaves; 1 clove; 12 sprigs of parsley; 1/2 teaspoon dried thyme; 2 large carrots (unpeeled), cut into large pieces; 1 small turnip, peeled and cut in half; and 2 diced tomatoes. Bring to a boil, reduce the heat, and simmer 3-4 hours. (Do not allow to boil).

Strain through a large sieve lined with 2 layers of muslin and set aside to cool. Remove the fat from the surface of cooled stock with a spoon to produce almost fat-free stock. To make the stock completely fat-free, strain again through 2 layers of muslin, or clarify as directed for Meat Stock (see below). Refrigerate for up to 2 days or freeze. Or reduce, if desired, to half the original volume by rapid boiling in an uncovered saucepan (to use in these recipes, use equal parts reduced stock and water) Cool before refrigerating or freezing.

To make approximately 1.7 litres/3 pints Meat Stock: Add 3 tablespoons olive oil to a heavy baking dish or roasting pan. Arrange a single layer of about 900 g/2 lb beef shin bones (sawn through by the butcher and thoroughly rinsed) in it, and bake 1 hour at 190C/375F/gas mark

5 or until well browned. Transfer to a large stockpot or saucepan, add 2.3 litres/4 pints Light Meat Stock, and bring to a boil. Cover, reduce the heat, and simmer 4-5 hours. Strain through a large sieve lined with 2 layers of muslin, let cool, and remove the fat from the surface of the stock to make it almost fat-free. Refrigerate for up to 2 days or freeze.

To make completely fat-free Meat Stock: Reduce the stock by rapid boiling to 1.1 litres/2 pints, and let cool. Add 2 egg whites and bring slowly to a boil, stirring with a wooden spoon. Simmer uncovered, without stirring, for 15 minutes. Slowly strain the stock through a sieve lined with 2 layers of muslin into a bowl, 1 ladleful at a time, disturbing the sediment on the bottom of the pot as little as possible. Remove any remaining fat by blotting the surface with paper towels.

See also **Chicken Stock**, **Lamb Stock**, **Fish Stock** and **Vegetable Stock**.

Meze (Mezedes) A small, usually savoury, dish served with ouzo or raki (page 338) or wine. From 4 to 25 *mezedes* are served at one time to compose a *meze* table. Small *mezedes,* such as olives, cucumber or tomato chunks, cheese, and almonds, are known as *mezedakia.* See Appetizers and First Courses (page 28).

Onion Juice This is used in Greece as a marinade to tenderize and flavour fish and meat before grilling (page 150). For the best flavour do not use metal utensils to prepare it.

To make onion juice: Chop 1 large onion, place it in a bowl, and stir in 4 tablespoons boiling water. Set aside to cool. Line a sieve with 2 layers of muslin and set it over a bowl. Pour in the onion and any liquid, pull up the edges of the muslin to make a bag, and squeeze as much juice as possible into the bowl. Use immediately.

Orange Flower Water Used to flavour syrups for filo pastries (page 267) and cakes (page 280). Available from Greek and Middle Eastern shops, and many supermarkets.

Orange or Lemon Zest When a recipe calls for just a delicate hint of citrus zest, remove the zest from the fruit with a stripper or zester and either blanch it or dry it. To blanch zest, drop it into boiling water for a minute, then drain, cool, and blot dry with paper towels before using. To dry zest, spread the strips of zest on a baking tray and dry them for 30 minutes in a very low oven. Store dried zest for up to 3 months in an airtight container and use it in casseroles and pastries.

Partridge In Greece these game birds are in season from late October until the end of November. When choosing partridges, you need to know their age since this dictates the length of time you should cook them. (You can recognise an old partridge by the large knots on its lower legs, not present in young birds.) One large partridge will serve two. They are delicious spit roasted; wrap first in vine leaves to flavour and protect from the fierce roasting heat. Always request the giblets from your supplier; they improve the flavour of the accompanying sauce.

Pastourmas Highly spiced and salted veal or pork. Thin slices of *pastourma* are served with pickles as a meze. *Pastourmas* also describes a type of flavour (page 176).

Pigeon/Squab Pigeons, or squab, are best braised, as in recipes such as Hunter's Pot (page 136); simply roasted, they tend to become dry. Always request the giblets from the supplier; they add to the flavour of the accompanying sauce.

Pilaf A savoury rice dish flavoured with herbs, to which can be added vegetables, fish or shellfish, chicken, or meat (pages 224-234).

Pitta Soft, flat bread, shaped into rounds or ovals (page 252) that can be split through the centre to make "pockets" to hold *souvlakia* and/or salads. Perfect with grilled meats or dishes served with a sauce, or with *mezedes,* especially *salates* (see below).

Pork Caul Fat This is the outer lining of a pig's stomach. In Greece it is sold in small blocks by street vendors as well as in butcher's shops; here it is available from many butchers, in the same block form. Pork caul fat (*panes*) is stiff and easily torn; to separate the pieces, soak block in lightly vinegared tepid water. Use to make sausages or packets of minced or chopped meat for grilling, spit roasting, or baking. During cooking the fat melts away, leaving moist and tender aromatic meats.

Rosewater   A favourite flavouring for filo nut pastries (page 266) and *kataifi* (Kataifi Custard Pie in Rosewater Syrup, page 269).

Salata (Salates) Literally, this means "salad", but Greek salads do not always conform to our expectations of a salad. Many are purées (see the chapter on Appetizers and First Courses), others are composed vegetable salads. A green salad is called *salatika,* and one consisting of wild greens, *khorta salatika* (see the chapter on Vegetables and Salads).

Sardines in Olive Oil Greek sardines – lightly salted, immersed in fruity olive oil, and packed in barrels – have an unusual and appetizing flavour. Garnished with capers, cracked black pepper, and a little chopped mild onion they make a delicious *meze*. Greek shops occasionally stock barrels of sardines from Greece; other imported tinned sardines packed in olive oil are the best substitute.

Sausage Casings To make a long sausage for smoking you need a long intestine – the ancient Greeks used pig's intestine but villagers today use a sheep's intestine. It is scrubbed inside and out with vinegar or wine, rinsed well, and then stuffed (pages 176 and 178). Speciality butchers occasionally stock cleaned and salted sheep's intestines; to prepare them, soak overnight and rinse thoroughly. Frozen sausage casings for 10-12 cm/4-5 inch sausages are sold in most butcher shops – just rinse them before using.

Sea Urchins Only the roe (eggs) of sea urchins are eaten (page 116), and it is easiest to buy them ready to use. However, collecting sea urchins can be an enjoyable way to pass a few hours. You can find sea urchins in small clusters on rocks just below the water's surface (experienced divers will find a better harvest on rocks 3.6-4.5 m/12-15 feet below the surface). Look for female urchins, which are a deep reddish or chestnut brown. The greenish-black males can be left alone. The urchin's hard round shell is covered entirely in spikes except on the flattened underside where the mouth is. (See recipe page 116 for instructions on how to prepare them.) For the best harvest, gather sea urchins at the full moon. Greek sea urchins are usually quite small (2.5-7 cm/1-3 inches across) but those found in British waters are often larger. Sea urchins must be very, very fresh so either collect them yourself or use a reputable supplier; they are usually inexpensive.

Skordalia The best version of this pungent, powerful garlic sauce is made with almonds (page 314). Serve with Tiny Fried Fish (page 31), *khorta* (page 221), or as a dip, with pitta bread (page 252).

Snails Snails are very popular in Greece, especially on the islands, where they are made into *meze* (recipe, page 37), *pilafi*, and a winter casserole. Gathered after a rain (the only time villagers consider them safe to eat), they are kept in large baskets containing bran, to dry the snails, and thyme, to sweeten their flavour. To deter the snails from escaping salt is spread round the basket rim. The snails are left in a cool place for 3 or 4 days and thoroughly rinsed in lightly vinegared cold water before cooking.

When buying fresh snails make sure that the shell and the membrane covering the opening are both intact; at home discard any that break during preparation. Simmer snails 1 hour (or until cooked), adding a few tablespoons vinegar once the water boils (skim off the scum that forms on the surface). Remove membranes with a small paring knife, discard the tiny black "tail" of each snail – and they are then ready to use. Of course, although some flavour is lost it is much easier to buy tinned snails – all you have to do is drain them.

Souvlaki (Souvlakia) Flavourful chunks of meat, fish, or vegetables are threaded on a skewer (*souvla*) and roasted over an open fire or grill. Lamb is the most popular meat but pork and chicken are also used and minced meat is wrapped in pork caul fat (see above) to make *sheftalia* (page 175). These are more familiar to many of us as *kebabs,* the Turkish name for the ancient cooking technique used. See also page 148.

Squid In Greece, succulently tender, flavourful squid (*calamaria*) is a favourite summer dish. Larger squid are stuffed, tiny ones (*calamarakia*) are fried whole. Fresh squid is firm and shiny with a lightly mottled, pink skin.

To prepare squid: Gently pull the head from the body or bag and cut off the two attached fins. Discard the contents of the bag (use your finger, or slit the bag from end to check) except for the elongated ink sac – set this aside in a small bowl. Cut off and discard the strip containing the eyes and press out the tough beak. Thoroughly rinse the squid, rubbing both tentacles and body bag with your fingers to remove any sand or purplish skin. Leave the body bags of small squid (and those to be stuffed) intact; cut others into 2.5 cm/1 inch strips for sautéing; leave in iced water until ready to use.

Taverna Despite its name, the Greek taverna is not primarily a drinking place but rather an eating place. Simpler, less expensive, and less pretentious than restaurants, many tavernas are located in spectacularly beautiful places – on terraced hillsides, in village squares, alongside beaches. Many (even in the heart of Athens) have vine-covered or shady courtyards or terraces and in most the owner stamps his personality on the décor in a very idiosyncratic way!

The way to find the most interesting food in a taverna is to follow the Greek example and take a look around at what's bubbling in the kitchen – written menus do not always alert the visitor to the day's speciality. Family-run tavernas usually have a welcoming casual atmosphere with the emphasis on relaxation – so don't expect a meal in a hurry. Tavernas often specialise – harbour-side establishments serve mostly fish, mountain tavernas mainly meat, while others make a speciality of a certain cooking method or type of dish.

Most tavernas serve local wine measured by the jug and perhaps a few bottles of national brands too. You will not be offered fancy desserts – fresh fruit or perhaps yogurt and honey are traditional endings for a taverna meal – nor is coffee usually available. These will be found at the nearby pastry shop, or *zacharoplasteion*.

Toursi (Toursia) Vegetables pickled by a traditional method and with a distinctive flavour (page 326).

Vegetable Stock This simple, fresh-tasting stock can be used as a substitute for meat or chicken stocks. Celery is the dominant flavour but add or substitute turnips, parsnips, or leeks if you prefer.

To make approximately 1 litre/1¾ pints stock: Combine 3 sticks of celery, finely diced, 2 medium carrots, finely diced, 1 large onion, chopped, 2 bay leaves, 2 sprigs of fresh dill, (or fresh or dried thyme or marjoram), 2 sprigs of parsley, a pinch of salt, and 450 ml/16 fl oz water in a heavy saucepan. Bring to a boil, cover, reduce the heat, and simmer 40 minutes. Discard the bay leaves and herb sprigs, transfer vegetables and cooking liquid to a blender or food processor, and purée until smooth. Or pass the vegetables through a moulis-légumes fitted with the fine disk into a bowl containing the cooking liquid. Set a fine-meshed sieve over a bowl and press the purée through with a wooden spoon. Discard any solids left in the sieve. Thin with water if desired, and season to taste with salt and pepper. Refrigerate for up to 2 days. See also **Meat Stock**, **Chicken Stock**, and **Fish Stock**.

Vine Leaves The vine leaves used to make *dolmades* (page 344) must be tender enough to be edible, so they are picked from the top third of the vine and only a few are taken from each plant, in the spring and early summer. The leaves used to protect baked or grilled foods are discarded before the dish is served, so they are picked from any part of the vine, throughout summer. For a delicious country flavour cover trays of stuffed vegetables or young broad beans in the pod with vine leaves before baking (page 194) or wrap *kephtedes* (page 160, made with rice instead of bread) in vine leaves and bake moistened with water, olive oil, and lemon juice. Both fresh leaves and those preserved in brine are used to make *dolmades;* only fresh leaves are used in grilled dishes.

Wild Celery A very popular flavouring in meat and fish casseroles, soups, and salads, and the most commonly available celery in Greece, Its natural habitat is marshland near the sea but in Greece it is semi-cultivated. The leaves, similar in appearance to flat-leaf parsley, are a beautiful shade of dark green; they have a mild, almost sweet, flavour, without any trace of the slightly bitter aftertaste of the pale leaves of large cultivated celery. During spring and summer Italian markets stock wild celery; if unavailable, use the darkest leaves of rib celery, but first blanch them briefly in boiling water.

Menus for Different Occasions

Newcomers to Greek cooking may at first be unsure how to compose a balanced menu with dishes from various sections of this book. To help with this problem (although I am sure it will not remain a problem for long) I have suggested below a range of complete menus suitable for family meals, quick lunches or suppers, and for entertaining (both for small dinner parties and larger gatherings). Represented here are authentic, traditional dishes in which a variety of distinctively Greek flavours contrast and complement: Any of these menus will give you and your guests an ideal introduction to the enticing tastes and aromas of Greek food. The selection begins with menu suggestions for well-known Greek celebrations and the Lented fast.

An Easter Feast

Mezedakia

Spit-Roasted Easter Sausages
Easter Bread
The Paschal Lamb
Potatoes in a Clay Pot
Marinated Asparagus
Easter Greens Salad with Latholemono Sauce
Kos Lemon Pie

Drinks

White: Santorini Boutari
Reds: Semeli Nemea *or* Ktima Mercouri

A Christmas Table

Mezedakia

Christmas Bread
Duckling Thessalia-Style
Turnips and Grapes in Aromatic Sauce
Garlic Potatoes with Juniper Berries Island Greens Salad
Fruits in Sweet Wine and Honey
Honey Cakes

Drinks

Aperitif: Spyropoulous Mantinia
White: Strofilia Nafsika
Reds: Boutari Grand Reserve or Chateau Semeli

Dessert

Muscat of Samos

New Year's Day

Mezedakia

Leeks the Classic Way
Saint Basil's Bread
Pheasant over a Fire *or* Hunter's Pot
Potatoes in a Clay Pot
Purslane and Young Beetroot
Platter of Fresh Fruit
Manouri or *myzithra* cheese with aromatic Greek honey
Honey Cakes

Drinks

Aperitif: Kouros white
White: Adoli Ghis (Anotonopoulos)
Reds: Gerovassiliou Red *or* Boutari Goumenissa *or* Katogi Averoff

Dessert

Muscat of Limnos

The Lenten Fast

Salt-Dried Fish Roe Salata
Chickpea and Garlic Salata
Potato and Vegetable Kephtedakia
Marinated Olives
Peppered Dried Figs
Pitta Bread
Broad Beans and Sweet Carrot Pilaf
Wild Greens Salad
Almond Creams
Platter of Fresh Fruits

Drinks

A selection of waters

Easy Lunch

Macaronia with Chicken and Wild Greens *or* Kritharaki with
Brown Butter and Cheese
Fragrant Aubergines with Olives
Sweet-Baked Figs *or* Anoula's Dried Figs

Drinks

White: Gaia Notios

Dessert

Mavrodaphne of Patras

or

Peppery Grilled Liver
Rigani Cheese Bread *or* Olive Bread
Vanilla Rice Pudding

Drinks

White: Anotonopoulos Mantinia
Red: Tsantalis Rapsani

A Casual Dinner Party

Sesame Spinach Pies
Bay-Scented Chicken
Tiny Cracked Potatoes
Kataifi Nut Rolls with Caramel Syrup

Drinks

White: Gaia Thalassitis
Rosé: Semeli

or

Baked Aubergines to Make the Sultan Swoon
Yogurt Lamb Souvlakia with Saffron Rice
Purslane and Young Beetroot
Kataifi Custard Pie in Rosewater Syrup

Drinks

Red: Ktima Papaioannou

Family Dinner

Chicken Avgolemono Soup
Smyrna Sausages
Potatoes in a Clay Pot
Cucumber Salad with Honey Vinegar Sauce
Honey Sesame Sweetmeats with Vanilla Ice Cream

Drinks

White: Retsina
Red: Skouras Cambello

Dessert

Muscat

or

Potato Kephtedakia with Cheese
Pork Cutlets with Mustard Sauce
Pilaf with Green Lentils
Honey-Glazed Onions
Sticky Yogurt Cake

Drinks

White: Retsina
Red: Gerovassiliou

Dessert

Samos Nectar

Dinner Party

Mezedakia served with Drinks

Pork in Aspic
Marinated Olives
Purslane Salad
Cinnamon Lamb with Aubergines
Pilaf with Currants and Pine Nuts
Island Greens Salad
Minoan Dates and Prunes

Drinks

White: Antonopoulos Chardonnay
Red: Skouras Megas Oenos

Dessert

Mavrodaphne of Patras

or

Mezedakia served with Drinks
Tiny Stuffed Vegetables
Cretan Chicken Pie
Green Salad with Feta Cheese and Olives
Honey Ice Cream with Fresh Fig Compôte
Shortcakes

Drinks

White: Gerovassiliou
Reds: Gaia Notios *or* Ktima Mercouri

Dessert

Samos Nectar

Vegetarian Dinner Party

Mushrooms à la Grècque
Spinach Bread or Fennel Bread
Baked Stuffed Aubergines, Tomatoes, and Peppers
Purslane Salad *or* Island Greens Salad
Baked Figs
Hazelnut Biscuits

Drinks

White: Oenoforos Asprolithi
Red: Boutari Naoussa

Quick Supper for Friends

Black Olives and Lentil Salata
Pitta Bread
Country Vegetable Omelette
Purslane Salad
Glazed Sweet Chestnuts

Drinks

White: Ktima Kosta Lazaridi

Dessert

Mavrodaphne of Patras

or

(mostly made ahead)
Baked Cheese and Spinach Pies
Chicken in a Pot
Perfect Pilaf
Fruits in Sweet Wine and Honey

Drinks

Rosé: Ktima Kosta Lazaridi

Meze Party

Most of the work for this menu can be done one or two days ahead,
and some of the dishes can be frozen; last-minute work is minimal.

Mezedakia, large selection

Grilled Aubergine Salata
Chickpea and Garlic Salata
Stuffed Vine Leaves with Latholemono Sauce
Kephtedakia
Tiny Stuffed Vegetables
Honey-Glazed Onions
Purslane and Young Beetroot
Tiny Cracked Potatoes
Smoked Fish Salad
Small Pies
Souvlakia
Cheese Mint Bread
Olive Bread

Drinks

Whites: Semeli White *or* Boutari Moschofilero
Red: Boutari Nemea

A Summer Buffet

Mezedakia

Green Lentil Salad
Traditional Tomato Salad
Fennel Bread, made with fresh fennel *and/or* Pitta Bread Moussakas
Potatoes in a Clay Pot
Nut Pastries in Fragrant Honey Syrup
A Platter of Fresh Fruits
Myzithra or manouri cheesewith aromatic Greek honey

Drinks

Whites: Strofilia *or* Cambello White
Rosés: Semeli *or* Tsantalis Agoriotiko
Red: Strofilia

A Barbecue

(with some dishes baked *and/or* prepared ahead)

Mezedakia

Black-Eyed Peas with Capers
Snails in Vinegar
Small Pies
The Villagers' Grilled Lamb *or* Souvlaki Sausages

or

Mani Pork Souvlaki
Baked Summer Vegetables
Green Salad with
Feta Cheese and Olives
Shepherd's Bread
Country Bread
Filo Custard Pie

Drinks

Whites: Vin de Crete *or* Boutari Kretikos
Red: Kourtaki Kouros

A Picnic

Marinated Olives
Peppered Dried Figs
Summer Bean Salad
Island Aubergines
Olive Bread *and/or* Pitta Bread
Beetroot Island-Style
Cheese and Spinach Pie
Almond Cake in Honey Syrup
Platter of Fresh Fruits

Drinks

Whites: Retsina *or* Emery Villaré
Red: Vin de Cret

Bibliography

While writing this book I consulted many written sources. Some were manuscripts and stored in archives, others were books long out of print and quite difficult to find. These are some of the more easily accessible works.

Brillat-Savarin, Jean Anthelme. *The Physiology of Taste*. Translated and annotated by M.F.K. Fisher. San Francisco: North Point Press, 1986.

Chatto, James & Martin, W.L. *A Kitchen in Corfu*. London: Weidenfeld and Nicholson, 1987.

Clusells, Sylvain. *Cooking on the Turning Spit and Grill*. London: Arthur Barker Ltd., 1961.

D'Andrea, Jeanne. *Ancient Herbs in the J. Paul Getty Museum Gardens*. Malibu, CA: J. Paul Getty Museum, 1982.

David, Elizabeth. *Mediterranean Food*. Revised ed. London: Penguin Books, 1955, and *Elizabeth David Classics*, Grub Street, 1999.

Davidson, Alan. *Mediterranean Seafood*. London: Penguin Books, 1972.

Durrell, Lawrence. *Prospero's Cell*. London: Faber & Faber, 1963.

Fermor, Patrick Leigh. *Roumeli*. London: John Murray, 1966, Penguin Books, 1983.

Gissing, George. *By the Ionian Sea*. 1901. Reprint. London: Richards Press, 1956.

Graves, Robert. *Greek Myths*. 2 volumes. London: Penguin Books, 1956.

Gray, Patience. *Honey from a Weed*. London: Prospect Books, 1986.

Grigson, Jane. *Jane Grigson's Vegetable Book*. London: Michael Joseph, 1978.

Harrison, S. G.; Masefield, G.B.; and Wallis, Michael. *The Oxford Book of Food Plants*. Illustrations by B.E. Nicholson. London: Oxford University Press, 1969.

Homer. *The Odyssey*. (Many editions available.) London: Penguin Books, 1985.

Homer. *The Iliad*. (Many editions available.) London: Penguin Books, 1950.

Kochilas, Diane. *The Food and Wine of Greece*. New York: St. Martin's Press, 1990

Lambert-Gócs. *The Wines of Greece*. London: Faber & Faber, 1990

McConnell, Carol and Malcolm. *The Mediterranean Diet*. New York: W.W. Norton & Co., Inc., 1987.

Marks, Theonie. *Greek Islands Cooking*. Boston: Little Brown & Co., 1972.

Miller, Henry. *The Colossus of Maroussi*. 1941. Reprint. London: Penguin Books, 1963.

Niebuhr, Alta Dodds. *Herbs of Greece*. Sponsored by the New England Unit of the Herb Society of America, 1970.

Roden, Claudia. *A New Book of Middle Eastern Food*. London: Penguin Books, 1986

Salaman, Rena. *Greek Food*. London: Fontana Books, 1983.

Sculley, Victor. *The Earth, the Temple, and the Gods*. New Haven: Yale University Press, 1979.

Soyer, Alexis. *The Pantropheon*. New York: Paddington Press, 1977.

Stavroulakis, Nicholas. *Cookbook of the Jews of Greece*. New York: Cadmus Press, 1986.

Stobart, Tom. *Herbs, Spices, and Flavourings*. London: Grub Street, 1998.

Stubbs, Joyce M. *The Home Book of Greek Cookery*. London: Faber & Faber, 1963.

Tselementes, Nicholas. *Greek Cookery*. New York: D.C. Divry Inc., 1950.

Wolfert, Paula. *Mediterranean Cooking*. New York: Quadrangle/The New York Times Book Co., Inc., 1977.

Index